A Language
of
Our Own

Oxford Studies in Anthropological Linguistics
William Bright, General Editor

A LANGUAGE OF OUR OWN

The Genesis of Michif,
the Mixed Cree-French Language
of the Canadian Métis

Peter Bakker

New York   Oxford
Oxford University Press
1997

Oxford University Press

Oxford   New York

Athens   Auckland   Bangkok   Bogota   Bombay   Buenos Aires
Calcutta   Cape Town   Dar es Salaam   Delhi   Florence   Hong Kong
Istanbul   Karachi   Kuala Lumpur   Madras   Madrid   Melbourne
Mexico City   Nairobi   Paris   Singapore   Taipei   Tokyo   Toronto

and associated companies in
Berlin   Ibadan

Published by Oxford University Press, Inc.
198 Madison Avenue, New York, New York 10016

Oxford is a registered trademark of Oxford University Press

Library of Congress Cataloging-in-Publication Data
Bakker, Peter.
A language of our own : the genesis of Michif, the mixed Cree-French
language of the Canadian Métis / Peter Bakker. — [Rev. ed.]
p.   cm. — (Oxford studies in anthropological linguistics : 10)
Revision of thesis (doctoral)—Universiteit van Amsterdam, 1992.
Includes bibliographical references and indexes.
ISBN 0-19-509711-4; 0-19-509712-2 (pbk.)
1. Michif language—History.   2. Michif language—Grammar.
I. Title.   II. Series.
PM7895.M53B35   1997
497'.3—dc21   97-7301

PM
7895
.M53
B35
1997

1 3 5 7 9 8 6 4 2
Printed in the United States of America
on acid-free paper

CONTENTS

PREFACE

In Native communities in Canada, people often wondered why a Dutchman traveled so far to learn and study the Michif language. Actually, I became involved in this language by chance. I was studying linguistics with an emphasis on language contact, and I happened to read an article called "Indian Lingua Francas" by Allan Taylor, in which a language that allegedly consists of Cree Indian verbs and French nouns was mentioned in passing. Because this seemed to violate so many theories and presumptions taken for granted in linguistics, I mentioned this language, called Michif, to Norval Smith. Within half a minute he retrieved from his archives a photocopied article called "French Cree: A Case of Borrowing" by Richard Rhodes, which was a detailed grammatical sketch of the Michif language. From that moment I felt the urge to find out more about this fascinating language. Fortunately, I received a nine-month grant from the Canadian Embassy in the Netherlands to study the language on the spot, and after that a grant from the Netherlands Organization for Scientific Research (NWO) in The Hague to write this book and do more fieldwork on location. This book contains the results of my research and my ideas about the genesis of this unique language.

ACKNOWLEDGMENTS

I want to express my gratitude to the Michif, Cree, Michif French, and Ojibwe speakers who were willing to share their time and knowledge with me during my field trips in 1987–1988 and 1990. They translated material I supplied; told me stories and legends; and granted interviews, some lasting many hours. I am grateful to the following people:

Alice Aubichon, Elizabeth Bouvier, Georgina Bouvier, Victoria Daigneault, Jean Daigneault, Rose Laliberté, Claudia Larivière, Marie Jacobson, Nap Johnson, Teresa Morin, Vital Morin, and Rose Roy of Ile-a-la-Crosse, Saskatchewan.

Celina Doré-Moberley, Jeffery Morin, Agnes Morin-Moberley, and Florence Petit of Buffalo Narrows, Saskatchewan.

Annie Johnstone from Pinehouse, Saskatchewan.

Morris Amyotte, May Desjarlais, Margaret Desjarlais, Florence Desjarlais, Edward Fayant, John Gosselin, and Harry Poitra from Balcarres, Katepwa, and Lebret in the Fort Qu'appelle Valley in southeastern Saskatchewan.

Lawrence Allard, Ida Rose Allard, Marie Azure, Rose Azure, Sara Belgarde, Lawrence and Marie Bruce, Edna Cloud-Martin, Francis Cree, Ernestine Davis-Malaterre, Pete Delorme, Julius Grant, Emma Greatwalker, Victor Johnson, Elizabeth Keplin, Walter LaFontaine, Patline Laverdure, Mathilde Poitra, Beatrice Poitra-Decoteau, and George Wilkie from the Turtle Mountain Reservation and surroundings in North Dakota.

Adelard Belhumeur, Florence Belhumeur-Allery, Henry Chartrand, Verna Delaronde-Godard, Joe Fagnan, Bill Fiddler, Jack Flamand, Rita Flamand, Julia Flamand-Nikinak, Filiou Guiboche, Archie Lafrenière, Leon and Maggie Lafrenière, Maggie Ledoux-Fagnan, Louison Ledoux, Pauline Richard-Flamand, and Grace Zoldy-Ledoux from Camperville, Manitoba.

Christine Hatcher, Marie Lavallée, Peter Parenteau, and Stanley Parenteau from Duck Bay, Manitoba.

Brian Beauchamp, Adelard Dumas, and Verna Debaere-Mercredi from Crane River, Manitoba.

Cecilia Burns, Della Genaille, Clara Leclair-Genaille, William Leclair, Joe L. Pelletier (Harry), and Mathilde Prescott-Tanner from Brandon, Manitoba.

Albert Langen from Boggy Creek, Manitoba. Justin Larocque from San Clara, Manitoba. Annie Funk from Roblin, Manitoba. Bertha Chartrand from Dauphin, Manitoba.

Joseph Boucher and Peter Vilbrunt of Regina, Saskatchewan.

Joe Bell, Agnes Boyer, Ernest "Chickadee" Moule, Peter Fleury, and Robert Lepine from Saint Lazare, Manitoba.

Dan DeMontigny, Lena Fleury, and Victoria Genaille from Binscarth, Manitoba.

Henry Daniels, Malcolm Daniels, and many others from Sturgeon Lake, Saskatchewan.

Claudia Snell-Gerard, Elizabeth Vandale, and Cecile from Big River, Saskatchewan.

Reggie Boucher, Vital Boucher, Hilaire Ladouceur, and Stanley Lavallee from Lac La Biche, Alberta. Willie Ladouceur from Buffalo Lake, Alberta.

I also want to thank my guides and hosts: Claire Bélanger, Mathilde Belhumeur, Ken and Diane Cornett, Henry and Marlene Daniels, Verna and Emile Debaere, Jim and Marie Favel, Sonny Grant and Loretta Keplin, Murray Hamilton and Cathy MacKay, Jackie and Tim Hansen, Liza Keplin, Michael K. Keplin, Guy and Grace Laramee, Rick Leclair, Louison Ledoux, Florence and Elmer Nayneecassum, John Nichols, Ron Richard, Chris and Julianne Wolfart, and Grace Zoldy. Further thanks go to George Lang for his valuable role on the side as a voluntary bureaucrat, the Manitoba Métis Federation in Winnipeg for technical facilities and permission to use their taped Michif materials, and to the Universities of Brandon and Winnipeg, Manitoba. I am grateful to The Federation of Saskatchewan Indian Nations in Prince Albert; Claire Bélanger; the school board of the Rossignol school in Ile-a-la-Crosse; Mirja Akkerman, Anne Mars, Elly Borghesi, and the Institute for Functional Research into Language and Language Use (IFOTT) staff in Amsterdam; and the Netherlands Institute for Advanced Studies (NIAS) staff in Wassenaar for technical assistance and computer facilities.

I am grateful to Joan Kensmill, who used her drawing talent for some of the maps and also Valérie Blain, François Tremblay, Jean Séguin, and Tom and Leo of the P.J. Meertens Instituut in Amsterdam for their help with the maps. I also want to thank Adriënne Bruyn, Robert Papen, Vincent de Rooij, Rob Schoonen, and Hein van der Voort, who commented on parts of this book. They cannot be held responsible, however, for any errors or opinions expressed here. Neither can Petra Sjouwerman, who was there when I needed her.

A number of people also gave comments on parts of an earlier version of this book. The following were useful in preparing it for publication: four anonymous commentaries, Fred Field, Anthony P. Grant, George Lang, Petra Sjouwerman, H. Chr. Wolfart, and especially Denys Delâge for his comments on Chapter Two and David R. Lipscomb for revising my English.

Chapter Four draws heavily on parts already published in Bakker and Papen (in press). I thank Robert Papen for his kind permission to quote from that paper.

I am grateful to a number of Algonquianists with whom I had the opportunity to discuss Michif and my field experiences: Lynn Drapeau, Murray Hamilton, John D. Nichols, Robert A. Papen, David Pentland, and Chris Wolfart. Some of them will find their ideas reflected in this book; others may not agree.

I owe the most thanks to Pieter Muysken, who made this whole project possible with his initiative, enthusiasm, ideas, knowledge of the funding agencies, energy, comments, criticism, time, and stimulation.

Finally, I thank the Canadian Embassy in Holland for the Canadian Studies Graduate Student Award, which allowed me and my partner to spend a year in Canada in 1987–1988 for fieldwork. Our stay on the Cree reserve and in the Métis communities was unforgettable and changed our lives in many ways. Furthermore I am grateful for the financial support from the Foundation for Linguistic Research, which is funded by NWO, who supported this research project financially during 1988–1991. A postdoctoral grant from the Royal Academy of Arts and Sciences in the Netherlands (KNAW) allowed me to do more research on contact languages between 1993 and 1996. During a stay in Montreal in 1993, I collected code-switching and other fieldwork data on Attikamek, Algonquin, James Bay Cree, and Naskapi. I am grateful to the Department of Linguistics of Université du Québec à Montréal (UQAM) especially Lynn Drapeau, for its hospitality. A stay at the Netherlands Institute for Advanced Studies in the Humanities and Social Sciences in Wassenaar during the academic year 1995–1996 made it possible to revise my dissertation for publication.

REMARKS ON SPELLING

Devising a spelling system or even a consistent, broad phonetic transcription style is almost an impossible task for a language like Michif, which has two phonological systems: one for the Cree part and one for the French part. The standard spellings for both languages would have been an easy solution for me and probably also for the reader, but it would have done great injustice to the language.

One alternative would have been to use the standard spelling for Michif in the excellent Michif dictionary (Laverdure and Allard 1983), which was compiled by two native speakers of the language. That spelling, however, is based on English and shows some inconsistencies; therefore, it is not usable in a study like this, where exactness is a requirement.

In this book I use the standard spellings for Plains Cree and for French, but for Michif I use most often a broad phonetic transcription. In some chapters, however, I mainly use the standard spelling of both source languages involved (where I think that phonetic detail would only obscure the argument). In my transcription I respect phonological and dialectal peculiarities of the speakers. In this way some of the variation is visible in the texts and examples.

The spelling I use for Michif is therefore actually a kind of compromise. On the one hand, it shows the differences among the various speakers and some of the variation in Michif; on the other hand, it shows the phonological differences between the Cree part and the French part in a more transparent way. Therefore I sometimes use different symbols for similar phonemes in the Cree part and the French part. For instance, both languages have an /i/ and /I/. Cree grammarians stress the length difference between the two vowels (long "i" and short "i"), whereas French grammarians stress the quality differences. In my transcription system, I use "i" for French "long /i/" and "ɪ" for French "short /i/." However, I use "i:" for Cree "long /i:/" and "I" for Cree "short /i/" because the phonetic range of these phonemes differ. Rhodes (1986) has shown that the allophones of the other vowels as well, in both components, differ considerably.

I have not done this consistently, however. For the other vowels I do not use different symbols for similar phonemes in the different components. It has to be kept in mind that a short /a/, for instance, can sound very different in the two components.

My transcription system is close to the International Phonetic Alphabet, except that I use /ž/ for IPA /ʒ/ and /š/ for IPA /ʃ/. Throughout this book, I use a broad phonetic transcription when I discuss Michif but standard spellings for French and Cree (as outlined in Wolfart and Ahenakew 1987) when I speak about these languages. For the Cree part, the languages are easily distinguishable since in the standard spelling, long vowels have a macron (^) on top and in Cree following a colon, for example, *wâpamêw* "he sees him" for Cree versus *wa:pame:w* for Michif. Cree and French are easily distinguishable in all Michif example sentences and texts because all Cree elements are consistently italicized throughout the book. As for the French part, it is easy to see whether standard or phonetic spelling is used when looking at diacritical marks, especially the tilde (~), which is used for nasal vowels in the phonetic system.

I deviate from this system only in a few cases. When I show texts in Michif, I mostly use standard spelling for the Cree and French parts. For the rest I have tried to make it as clear as possible when I am discussing Michif and when Cree or French. Although this is not totally satisfactory, it seems the best thing I can do. I hope this compromise satisfies the readers.

In all examples of Michif and other mixtures of French and Cree, the Cree elements are italicized. In the glosses, morphemes are separated by hyphens, and portmanteau morphemes have points that separate the elements conveyed in the morphemes (e.g., "1.PST" stands for "first person, past tense"). An arrow separates subject and object in the glosses; for example, "2 → 1" means "second-person subject, third-person object." A list of abbreviations used in the glosses follows.

ABBREVIATIONS

In the morphemic glosses, the following abbreviations are used:

ABL	ablative	DAMS	definite article, masculine singular
ABS	absolutive (transitive object, intransitive subject)	DEAN	deanimatizer
		DEF	definite
ADV	adverb	DEM	demonstrative
AI	animate intransitive verb	DETR	detransitivizer
AN	animate	DETRANS	detransitivizer
AOR	aorist	DIM	diminutive
APPL	applicative	DIR	direct marker
ARG	argument	DIST	distal
ART	article	DUB	dubitative
ATT	attitudinal particle	DUR	durative
BEN	benefactive	EMPH	emphatic marker
C	class	ESS	essive
CAS	case	EXCL	exclusive
CAUS	causative	F	feminine
CLASS	classificatory element	FIN	final
COM	comparative	FUT	future
COMIT	comitative	IAMS	indefinite article, masculine singular
COMP	complementizer		
CON, CONJ	conjunct order verb	IAFS	indefinite article, feminine singular
COND	conditional (called "subjunctive" by Algonquianists)		
		II	inanimate intransitive verb
		IMP	imperative order verb
COP	copula	IMPERF	imperfect
DAFS	definite article, feminine singular	IMPRS	impersonal
		INAN	inanimate

INCL	inclusive
IND	independent order verb
INDF	indefinite
INDFZR	indefinitizer (makes object indefinite)
INF	infinitive
INFER	inferential
INFL	inflection
INIT	initial
INT	interrogative
INTR	intransitivizer
INV	inverse
ITER	iterative
LOC	locative
M	masculine
MAN	manner
MDL	modal
N	noun
NA	animate noun
NAD	dependent animate noun (obligatorily possessed)
NEG	negation
NI	inanimate noun
NID	dependent inanimate noun
NOM	nominalizer
NON3	not third person; hence first or second
O, OBJ	object
OBL	obligational
OBV	obviative
P	plural
PA	plural article
PART	participle
PASS	passive
PC	uninflected particle
PERF	perfect
PL	plural
PN	prenoun
PO	possessed object
POSS	possessive
POSSD	possessed
POT	potential
PR	pronoun
PRE	prenoun and preverb
PREP	preposition
PRET	preterit
PROX	proximal

PST	past
PV	preverb
Q	question marker
RD	reduplication
REC	reciprocal
REDUP	reduplication
REFL	reflexive
REL	relative marker
RELR	relator (relative case)
RES	resultative
S	singular
SUB	subordinator
SUBJ	subject
T, TO	topic
TA	transitive animate verb
TI	transitive inanimate verb
TOP	topic
TRANS	transitive/transitivizer
VLNC	valency
VOL	volitional

1	first-person singular ("I")
11	first-person exclusive plural ["we (but not you)"]
1p	first-person exclusive plural ["we (but not you)"]
2	second-person singular ("you")
21	first-person inclusive plural ["you and me (and others)]"
2p	second-person plural ("you guys")
3	animate third person singular ("he," "she," "him," "her")
3p	animate third-person plural ("they")
3'	animate obviative ("the other")
4	inanimate singular ("it")
4p	inanimate plural ("them")
*	marks ungrammatical phrase or utterance
1→3	1 subject, 3 object (etc.)

Other abbreviations:

HBC	Hudson's Bay Company
NWC	North West Company
n.a.	not attested

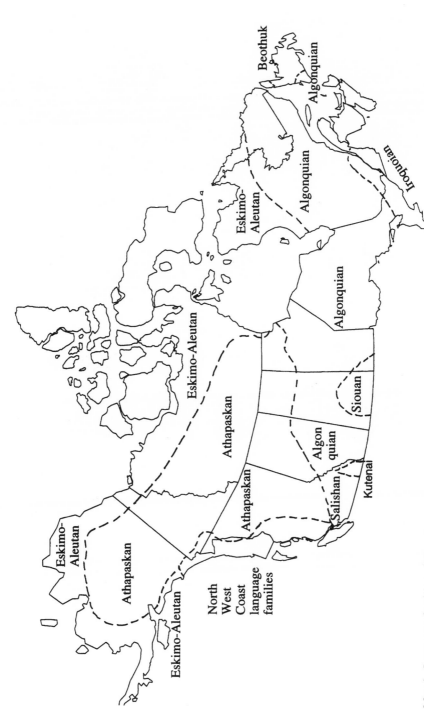

MAP 1. Language families of Canada.

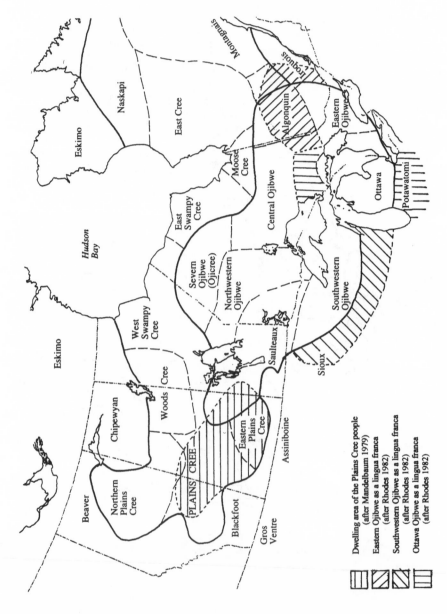

MAP 2. The Canadian Northwest: Cree and Ojibwe dialect areas.

Dwelling area of the Plains Cree people
(after Mandelbaum 1979)
Eastern Ojibwe as a lingua franca
(after Rhodes 1982)
Southwestern Ojibwe as a lingua franca
(after Rhodes 1982)
Ottawa Ojibwe as a lingua franca
(after Rhodes 1982)

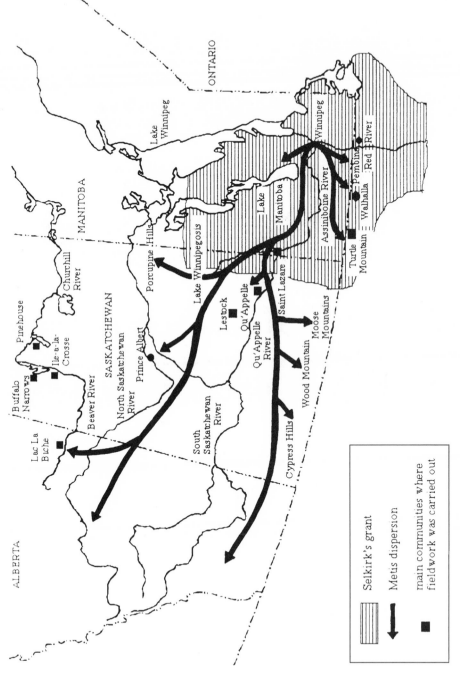

Map 3. The Canadian Northwest.

ALBERTA

SASKATCHEWAN

MANITOBA

ONTARIO

Lac La Biche

Buffalo Narrows

Ile-à-la-Crosse

Pinehouse

Churchill River

Beaver River

North Saskatchewan River

Prince Albert

South Saskatchewan River

Porcupine Hills

Lake Winnipegosis

Lake Winnipeg

Lake Manitoba

Lestock

Qu'Appelle

Qu'Appelle River

Saint Lazare

Assiniboine River

Winnipeg

Pembina

Walhalla

Red River

Turtle Mountain

Wood Mountain

Moose Mountains

Cypress Hills

Selkirk's grant

Metis dispersion

main communities where fieldwork was carried out

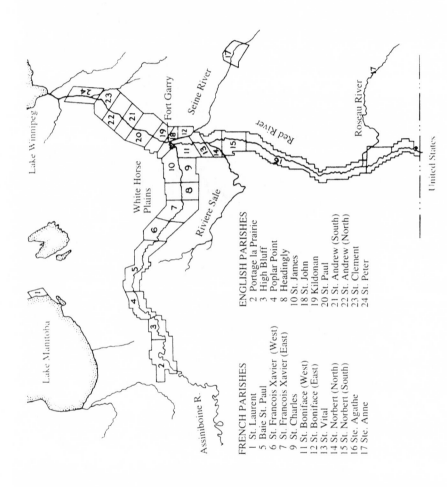

FRENCH PARISHES
1 St. Laurent
5 Baie St. Paul
6 St. Francois Xavier (West)
7 St. Francois Xavier (East)
9 St. Charles
11 St. Boniface (West)
12 St. Boniface (East)
13 St. Vital
14 St. Norbert (North)
15 St. Norbert (South)
16 Ste. Agathe
17 Ste. Anne

ENGLISH PARISHES
2 Portage la Prairie
3 High Bluff
4 Poplar Point
8 Headingly
10 St. James
18 St. John
19 Kildonan
20 St. Paul
21 St. Andrew (South)
22 St. Andrew (North)
23 St. Clement
24 St. Peter

MAP 4. Parishes of the Red River Settlement in 1870.

A Language
of
Our Own

1

Introduction

The Problem of Michif

The Michif language is spoken by Métis, the descendants of European fur traders (often French Canadians) and Cree-speaking Amerindian women. It is spoken in scattered Métis communities in the provinces of Saskatchewan and Manitoba in Canada and in North Dakota and Montana in the United States. There are also pockets of speakers in northern Alberta and the Northwest Territories in Canada and in Minnesota and Oregon in the United States. It is spoken outside the French-speaking part of Canada and the Cree-speaking areas of North America. At present, the number of speakers is estimated at fewer than 1,000. It was probably double or triple this number around the turn of the century but never much higher. Michif is a rather peculiar language. It is half Cree (an Amerindian language) and half French. It is a mixed language, drawing its nouns from a European language and its verbs from an Amerindian language. It has been called the "nec plus ultra of grammars in contact" (Papen 1987c). Michif speakers, however, rarely know both Cree and French. No such mixture of two languages has been reported from any other part of the world. There are some other mixed languages, but these are all of a different type, dissimilar to Michif. Michif is unusual, if not unique, in several respects among the languages of the world. It poses challenges for all theories of language and of language contact.

First, it is a problem for the "family tree" model of language. In this model, every language has one parent language, from which it differs slightly. One "parent" can have different "daughter" languages. These daughter languages and the parent language are said to be "genetically related": they belong to the same "branch" of a "language family." Michif cannot be classified by this model. Being a mixture of Cree and French, it cannot be classified as an Algonquian (Amerindian) language or as an Indo-European (or Romance) language. Therefore, Michif is a problem for classification and a challenge to this model (Orser 1984).

3

Second, Michif is a problem for theories of language contact. A number of processes of contact-induced change and a number of types of contact languages have been formulated by scholars in this field, but Michif appears to be different from all these, as I show. Mixed languages are rare, but Michif appears to differ strikingly even from those.

Third, Michif challenges all theoretical models of language. It is a language with two completely different components, with separate sound systems, morphological endings, and syntactic rules. For psycholinguists this is a challenge: how does this work in the brain? For language theoreticians it is also a problem: how can one make a grammatical model that combines two grammatical systems in one language? How can one construct a model that accounts for different phrase structures in one language depending on the source language from which the morphemes are drawn? How can one account for the presence of two phonological systems in one language?

In many respects, Michif is an impossible language. I know several professional linguists who contest its existence since it does not fit into their model of how a language, or a mixed language, should look. It is therefore of the utmost importance that we study, describe, and preserve this unique language. In this book I do not deal with all the challenges just formulated. I limit myself to the question of the genesis of Michif: how, why, and when did this language come into being? Although my background in linguistics is obvious throughout the book, this study is interdisciplinary in its approach. There are historical, anthropological, and psychological aspects to the genesis of this language. I hope to show that Michif came about as the result of a process of language mixture I call "language intertwining," which has led to this peculiar case because of the typological properties of the languages in contact. The impetus for its emergence was the fact that the bilingual Métis were no longer accepted as Indians or as French, and they formulated their own ethnic identity, which was mixed and in which a mixed "language of our own" was considered part of their ethnicity.

In this chapter I outline the problem Michif poses for theories of language contact. For this purpose, a brief sketch of the Michif language is needed to show the striking and regular mixture of French and Cree elements. Some grammatical categories are consistently Cree, others are consistently French, and some can be derived from both languages. Then, to show the exceptionality of Michif, I present a brief overview of theories of language contact and contact languages. It will be clear that Michif does not fit into any of the types or categories that studies of language contact have brought to light. The main function that contact languages originally had and their linguistic nature are intimately connected, as has been shown convincingly by Thomason and Kaufman (1988) for other types of language contact, and this must be the case with Michif, too. In the next section I review a number of hypotheses concerning the genesis of Michif. Only a few of these appear to be worth serious consideration, and these are the ones that recur in the rest of this book. I end the chapter with some conclusions and an outline of the book.

Short Structural Sketch of Michif

Only a brief sketch of the Michif language is presented here. A more detailed grammatical description is given in Chapter Four. An understanding of the facts presented in this chapter will enable the reader to grasp the problems and the general discussion on language contact and also to see how Michif fits into the language contact models, or rather how it does *not* fit in.

The structure of Michif is best illustrated by presenting a text and then illustrating its structural characteristics. I first present the English version as told by the speaker and then the same story as he told it in Michif. The story was told in both languages by Modeste Gosselin of Lebret, in the Fort Qu'Appelle Valley in Saskatchewan.

(1) That old trapper, way up north, he was old, the old bugger. He was trapping up there in a cabin. He took sick, you see. And when he got up in the morning he was sick, but still he had a little bit to eat and then he had to go and see, visit his traps. So he went anyway and a storm come up, he got lost, he couldn't find his way back to his cabin, and he walked and he walked and he walked. He was sick, he was old, and he played out and he was real sick then. And he thought, well, if I'm gonna die, I'll sit down beside this tree, a good place to die. So he sat beside the big tree there. He was looking and all of a sudden he see that timber wolf coming straight for him. So he just sat there and watched, looked at him. The timber wolf come right for him, you see. And when the timber wolf come to him, he open his mouth to grab the old man. The old man stuck his arm in the wolf's mouth, right through the wolf, and he grab him by the tail and he pull you see, and he pull that wolf inside out! So the wolf went back the way he come, ha ha ha!

The Michif version is given in standardized French and Cree spelling (for Cree, see Wolfart and Ahenakew 1987). All the Cree elements are printed in italics:

(2) un vieux *ana ayi*. . . . un vieux *ê-opahikêt ê-nôcihcikêt*, you see, *êkwa ayi*. . . . un matin *ê-waniskât âhkosiw*, but *kêyâpit ana wî-nitawi-wâpahtam* ses pièges. *sipwêhtêw. mêkwât êkotê ê-itasihkêt*, une tempête. *maci-kîsikâw*. pas moyên *si-miskahk* son shack. *wanisin*. pas moyên son shack *si-miskahk. pimohtêw, pimohtêw. êy-âhkosit êkwa* le-vieux-*iw-it nôhtêsin*. d'un gros arbre *pimi-cipatapiw*. "*ôta nipiyâni*," *itêyihtam êsa*, "une bonne place *ôma si-nipi-yân*." *ê-wâpamât ôhi* le loup de bois *ê-pâ-pahtâ-yi-t*. ha, ha. *pêhêw, ka-kanawâpamêw*. le loup *awa pê-isipahtâw êkota itê api-yit. êkwa ayi* . . . *pâstinam* sa bouche *ôhi* le loup *ê-wî-otinât. pastinên*, son bras *yahkinam*, right through *anihi* le loup. the wolf dans la queue *ohci-otinêw*, par la queue *âpoci-pitêw*! *kîhtwâm* le loup *asê-kîwê-pahtâw*! ha ha ha!

Here is the same text in a morpheme-by-morpheme translation, from which false starts have been deleted[1]:

(3) un vieux *ê-opahikê-t ê-nôcihcikê-t*,
     an.M old trap-he.CONJ COMP-trap-he.CONJ

(4) *êkwa* un matin *ê-waniskâ-t âhkosi-w*,
     and an.M morning COMP-wake.up-he be.sick-he

(5) but *kêyâpit ana wî-nitawi-wâpaht-am* ses pièges.
     but still this.one want-go-see.it-he.it his.P trap.

(6) *sipwêhtê-w. mêkwât êkotê ê-itasîhkê-t,* une tempête.
     leave-he. meantime there CONJ-be.busy-he. a.F storm

(7) *maci-kîsikâ-w.* pas moyên *si-misk-ahk* son shack. *wanisi-n.*
bad-weather-3. no way COMP-find-he.it. his cabin be.lost-he

(8) pas moyên son shack *si-misk-ahk.*
no way his cabin COMP-find-he.it

(9) *pimohtê-w, pimohtê-w. êy-âhkosi-t êkwa* le-vieux-*iwi-t nôhtêsi-n*
walk-he, walk-he. COMP-be.sick-he and the.M-old-be-he play.out-he.

(10) d'un gros arbre *pimicipatapi-w.* "*ôta nipi-yân-i,*"
of-a big tree sit.upright-he here die-1.CONJ-COND

(11) *itêyiht-am êsa,* "une bonne place *ôma si-nipi-yân*"
think.of.it-he.it it.is.said a.F good.F place this COMP.FUT.-die-1S

(12) *ê-wâpam-ât ôhi* le loup de bois *ê-pa-pahtâ-yi-t.*
COMP-see.him-he.him that.OBV the.M wolf of wood COMP-RD-run-OBV-he

(13) *pêhê-w. ka-kanawâpam-êw* le loup
wait.for-he.him. REDUP-look.at-he.him the.M wolf

(14) *awa pê-isipahtâ-w êkota itê ê-api-yi-t.*
this come-thus-run-he there where COMP-sit-OBV-he

(15) *êkwa pâstin-am* sa bouche *ôhi* le loup *ê-wî-otin-ât.*
and open-he.it his.F mouth this.OBV the.M wolf COMP-want-take-he.him

(16) *pastin-ên* son bras *yahkin-am* right through *anihi* le loup.
open-he.it his.M arm push.forward-he.it right through that-AN the.M wolf

(17) the wolf dans la queue *ohci-otin-êw,*
the wolf in the tail from-take-he.him

(18) par la queue *âpoci-pit-êw*!
by the tail inside.out-pull-he.him

(19) *kîhtwâm* le loup *asê-kîwê-pahtâ-w*! ha ha ha!
again the.M wolf back-go.home-run-he

This text is a representative example of the Michif language of the 1980s. The man who told this story speaks French fairly well, but he is not able to understand or speak Cree sufficiently to hold a conversation in the language. His active knowledge of Cree words is much too limited. Therefore, he is fairly representative as a Michif speaker: virtually no Michif speakers are able to speak or understand Cree, and only a minority speak and understand French.

In this short story, a number of things may strike the reader, for example, that Cree and French words are used in roughly equal proportions. This can be seen easily, as all Cree elements are italicized in the text. Further it must be noticed that *all* of the verbs in this story are Cree and *all* of the nouns are French. The only words that are not French or Cree are a few English words ("but," "shack," and "right through"). It is clear that not only French nouns but also French articles, both definite and indefinite and both masculine and feminine (*un matin, une tempête, le loup,* and *la bouche*), are used exactly as they would be in French. Also the French possessive pronouns *son* and *ses* are apparently used with the gender and number they would have in French (*son bras, son shack*, and *ses pièges*). French prepositions (*dans* and *par*) are also used. Thus one surmises at first that all noun-related parts of speech appear to be French, but this is not entirely correct: the demonstratives are Cree (*ana* and *awa*). In Cree there are different demonstratives for animate and inanimate nouns [*ana* "that" (animate); *ôma* "that" (inanimate)], and for close, far, and very far entities (e.g., *awa* "this"; *ana* "that"). In Cree there are also different forms of the demonstratives for animate nouns that are the topic of the story (e.g., *ana*) and animate nouns that are new in the story (e.g., *anihi*), the latter being called "obviative" forms. All of these are used in Michif, too. The Cree demonstratives in Michif apparently agree in number, animacy, and obviation with the noun, as in Cree.

Further the few French adjectives in the text have a masculine form (*un gros arbre*) or a feminine form (*une bonne place*) according to the noun they modify, just as they would in French. Apparently the French part of this story is very close to other varieties of French. There seems to be one exception. When the man took the wolf by its tail, the narrator says, "*dans* la queue," whereas a Frenchman or French Canadian would have used a different preposition, that is, *par*. These kinds of differences are relatively insignificant compared to the similarities. Whereas French has a number of locative prepositions (*sous, à, sur, dans*, etc.), Michif generally has only one, *dans*, often pronounced as /da:/ or /da/. Of course, Michif can express more precise location, too, through additional prepositions like *en arrière* "behind." Also, the meaning of words in Michif is sometimes slightly different from that in French or Cree. For example, in Michif the word *gros* means "big," but in Canadian and European French this word generally means "fat," with "big" as a secondary meaning.

In this text no French verbs are used; all the verbs are Cree. We see that these Cree verbs can be quite complex. They have agreement markers, like *-t* and *-w* for "he" and *-yân* for "I." Some verbs can express things in one word, whereas English needs almost a whole sentence: *wî-nitawi-wâpaht-am* "he wanted to go and see it/them." In the text, different verb forms are used for subordinate clauses and main clauses, called by linguists the conjunct order/mode and independent order/mode, respectively, just as in Cree. The conjunct forms have a complementizer type of prefix ("that," "when," etc.). Further, there are reduplicated verb forms in the text, like *ka-kanawâpamêw*. The first syllable of the stem is reduplicated to express "ongoing action," just as it would occur in Cree to express the same aspect (Ahenakew and Wolfart 1983). Cree verbs have different stem forms for animate and inanimate objects (in transitive sentences) or for animate and inanimate subjects (in intransitive sentences). The same occurs in the Michif verbs. There are transitive inanimate stems like *wâpaht-* "see it" and transitive animate stems like *wâpam-* "see him/her" in this text. The Michif French nouns have the same animate or inanimate gender as their Cree semantic equivalents. In short, all the verbs are used exactly as they would have been used in Cree or, to be more precise, in the Plains Cree dialect.

We also see that in this text all the words are either all French or all Cree, with one exception: in the word *le-vieux-iw-it* "he who is old," the first half is French and the second half is Cree. This is a French noun (in Michif *le vieux* means "old person" or "husband") with Cree verb endings. This, too, occurs in Michif, although it is fairly rare. It will be discussed in more detail in Chapter Four.

Word order seems to be more like Cree than like French. For example, in sentence (20), the verb is in the final position of the sentence, which is common in Cree but impossible in French.

(20)   The wolf dans la queue *ohci-otin-êw*.
        The wolf by the tail he-took-him-from.

In the noun phrase, however, French rules are followed closely. Some adjectives like *bonne* and *gros* are placed before the noun, as in French. Most of the French adjectives are placed behind the noun in Michif, following French rules for each individual adjective.

If the verbs are Cree and the nouns are French, the next question is, what about adverbs and other grammatical function words that do not belong to either category? We have seen that demonstratives are Cree, adjectives can be French or Cree, and adpositions (prepositions and postpositions) are usually French. Personal pronouns (used only for emphasis in Michif, as in Cree) are derived from Cree. In this short text there are only four adverbs: *kêyâpit*, which is the Cree word for "still"; *mêkwât*, which here means "in the meantime"; *êkotê* or *êkota*, which means "there"; and *êkwa*, which means "and, now." All of these words happen to be Cree, but this is not necessarily so. We see later (Chapters Four and Five) that adverbs can be both Cree or French, depending on the speaker and on their meanings. This is true not only for adverbs but also for other function words, which can often be taken from either language. Quantifiers can be either French and Cree, but numerals are always French.

English words are also common in Michif since today all its speakers know English, which is the language most of them ordinarily speak. However, except for words that do not have equivalents in Michif—often objects recently introduced into Métis society—the English words are usually not considered an integral part of Michif. In careful speech, English is usually avoided.

In the preceding text a standardized spelling was used for both the French part and the Cree part. I now repeat this text in a broad phonetic transcription in order to make some remarks about the phonological system of Michif.

(21)   "æ̃ vjɸ *ana:ji*, æ̃ vjɸ *upahike:t e:nu:čIsčikI:t* ju si:, *ekwa aji*. æ̃ matæ̃ *wanIška:t a:hkuši:w*,
        bAt *ke:ja:pIt n wi:ndowa:pAhtAm* si: pji:ž. *šIpwe:hte:w. me:kwa:t e:kote: taši:hkI:t*
        ɛn tãpɛt. *mAčiki:šikA:w.* pɔmjæ̃ *šImIška:* sõ šæk. *wAnIšIn.* pAmjæ̃ sõ šæk *šImIška:h.*
        pmuhte:w, pmuhte:w. eja:hkušIt e:kwa IIvjɸwIt nuhte:šIn. dæ̃ gru: za:b *pičipAtapIw,*
        uta nIpuja:ni Ite:htAm e:sa, ɛn bɔn plAs *uma šI-nIpuja:n. awa:pama:t uhi* Ilud bwa:
        e:wa:pahtajIt. ha, ha. *pe:he:w. kakana:pame:w* II lu *wa pe:špahta:w ekta te:pajIt. e:kwa*
        ajIh. pA:šte:nAm sa buš *uhI* Ilu *e:wycina:t* æ̃h. *pašte:n* sa . . . sõ bra *jahkinAm*, rait tru
        dɘ . . . *anI* Ilu. dɘ wulf *e:kwa ajI* . . . dã la čy osi *u:čicIne:w* par la ky, hæ̃ *a:pučipite:w.*
        ki:htwa:m 1 lu *še:kiwe:pahta:w*. ha, ha ha.

There are apparently two different phonological systems in the language, one for the Cree and one for the French. Only in Cree is vowel length distinctive (e.g., *ši-nipija:n* "that I sleep"; *ši-nipijan* "that you sleep"). In the French part there are nasal vowels (marked with a tilde) but not in the Cree part. In the Cree part of Michif there is a sound /e/, whereas in the French part there is not; whereas "normal" French has an /e/, Michif has an /i/, for example, in *si: pyi:ž* (Fr. /se: pjɛž/). Also, the French /o/ is pronounced as /u/ in Michif, and the French /ø/ is often pronounced as /y/ (*queue* is /ky/ or /čy/). The Cree part has only the sibilant /š/, whereas French has both /s/ and /š/. Phonemes like /f/, /r/, /y/, and so on occur only in the French part, and the preaspirated /hk/ and /ht/ are not used in French. There are other differences between the two components of the language, but these are sufficient to show that the Cree and the French parts of the language preserve their own sound systems.

We also see that there is some variation in the words. The first time the French word *queue* is used in the text, it is pronounced [čy]; the second time, just a few words away, it is [ky]. The stops /t/ and /k/ can be palatalized in front of a non–low front vowel in the French part and /k/ can also be labialized to [kw] before back vowels. None of these variations exists in the Cree part.

In summary, we can say that Michif is a mixed language of Plains Cree and French words plus a few English ones. The French and Cree elements are about evenly distributed. English words intrude into Michif because that is the language mostly used by speakers of Michif. Verbs, personal pronouns, and demonstratives are always Cree; nouns, numerals, and articles are always French. Michif verbs have the same complexity as the Cree verbs. Michif nouns are used and categorized as in French. Word order mostly follows Cree, that is, almost completely free, but order in noun phrases is like that in French. The agreement system of Michif combines the agreement systems of French (masculine or feminine) and Cree (animate or inanimate). French nouns are classified as animate or inanimate as if they were Cree nouns and showed the appropriate gender agreement in the verb. Michif adjectives from French are used as are French adjectives, Cree adjectives in the Cree way. Other categories associated with noun phrases, such as prepositions, are often French. Adverbs can be Cree or French. A very few words have French stems and Cree affixes. Cree and French lost very little of their complexity in Michif. Michif has two phonological systems, one for the Cree part and one for the French part, each with its own rules. The Cree part is almost identical with Plains Cree, and the French part is almost identical with the Métis French dialect, which is a derivative of eastern Canadian French dialects. Although in Chapter Four we see that this sketch is not accurate in all details, in the meantime it does give an impression of the Michif language.

The Place of Michif in the Study of Language Contact

Michif is obviously a result of language contact, in particular Cree and French. The study of language contact is a subdiscipline of linguistics that is receiving more and more attention. It is a broad field, with ramifications in psychology, anthropology, sociolinguistics, and creole studies. The more language-centered approach covers fields like word borrowing, code switching, or code mixing (the use of two languages in one and the same sentence); language change induced by contact; interlanguages and other results of imperfect second-language acquisition; and the emergence of new languages such as trade jargons, pidgins, and creole languages.

In this section, I briefly discuss some of the findings of research in contact linguistics, but one can easily see that Michif appears not to fit into any of the classifications formulated in this field. It must be stressed at this point that monolingualism is by no means the "normal case" that most Westerners take it to be. Only in industrialized, Western societies are most people monolingual. In large parts of the globe people grow up learning two, three, and sometimes even four or more languages. In this section I speak of bilingualism, although people may know more than two languages. What is said here is probably valid for multilingualism, too. So, for reasons of simplicity, I take two languages as a point of departure.

A *pidgin* is a language that may develop between groups who do not know each other's language but who want to communicate, for instance, in trade or labor relations. Only a limited set of words is used, and the grammatical structure is simplified and not fixed. Pidgins have to be learned as such. Although Michif is associated with the fur trade in Canada, where one could expect a pidgin to develop, Michif is very much unlike a pidgin in that it has neither a reduced lexicon nor a simplified grammatical system. Many pidgins are simplified forms of one language, but Michif is based on two languages. *Jargon* is a term sometimes used for a primitive and rudimentary form of a pidgin. It is clear that Michif is not a jargon either.

A *lingua franca* is a language—not necessarily reduced in lexicon or in its grammatical system—used by people who have different mother tongues in order to communicate with one another, for example, English at an intertribal Amerindian celebration or an international scientific congress. However, Michif is used by Métis only to communicate with other Métis, not with other ethnic groups. It is also unlikely that it was once used for communication between Cree Indians and French fur traders. The first speakers must have had such a good knowledge of both French and Cree that the use of either would have been the obvious choice, not a complicating mixture of the two. Furthermore, lingua francas are always important languages that are well documented in historical sources. There is no mention in print of Michif before the 1930s, although it must have been spoken at that time by several generations of Métis. This also points to the fact that it was not a generally used language like a lingua franca.

Trade language is sometimes used as a general term for pidgins, jargons, and lingua francas. Since Michif is unlike any of these three subtypes, it is not a trade language either. Neither is Michif a form of *foreigner talk*, which is a simplified form of one's language that people may use when speaking to people who do not know the language. Michif is in no way simplified, and it is not used with outsiders. A *creole* is a language with few or no morphological markers and with a lexicon basically derived from one language, spoken as a first language. Many creole speakers are descendants of slaves or members of a multilingual work force. Michif is not a creole language since it has all the morphological complexities of Cree and French, unlike all creole languages. Neither did it emerge among a multilingual work force.

Languages can take over words from other languages. These are called loanwords or *borrowings*. Michif clearly has elements from two languages. Could the Cree or the French part be considered a borrowing? It does not seem so. Even in the most extreme cases of borrowing, the proportion of loanwords is not so enormous as in Michif. Furthermore, loanwords are usually adapted to the sound system of the borrowing language, but in Michif both components preserve their own sound systems. Also, no cases are known of such categorial borrowings (only nouns, only verbs, or something like it) as in Michif. Therefore Michif does not seem to be a case of Cree borrowing into French or French borrowing into Cree.

There is also a fairly rare process called *relexification*. In this process all the stems of a language are replaced by stems from another language. In Michif, one could say that, for example, all Cree noun stems are replaced by French noun stems, but none of the Cree verb stems has been replaced by French verb stems. Furthermore, there are also French adverbs, prepositions, and so on in Michif, which one would not expect here: they should be derived from Cree. Therefore Michif is also unlike relexification.

People in many bilingual communities are reported to mix the languages they speak spontaneously when they are among themselves. This is called *code switching* or *code mixing*. However, virtually none of the speakers of Michif speaks Cree, and only few of them speak French, although it is clear that the first speakers of Michif must have been Cree-French bilinguals. Could they have been code mixing or switching? This is unlikely at first sight since nowhere in the world are there reported cases of code mixing in which only certain categories (e.g., only nouns) are taken from the other language. In code mixing, in principle, anything can appear in any language.

When people learn a second language, one speaks (not surprisingly) of *second-language acquisition*. Michif is not such a case: no Cree speakers are acquiring French, and no French speakers are acquiring Cree. Could it have been second-language acquisition in the past? When people acquire a second language, they construct *interlanguages*: conceptual approximations of the target language of the language learner. They may stop making progress. A *fossilized* form of parts of a second language can be the result. Such an in-between form between the first and second language can be an intelligible but still a far from perfect form of the second language. Michif did not come about as a fossilized second language nor as an interlanguage. The Cree and French components are so close to the source languages that this mixed language cannot have been imperfect second-language acquisition: the Cree half is virtually flawless Cree, and the French half is virtually flawless French. Its first speakers must have been fluent bilinguals rather than language learners.

When people shift from one language to another, their second language may show traces of the first. These are called *substrate features* of a first language in a second language. In the case of Michif, one cannot speak of Cree with a French substrate or the other way around because both components are too well preserved.

Although Michif itself is now a dying language, its genesis is not related to *language death*. Dying languages show a reduction of the morphological system (attrition), monostylism, frequent word borrowings, and word-finding problems by its speakers. These signs of decay indeed show up in the speech of some modern speakers, but it has nothing to do with the genesis of the language. The fact that people learned it as their first (and only) language shows that there was no question of a dying language then.

These are all the relevant phenomena related to language contact, but Michif is unlike any phenomenon reported in studies on this subject. It is the goal of this book to explain the genesis of Michif, both from an ethnological viewpoint and from a linguistic viewpoint. Is Michif really as unique as it seems? A number of suggestions have been made about its genesis, and these are discussed in the next section. A few of the language contact phenomena just mentioned, such as borrowing, relexification, and code mixing, recur there.

Some Hypotheses on the Genesis of Michif

I have shown that Michif in linguistics is like the duck-billed platypus in biology— in many ways unclassifiable. Michif does not fit into the family tree model of languages since it is equally French (Romance, Indo-European) and Cree (Algonquian). Michif is a contact language, but it is also very different from other reported results of language contact. It is not a pidgin, a creole, an interlanguage, a relexified language, a case of code switching or code mixing, or anything else reported from language contact studies. It is unique. Still, people have expressed opinions concerning the type of language that Michif is. In this section I discuss these briefly. Some were presented by the Métis themselves, others by scholars. Some are mentioned just for amusement; they give an impression of the ideas that outsiders and Michif speakers themselves have developed to explain the unusual mixed quality of this language. A number of these opinions can be refuted easily, but there are a few that may be relevant. These are discussed in more detail than the ones that are too implausible. Some of the hypotheses concerning the genesis of Michif involve social circumstances; others are hypotheses about psycholinguistic mechanisms. It is obvious that both types complement each other. The hypotheses are discussed here briefly and later in some detail.

- *New nation / mixed identity hypothesis.* As the Métis became a new ethnic group, consisting of bilinguals of mixed ancestry, a new language to express this identity would be part of their ethnicity. A new language was created out of the two already spoken or was developed from mixed patterns already existing.
- *Trade language hypothesis.* When the French and the Cree came into contact, they created a mixed language to be able to communicate with each other.
- *Laziness hypothesis.* The Frenchmen were lazy and let the Indian women (their wives) do all the work. Hence the verbs, expressing action, are in the Indian language and the nouns are in French.
- *Separate task hypothesis.* The vocabulary split is related to the separate tasks of the fathers and mothers of the first generation of Métis. The French fathers and the Indian mothers each brought in a part of the vocabulary. That is, the women brought their own special vocabulary and so did the men, leading to this mixed language.
- *Pointing hypothesis.* The Indian women who married French-speaking traders did not know French. The French traders pointed to all kinds of objects, so that the women learned the French words for objects and taught these to their children.

Of these five "social" hypotheses, the last three all presume that the French men and Amerindian women were different enough to learn a new vocabulary from their partners. The four following are all linguistic hypotheses, mostly about the reason and manner in which the languages were mixed.

- *Verb-noun mixing hypothesis.* The first generation started mixing the two languages by taking the verbs from one language and the nouns from the other. This would be a rare, but presumably not unique, phenomenon.

- *Code-mixing hypothesis.* The language is the consequence of code mixing, which occurs in communities of fluent bilinguals, who mix their languages within one sentence. Michif would have emerged from French-Cree code mixing.

- *Relexification hypothesis.* Relexification theory claims that a language can replace all of its vocabulary items with items from another language. Michif would be an anomalous instance, whereby not the whole vocabulary but only the Cree nouns were replaced by French nouns.

- *Difficult parts hypothesis.* In Cree the structure of the verb is notoriously complex, and in French the noun is more complex than the verb. It has been suggested that Michif combines the difficult parts of these two languages.

I discuss these hypotheses in the following section.

New Nation/Mixed Identity Hypothesis

The Métis nation emerged under special circumstances. The man and the woman brought different bodies of knowledge and ideologies. The Métis are a new nation, both in their own eyes and in the eyes of other peoples, from the early 1800s onward (see Chapter Three). The Métis are not only a new nation with their own ethnic identity but also a mixed group. It can safely be assumed that the Michif language arose as a consequence of the contact of French-speaking men with Cree-speaking Amerindian women. Their descendants speak the mixed language. Considering the rather unusual social circumstances under which the Métis emerged, it is reasonable to assume that the atypical linguistic result is somehow a consequence of these atypical social circumstances (Thomason and Kaufman 1988: 233). Therefore it is possible that the emergence of the Michif language involved this new and mixed identity.

These circumstance are not unique, however. If we look at other cases in which groups of men who spoke one language married women who spoke another, we find striking results. Their descendants speak mixed languages. The Griekwas and Basters (Afrikaans fathers and Khoekhoen mothers in the first generation) in South Africa speak a mixture of Afrikaans and Hottentot. The Island Carib (Carib fathers and Arawak mothers) spoke a mixture of Carib and Arawak. The same is true for the Krojos (Javanese mothers and Dutch fathers) and the Pecus (Malay mothers and Dutch fathers). All these groups—or in some cases, peoples—speak a mixed language. Of

course, this did not happen very often in the history of the world, but the cases mentioned are clear. These people seem to have expressed their dual identity through a
mixed language, although there are a number of additional conditions, for example,
that there must have been a fair number of these mixed people (to be discussed in
Chapter Seven).

Therefore, there seems to be a relation between separate groups with dual ancestry and a new ethnic identity and mixed languages. Do these languages have
the same dichotomy as in Michif, with verbs from one language and nouns from
another? No. None of the others looks like Michif. In those cases, the languages
are mixed, but they have stems from one language and affixes from another. The
lexicon is from one language and the grammatical system is from another (see
Chapter Seven).

Despite these linguistic differences between Michif and the other mixed languages that emerged under similar social and historical conditions, there are good
reasons to study the latter in more detail. Although Michif differs structurally, the
social circumstances are similar and led to a similar result. We thus study these cases
in Chapter Seven, hoping to explain both the differences and the similarities between
them and Michif.

Trade Language Hypothesis

What we know about trade languages is that they are always, more or less, simplified versions of other languages (lingua francas or pidgins) or some kind of mixture
that is also strongly simplified (mixed-lexicon pidgins).[2] Lingua francas are only
slightly simplified versions. Michif, however, is no less complex than either French
or Cree. One could even claim that it is more complex: the intricate Cree verb system has been preserved, as well as the French nominal system with its unpredictable
gender assignment in the article and its definite and indefinite forms. French nouns
have a great number of derivational suffixes, many of which are preserved in Michif.
Cree nouns have only two inflectional suffixes and a handful of derivational suffixes,
and they do not have overt gender marking. Therefore it seems that the most complex categories of each language are part of Michif instead of the most simple. Furthermore, one of the two inflectional noun affixes from Cree (the obviative) is also
used in Michif. It has also been made clear that Michif has preserved both Cree and
French gender systems (see also Chapter Four), which cannot be regarded as a simplification of the language. Michif is in no way structurally similar to a simplified
language such as a pidgin. Contrary to pidgins, Michif has preserved virtually all
original morphology. Furthermore, if Michif was indeed the trade language used in
European-Amerindian trade contacts, there would have been extant documents and
vocabularies, in manuscript and in press (Bakker 1988–1989). None of the traders
or missionaries or travelers, however, mentions it. Therefore Michif cannot have had
the importance of a trade language.

The Michif language preserves so many features of both French and Cree that
the language must have been formed by French-Cree bilinguals. On the one hand, if
the French trader and the Indian (whether trader or wife) did speak each other's languages, the trade would naturally take place in either French or Cree instead of in

some complicating mixture. There would be absolutely no need for a new language. Fluency in two languages would not lead to a new language in which the message is the impetus for communication. On the other hand, if the French trader and the Indian did not speak each other's language, other, similar situations show that a simplified version of one of the languages would have been used, often a pidgin. Nowhere in the world did a trading situation trigger a language with a morphological complexity and a mixed nature like Michif.

In fact, in the whole fur trade area in Canada—where Michif is said to have emerged—no pidginized form of Cree seems to have arisen (Bakker in press), although a pidginized form of Ojibwe was in use both between Indians and between Indians and Europeans (Nichols 1992, 1995; Bakker 1994a). There are three factors in the area that hindered the genesis of a pidgin: the presence of multilinguals, the widespread existence of lingua francas, and the presence of interpreters. The first and most important explanation is given by Taylor: "Many American Indian groups solved their problems of communication at tribal and language boundaries through the mediation of bilingual persons. Often such bilingualism resulted from accidental factors such as intermarriage or a period of residence in a foreign tribe" (1981a: 175). In other words, in almost any tribal group there were one or more individuals who spoke the language of a neighboring tribe. As the Indian bands were often patrilocal in North America, bilingualism by intermarriage especially was widespread on this continent (Owen 1965).

The second reason for the rarity of pidgins in North America is the existence of lingua francas, which are mother tongues for one powerful tribe but second languages for a number of neighboring tribes. In Canada, Huron (Iroquoian) was a lingua franca in the area east of the Great Lakes before 1650. West of this area Ojibwe was (and still is) a lingua franca, and farther west it was (and sometimes still is) Plains Cree (Lacombe 1874a: xi; Rhodes 1982). These three lingua francas were all spoken in fur-trading areas, as were other lingua francas in other areas: for these see Silverstein (1973), Taylor (1981a), and Bakker and Grant (1996). Together they cover most of the territory where the French Canadian fur traders traveled on their canoe routes to the West. This must have contributed to the fact that no pidgins or trade languages are reported from the fur trade.

A third and last reason for this absence may be the presence of a great number of children from mixed European-Indian marriages, who must have been bilingual in the languages of both parents. There is some evidence that most of the French Canadians also spoke a number of Amerindian languages and lingua francas (Lang 1991; see also Chapter Two). These bilinguals regularly acted as interpreters.

So we can conclude that in North America, pidgins and trade languages were relatively rare despite the linguistic diversity on the continent. Because of the presence of Indians and Europeans who spoke several Amerindian languages (and possibly a European tongue, too) and children of mixed marriages, who knew both French or English and some Amerindian language, and the widespread knowledge of lingua francas in the most important areas of the fur trade, there was no need for the formation of trade languages. That is, there was no need for a new language to develop, Michif or any other. In short, Michif did not develop as a trade language between the French and the Amerindians, nor was it ever used as such.

The Three Men/Women Hypotheses

In this section I discuss together the three hypotheses that claim that the mixed nature of Michif involves the man-woman dichotomy.

LAZINESS HYPOTHESIS

The laziness hypothesis was suggested to me by a historian, not without irony, at a meeting on the history of the fur trade. He speculated that the Frenchmen were lazy, and the Amerindian women had to do all the work. Hence the words that denote activities would be in the Amerindian language, and the words for "chair"—in which the Frenchman would be sitting, looking out of the "window" and smoking his "pipe"— would be French. This idea must be rejected. Even if men did not engage in certain actions, they must have been able to speak about them—perhaps even more so. Also, historical sources show that the Métis men and the French fur traders had to work hard for their survival in fishing, hunting, trapping, and so on.

SEPARATE TASK HYPOTHESIS

The separate task hypothesis is also based on the assumption that men and women, speaking different languages, had different tasks in the family and in the community, and therefore the vocabularies would reflect the separation of their roles. This hypothesis is untenable. An important objection is that the Cree and French languages are always associated with one and the same task. Both nouns and verbs are involved in any job. Berry picking, for instance, is traditionally a woman's job, both in Indian society and Métis society. But the verb for "berry picking" is Cree, and the names for all the different berries, except for one, are French. Handling guns was more a man's task, but the Michif word for "gun" is French and the word for "shooting" is Cree. Things men and women did together also have French and Cree words. The Michif words for "house" or "tipi" and the objects one can find inside are French, but the words for "to live," "to cook," "to sleep," and so on are Cree-derived. Therefore, this hypothesis must also be rejected.

POINTING HYPOTHESIS

The pointing hypothesis was suggested orally to me by various people independently. It is based on the fact that in Michif most visible objects are derived from French. Thus objects like "table," "window," "axe," "knife," and so on were taught in French by the fur traders to the Amerindians they were in contact with, more specifically the women they married, that is, the mothers of their children. The hypothesis is implausible for a number of reasons. There are also genuine Cree names in Cree communities for these objects, and few of the French nouns denote cultural innovations for the Cree. In addition, the typically Amerindian items, such as "tipi" (*la loge*) and "moccasins" (*les souliers moux*), are also expressed by French nouns, and virtually all of the local plants and animals have French names, not Cree names.

Many French nouns denote things that cannot be made clear by pointing, for example, abstract nouns like "love" and "wisdom" or uncommon or nonexistent beings such as "werewolves." Further, many actions are concrete and can easily be made clear by pointing, as well as with signs, like "swimming," "kicking," and so on. These actions, however, are expressed in Cree. Nor does this hypothesis explain the presence of those few nouns commonly used in Michif that are derived from Amerindian languages, such as "bee" and "chokecherries," whereas all other insects and berries have only French names. Finally, if actions are associated with tools, the tools are expressed in French and the action in Cree, although both can easily be made clear by pointing and gesturing. Other objections can be added without too much effort. Therefore, this hypothesis must be rejected.

The Verb-Noun Mixing Hypothesis

The verb-noun hypothesis claims that somehow the people who felt the need to develop a new language out of the two that were already spoken in the community could do so by taking verbs from one of the languages and nouns from the other. Michif gives the impression of being mixed in this way, as we have already seen. However, there are numerous reasons not to accept this hypothesis.

But first we have to distinguish the donor language from the borrowing language. The question is, were Cree verbs borrowed into French or French noun phrases borrowed into Cree? It would most plausibly be French nouns borrowed into Cree, following the often made observation that nouns are the most easily borrowed categories. This is discussed in the following section. Then I discuss a typology of verb borrowing, in which Michif appears to be a very different case. Finally I deal with two languages that do show some form of verb-noun dichotomy.

Noun Borrowing

Several hierarchies of borrowing have been proposed in the literature (e.g., Haugen 1950; Muysken 1981; Appel and Muysken 1987: 170–171). These invariably show that nouns are borrowed most easily. For Michif this could be taken to mean that French nouns werre borrowed into otherwise Cree structures, but for some reason in such a massive way that all Cree nouns were replaced by French nouns. This is what was initially suggested by Richard Rhodes (1977) in his pioneering paper on Michif. Later, however, Rhodes (1986) rejected this hypothesis in favor of a mixed language hypothesis. Still, as this is something other people suggested, too, I discuss it here in some detail.

Although I do not think that any research has been done on this subject, there seem to be at least some languages that borrowed *only* nouns and no verbs (we leave the matter of borrowing other categories, like conjunctions and numerals, for the moment). Examples are Slave, an Amerindian language of the Athapaskan family spoken in Canada (Rice 1989), and some other Amerindian languages that borrowed only nouns from French. In these languages, however, the extent of the borrowing was fairly limited, perhaps a few dozen words, not the complete nominal lexicon as in Michif. There are also languages that borrowed categories in very different proportions: many nouns and few verbs. This is in line with the often made observation that nouns are much more easily borrowed than verbs.

In Drapeau (1980) only nominal borrowings from French into Montagnais (an Amerindian language of the Algonquian family, like Cree, spoken in Quebec) are discussed, but later studies (Drapeau 1991) show that French verbs were also borrowed (or perhaps code-mixed) into Montagnais, with a Montagnais helping verb meaning "to do." Nevertheless, the proportion of French nouns used in Montagnais seems to be significantly higher than the proportion of verbs—at least in the early stage. The Montagnais case is discussed in more detail in Chapter 6.

It must also be stressed that some French and English verbs were borrowed (or code-mixed) into Michif, but non-Cree verbs are relatively uncommon. The ways in which these borrowed verbs are used differ significantly from other cases of verb borrowing, including the borrowing of French verbs into Betsiamites Montagnais (see the next section).

Noun borrowing is unlikely as an explanation for the nature of Michif for several reasons. First, borrowing in Michif was not limited to nouns. Adjectives, adverbs, numerals, conjunctions, prepositions, and articles also came from French. Prepositions and articles especially are rarely reported to be borrowed in other cases of language contact, but the nouns in Michif were borrowed with these other word classes. This type of borrowing—nouns complete with determiners, prepositions, and so on—is highly unusual, if not unique. Second, Michif is unique in borrowing the complete basic nominal vocabulary. This cannot be a case of borrowing because of its extent and its nature, which have no parallel in the rest of the world. In short, it must be something else.

Verb Borrowing

Moravcsik (1975) discusses the universals of verb borrowing, distinguishing three types. In the first type, borrowed verbs go with an indigenous lexical item meaning "to do," for example, English verbs in Urdu, where *karo* means "to do":

(22)   *arrange* karo "to arrange"; *begin* karo "to begin"

The second type has a suffix added to the borrowed verb, for example, the suffix *-l* in Hungarian:

(23)   az emberek *gesztikulá*-l-nak "The people are gesticulating."

The third type is one in which inflectional suffixes are directly added to the verb stem, for example, German, which has forms like those in (24):

(24)   *manag*en "to manage"

German, of course, also has the second type in Romance borrowings, like "*glorifi*zieren."

Moravcsik argues that in all three cases the borrowing of verbs follows the pattern of verbalizing indigenous nouns in the language.

If one were to support the notion that Michif has verb borrowing, it would have to be a form of borrowing that includes all verbal morphology, which is not attested to in Moravcsik's (1975) study. The Michif type of verb borrowing is highly uncommon, if not unique, in the languages of the world; Moravcsik does not mention anything like it. Therefore verb borrowing is unlikely. Furthermore, not only verbs are used from the supposed source language, Cree, but also many other categories, including syntax. Again, both the nature and extent of Cree dictate that Michif cannot be the result of verb borrowing into French.

"Mixed" Languages with some Verb-Noun Dichotomy

There seem to be only two other languages in the world with a kind of verb-noun dichotomy. Both cases only vaguely resemble Michif. The first is the language spoken in a Gypsy community in the Athenian suburb Ajia Varvara. The language has been described by Messing (1987) and Igla (1989). Virtually the whole community is bilingual in Greek and Romani, the Gypsy language, which belongs to the Indic branch of Indo-European. A few elderly people also speak Turkish. This group immigrated into Greece from Turkey in the 1920s. About three hundred Turkish words are used in the community, although young speakers use only about one hundred. All generations use about thirty or more Turkish verbs, in a rather peculiar way: they are conjugated according to the Turkish system, not the Romani system. The large majority of the verbs in this language (of both Romani or Greek origin) are inflected with the inherited Romani affixes, both in present tense and past tense. An example (from Igla 1991) shows the Turkish verbs (italicized):

(25) and o sxoljo ka sikl-os te *okur-sun* ta te *jazar-sun*
      in the school FUT learn-2 COMP read-2 and COMP write-2
      "In the school you will learn how to *read* and *write*."

The speakers of this Romani dialect, at least those who do not know Turkish, consider these words to be genuine Romani verbs and are not aware of their Turkish origin or their deviant inflection.

I counted the etymological origin of all the verbs starting with the letters "A" and "B" in Messing's (1987) glossary of this language. Two verbs appear to be of Greek origin, ten of Turkish origin, and twenty-two of Romani origin. Most of the verbs are apparently Romani in this language. If we look at the semantics of these verbs, we find the following for the Turkish verbs (starting with "A" and "B"):

(26) to learn, be in heat/angry, to step/press, to sink, to lose (at games), to faint, to wait (for), to like, to resemble, to finish

The semantics of the verbs make clear that they do not denote cultural innovations exclusively. Indeed, they seem to be "arbitrary" borrowings if we look at the meaning. In a number of cases, verbs of different origin with apparently the same meaning coexist, for example, *siklivav* (Romani) and *aleširim* (Turkish), both "to learn"; *pirkasarav* (Greek) and *dokonúrum* (Turkish), both "to bother."

Yet this language is very dissimilar to Michif. It is improbable that there ever was a rigid verb-noun dichotomy in the language of the ancestors of the Ajia Varvara group (Turkish verbs and Romani nouns). First, most Romani and Greek verbs are inflected as Romani verbs. Neither the semantic content nor the phonological form nor the inflection of these verbs is lost. Second, only a minority of the verbs are of Turkish origin in this dialect. Probably the number has always been small. The most plausible explanation for the presence of more or less arbitrary Turkish and Greek verbs in this Romani dialect is probably extensive Romani-Turkish code mixing in the past and Romani-Greek code mixing in the present-day community. The borrowed words, for which present-day Romani forms are lacking are still in the minority. The language remains a Romani dialect, albeit with a significant amount of borrowing and spoken in a community with extensive code mixing.

Could it be that there are Romani dialects with exclusively borrowed verbs? Igla (1991) reports that in another Gypsy dialect in Athens (Ano Ljosia) a small number of Turkish verbs is also used. This group does not have historical connections with the Ajia Varvara. The same is true of a Romani dialect spoken (perhaps formerly) in northeastern Bulgaria and European Turkey. Marcel Cortiade (pers. comm., 1990) and Hristo Kyuchukov (pers. comm., 1994) report the same about some Romani dialects in Albania and Bulgaria, respectively. In all these cases the Turkish verbs are fairly infrequent. If in all of these cases only a limited number of verbs is borrowed, it is improbable that there has ever been a Turkish-Romani mixed language in the way Michif is a mixed language.[3]

Therefore we must conclude that the formal similarity between this Romani dialect (and the others mentioned) and Michif is only superficial. In Romani, there is only a limited number of verbs from another language, but in Michif all the verbs, along with their inflection, come from another language.

The only other language in which there may be a form of dichotomy between verbs and nouns is the Aleut dialect of Copper Island in the Bering Strait.[4] Aleut is a language related to the Eskimo languages. Copper Island Aleut or Mednyj Aleut, as reported in Golovko (1994) and Thomason and Kaufman (1988: 233–238), following Menovshchikov (1969), has Aleut stems but Russian inflectional affixes in the finite verbs. The language is spoken by a group called "creoles," Aleuts whose ancestors were Russian seal hunters, who settled there soon after the Aleuts themselves in 1826. Russian seal hunters intermarried with the Aleuts, and it seems that Russian ceased being spoken in the late 1800s. Thomason and Kaufman say little about other Russian grammatical or lexical influences, apart from the restricted use of Russian pronouns. More recent studies (Golovko and Vakhtin 1990; Golovko 1994) show that this language also borrowed a significant part of the Russian lexicon, and it proposes theories about its genesis. A. G. F van Holk (pers. comm.), who briefly looked at the texts appended to these articles, states that quite a few nouns are borrowed from Russian, with Aleut case markings, and the verb phrase is Aleut with Russian inflectional suffixes. The following is a short text fragment from Golovko and Vakhtin (1990: 123) with an unusually high number of Russian elements, which are italicized:

(27)   *mi cāynika-x̄* inka-ča-*l-i*,
        we kettle-3S.ABS hang-CAUS-*PST.1P*,

kamīna-kuca-x̄ ani-l *čayu*-ča-*l-i*.
stove-small-3S.ABS burn-CON *drink.tea*-CAUS-*PST-1P*

putum gōroda-m haya timis huyā-sā-*l-i*.
then city-RELR.S. to.3S OBJ go-TRANS-*PST-1P*

tunu-xta-*l-i gōroda*-x̄ agita-l súnn-ax̄ tama-ga.
utter-RES-*PST-1P town*-3S.ABS together.with-CON ship-3S.ABS meet-INT.3PL

"We put the kettle on the fire, made fire in the stove, and drank tea. Then we started for the city. They said that a ship left the city (to meet us)."

Because of a lack of sufficient data, it is hard to reach any firm conclusions about possible typological similarities between Mednyj Aleut and Michif. In the former, personal pronouns, higher numerals, many nouns, the verb "to be," subordinating elements, some particles, and verbal inflectional affixes seem to be Russian, whereas most case markers, most verb and noun stems, some particles, lower numerals, and postpositions are from Aleut (Golovko 1994). In a way, Michif and Mednyj Aleut seem to have emerged in fairly similar circumstances: invading fur traders who married indigenous women.

In conclusion we can say that the Romani cases are too different from Michif to be of interest, and so is Mednyj Aleut. There are many differences between Mednyj Aleut and Michif. The source languages of the different grammatical categories are different. Most important, the verbs have different source languages for the stems (Aleut) and the affixes (Russian), whereas in Michif both stems and affixes are Cree. As for Mednyj Aleut and the Aleut dialect that was one of the source languages, we lack sufficient analyzed data. Thus, Michif, as far as is known, remains unique in the world in its distribution of verbs and nouns. One has to notice that in Copper Island Aleut only the verbal inflection was affected and not the nouns. No closer comparison is possible here. In short, the verb-noun hypothesis does not seem to make sense for the genesis of Michif.

Code-mixing Hypothesis

In many bilingual societies people may spontaneously mix the languages spoken. This is called code switching, if switches occur between sentences, or code mixing, if switches occur between words and phrases. In this discussion I use "code mixing" as a general term. Code mixing is especially prevalent among fluent bilinguals. It is only very recently that researchers have begun to work on the typology of code-mixing communities (e.g., Pieter Muysken), and general results are not yet available. More research has been done on structural constraints in code mixing, which appears to be not a haphazard mixture of two languages but a sophisticated, rule-governed form of language use. Several universal constraints have been proposed for code mixing, such as the free morpheme constraint, which basically means that bound morphemes must belong to the same language as its stem (i.e., no word-internal switches are possible), and the equivalence constraint, which means that a switch is possible only where the two languages have the same surface-structure word order (Poplack 1980). The following is an example of French-English code mixing (from Heller 1991: 67):

(28) c'est ça qui choque tout le monde asteur *it's creating hard feelings* avec les Anglais
      pis j'aime pas ça *because* moi j'en connais trop des Anglais. . . .

      "that's what's upsetting everyone these days it's creating hard feelings with the En-
      glish and I don't like that because I know too many English people. . . ."

This is not a sign of "language decay" or something like it, as it is sometimes interpreted by outsiders and laypeople. Indeed, it is a rule-governed pattern in which the
most fluent bilinguals are the most competent (Poplack 1980; Nortier 1989).

      Could Michif be a case of code mixing? At first sight one would answer this
question negatively. It is clear that the equivalence constraint is not valid in Michif
because the linear order of Michif sentences is sometimes heavily different from the
French word order, as is clear from the story in (3). And if one takes the rather rare
instances of French stems with Cree inflectional affixes (e.g., *le-vieux-iw-it* in the
text discussed earlier) as counterexamples against the free morpheme constraint, this
other constraint is regularly violated, too. Moreover, for people to mix codes, they
have to be bilingual, and Michif speakers rarely know Cree and usually do not know
French either. In a contemporary analysis, Michif cannot be an instance of code
mixing.

      Michif is not a case of code mixing today, but what about in the past? Could
Michif have emerged from code mixing? Recent research on Swahili-French (Fabian
1982), Finnish-English, and Turkish-Dutch code mixing (Boeschoten 1991; Backus
1996) shows that for some language pairs, word-internal code mixing is common, if
not the norm (contra Poplack 1980), as has been shown in the work of Myers-Scotton
(1993). Swahili, Finnish, and Turkish are agglutinative languages. It may be that the
nature of these languages, that is, a type with a complex word structure, makes word-
internal code mixing possible or perhaps even necessary (as already observed by
Muysken 1991). Could it be that Cree is of a different type again, necessitating noun-
verb code mixing with French and Cree? Cree is indeed a polysynthetic language, a
type that may show still other constraints.

      The hypothesis that Michif came about as a consequence of massive, spontane-
ous language mixture (code mixing) by bilingual Métis was first implicitly suggested
by Drapeau (1991), based on data showing the spontaneous mixture of Montagnais
(East Cree) and French by bilingual speakers in Betsiamites, in Quebec. This mixture was compared to Michif, and striking parallels were noted. It was suggested
explicitly as a possible explanation for the dichotomy of Michif, on the basis of
Drapeau's data, in Bakker (1991c). The striking similarities in what is expressed in
French and what in Cree-Montagnais make this hypothesis possible. The following
utterance of a child with Montagnais as a mother tongue is virtually identical to Michif:

(29) ekw ni:l *une pomme*, mia:m *une orange* eshi-matshishikant   (Montagnais-French)
      êkwa nîya *une pomme*, tâskôc *une orange* ê-isi-manisoht   (Michif)
      and me *an apple* like *an orange* that-is-thus-cut
      "And me, (I want) an apple that is cut like an orange."

It is, for instance, not axiomatically impossible that code-mixed languages, once
they become the only code available to children, change to a type of mixed language

like Media Lengua, with Spanish stems and Quechua grammar (see the following section), or Michif. Such a suggestion would explain the fact that mixed languages spoken as mother tongues look structurally very different from spontaneous language mixture by bilinguals. This hypothesis must be taken seriously, and I return to it in Chapter Six.

Relexification Hypothesis

"Relexification" is a term that does not have a precisely circumscribed meaning. It is sometimes used just as an alternative term for lexical borrowing, especially when this is a massive process. Still others use it as a descriptive term for the process that leads to languages with the affixes of one language and the stems of another. Finally, in creole studies, the term is used for a process in which the phonological shapes of all stems and morphemes of an African language are replaced by the closest semantic equivalents from a European language (after Stewart 1962). Haitian Creole, for instance, would be a French relexification of the Ewe-Fon language of West Africa. In this section, I am concerned with the second type. An example is Media Lengua, a language with Quechua affixes and Spanish content morphemes (Muysken 1981). In Media Lengua, the grammar (syntax, morphology, phonology) is identical to Quechua, but the stems are more than 90 percent Spanish. An example (Quechua morphemes are italicized) follows:

(30) dimas-*ta* llubi-*pi-ga*, no i-*sha-chu*   (Media Lengua)
      yalli-*da* tamia-*pi-ga*, mana ri-*sha-chu*   (Quechua)
      too-much rain-SUB-TO, not go-1FU-NEG
      si llueve demás, no voy a ir   (Spanish)
      "If it rains too much, I won't go."

One can see that Media Lengua is quite different from Michif. First, in Media Lengua, the content words are Spanish and the grammatical morphemes are Quechua. One word typically contains Spanish as well as Quechua elements, the root being Spanish and the affixes being Quechua. In Michif it is only very marginally possible to combine French and Cree in one word. Second, Spanish elements are phonologically integrated into Quechua in Media Lengua. This language has one phonological system. In Michif the Cree, French, and English words basically retain their phonological systems. Third, Media Lengua is a mixed language, although neither the lexicon nor the grammatical system is mixed: the lexicon is Spanish, but the grammatical system is Quechua. In Michif both the grammar and the lexicon are mixed.

Bakker (1989c, 1990b) suggests that something like relexification was involved in the genesis of Michif, without distinguishing the different types and without specifying which type of relexification was meant. Bakker (1989a) shows that in a number of Michif constructions, the lexical material is French but the underlying language is Cree. Michif has one general locative marker, *da* or *dã*, meaning not only "in," as in French, but also "on" and "at," like the Cree locative suffix *-ihk*. The *da* locative is sometimes used in combination with other French or Cree prepositions, just like Cree *-ihk* (see Chapters Four and Eight). The preposition *da*, it is argued, functions exactly like the Cree locative suffix *-ihk* and would thus be relexified.

Bakker (1990a) argues that Michif in fact has Cree grammatical affixes and a French lexicon. Cree verbs, he says, consist solely of grammatical affixes (some of which also have lexical meaning), so that these verbs do not have stems that could be replaced by French stems. Because of the infrequency of Cree noun inflection, Cree affixes rarely appear with French nouns. There are phrases like the following:

(31) la jument l'étalon-*wa otinêw*
      the mare the stallion-OBV he.takes.the.other
      "The mare takes the stallion."

Here the French object is marked with a Cree grammatical suffix. The obviative suffix (explained in Chapter Four) is fairly common with animate obviative forms in Michif. There are a few other Cree suffixes that appear with French stems (see chapters Four and Eight).

Lefebvre and Lumsden (1989) consider Michif to be a case of relexification in a slightly different sense. Media Lengua would have only the Quechua stems relexified and Haitian Creole both Ewe-Fon stems and affixes. In Michif, however, only nouns would have been relexified.

Michif and relexified languages are in some ways similar: they can be the only languages spoken by an individual, whereas code mixers always must know two languages. Despite the structural differences between relexified languages, on the one hand (roots from one language, affixes from another), and Michif, on the other (verbs and demonstratives from one language, nouns from another), it seems worthwhile to make a more detailed comparison between Michif and relexified languages.

The suggestion that it was a process of relexification that led to Michif seems to make some sense. Therefore it is discussed in more detail in Chapter Seven (for the sociohistorical dimension) and Chapter Eight (for the linguistic dimension).

Difficult Parts Hypothesis

According to some, Michif combines the difficult parts of two languages. In French the verb is relatively simple, and the noun phrase is relatively complex. For every noun one has to learn whether it is masculine or feminine, there are all kinds of morpho-phonological processes such as liaison, and there is no fixed position for the class of adjectives. The Cree verb is notoriously complex and the noun inflection simple. In Cree, the unpredictable features are found in the verb; in French they are in the noun.

There are a number of objections to this hypothesis. There are no objective criteria to decide what is complex and what is simple. All natural languages are learned without effort by children. Also it seems unlikely that people would be able to judge what would be a complex part of their language or languages, which is necessary to combine it with something else. It is more important to know the reason for this combination. The only reason would seem to be the creation of a secret language that is difficult for outsiders to understand. Any other combination of the two languages would probably also serve that purpose or even one of the languages (unless the outsiders also speak both). Therefore the fact that the more "complex" parts of both source languages are found in Michif seems to be stimulated by other factors, not by their complexity.

Summary

I present in this section hypotheses about the origin of Michif. The hypotheses that involve the man-woman relation of the French and Indians are rejected. Also rejected is the suggestion that it was originally, or at any time in history, a language used between Cree speakers and French speakers. The fact that the Métis are a new and mixed ethnic group appears to be a possible causal connection for such a language to emerge. So this may have been the impetus for the genesis of the Michif language. We go deeper into this hypothesis in Chapter Seven.

This does not explain, however, the particular mixture of the two languages, with Cree verbs and French nouns. It had nothing to do with the separate tasks of the French husbands and the Cree wives. Four other possibilities are discussed: first, that there are languages that have verbs and nouns from different languages and that Michif is one of them; second, that Michif is fossilized code mixing; third, that it is relexification. It is not likely that nouns from one language were consciously combined with the verbs from another language. This is not documented from any part of the world, and it is unlikely to be a possible process. No reason could be detected for the combination of the so-called "difficult parts" of both source languages. Fourth, two hypotheses seem plausible: that Michif was in fact originally a case of code mixing that became fossilized or that it is a form of relexification. I evaluate both possibilities in more detail in following chapters.

Conclusions

In this chapter we have seen that Michif is an unusual language in a number of respects. First, it is not classifiable as belonging to a single language family. Michif is just as much an Algonquian as an Indo-European language, so it can be said to belong to two language families at the same time. Michif has grammatical and lexical features from the two languages in roughly equal numbers, which may very well make it unique among the languages of the world. It is certainly distinctive in its distribution of the elements from the two source languages: no mixed language shows nouns from one language and verbs from another.

Second, Michif appears to be unlike all of the language contact phenomena discussed in this chapter. In particular, Michif is not a trade language, a pidgin, a creole, an interlanguage, a case of code mixing, nor a case of second-language acquisition.

Third, concerning the social circumstances under which Michif arose, only one suggestion makes sense: the fact that its speakers, having double ancestry, form a fairly atypical group. It is possible that the mixed nature of Michif is associated with the mixed nature of the people who speak it.

Fourth, the only linguistic phenomena to which Michif shows vague similarities are code mixing and relexified languages, both of which are cases of language mixture by bilinguals. Code mixing is a spontaneous, ad hoc mixture, and relexified languages are mother tongues. There are also important differences, however, so that neither provides obvious clues to the genesis of this strange mixed language. These phenomena are discussed again later.

Outline of the Book

This book deals with the question, what kind of language is Michif and why, when, and how did it come into being? This is a rather complex problem with ramifications into linguistics, anthropology, ethnohistory, Native studies, and other disciplines. It is therefore necessary to deal with the question from a number of viewpoints. For my scenario for the genesis of this mixed language, I use a variety of data, including the structure of the language and the nature of the mixture of French and Cree. Because dialect differences and similarities also provide clues, I did comparative research on dialects of the language spoken in diverse communities. I also looked at the precise language input: to which dialects of Cree and French is Michif most closely related? In addition, I looked at mixed languages from other parts of the world and the sociolinguistic circumstances under which these have emerged. Finally, I did some modest historical research: what do the speakers themselves know about the genesis of the language, and what did people in earlier periods say about this mixed language and the language use of the Métis?

The results of the different approaches seem to be parallel to one another to a great extent. It is striking that the language is never mentioned in historical sources. This suggests that it was intended only for internal use by the Métis. Nevertheless, there are indications that the language must have come about in the first decades of the nineteenth century, when the poorer Métis from the southern part of Manitoba traveled west in great numbers twice a year for the bison hunt (from about 1821). The moment at which the offspring of mixed European-Amerindian marriages started to consider themselves a separate nation occurred just before (ca. 1812). According to orally transmitted Métis traditions, the language was already spoken in 1820–1840. In that period some of the villages that are now Michif speaking must have been established as winter camps for the Métis buffalo hunters.

It is beyond doubt that the Métis as a people were a product of the fur trade. The quest for furs brought French and British entrepreneurs and adventurers to new Indian tribes. The Métis speak a mixture of the languages of their paternal and maternal ancestors. Therefore I discuss the history of the fur trade in Chapter Two.

The Métis are the only speakers of the Michif language. The existence of these people, who constitute an ethnic group with their own culture and history and who recognize their double ancestry, seems to be related to the existence of a language with a double genetic origin. The history of the genesis and the contemporary culture, including the linguistic situation, of the Métis is discussed in Chapter Three.

In a study on the genesis of a language, a structural sketch of it is indispensable. In Chapter Four, I present a grammatical outline of the Michif language. It contains information on the sound system, word formation, and sentence structure, as well as information on the contribution of Cree and French to the language. The specific ways in which French and Cree elements interact and the source language of the diverse linguistic categories are also discussed.

This structural sketch is based on the dialect of one locality, Turtle Mountain in North Dakota. Are all mixtures of French and Cree identical, or did they develop independently on different locations in North America? In Chapter Five I show that other Michif varieties, as became clear through fieldwork on location, differ only minimally from the one described in Chapter Four. There is no doubt that the language as spoken in scattered communities in southern Saskatchewan, Manitoba, and North Dakota is identical, except for some minor local variations. These dialects must stem from one common source language, which was already mixed. Nevertheless, there also appear to be varieties of French and Cree mixtures in northwestern Saskatchewan and Alberta that do show some similarities to Michif but which cannot stem from that same source because of extensive differences. These must be mixtures that occurred independently. There appear to be three types of Cree-French contact phenomena: Cree-French code mixing, Cree with French borrowings, and Michif. The three processes mix French and Cree in clearly different ways.

In Chapter Six, I discuss these three types of mixtures of Cree and French in more detail. They appear to be three distinguishable phenomena, with different results. Michif differs both from borrowing and from code mixing, so it must have emerged through a different process. In Chapter Seven I present a model of language mixing called "language intertwining"; I claim that Michif is a special case because of the typological properties of the languages in contact, French and Cree (Chapter Eight). Language intertwining occurs when bilingual people need a secret language or, in cases of a mixed, negative identity, a language of their own. The Métis belong to the latter subgroup. Michif differs in its mixture from the other intertwined languages because its grammatical affixes cannot be separated from the verb stems.

In Chapter Nine I discuss the source languages of Michif. These linguistic facts are combined with historical and geographical aspects. I try to show with which dialects these are most closely related. I also provide an explanation for the presence of Ojibwe elements in the language. In the conclusion (Chapter Ten) I summarize this work and indicate some further points to be studied.

The genesis of Michif is the subject of this book. Soon the language will be lost if the attempts at revival at diverse locations in Canada and the United States fail. Then it will follow the fate of the great auk, the Eskimo curlew, and the traveler pigeon, North American birds that had to give way to "civilization." The Michif language is now on the verge of extinction. Most speakers are in their 70s and 80s, and it is no longer learned by children. There is little or no hope for survival. Although this book cannot save the language, I hope it will contribute to a better understanding of the Métis and their role in Canadian history. We cannot save the language, but at least we can save it from oblivion.

European-Amerindian Contact
in the Fur Trade

The influence of the fur trade on Canada has been enormous. Since the Europeans arrived in North America, they exchanged tools, utensils, clothing, and other items with the natives for precious furs. The fur trade brought a significant number of European men, of different ethnic backgrounds, in contact with a variety of Amerindian nations. Among the consequences were the birth of a significant population of "mixed bloods" (unfortunately there is no other term to express this), of which the Métis, of French ancestry, are the most important, and the emergence of a new, mixed language, Michif. The Métis are all aware that their ancestors are, on one side, Amerindians and, on the other, French-speaking fur traders. At least from the early 1800s onward, they have considered themselves a separate nation, different from other people, including the Indians and the French.

In this chapter I discuss the fur trade and the different European and Amerindian groups that came into contact with one another. The contacts between Cree-speaking Indians and the French are the most important, as they provided the source languages of Michif. No mixed language emerged in the contacts between the Scottish fur traders and the Indians.

We must face a paradox, which I try to resolve in this book. The fur trade is mainly an activity of the woodlands. The Cree part of Michif, however, is basically the *Plains* dialect, spoken almost exclusively on the prairies, where the fur trade was less important. Although it is undoubtedly the case that the Métis as a people emerged as a consequence of the fur trade, this is not so obvious for the genesis of the Michif language. Nevertheless, the fur trade and the contacts between Europeans and Natives are of great interest for a discussion of the origin of Michif. The fact that the Métis are biologically and culturally mixed is related to the fact that their language is mixed.

I first present a general overview of the different Native peoples in the northern part of North America and their cultures and languages, followed by a presentation of the French in North America. Then I focus more specifically on the fur-trading area and the natives residing there. I also discuss the fur trade companies and the groups involved, focusing on their contacts with native women.

Native Peoples in North America

North America has been inhabited by a wide variety of people for a very long time, and thus there is a great diversity of languages and cultures. The different Amerindian nations can be classified more or less naturally in two ways: according to the languages they speak (language families), which can be related or not, or according to the geographical features of the area they live in (e.g, woodlands, coast, and mountains). These two kinds of groupings rarely coincide.

The number of language families in North America has been estimated to be as high as fifty-eight (Powell 1891) or fifty-five (Boas 1911). Sherzer (1976) lists twenty-two[1]—an enormous number if we compare it with the only three or four families existing in Europe. Many attempts have been made to reduce this number by linking certain language families with others, but none of these has gained wide acceptance. The most radical proposal is Greenberg's (1987) classification of all of America's languages (North, Central, and South) into three superfamilies, but this met with vehement reactions from linguists who specialize in Amerindian languages and it remains highly controversial. The total number of different languages in North America has been estimated to be between 200 and 500, which is roughly equal to the number of Amerindian tribes or nations. Despite cultural or linguistic similarities between some of the tribes, there have always been clear ethnic boundaries between them. Neighboring tribes may differ considerably not only for European observers but even more for the Natives themselves. The linguistic boundaries often do not coincide with the cultural ones.

We can distinguish six culture areas in Canada, following MacLean (1982) (see also the *Handbook of American Indians* of the Smithsonian Institution, Sherzer 1976, and Sauvé 1989). These areas have common culture traits, such as the use of fur for clothing in the cold season and the use of stone tools. There are also commonalities in religion and interpersonal behavior that go beyond linguistic and cultural boundaries. Among the six areas, however, the differences are significant. Three of them are not, or are only marginally, related to the subject matter of this book. The Arctic culture of the Inuit and the Pacific Northwest cultures of the peoples who inhabit British Columbia are irrelevant for this study and therefore are not discussed. Of only minor importance is the Atlantic Coast culture area, where the French initially settled in the early 1600s. The French and the Natives of the area had fairly close ties, as we see later, and this had consequences for French-Indian relations in later periods. In this area, seafood and game were the most important food sources.

The three culture areas most relevant to this study are the northern forest area, the Great Lakes area, and the northern Plains. The cultural differences within these areas are minor compared to the similarities.

In the northern forest, nomadic Amerindian nations lived off the resources in the woods and the lakes, mostly by hunting and gathering. Meat, berries, wild rice, and some wild vegetables were the most important foods. The people did not grow vegetables or corn, with very few exceptions (Giraud 1945: 51), but they did eat fish. The area can roughly be equated with the Canadian shield, the vast rocky belt covered with woods and lakes. These Indians spent the winters mostly in the interior and the summers on lakeshores or riverbanks. Birchbark canoes provided transportation on the rivers, lakes, and streams. These canoes were glued with gum composed of locally available materials. Dwellings were also made of birchbark. Most of the inhabitants of this area spoke, and still speak, Algonquian and Athapaskan languages. The most important groups are the Ojibwes, Crees, and Chipewyans.

The Great Lakes area stretches from the Saint Lawrence River and northern New York State to the Great Lakes. The people, Algonquians and Iroquoians, were farmers, growing mainly corn, squash, and tobacco. Fishing, hunting, and trapping brought in supplementary food. Meat was also obtained by trading. The people used canoes but not as much or as deftly as the woodlands Indians; also the canoes were heavier because they were made of the bark of the elm tree, which is not as light as birchbark (Delâge pers. comm., 1995). The Hurons were competent in canoes, as were the Algonquians. The Hurons and Iroquois lived in more or less stable villages, which were moved from time to time when supplies, such as firewood, became exhausted. These villages consisted of multifamily houses. Women traditionally played an important role in these Iroquoian communities.

The northern Plains area traditionally comprises vast prairie grasslands, sometimes interrupted by brushes and bushes, sloughs, and rivers. Its inhabitants were and are the Blackfoot, the Ojibwes, the Crees, the Sioux, and the Assiniboines. They lived off the buffalo herds that roamed the area and were, therefore, nomads. Wild meat was an important source of food. Fish, considered dogfood, was not eaten except in periods of extreme shortages. Berries and some wild vegetables were gathered and eaten. The people lived in tipis, wooden frames covered with hides. Transportation was originally by foot, with domestic dogs as beasts of burden. Later, horses were used for transportation, after the introduction of these animals to the continent. The *travois*, a wooden construction that was dragged by people or animals, was used to transport goods. Canoes were not used. Today, the prairies are almost exclusively an agricultural area, mostly for the cultivation of grain. There is also extensive dairy farming, although there probably used to be more buffalo than there are cows today. Between the Plains and the northern forest, there are regions that combine wooded areas with prairie land. These are commonly called the Parklands. This area may have played a role in the "invasion" of some woodland tribes onto the prairies.

The fur trade area is roughly the area around the Great Lakes, the woodlands of the Canadian shield, and the northern prairies. For this study, the French activities in the West (roughly the prairie provinces and the western woodlands) are the most important, for it must be here that the French came into contact with Cree-speaking Natives. Before I discuss the Natives of this area in more detail, I consider the French in Canada.

The French

In the early history of Canada, the French were the first successful settlers in the northern part of North America. By then, almost a century had passed since the start of continuous and regular visits by European fishermen to the coast of Canada and the banks of the Saint Lawrence River (Morison 1971). The French Captain Jacques Cartier from Saint-Malo in Brittany, who sailed to what is now Canada in 1534, figures in many Canadian history books as the first European to visit Canada. There are documents that point to the presence in the "New Founde Land" of English fishermen in 1502, Normans in 1506, Bretons in 1510, and Basques in 1520 (Morison 1971; Huxley 1987; Turgeon 1990). Although Cartier is the official "discoverer" of Canada, several other explorers had preceded him (Caboto, Corte Real, Fagundes, Verrazzano, and anonymous fishermen). His name was made famous because he was the first official Frenchman, but anybody who reads his travel reports will immediately understand that he could not have been the first. The natives that he met knew Christian symbols (the cross), and other natives tried to persuade him to trade hides, which they would have done only if they had met such strange people in unusual clothing before. Also, some of Cartier's French place names clearly already existed, whereas others were given by Cartier on the spot.

Thus, undoubtedly as early as 1534, trade contacts between Natives and Europeans had been established. The Basques would become the most important Europeans in Canada in the sixteenth century. Apart from their fisheries and whaling activities along and on the shores, they also established a trade network with the Natives of the area (Turgeon 1982, 1990; Bakker 1989b). In a way they were the pioneers who made the first contacts with Native groups like the Micmac, the Montagnais, and the Labrador Inuit. This made French settlement a relatively easy task, as the Natives were already fully acquainted with the Europeans and their technology when the French arrived in the early 1600s with the purpose of settling in North America.

The French in Eastern Canada: New France and Acadia

The French first came to the New World in the first decades of the seventeenth century. They settled on the Atlantic Coast in what was then called Acadia, in present-day Nova Scotia (Eccles 1983) in the early 1600s. Settlement in the Saint Lawrence River Valley soon followed, in a colony called Canada. These two areas have partly different histories. They did not grow to be very large in the first century of their existence. The population of the colonists is estimated at 15,000 by the end of the seventeenth century and at 18,000 in the second quarter of the eighteenth century (Wade 1968: 25, 29). More recent estimates give 24,000 in 1720 and 34,000 in 1730 (Delâge, pers. comm., 1995). It was mostly men who arrived in New France. The man-woman ratio of the French people in 1663 was still six men to one woman (Brown 1980: 4), for young adult bachelors at least (Delâge, pers. comm., 1995). Later this difference was reduced when orphan girls (*Filles du Roy*) arrived from France. Nevertheless, it was a diverse society, with farmers, traders, craftspeople, and artists. After around 1680 the fur traders could mostly be found on the frontier of New France

(Brown 1980: 3–4). Before then, Natives had traveled to Montreal for trading. The fur trade was for a long time the main economic activity of the colony (Delâge, pers. comm., 1995). Still, the settlers did not thrive economically in New France. Neither agriculture nor commerce nor industry was sound throughout the seventeenth century (Wade 1968: 31).

From the beginning there was a strong Roman Catholic tradition in New France, even stronger than in the Old World (Wade 1968: 24, 37–38). Nuns and priests were present at the outset. Catholic clergy from several religious groups were active as missionaries from an early date among the diverse Native groups of New France (Hanzeli 1969), perhaps even more than as priests among the French (Wade 1968: 37). In New France, the power of the church was said to be stronger than the power of the French king before 1663, when the state strengthened its political authority in the colony.

There were class differences between the ruling class of the *seigneurs* (religious communities, small patricians, and traders) and the general population. The small group of seigneurs was similar to the continental monarchy and aristocracy, erecting spacious houses for their administration. The rest of the population was made up mainly of small farmers, merchants, and traders, with only little social stratification. The seigneurs did not have any real power over the traders.

New France was surrounded by English-speaking colonies. In the east, British fishermen established permanent and seasonal settlements on the island of Newfoundland. The British claimed ownership of Newfoundland, Acadia, and Hudson Bay. In 1713 they obtained official sovereignty at the Treaty of Utrecht. To the south, New England and New York were English strongholds. In the northwest of New France, British traders were active on the coasts of Hudson Bay from the second half of the seventeenth century. Only in the west were there no British, just Natives. It is not surprising that many French Canadian fur traders, the *coureurs de bois* "woodrunners," traveled westward in search for riches and adventure.

The differences between the French and the English in their North American activities were not limited to the different languages they spoke. There were also religious and cultural differences. In New France non-Catholic immigrants were turned away, whereas in New England, Catholics were disfavored; thus New France was to be Catholic and the English areas generally Protestant. The relations between the two groups varied according to the ups and downs of the relations in their respective mother countries. The competition between the two was strong, especially in the economically important fur trade (Wade 1968).

There were also differences in the lifestyles of the two groups. Charlevoix (as cited in Wade 1968: 42), who traveled widely throughout North America, characterized them in 1746 as follows:

> The English colonist amasses means and makes superfluous expense; the French enjoys what he has and often parades what he has not. The former works for his heirs; the latter leaves his in the need in which he is himself, to get along as best they can. The British Americans dislike war, because they have so much to lose; they do not humor the Savages, because they see no need to do so. The French youth, on the contrary, loathe peace and get along well with the Natives, whose esteem they easily win in war and whose friendship they always earn.

Here we already see some of the differences between the French and the English, which will become important in explaining the genesis of Michif: the contacts of the French with the Native peoples were more extensive than those of the British. The French resembled the Natives more in that they did not amass extensive supplies and stocks for the future. Also, among the British, class differences seem to have been more important than among the French in the New World (with the exception of the seigneurs). Still, this view is somewhat one-sided in that it compares English colonists with the French of the frontier.

Other differences between the two groups of colonists are the following. The number of colonists in New England was higher than in New France, which meant more need for land and thus more conflicts with the Natives. Also, most French colonists settled in an area between Montreal and Quebec, from which the Native population had disappeared in the sixteenth century. The New England economy became diversified quickly (agriculture, timber, and fishing), which marginalized the fur trade, but not in New France. New England, like New Netherland, was more on its way toward a capitalist society. The importance of the fur trade in New France led to more intensive relations with the Native people (Delâge 1985, 1991).

The fur trade had a lasting influence on New France. In the long winters, it was one of the few possible enterprises (Wade 1968: 32). A significant number of inhabitants left the colony for fur-trading ventures. Wade (1968: 25) estimates the number to be some 15,000 people during the seventeenth and eighteenth centuries. In 1680, for instance, there were 800 *coureurs de bois* who spent the winters trading furs in the woods (Brown 1980: 5). Some of them traded with, and wintered with, Natives in New France; others traveled west to the Great Lakes and perhaps even beyond. The material gains and food that were supplied by the fur trade were sufficient to make a living, at least for a significant part of the population. Agriculture was limited for a long time because of the lack of external markets for its products (Delâge, pers. comm. 1995).

In the eighteenth century the economy of New France seemed to get somewhat stronger, but in the meantime the competition with the English was felt everywhere. From the 1670s onward, British fur traders had been active in Hudson Bay. In the same century, they took over much of the Dutch fur trade in New York. In 1713, through the Treaty of Utrecht, the Hudson Bay was officially assigned to the British.

In 1759 and 1760 the British conquered Quebec and Montreal, and in 1763, through the Treaty of Paris, the French ceded their North American possessions to the British. This treaty consolidated the British dominance over what was formerly called New France, as well as over Canada and the Great Lakes. After this, there was an important migration of rather well-to-do Scots from the south to New France, partly because of the independence movement in the American colonies, where the Scots often had pro-British sympathies. Most of the French-speaking inhabitants of Acadia —but not of the Saint Lawrence River Valley—were deported to the West Indies, Europe, and elsewhere. Later they gathered in Louisiana in the southeastern United States, where they are still known as Acadians (Cajuns). The Scots were to dominate the Montreal fur trade, in the sense that they provided all the capital and the managers, but throughout its history, the French Canadians remained the laborers, canoeists, and interpreters.

New France is important for the history of Michif for two reasons: it is from here that the French people in the West (who were ancestors of the Métis) came. Also, it is here that the contacts between the French and the Native peoples started and from where the enterprising free traders, who were familiar with the Natives, traveled west from an early date. Therefore I discuss the relations of the French with the Natives in the New France era in more detail.

The French and the Natives in New France

French people continued to arrive from France, although in relatively small numbers. Most of them came from the Paris region and the coastal areas of Normandy, Poitou, the Loire estuary, and Brittany (Hewson 1989: 12–14). As only very few Frenchwomen crossed the ocean in the early decades of colonization, Native women were often the only partners for the men who arrived in New France. Thus, mixed unions were common. Samuel de Champlain, called "the Father of New France," was reported to have said on two occasions to Natives of the area: "Our young men will marry your daughters, and we shall be one people." (Thwaites 1896–1901: 5:211, 10:26). In fact, he meant that the Natives were supposed to become like the French. Dickason (1985) shows in an insightful study that the biological mixture of the French with the local population was the general French policy of colonization, not only in New France. At that time, a large population meant greater power in Europe; thus power could be increased by enlarging the population. By intermarrying and thus producing new French nationals, the French hoped to enhance their power in Europe through numerical strength. The Company of New France included an article in its charter that had the same objective: "The Savages who will be led to the faith and to profess it will be considered natural Frenchmen, and like them, will be able to come and live in France when they wish to" (cited in Dickason 1985: 22).

It was not only the demographic policy of the French but also crucial to survival to have intimate relationships with the Native people of New France. Earlier attempts at settlement in Canada had been doomed because the Europeans in the New World did not interact with the Natives to learn their many useful skills. In fact, Native women were indispensable for survival during the early period of colonization (Delâge 1992a and b). The harsh climate and the low winter temperatures, problems with agriculture, travel difficulties, and the different foods made survival difficult for a Frenchman unless he had a wife who knew the techniques of food preparation and preservation, how to make snowshoes for winter travel, how to sew clothes, which plants to use for medicine, and so on (Dickason 1985: 29). French-Indian marriages, either officially approved by the priests or à la façon du pays "according to the custom of the country", were prevalent at the time (Dickason 1985: 22–25), especially in Acadia. In some cases these couples and their children lived with the Native groups, but frequently they would spend their lives among French Canadians.

The economic interests of the fur trade triggered intensive contacts with Native women. In certain periods, sums of money were paid for mixed marriages by the authorities, as stimulation premiums. By the end of the seventeenth century, most of the mixed marriages took place on the frontier of New France (Dickason 1985: 28) west of Montreal, especially around the Great Lakes. They were no longer so frequent, it seems, within the colony itself. It was only in the eighteenth century that opposition to intermarriage began to grow.

The relations of the French with the Native groups in New France were generally friendly, partially because the Amerindian and Acadian lifestyles were similar, and no land of value to the Natives was being used for agriculture by the French. For the Natives, the contacts with the Europeans were also profitable, as this was a way to procure knives, axes, and other goods of superior quality.

Nevertheless, despite the frequency of intermarriage, a Métis group—that is, a group that identified itself as such—did not emerge in New France. Dickason (1985: 29) shows that "the children of mixed unions tended to identify with either the French or the Amerindians rather than considering themselves a separate entity." It depended partly on the place they were living, and possibly on their occupations, whether these children, once they were grown up, would identify with the Natives or the French. In the fur trade, in the diplomatic services with the Amerindians, or in the anti-English guerrilla groups, identification would have been as Indian; all other activities would lead to identification as French. Already in the earliest period, a significant number of French immigrants preferred to live with the Natives (Charlevoix 1744: III 322; Giraud 1945: 194). There were Frenchmen who were adopted into Iroquois communities. Some of them even became leaders of Indian bands (Giraud 1945: 316, 319– 320). Also it was common for fur traders in New France to live with the Natives, and attempts to get them back into the colony apparently failed:

> The Vagabonds [French Canadian *coureurs de bois*, who traded beaver pelts with the English in New York], who had got the taste of the freedom of a nomadic life and of independence, stayed with the Indians, from whom they were not distinguishable, except for their vices. Several times the means of Amnesty was tried to call back these defectors, and at first these were rather useless.[2] (Charlevoix 1744: III 322)

Already in 1688 the governor general of Canada, René de Brisay, Marquis de Denonville, lamented the detrimental effects of these habits on the colony: "Mr. de Denonville next returns to the Coureurs de Bois, about whom he states that they are so numerous that it depopulates the Country of the best men, makes them unruly, intractable and leads them astray, and further that their children are raised like Indians"[3] (Charlevoix 1744: I 532–533). The agricultural colonists in New France, who constituted the large majority of the European population, did not share this lifestyle.

Despite these facts, many French Canadians and Quebecois historians have stated that the French Canadians have no Amerindian ancestors (Delâge 1991); but according to Dickason (1985: 22), "It is unrealistic to deny that racial mixing occurred within French communities (particularly in Acadia) on the grounds that it was so seldom recorded as such, on the other hand it is extremely difficult, if not impossible, to determine just how prevalent it was." This is true for Acadia and the area west of Montreal rather than the colony between Montreal and the Gulf of Saint Lawrence.

The French in the West

Enterprising Frenchmen, looking for riches and adventure, traveled westward from the first decade of their arrival in the New World. These explorers and traders came from New France, more specifically from Montreal, and not from Quebec and the seacoast. At one point fur traders made up 20 percent to 25 percent of the population of Montreal. They paddled on the intricate system of waterways in Canada, the network of rivers and lakes through which one can travel from the North American East Coast to the Rocky Mountains. The distances these *coureurs de bois* "woodrunners" and *voyageurs* "travelers" covered were enormous, several thousand kilometers each summer. They used canoes built in the tradition of the Algonquian Indians, made from watertight birchbark glued to a wooden frame. These canoes were very well adapted to traveling in that area and could be repaired almost anywhere with locally grown supplies. In other aspects of their way of life, they were also influenced by Amerindian traditions, for example, religion (Beaudet 1992; Delâge 1992c: 75–70). The goal of most of these travelers was to obtain furs, which could be sold at the Montreal fur market or to English traders in New York. Naturally, they made contact with Native people during their travels westward. The nomadic Natives always tended to spend an important part of the year (the summers) on lakeshores or riverbanks, so they were quite easily encountered by the traders.

It is not known when the first French people arrived in the Great Lakes area or in the West. The French were already on the west coast of Lake Michigan in the second half of the seventeenth century. Few of these Europeans from New France could write, and very few left traces. It is unfair to ascribe the pioneering European explorations to those few who were able to write about their travels into the interior. Close reading of some of their accounts makes it clear that they had French Canadian or Métis guides; apparently Europeans (and of course Natives) had preceded them in those areas. Some even mention French people living with Native groups.

Like the other Europeans, the French Canadians were not homogeneous either. The *voyageurs* "travelers" were the paddlers. They were the ones who transported the trade goods to the West over the rivers and streams in their Indian-style birchbark canoes. They had contracts with the fur-trading firms in Montreal, and they had their base in New France. The *coureurs de bois* "woodrunners" were the traders who left the French colonies, sometimes just for a season, sometimes for longer periods. They had no contract with fur-trading firms. Some of them never came back, and they lived with Natives in the woodlands west of the French colony. The *gens libres* "freemen," or free traders, were like the *coureurs de bois* after the British conquest of New France in 1760. The *gens libres* are encountered in many traders' journals and travel accounts, often living with or close to the Native peoples. Some of them may have been part Indian, too.

For the *voyageurs*, a distinction is made between the *hivernants* "winterers" and *mangeurs de lard* "pork eaters." The winterers, who operated in small groups, were the voyageurs who spent the winters in the woods, around the Great Lakes or farther west, close to the Indians. The pork eaters were those who traveled back and forth between Montreal and the Great Lakes, transporting goods between them (Innis 1970: 239, 242). Usually the *voyageurs* had contracts for three years (Brown 1980: 85). The first ones had higher prestige; the pork eaters were often novices (Nute 1931: 5). During a long period of the fur trade, licenses had to be bought in Montreal, but these were limited in number. The free traders operated without licenses. There were independent *voyageurs*, but many were in the service of the North West Company as paddlers (Innis 1970: 50), the largest group on the payroll.

The French Canadians were almost all illiterate and left no records, except through their orally transmitted songs. Their way of life can be reconstructed only through the casual remarks that the literate (often Scottish or English) fur traders made about them. Unfortunately, most of the literate traders did not find them worthy of mention, although it is clear that many of the chroniclers had *voyageurs* as paddlers in their company (Nute 1931: 227–228). The free traders, who stayed in the woods, are even more obscure. Still, their importance as explorers, settlers, guides, and cross-cultural liaisons (Lang 1994) cannot be underestimated. Nute's monograph on the *voyageurs* contains a wealth of documentation gathered from scraps here and there.

The *voyageurs* were readily distinguishable from other groups (Nute 1931): "The voyageurs had their own distinctive ethnic identity and social and cultural attributes—distinctive values, lifestyle, tastes, music, and so forth" (Brown 1980: 47–48). They had a distinctive dress, spoke French (and often Amerindian languages in addition), smoked pipes, wore a sash, and carried a beaded tobacco pouch. They were hard and lively workers and had their own habits and rituals during their travels. Their food was partly Amerindian (corn bread and wild meat) and partly European, such as the unleavened bread called *la galette*, which is Scottish in origin (Innis 1970: 167–168, 224; Nute 1931: 53, 85). According to witnesses, they were constantly singing French songs.

The relations of the French Canadians with the Natives were usually said to be good by contemporary observers. Many state that the French living among the Indians were "almost like one of themselves" (Brown 1980: 82). The British jealously noted this relationship, such as this trader from York Factory in 1794: "The number of Canadians impresses the Natives, their influence increases every day and they secure their esteem with the generosity of their presents"[4] (Giraud 1945: 242).

In many contemporary studies, these different groups of French Canadians were, in my opinion, insufficiently distinguished. The *gens libres* especially have not received the attention they deserve. They have never been studied as a separate group, to my knowledge, but they may have been numerous and important, perhaps more important than the French Canadians in the service of the companies. When mentioned, they were said to hunt with the Indians, to steal horses like the Indians, and to carry out other typical activities (Giraud 1945: 374, n. 2). They were already breeding horses in the Red River area around 1800, where they must have been numerous (Giraud 1945: 375, n. 2). Freemen were already active in the Edmonton area at the end of the eighteenth century (Giraud 1945: 504–505).

The influence of the *voyageurs* and freemen on the culture of the French Canadian settlers in the West may have been considerable. One measure of distance on land, for instance, was *la pipe*. This measure originated with the paddlers' habit of pausing when their pipes became empty after they had gone a certain distance, so that a time measure on water became a distance measure on land. A number of traits were common to these voyageurs, and to the Métis as well. Perhaps they cannot be distinguished, as many nineteenth-century sources refer to the Métis and the French Canadians in one breath. Some descriptions of the *voyageurs* as a distinct group are almost equally applicable to the Métis, so that it is likely that these *voyageurs* are the ancestors of the Métis.

Native Peoples in the West

With which Native groups did the French make contact in their travels westward? I limit myself to the vast areas around the Great Lakes and the plains and woodlands west of the Rocky Mountains, which is where the activities of the Cree-speaking Indians and the French coincided and where they traded with each other and had intimate relations of all kinds. The latter area is called the West or Northwest and can be equated with the prairies and forest areas in the Canadian prairie provinces of Manitoba, Saskatchewan, and Alberta.

It is not always possible to say with certainty which Native group lived where in former times. The different sources are often contradictory, if not lacking altogether. Archaeological remains are often hard to ascribe with certainty to a particular group (Meyer 1987; Chapdelaine and Kennedy 1990). Oral histories of the Natives have not always been adequately recorded before this knowledge was lost. It is reasonably well known which Amerindian nations live in which community today. By plotting these data on a map, tribal areas can be established. In maps like these, joint areas are usually omitted, as well as the fact that the Natives are minorities there, their small reserves being surrounded by Euro-Canadian settlements.

In trying to make maps of the tribal distribution for the past, one runs into a number of additional problems. The Natives tended to migrate, which makes it difficult to assign tribal areas. Tribal boundaries tended to be fuzzy, too. Sometimes migrations forced neighboring tribes to move away or brought bands to join other tribes, perhaps fusing into one new tribe (Moore 1994). These tribal maps do not usually account for shared areas, migrations, tribal subdivisions, groups living in other tribal areas, and so on. Nevertheless, maps 1 and 2 give a fair impression of the tribal distribution.

For the historical period, there are a number of clear cases of migration. The fur trade seems to have had drastic consequences on the tribal areas in the West. Many tribes now live westward of their original area. There are also cases in which two tribes, or two bands of different tribes, fused into one new tribe, such as the Cree-Assiniboines (Sharrock 1974) and possibly the Ojicree (Bishop 1975; see also Albers 1993 and Moore 1994 for a study on tribal fusion on the northern Plains). Furthermore, it is often difficult to link the names of tribes used in the older sources with twentieth-century data. Only in very rare cases is the name by which the tribes are known to us in the literature the name they use for themselves. "Iroquois" is a Basque word (Bakker 1990a, 1994b); "Montagnais" is a French word; "Assiniboine" and "Cree" are probably Ojibwe words; "Ojibwe" and "Chipewyan" are probably Cree words; and so on. Usually neighboring tribes or trading partners supplied the Europeans with a tribal name for other tribes that were not yet known to the Europeans. In older sources the general name was not often used (such as "Cree"); the local name (such as "Long Lake People") was used instead. Therefore, in many cases, names of bands and tribes that no longer exist are mentioned in the sources, and migrations, as stated, were very common throughout North America. In other words, even the names in printed sources are not easily equated with modern tribal names.

Sometimes there seem to be contradictory facts about the tribal membership of bands met by traders or missionaries. A group is said to be Ojibwe, for instance, but the language they used is beyond doubt Cree. Or the same community is sometimes called Cree, at other times Ojibwe (Rhodes and Todd 1981; Rhodes 1982). In other cases some group has a double name, for example, "Cree-Assiniboine," in several sources. Are they then Assiniboine (Siouan) or Cree (Algonquian)?

All these potential problems become actual as I try to resolve the origins of Michif, especially in the later chapters. The language is a mixture of French and Cree, so the question is, where did the French and the Cree speakers meet each other? Or, in a broader context, which were the tribes the French met in their travels westward? First I discuss from a linguistic viewpoint the different Amerindian groups that the French may have encountered.

Native Languages in the West

I have already mentioned the enormous number of unrelated Amerindian languages spoken in North America. If one limits oneself to the area relevant to this study, roughly the part that is now Canada between the Great Lakes and the Rocky Mountains, there is a much smaller number of language families. The distance from Montreal (where the North West Company had its headquarters) to Calgary in the foothills of the Rocky Mountains is no less than 4000 kilometers. This is the distance that had to be covered by the people who transported the furs. Despite the enormous size of this land, this area is relatively homogeneous in physical features and population groups; only four language families are encountered here: Iroquoian, Algonquian, Athapaskan, and Siouan.

Iroquoian languages were and are spoken in the Saint Lawrence River Valley and southward. Only two Iroquoian languages, Mohawk and Huron, are relevant to this study. Mohawk is spoken today in southwestern Quebec, southeastern Ontario, and the northern part of New York State, and it was perhaps once used as a lingua franca in the fur trade around the Great Lakes. Many Mohawks became excellent trappers, and they were also hired as trappers and *voyageurs* in the West by the North West Company (Giraud 1945: 248; Innis 1970: 264). Abenakis from Odanak were also hired (Delâge, pers. comm.). The Huron language is now extinct, but it was once spoken between Lake Ontario and Lake Huron and also used as a lingua franca before 1650 by other tribes that spoke Algonquian and Iroquoian languages.

Algonquian languages are spoken from the Atlantic Coast to the Rocky Mountains. They can be divided into four subgroups, which differ considerably (see figure 2.1), but only three branches are relevant to this study: Blackfoot, Eastern Algonquian, and Central Algonquian. Blackfoot is a branch of Algonquian by itself. Its speakers live on the western prairies, but they were hardly involved in the fur trade. Eastern Algonquian languages, for example, Micmac, Maliseet, and Abenaki, are spoken on the Atlantic Coast by tribes with which the French were in contact in New France and Acadia (roughly what is now Quebec and the Maritime Provinces, which border the Atlantic Coast). Central Algonquian languages include, for example, Cree

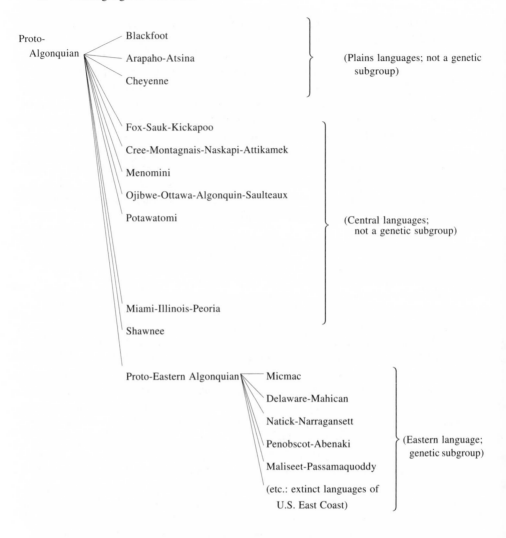

FIGURE 2.1. Classification of Algonquian Languages
Based on Ives Goddard, Eastern Algonquian languages, *Handbook of North American Indians*, vol. 15, *Northeast*, ed. Bruce G. Trigger (Washington, D.C.: Smithsonian Institution, 1978), p. 70; and J. Randolph Valentine, Ojibwe dialect relations, Ph.D. dissertation, University of Texas, Austin.

and Ojibwe. Montagnais—closely related to Cree, and for comparative purposes often considered as a dialect of the same language—is spoken on the north shore of the Saint Lawrence River; the French had regular contacts with the Montagnais since the early colonial period. Ojibwe is known under different names and is spoken in different dialects, from Lake Ontario to eastern Saskatchewan. In this study, the term "Ojibwe" is used to cover all Ojibwe dialects, for example, Ottawa, Algonquin (province of Quebec, which gave rise to the name of the language family, "Algonquian"), Chippewa (United States), and Saulteaux (Plains). The canoe routes of the fur trade passed mainly through Ojibwe territory, and not surprisingly, the Ojibwe language was widely used in the fur trade, especially by the French traders in the early period. Cree, spoken from northern Quebec to the foothills of the Rocky Mountains, also in different dialects, is discussed in Chapter Nine. Cree was also used in the fur trade (Bakker 1996) and, of course, of the utmost importance in this study as one of the component languages of Michif.

Athapaskan languages are spoken, among other places, in the northern parts of Manitoba, Saskatchewan, and Alberta. Several tribes traded with the fur-trading companies, and here I mention only the Chipewyans (not to be confounded with the Chippewas), who live in northern Saskatchewan and Manitoba and in the Northwest Territories (see map 2). They call themselves Dene.

The Siouan family is also relevant, mainly the Sioux language, which includes the deviant variety Assiniboine. Sioux is today spoken in several dialects, mainly in the Dakotas in the United States but also in Manitoba and Saskatchewan. The Sioux did not trade as intensively with the relevant fur trade companies, however, and they often resisted the intrusion by other tribes and the Europeans into their territories (see, e.g., Hickerson 1956). Part of the fur trade occurred in an area that formerly belonged to the Sioux, namely, the woodlands southwest of the Great Lakes. The Assiniboine language is relevant because the Assiniboines were active in the fur trade. They were also allied with the Cree from an early date onward, despite the diversity of their languages. Many of the Assiniboines spoke, and speak, Cree as a second language.

Other language families spoken in Canada but not relevant to this study are the Eskimo languages of the Arctic, the Salishan languages of British Columbia, the Wakashan and Tsimshian and Salishan language families of the Northwest coast, Tlingit and Haida of the Northwest, and the language of the small and isolated group of Kutenai of the Rocky Mountains and extinct Beothuk of Newfoundland. For our purpose only the four language families already discussed are important.

As noted, linguistic family boundaries differ from culture boundaries. Members of the same language family, or even members of the same language or dialect, may belong to different culture areas. The reverse is also true: one culture area as a rule contains languages from different families. It is also important to note that several Amerindian languages were widely known by other tribes as contact languages.

Lingua Francas in the Fur Trade Area

It is not only important to know which languages were spoken as mother tongues but also which languages were spoken in intertribal contacts. Some languages were widely used as a second language by different native peoples. Plains Cree, the Amerindian part of Michif, is among these contact languages, which are also called lingua francas. A lingua franca is a language commonly used between people who have different mother tongues. In large parts of North America, there were tribes in which most of the members could also speak another Amerindian language, in addition to the ordinary language used among the tribal members. The technical term for such a language, *lingua franca*, literally means "language of the Franks" (Holm 1989: 606–607). This was originally the name of the mixture of French, Provençal, Spanish, Italian, Arabic, and perhaps other languages that was used by the sailors and soldiers of the Mediterranean, at least from the late Middle Ages. From this time on, the term has also been used for languages employed to bridge the communication gap between people who do not speak each other's language. This is not necessarily a mixed language or a radically simplified language like the original Lingua Franca. English, in the modern world, can be seen as a lingua franca in many situations that involve people who do not speak each other's language. Today the lingua franca among Amerindians is also English, rather than a Native language.

In different parts of North America, Amerindian lingua francas were spoken. Rhodes (1982) provides an overview of lingua francas in the Great Lakes area (see map 2). Although he uses the term "trade language," it is clear that most of these are of the "lingua franca" type and are not pidginized (radically simplified) forms. There is an exception: a pidginized form of Ojibwe (Nichols 1992, 1995). Rhodes distinguishes four lingua francas: eastern Ojibwe east of the Great Lakes, Ottawa Ojibwe around Lake Huron and east of Lake Michigan, southwestern Ojibwe between Lake Superior and Lake Michigan, and Cree (dialect not specified) north of the Great Lakes. Apart from these Algonquian trade languages, I can mention Huron (Iroquoian) as a lingua franca east of Lake Huron before 1650 (Trigger 1976), which is not dealt with by Rhodes. This language is too far outside our area to be directly relevant, but it emphasizes the extended use of these trade languages in North America. Rhodes was able to detect the earlier existence of a lingua franca from both ethnographic and linguistic data. These facts can be summarized as follows.

First, where these lingua francas are used, there is extensive but asymmetric bilingualism, in which speakers of language A also speak language B (the lingua franca) but no speakers of language B speak language A. Thus there is a hierarchical system of language status and use. For instance, in some areas all Potawatomis also speak Ojibwe, whereas no Ojibwes speak Potawatomi. Indeed, the neighboring Ojibwe often do not know that the Potawatomis speak a language of their own (John D. Nichols, pers. comm., 1990), as the Potawatomis always address the Ojibwes in Ojibwe.

Second, there may be some confusion about the name of the language. Often the ethnic group shifted from its ancestral language to the lingua franca in the past, but it still gives the newly adopted language the name of its original ethnic affiliation. Sometimes it also claims to speak a mixture of languages, the old tribal tongue and the new one. Some of the Ottawa speakers Rhodes worked with, for instance, call the language that they speak Chippewa because they were descendants of American Chippewas. As they were originally speakers of Chippewa, with Ottawa as their lingua franca, they shifted to Ottawa as a mother tongue, but they still named their language after their former tribal affiliation, Chippewa. Other Chippewas who had shifted to Ottawa in the past called their language "a mixture of Chippewa and Ottawa." So in both cases there is discongruence of the tribal name and the language spoken.

Third, communication with outsiders takes place in the lingua franca rather than in the tribal language. There are cases, for instance, of published vocabularies of a language that is called Potawatomi, which appear to be nothing but southwestern Ojibwe (John D. Nichols, pers. comm., 1993).

Finally, there are also linguistic differences between the lingua franca and the original language of the same name. The lingua franca, always a second language, may be a slightly simplified version of the source language, but this has never been studied systematically. It is certain that the phonology of the lingua franca often shows some differences with the source language on which it is based, usually influences of the speaker's mother tongue. There may also be some substratal words from the first language in the lingua franca. Rhodes (1982: 8) gives examples of both from the Ottawa lingua franca area: there are some Potawatomi words used by speakers of Ottawa, and there are a number of phonological differences between the two varieties of Ottawa, the one spoken as a first language and the one originally spoken as a second language. This is exactly what we would expect as the result of language shift (Thomason and Kaufman 1988).

Not only Ojibwe but also Plains Cree was a lingua franca, specifically on the northern Plains. I discuss this in more detail in Chapter Nine. This is, of course, important since Plains Cree is one of the source languages of Michif.

Natives Contacted by the French

On the shores of the Great Lakes, the culture area of the Natives is relatively homogeneous, at least in the later historical period. It is all forest economy, that is, hunting and gathering. Different subgroupings of the Ojibwes are living on the northern shores. They all speak the same language of the Algonquian language family. To the north, a significant distance from the lakes, Cree is spoken, in different dialects. On the southern shores of the Great Lakes there is at least some sort of agriculture (corn, beans, squash), and therefore it is more heterogeneous. There one can find, as well as the Ojibwe, the Menomini, Potawatomi, and Sauk/Fox /Kickapoo tribes, all speakers of Algonquian languages, and some Winnebagos, who speak a Siouan language. These tribes also spoke, and sometimes still speak, Ojibwe as a second language. The north shore must have been the most important route to the West, and thus speakers of Ojibwe were the Natives the French mostly met. According to the oldest sources, the situation was only slightly different in the eighteenth century (Tanner 1987: map 13). Some sources place Cree speakers on the eastern shores of Lake Superior (Pentland 1978a: 104–105), in what is now Ojibwe territory. There is more Ojibwe spoken south of the Great Lakes today than in the past because of migrations and language shift.

The wooded area west of the Great Lakes is now Ojibwe territory as far west as roughly the Fort Qu'Appelle Valley. The Ojibwes are locally called Saulteaux in Canada and Chippewa in parts of the United States. The whole southern forest area is Ojibwe speaking, as is the eastern part of the prairies in Manitoba. West from there one can find the Assiniboines, often sharing reserves with the Cree. The Cree live in the area north and west of Ojibwe territory. They speak an Algonquian language, fairly similar to Ojibwe, and the Assiniboines speak a Siouan language. These three Plains tribes have lived in peace with one another for most of the historical period. The Crees and the Assiniboines seem to have been allied before around 1670 (Innis 1970: 46–50.) There are also some pockets of Sioux in Saskatchewan and Manitoba. They came from the United States in the last quarter of the nineteenth century. The Blackfoot live in the prairies west of the Cree territory (in western Alberta), and they have been the traditional enemies of the Cree for centuries. They speak a very divergent Algonquian language. The Chipewyans, who speak an Athapaskan language, live north of the Cree, from north central Manitoba westward to northern Alberta. The Chipewyans live only in the boreal forest, the Crees partly in the prairies and partly in the forests.

In the earliest contact period the situation was slightly different. One could roughly say that all of these tribes west of the Great Lakes, except the Chipewyans, have migrated westward. In earlier times, Crees were living around the Lake of the Woods (now Ojibwe territory), Assiniboines were living in southern Manitoba (now Ojibwe), and Gros Ventres were living in southern Saskatchewan (now Cree and Assiniboine territory) (Innis 1970: 48). The boundary between the Crees and Chipewyans fluctuated over time. It is certain that some of the northern Crees are now living in former Chipewyan territory. The Crees also gained some territory from the Blackfoot, who in their turn ousted other tribes (Dickason 1980). In Charlevoix's time (in the middle of the eighteenth century) it was thought that the Cree originally came from the area north of Lake Huron (Charlevoix 1744 I: 397–399) and had migrated west from there (Mandelbaum [1940] 1979). Others believe that the Crees have lived in the Alberta woodlands since time immemorial (e.g., James Smith 1981; Meyer 1987; Russell 1991). Map 1 shows a reconstruction of the distribution of tribes based on language families at the period of the first white contact.

We have seen that the area in which the fur traders did their business is vast but not very heterogeneous: mostly forest with rivers and some prairie land. And as the traders were interested in fur, they mostly dealt with only one culture group: the hunters and gatherers of the boreal forest, who used fur-bearing animals as food sources. Especially in the areas most frequented by the traders, only a few different cultures and languages were to be found. Both in the forests and on the prairies, traders had contacts with Ojibwe- and Cree-speaking Natives. A number of tribes with other mother tongues also spoke either of these languages in their contacts with outsiders, so Ojibwe and Cree must have been the main tongues in trade contacts.

We also should mention the activities of French missionaries, who worked with many of the tribes just mentioned. They left an impressive amount of linguistic work and religious tracts, especially in Huron and Ojibwe (Hanzeli 1969).

In short, neither the geographical nor the linguistic features of the fur-trading area were very diverse or variable. The French and British traders in the Northwest apparently met with a relatively homogeneous Native population.

Why is it important to know these tribal territories? As stated previously, it is important to know where the French came into contact with Cree speakers in order to establish where and when Michif could have emerged. Because the Amerindian part of the Michif language is Cree, more specifically Plains Cree, it is not immediately obvious where the language arose. The French were fur traders, so they would obviously have relations with tribes in the forest. The forest was the source of the precious fur-bearing animals. Beavers, the main trade object until well into the nineteenth century (Innis 1970), need wood for food and building materials. These animals could hardly be found in the prairies. The Crees who live in the forest, however, do not speak Plains Cree but other dialects, such as Woods Cree or Swampy Cree. The relevant dialect of Plains Cree is spoken in the prairies, where the fur trade played only a minor role. Indeed, Plains Cree is not spoken in the eastern prairies (Saskatchewan and Manitoba), where most of the Michif speakers can be found today. There is only a very small overlap of Michif territory and Plains Cree territory in the Fort Qu'Appelle Valley. Therefore, Michif cannot simply be considered a language that emerged from the fur trade. Nevertheless, it is both widely accepted and obvious that the Métis nation, and thus their language, did come about as a consequence of this trade. I attempt to resolve this paradox in this book, in particular in Chapter Nine, where I discuss the source languages of Michif and possible influences from other languages in more detail.

The Métis people, however, were undoubtedly a product of the fur trade. In the rest of this chapter I discuss the fur-trading companies (both British and Canadian) in more detail and the intermarriage of Europeans and natives, as these, at one time, led to the genesis of the Métis nation.

The Fur Trade Companies

In the beginning of the settlements in North America, the Europeans expected the Natives to bring their furs to them. Montreal was the destination of many Indian canoes loaded with furs in the seventeenth century (Innis 1970: 45). Later the French and the English had to find the traders in the woods, for several reasons (Delâge, pers. comm., 1995). The Native populations were severely diminished because of epidemics, especially between 1634 and 1667 (Delâge 1985). Further, there was competition between the French and the Natives. Finally, as any given area could support only a limited number of fur-bearing animals, the French desire to increase fur production forced them to find new Native groups as trading partners. British and Canadian companies that traded in furs were established, and they sent personnel into the woods to trade with the Indians.

The fur trade conducted by the companies drew to an important degree on Amerindian technology. The canoes that were used by the fur traders were inventions of the woodlands Indians. The North West Company used both the Indian version (*canoe du nord* "northern canoe") and an enlarged version (*canoe de maître* "master canoe"). These canoes could fairly easily be carried over portages (places where paddling was impossible). Sleds and dog teams, used in winters for more or less local transportation, were also Amerindian inventions, as were the snowshoes that made travel over soft snow possible. Ice-fishing techniques also drew on Amerindian knowledge.

Many groups were active in the Canadian fur trade. There were independent traders, mostly of French language background, who could be found in vast areas from an early date. Dutch, and later English, fur-trading companies operated from New York State from the early seventeenth century. In 1670 the Hudson's Bay Company was established in London, England with the privilege of trading in the entire area whose rivers drained into the Hudson Bay—roughly all Canada from the Rocky Mountains to near the East Coast. The North West Company emerged in Montreal in the 1780s out of a coalition of independent traders and small businesses. It was financed by Canadian Scots, who coopted relatives for the higher management positions. Its personnel, however, consisted almost exclusively of French Canadians. Roughly summarized, the British had fur-trading posts close to the Atlantic Coast and Hudson Bay, and the Canadian French had posts in the interior. Supplies for the English could be brought by ocean-going vessels; the French had to use much smaller and lighter canoes on the rivers. The Hudson's Bay Company and the North West Company are discussed in more detail in the following section.

The Hudson's Bay Company of London

In 1670 the British King Charles II granted a charter to his nephew Prince Rupert (see Newman 1985: 428–446 for the text). Basically it decreed that the British had the right to trade exclusively on all waters draining into Hudson Bay. This was to be the beginning of an enormous trading empire, which led to important changes on the continent.

The birth of the company started with the two French Canadian explorers Radisson and Groseilliers, who traveled to the rich fur countries in the West in 1659–1660 and returned with an abundance of beaver pelts. Feeling mistreated by the Canadian French authorities, who were not very interested and who even fined them for illegal trading, they went to the British with their findings. The British king then claimed what he called Rupert's land, basically all of Canada between Labrador and the Rocky Mountains and parts of the United States, and gave a group of "adventurers" the right to exploit it for the Hudson's Bay Company (HBC). The goals of the company were initially to exploit the resources (especially fur) of the country, to look for the northwest passage, and to colonize the land. In fact, only the first goal was put into practice.

From the very beginning, management was located in London, and board members rarely, if ever, traveled to Canada. The employees, both high and low, in Hudson Bay were physically separated from the London Committee, where all the decisions were made (Brown 1980: 42–50). The employees of the HBC were Europeans who signed contracts for a number of years. Many of them were picked up on the Orkney Islands in the northwest of Scotland, although Londoners and lowland Scottish employees were also common. Because of their European connections and the temporary nature of their stay, many of these employees were not strongly attached to the new land of snow and frost. Usually they wanted to return to Europe as soon as their contracts ended. Many of them were not well equipped for their jobs either, having little or no useful experience (Brown 1980: 21, 30, 48). There were only a few opportunities for careers in the company. The apprentices, clerks, and other lower-class laborers could become heads of fur-trading posts (masters) or areas (factors) or even governors (Brown 1980: 32). At the fur-trading posts, the relations between the management and the personnel showed patterns familiar in Europe, from which a kind of master-servant relation was imitated (Brown 1980: 32).

The earliest HBC fur-trading posts were called "forts," and these were often fortified, but as the relations with the Natives became more peaceful, they were called "house" or "factory" (Brown 1980: 18), after the word "factor," the name for the district manager. York Factory—to give one indication of the population of a HBC post—had fifty-one servants listed in 1786 (Brown 1980: 28).

The economic results varied enormously in different periods. Dividends could range from zero (because of losses) to 50 percent from one year to the next. Prices depended on many factors, one of which was the competition from the French fur traders and the fluctuations in supplies of skins. During a good period, more than half a million beaver skins reached London in one year. These were mostly made into hats, so-called beaver hats, worn by the upper classes in Europe. Between 1853 and 1877, HBC accountants calculated that they had sold 3 million beaver skins in London. To give an indication of the local prices at a fur-trading post in 1733, twelve needles could be obtained for one beaver skin or one gun for fourteen skins (Newman 1985: 65, 67, 466–468).

The HBC management forbade any ties between their employees and the Native population except for business contacts. Its employees had to follow rules of celibacy and chastity, but we see later that practice was different. The existing mores forced the company to tolerate the contacts of their personnel with the Natives and to change their policy in this regard from time to time to adjust to the realities of the Hudson Bay area.

In 1821 the HBC, after the resolution of some important disputes, fused with its larger rival, the North West Company. The important consequences of this amalgamation will be discussed in the following section and in Chapter Three.

The North West Company of Montreal and Lower Canada

Independent traders in New France had been active for a long time, but they felt the need to unite against the competition of the English traders of the Hudson's Bay Company. The North West Company (NWC) was therefore established in the 1780s. Its headquarters were in Montreal, traditionally the important harbor for the French fur trade. Whereas the HBC was managed from Europe, the NWC was managed from the colony itself. The capital for the company came from Canadians of Scottish ancestry, and the management and higher personnel were also Scotsmen. They came both from Europe and from immigrant communities in New England in what is now the United States (Brown 1980: 36–37).

In the NWC, there were sharp demarcations between the laborers, who were French, and the clerks, who were Scots. The French *voyageurs* were often acquainted with Native customs and languages before they were put into business, and tradition and knowhow were built up by generations of *coureurs de bois* and *voyageurs* of New France. In any case, they had the advantage of being born and growing up in the New World, thereby having a closer connection to the land than the British. The fact that the *Nor'westers* traveled by rivers and streams (where the Natives spent the summers) made contact with the Natives both unavoidable and necessary.

The Fur Trade Company after 1821

In 1812 the HBC allowed the philanthropical Lord Selkirk, a Scotsman, to settle on land near the Red River Settlement with a group of Europeans. People with ties to the NWC were staying there already and living mostly off the natural resources such as bison. The NWC and the local people—many of them Métis—resisted the arrival of the settlers, which sharpened the conflicts between the NWC and the HBC. Negotiations to resolve conflicts and to prevent future violence led to the amalgamation of the two rivals into one new company in 1821, keeping the old name Hudson's Bay Company. This event marks a number of changes important for the Métis. Often the HBC and the NWC had trading posts close to one another, and obviously from that time on many posts could be dispensed with. Solutions had to be found for the personnel. Some were fired, although in other cases people who were in fact superfluous were still hired (Brown 1980: 199). The HBC also wanted to find a solution for their retired employees who did not want or were not able to return to Europe or to eastern Canada, for instance, because they had a Native wife and children in the West. The HBC decided to send these people to the Red River Settlement, where they were to receive land and where schools and other institutions were being set up for them.

The new Hudson's Bay Company now became not only a company but also the administrative center of something like a colony, and a colonial government had to be set up (Brown 1980: 199). In business, it now had an absolute monopoly of the fur trade in British North America (what is now Canada). Former free traders, many of them Métis, now became illegal traders (Innis 1970: 329). They often had regular dealings with the United States, mostly trading bison products (buffalo robes and meat products).

Transportation was also improved after 1821. More and more the water routes were abandoned and overland trails set up (Gilman, Gilman, and Stultz 1979). Horse- and oxen-drawn Red River carts were increasingly used overland, and York boats (small sailing vessels) were used on the larger rivers and lakes (Innis 1970: 218–222) instead of birchbark canoes. Some of these were in their turn to be replaced by steamships. Métis were often pioneers in these overland trails, both for the bison hunts and in free trade with the United States.

Another change after the fusion involved the fur sources. Before then, mostly beaver fur had been traded, but now other furs were exploited, too. The beaver had become scarce, sometimes even extirpated, in many areas where the animal was formerly common. Furthermore, there was less and less interest in beaver hats in Europe (Innis 1970: 397).

Intimate contacts between European men and Amerindian women had been common for all Europeans involved in the fur trade and all Native peoples. With the surplus of personnel and the increasing use of Métis as middlemen in the trade of bison products, the Métis were more and more becoming a separate group.

Contacts with Native Women

When Sylvia Van Kirk (1991) was researching the role of women in the fur trade, she was often asked whether there were any women in the fur trade. There was very little room for European women, but there were, of course, plenty of Native women. A question like this points to the ignorance of the average Canadian of the role, perhaps even of the mere existence, of Native people. In fact, Native women were crucial to the survival of the fur traders in the West, as it was for the first French settlers in Acadia and New France.

According to demographic data, the man-woman ratio was rather unbalanced among the Plains nations. Brown (1980: 88) mentions sources that claim a three-to-one ratio of women to men among the Blackfoot throughout the nineteenth century. She also cites a census taken by Alexander Henry in 1805–1806, which suggests that similar ratios were common among other tribes on the Plains. Henry listed a total of 16,995 Indian women and only 7,502 men in his district. The greatest imbalance was registered on the northern Plains, with 13,632 women to 4,823 men (Coues 1897: I, 282; Brown 1980: 88). Brown suggests that "high male casualty rate from their increasingly wealth-oriented warfare" and other factors led to this unbalanced ratio (see also Van Kirk 1980: 24, 37–38).

For Native people, marriage was mostly arranged by the heads of the household or hunting group. Often the father married off the daughters, and survival of the group was the decisive factor in these choices. Beauty and character were less important. A good hunter was a favorite husband for a daughter, as this meant abundant food for the family. For the husband, a good marriage partner was a woman with physical strength and the ability to work hard. In many of the Indian tribes in the fur-trading area, women did most of the physical work: they had to gather firewood, fetch the meat of the animals the hunters had killed, prepare hides, fish, prepare food, make birch syrup, snare rabbits, take care of the children, make moccasins and snowshoes, and so on (Giraud 1945: 1030; Brown 1980: 81; Van Kirk 1980: 17–18). Indian women were indispensable assistants to the explorers as well. Some explorers claimed that the absence of Native women in their crews led to a lower success rate (Brown 1980: 65).

Among the Indians, marriages were in principle for life, but they could also be dissolved fairly easily at any time (Van Kirk 1980: 24). There was very little ceremony about the wedding itself (Brown 1980). Premarital sex was common (Van Kirk 1980: 23), but the Indians were not promiscuous. Some Indian men forced women of other tribes to become their wives, after they had taken them as captives from their enemies. In the West, these captive women could be sold and traded, an activity in which the French Canadians sometimes engaged (Van Kirk 1980: 13–14).

Because of the importance of survival of hunting bands, most of the Native peoples in the area had a habit unknown in Europe: they would lend their wives or daughters to guests as part of their hospitality or to other tribal members when hunters had to leave for longer periods (Giraud 1945: 1031; Brown 1980: 59–60; Van Kirk 1980: 25). This could last anywhere from one night to several years (see Brown 1980: 61 and Van Kirk 1980: 40 for examples). When the man came back after such a period, any children born in the meantime would be an integral part of the wife's and her returned husband's family.

For the Indian chiefs, it was important to have strong bonds through marriage with the European traders, who could supply them with all kinds of useful tools and materials to make life easier (Van Kirk 1980: 28). In this way, they acquired access to the posts, too. Some chiefs "reserved" one of their daughters for a trader (Van Kirk 1980: 29). The trader's relationship with the Indian's family had the function of strengthening trade alliances. Europeans formed ties with the Indians, and a sexual partner could be part of the business deal. Their Indian wives could perform important tasks, such as making snowshoes, gathering food, and of course interpreting when necessary (Van Kirk 1980: 54). Marriage ties also ensured peaceful relations with the trading partners. The Indian leaders clearly considered marriage as a tool toward acquiring wealth and maintaining peace.

Indian women usually had about four children (Van Kirk 1980: 24). Many of the traders' wives had many more children, whether they were Indians (in the early period) or of mixed ancestry (later). The attitude of the traders toward the children they had with Native mothers changed over time. In the earliest years, many of these children grew up among the Indians and were raised by their Indian mothers (Giraud 1945: 1040). They were sometimes described in the records as Indians and at the same time the child of some trader (Brown 1980: 69). Some of them became Indian chiefs (Giraud 1945: 465), possibly because of the advantage of the skills learned from their fathers. Later, roughly after 1790, the traders would try to give their children a more European-oriented education (Brown 1980: 155–156). They regularly sent their sons to the city or even to Europe to be educated. When the women returned to their tribes after their European husbands had left, their children were accepted as their own people, as in cases of wife lending. Many generations of mixed-blood children had been born before they were distinguished as a separate group or before they considered themselves to be a separate group, as I show in the next chapter.

In short, several factors stimulated the intermarriage of Native women with traders: there were more Amerindian women than men, and the Native women found a life with European husbands easier. For Europeans it facilitated survival; habits like wife lending reinforced the trading relationships greatly and were wanted by both sides. It also guaranteed peaceful relations. Intermarriage was almost unavoidable, both for the Natives and for the Europeans, as there were no European women in the West between the 1680s and the 1820s. The *mariages à la façon du pays* ("marriages according to the customs of the country") would be a logical consequence of the meeting of European men and Native women. These marriages were neither blessed nor registered. Most of the partners came from the Cree, Assiniboine, Ojibwe, and Chipewyan nations (Van Kirk 1980: 29). Their offspring would ultimately become the Métis nation: *la Nouvelle Nation.*

Summary and Conclusions

We have seen that the fur trade brought about many changes in the northern part of North America, especially for the Native people. There were free traders, mostly

French Canadians, and a number of fur trade companies were active. Different groups of Europeans (Orkney Islanders, Englishmen, Scotsmen, and French Canadians), who worked for these companies, dealt with the Natives in different ways. Large numbers of them started sexual relationships with Native women. It must be stressed that this was not primarily for reasons of physical satisfaction. It was a way to stabilize trade contacts between the fur traders and the Natives and to maintain peace. The Indian nations also stimulated these contacts, hoping to get the best trade objects. The children born from these contacts were initially brought up by the mothers as Indians. Later, more and more mixed Amerindian-European households sprang up, whose children had a different status from those of the early 1800s. The role of the Indians, and their descendants the Métis, can hardly be overestimated in the history of the Canadian West and also in the development of Canada as a whole (Innis 1970: 383, 392).

It is clear that the contacts between the French and the Natives were more intimate than those of the diverse British groups. The French had a long fur-trading experience in New France. They were frequently of mixed origin themselves, and their lifestyle was close to that of the Amerindians. They stayed with the Natives in the woods for long periods. They were apparently easily accepted, whereas the Scottish and HBC personnel had stronger bonds with Europe and often had moral objections against mixed unions. These relationships were also against HBC regulations. The French contacts were mostly with Ojibwe- and Cree-speaking nations, and because of these contacts the Métis nation and the Michif language must have been born.

The languages used in the fur trade were probably few in number. French, of course, was widely used. Only two, related Amerindian languages, in various dialects, were probably sufficient for making oneself understood throughout the fur-trading area from the Great Lakes to the prairies. These languages were Ojibwe and Cree. Both were also lingua francas for other tribes: Ojibwe in the southern woodlands around the Great Lakes, and Cree close to Hudson Bay and in the northern Plains.

The Métis are a product of the fur trade. The genesis of the Métis nation is discussed in the next chapter.

The Métis Nation

Origin and Culture

Michif is exclusively spoken by Métis, descendants of French fur traders and Amerindian women. It is necessary for several reasons to discuss these people. First, it is difficult to conceptualize for those who are unfamiliar with them a mixed ethnic group like the Métis. Second, it is useful to have the necessary background information on the speakers of the Michif language. Their situation is, in a number of respects, unique. Finally, the existence of this mixed language seems to be connected to the mixed identity of the Métis. The name of the people and the language is *Métis*, *Mitif*, and *Métif*, pronounced as *Michif*, which mean "mixed." All three are varieties of the same word, *Mitif* being the oldest (Trudel 1960: 83). The word is related to *Mestizo*, a person of mixed ancestry. Métis history and culture are the topics of this chapter.

Mixed unions of European males and Amerindian females were common from the earliest colonization of New France through the fur-trading period. Neither in New France nor in the Great Lakes area, however, did their children consider themselves separate from their parents' groups. They usually grew up as Indians, although sometimes as Europeans and sometimes as bicultural people. It was only in the 1800s that these people of mixed French-Indian origin began to consider themselves a separate ethnic group, different from both Indians and Europeans.

The Métis do form an ethnic group, although they differ from most other ethnic groups in a number of essential points (Fishman 1977). Most ethnic groups have a homeland (country or region), where they are usually numerically dominant. The Métis do not have such a homeland. They are dispersed in scattered communities in an area as vast as western Europe, and they are the most numerous ethnic group in only a few communities. Between their communities, other ethnic groups—mostly English-speaking Canadians—live in much larger numbers.

Ethnic groups usually have a language of their own. The Métis do not have one ethnic language but at least four: Michif, which is particularly for the Métis, and

Saulteaux, French, and Cree, which are all slightly different from the same languages as spoken by the Indians or French. Virtually all Métis today also speak English. Only Michif is a uniquely Métis language.

Ethnic groups usually have a common core culture. Métis culture is highly diverse because of the different origins of their ancestors, as well as the different geographical areas in which they live. Some Métis live in cities, others on arid land, and some as trappers in log cabins in the woods.

Ethnic groups usually share the same history. This is only partly true for the Métis. They all have both European and Amerindian ancestors, but these have different origins and cultures. From the 1800s onward, they seem to have had many common experiences, however, and this can be seen as their shared history.

The Métis are a separate ethnic group. Their common history and the cultural traits originating in their history may be the most important elements of their identity. The Métis themselves recently formulated their culture and identity as follows:

> Our Métis culture developed from a blend of Indian and European values and lifestyles. It still features commercial and domestic forms of living off the land; notably hunting, fishing, trapping, the gathering of wild rice, herbs, roots and berries, and farming. It includes our socials, music, jigging, country food, art, religious beliefs, historical knowledge, and our mixture of mainly Cree, English, Ojibwa, and French languages. All of this is bound together by close family ties, a strong sense of community identity, and by our common struggles for land, better jobs, improved living conditions, self-reliance, dignity and recognition as a nation. (Manitoba Métis Rights Assembly, connected with the Manitoba Metis Federation, in 1983; cited in Krosenbrink-Gelissen 1989: 35)

The Emergence of a Métis Identity

It is not easy to pinpoint the time when the Métis emerged. This depends on the criterion one uses. It is a cliché that the first Métis was born nine months after the first Europeans arrived in North America. Almost certainly this newborn person or persons did not belong to a different or new ethnic group. As seen in Chapter Two, the people of mixed European-Amerindian descent in New France never thought of themselves as a separate ethnic group. Neither did this occur in the Great Lakes area, where a mixed group existed but where no self-identification as a separate group seems to have emerged (Peterson 1978).

In the earliest period, roughly until the first decade of the nineteenth century, children born in these mixed marriages could identify themselves as Indians or as Europeans. In the Hudson's Bay Company (HBC) records they were called from time to time in the eighteenth century "natives of Hudson's Bay" (Brown 1980: 159). Sometimes they were called "Indian X, son of trader Y." Mostly, however, references to the children seem to have been avoided in the HBC records. Other terms, used in the Great Lakes area, were "French Indians," "Creoles," "country-born," *chicot, bois brulé, gens de libre*, "Canadese," and so on (Peterson 1978: 54). None of these early terms refers to the mixed ancestry of this group. It was only after the 1810s that people began to use a special terminology for the mixed offspring. In the first decade of the 1800s the terms "half-breed" and "Michif" (spelled as "Maitiff," "Metif," "Métif," and earlier "Mitif") were first encountered in the Canadian fur-trading context (Brown 1980: 172). A book in 1817 called them "Metifs, Bois Brulés, or Half-breeds" (*Statement* 1817: 17). An early description in an anonymous pamphlet related to the HBC described this group of what they called "lawless banditti" as follows:

> These are the illegitimate progeny chiefly of the Canadian traders, and others in service of the North-West Company, by Indian women. They have always been much under the control of that Company, by whom they are frequently employed as hunters, chiefly for provisions—an occupation in which they are very expert; hunting and shooting the buffaloe on horseback. The Company also employs them occasionally in other temporary services; and some of them are engaged in their regular employment as clerks, having received, in Canada, an education fitted to qualify them for that situation. (*Statement* 1817: 17)

This statement coincides with their emerging self-identity as Métis in that same decade. It was at that time that they themselves began to use terms like "half-breed," "Métis," "Métif," and (*Bois*) *Brulé*, as witnessed by some documents and songs dating from that period. This was particularly the case in the Red River area, where they were beginning to settle as bison hunters and suppliers of the fur trade (Brown 1980: 172). In letters in English, they called themselves *Halfbreeds* (*Statement* 1817), and in French songs *Bois Brulés* ("burnt wood"). The Red River area, the forks of the Assiniboine River and the Red River at the present site of the city of Winnipeg in Manitoba, is a central point in the history of the Métis. It was here that many Métis settled around 1800 and from which they later migrated, especially after 1867. For this reason the descendants of this group are still called Red River Métis. This does not mean that the Métis were the only inhabitants of the area. In 1820, for instance, there were "between 500 and 600 Scotch and English settlers, a large number of halfbreeds and some native Indians" (Tucker 1851: 22). The mixed people could have either French or Scottish ancestry, as these were separate population groups.

Nevertheless, just a few years later the Métis claimed the area as their land. It was here that some of the Métis had gardens and lands bordering the Red and Assiniboine rivers. Others had their home base in the area, leaving the place from time to time for bison hunts.

A crucial event in the history of the Métis took place in 1812. As stated in Chapter Two, the Hudson's Bay Company allowed Lord Selkirk, with poor people mainly from Scotland, to settle on a huge area of land that was formally part of HBC territory. This was an area where the North West Company (NWC), the Canadian competitor of the HBC, had already been active in the fur trade and where a number of French Canadians and Métis, linked to the North West Company, were already living. Selkirk's colony was intended as an agricultural settlement and was called Assiniboia (see maps 3 and 4). The NWC resisted these plans of the HBC, as it was afraid they would threaten its trading activities in the area. Many of the inhabitants feared for their livelihood.

The years after 1812 saw varied reactions and fluctuating relations between the old inhabitants and recent arrivals. On the one hand, there were Métis, Scots "half-breeds," and French Canadians, who supported the new settlers and helped them build their homes, fed them through the winter, and guided them (Giraud 1945: 570–571, 577). On the other hand, there were also Métis who opposed the new settlement because it might damage the bison hunt, in which many Métis were involved. This discontent was encouraged by the NWC leaders, who stimulated nationalistic feelings and claims to the land among the Métis. Métis people were sent for in places like Fort Qu'Appelle, Cumberland House, and Ile-a-la-Crosse (some 1000 kilometres away) to come and assist the Red River Métis. This shows not only that the Métis were very mobile but also that they knew where to find one another.

Some skirmishes took place between the Métis and the settlers. In 1816 the Métis killed twenty-two of the new settlers (including the governor of Assiniboia), in what was called the Battle of Seven Oaks or La Grenouillère (Frog Plains), in what is now Winnipeg. Some eye-witness accounts from an HBC viewpoint can be found in *Statement* (1817). A song about the event composed by a Métis ended with the line "to sing the praise of the *Bois Brulés*." (Joseph Howard 1952: 35; MacLeod and Morton 1963). They considered themselves "Lords of the Soil" (*Statement* 1817: 35n., 132) and the real owners and inhabitants of the land. The first national flag of the Métis was now also used: a red flag with a blue infinity sign (today it is a blue flag with a white infinity sign). It may be that Lord Selkirk's arrival had a reinforcing effect on the self-identification of the Métis as a separate group.

Another consequence of these skirmishes was that the fur trade companies realized that cooperation was necessary to avoid troublesome events like these. In 1821 the HBC and the NWC fused. The period after the amalgamation of the two fur-trading companies was characterized by a number of changes, some of which were already mentioned in Chapter Two. After the 1820s, racial considerations started to surface in HBC hiring policies. At that time significant numbers of Métis were employed by the HBC (Giraud 1945: 987–988). The career possibilities for the Métis, however, grew smaller and smaller. The Scottish "half-breeds" had the better jobs at the trading posts (Giraud 1945: 988). Some Métis were employed as interpreters and freighters and as guides for surveyors and explorers, not only for the HBC but also for the missionaries, scientists, explorers, military, and other visitors (Giraud 1945: 971, 985–986, 1006, 1073). Still, the Métis were a fast-growing population group, who could no longer be assimilated into Indian tribes or sent to Europe or Canada or hired by the company. Many Métis were dismissed from company service between 1822 and 1824 (Brown 1980: 202). Some turned to hunting, specializing in bison; others to trading; others to some modest agriculture. This development also led to the inception of social stratification among the Métis. As these activities are important, I discuss them now, before continuing with later historical events.

The Métis Bison Hunt

A highlight of the Métis life was the bison hunts twice a year, in which whole parishes were involved. It caused "a massive migration of a whole population" (Giraud 1945: 802), especially in the summer hunt. Around 1820 the first organized Métis buffalo hunt took place, and after 1827 it had become an institution (Roe 1935; Giraud 1945: 801, 1156–1173). It continued, with varying degrees of success because of the increasing scarcity of buffalo, until the 1870s.

The hunts were family events. The men hunted the animals with guns from horseback, the women cut the meat and prepared pemmican, and the children assisted the women. Pemmican is ground, dried buffalo meat to which fat and sometimes berries are added. Lasting for years, pemmican was the main staple food in the area. The Red River carts (drawn by horses or oxen) were used for travel, to carry supplies, and to bring back buffalo meat and hides. Many hunters had between six and twelve carts (Roe 1935: 206), and they usually owned a number of horses (Giraud 1945: 1051).

In the summer hunt, which took place from early June until the middle of August, some 500 to 1000 people were involved, with 800 to 1400 carts. This hunt was especially intended for making pemmican, dry meat, and clothing (Roe 1935: 181). Pemmican was used partly for personal consumption and partly for trading with the HBC, who used it as food supplies for its employees. The Métis of Pembina (on the North Dakota/Minnesota/Manitoba border) and Saint François Xavier (Red River Settlement) were especially active in pemmican production (Giraud 1945: 815, 852). The fall hunt took place from the middle of September until the first freeze. It was intended mainly to obtain fresh meat for the winter and buffalo robes for trade. This hunt was less massive, with between 200 and 300 carts.

The families of the hunters gathered in Saint François Xavier, the main hunters' parish of the Red River settlement. They split into two or sometimes three groups. One group went south to Pembina, following the Red River. The other group went west along the Assiniboine and the Qu'Appelle rivers, then southwest into the Plains. The hunting grounds were mainly south of the international border, roughly between the Assiniboine River to the north, the Red River to the east, the Cheyenne River to the south, and the Souris River to the west. They camped in tipilike structures with cloth; some had buffalo hides as covers. The number of buffaloes killed each season was high: it was speculated that between 20,000 and 40,000 were killed on average per season (Roe 1935: 211), and one wonders what contribution this made to the almost final extinction of the animal. If one considers, however, that the bison population before the arrival of the Europeans was estimated at 60 million, it still seems a negligible number.

The hunt was very disciplined. A chief was chosen for each hunt, with twelve counselors. They had captains under their command, who commanded societies of ten warriors. They had tasks similar to a police force, and they also guarded against attacks from the hostile Sioux Indians. These warrior societies were characteristic of the Indians, as the Assiniboines had identical warrior societies during their buffalo hunts (Roe 1935: 178; Giraud 1945: 805–807; see also some studies in Corrigan and Barkwell 1991).

Contradictory claims have been made about the involvement of Indians in the Métis bison hunt, which according to certain sources, some Indians did not approve of. In 1857 the Plains Crees of the Qu'Appelle Valley decided not to allow the Métis or whites to hunt buffalo in their territory (Roe 1935: 187). Sharrock (1974: 113; following Cowie 1913: 303) states that the Assiniboines, Cree-Assiniboines, Crees, and Saulteaux "in common resented the intrusion of the Metis hunters onto the Plains." Other sources, however, claim that Indians joined the hunters, some on the prairies, and others came to the meeting point (Giraud 1945: 802). There are documented cases of the latter. In 1849, for instance, the White Horse Plains division contained 700 Métis and 200 "Indians"—the tribe not specified (Roe 1935: 207)—which amounts to almost one-quarter of the hunters. In 1851, 200 Saulteaux were counted among the hunters (Giraud 1945: 802). In the 1870s, there was talk of "Chippewa tribes and their associates, the half-breed hunters," in reference to Métis bison hunters recorded in the 1910s (Turtle Mountain Indian Reservation 1985: 231; see also 229).

Other sources show that Métis joined Indian buffalo hunts. The Métis freemen were reported to have hunted frequently with the Crees and Assiniboines around Edmonton in the 1830s. Isaac Cowie, an employee of the HBC, was present at an Indian buffalo hunters' camp near Cypress Hills, Saskatchewan, in 1868. The camp consisted of 2500 to 3000 people: Crees, Saulteaux, Assiniboines, Cree-Assiniboines, and "a few English and French Métis from the Qu'Appelle, Touchwood Hills, and Fort Pelly posts" (Cowie 1913: 302–303; cited in Sharrock 1974: 112). Métis hunters who joined Indian buffalo-hunting parties had to camp at a distance from the Indians, and they were under constant surveillance (Sharrock 1974: 113).

Métis as Traders

Especially after 1821, many Métis took up freighting jobs, transporting goods all over the northern prairies, both in an east-west direction (to Edmonton, Alberta, and beyond) and north-south (to Saint Paul, Minnesota, and beyond) across the international border (Giraud 1945: 888–896; Gilman, Gilman, and Stultz 1979). Sometimes this was done for the HBC, but more and more Métis tried trading, mostly in furs and bison products such as pemmican and bison robes. On the prairies, long caravans of hundreds of Métis carts appeared frequently. Traveling in these caravans can be seen as a way to prevent attacks by the Sioux (Giraud 1945: 970–985). Bison products were among the important items traded.

The inhabitants of the Northwest refused to recognize the authority of the Hudson's Bay Company. The Métis, the most numerous group, did not accept HBC's fur-trading monopoly, nor did the French Canadians or the English and Scots in the area. The Métis free traders had regular conflicts with the HBC about trading activities. They were also middlemen in the illicit trade of the HBC with the Americans (Giraud 1945: 941). After the release of one who had been arrested for illegal trading in 1849, the Métis shouted: "Le commerce est libre!" ("The trade is free!") They also asked for freedom in their bison hunts (Brown 1980: 173).

The Beginnings of Social Stratification

Métis society is usually not thought of as being socially stratified,[1] and many studies do not even consider this possibility. Moreover, since almost all Métis today are among the lower classes of society, the stratification seems less important now than it actually was in the past. In the oral history of the Métis, many stories deal with political conflicts among the Métis in former times, some families choosing a certain side in a conflict, others joining the other side (see, e.g., Giraud 1945: 1106). Actually, on close reading of the sources of the conflicts of 1812, 1867, and 1885 between the Métis and the invading authorities, in all cases factions of Métis appear to have supported both of the opposing parties (Lee 1989). In other words, there were Métis who joined the supposed enemies of the Métis.

Most of these cases seem to have been based on what one may consider class differences among the Métis. In fact there were two clear classes in Métis society during the nineteenth century, those of the French-speaking agriculturalists and those of the "Indian"-speaking (perhaps Michif-speaking) buffalo hunters and freighters and traders. This was already noted in print by Giraud (1945), and according to Tough (1989) it was one of the Métis leaders with whom Giraud was in contact who had pointed this out to him. This analysis of class differences was confirmed later by, among others, St.-Onge (1985, 1990). Actually, Alexander Morris in 1880 had already observed clear distinctions. He divided the Métis into three groups: ". . . (1) those who . . . have their farms and homes; (2) those who are entirely identified with the Indians, living with them and speaking their language; (3) those who do not farm, but live after the habits of the Indians, by the pursuit of the buffalo and the chase . . ." (Roe 1935: 204). I want to suggest that the first group was mainly French speaking, some of them being absorbed later into the local French Canadian society. The second group was absorbed into the Indian tribes, speaking an Indian language, and the third group was the Michif-speaking group. This will be examined in more detail in Chapter Nine.

The French-speaking agriculturalists held the important positions in the Métis institutions. They cultivated land and planted gardens, combining these activities with fishing. A number of them were merchants or shopkeepers, but they were only slightly involved in hunting. Some of them were literate. This Métis "bourgeoisie" emerged after the 1830s. In the beginning, they did not think of organizing their own political institutions, but they were opposed to the HBC, as were the lower classes. Nevertheless, contacts with the hunting Métis were very limited. Research on the community of Pointe à Grouette (today Sainte Agathe, 70 kilometers south of Winnipeg) in the second half of the nineteenth century shows that the farmers and the hunters lived side by side, without much interference from each other. They rarely intermarried. St.-Onge (1985) indicates that the farming elite was neutral or even hostile to aspirations of Métis self-government. Only those farmers occupied official local positions. Both classes, however, were ultimately forced to leave the land because of manipulations with the scrips and land speculation (see the following discussion and, e.g., Giraud 1945: 1128–1131).

Different groups lived in the Red River parishes (Giraud 1945: 773–774; Spry 1985; see also map 4). These parishes of the Red River settlement were differentiated not only in language and ethnic background but also in religion, culture, and means of subsistence (Pannekoek 1991). There were English-speaking parishes, which were Protestant or Anglican, and French-speaking parishes, which were Catholic. The retired HBC workers and their Scottish-Indian mixed families lived at the lower reaches of the Red River, that is, in Saint Andrew parish. The descendants of the Selkirk settlers from Scotland lived south of them, in the parish of Kildonan. The higher personnel of the HBC and British settlers made their living around Upper Fort Garry. French Canadians and Métis of French descent were upstream of the forks, with Saint Boniface as its central point. The Indians could be found on the extremities. In Saint Paul there was a Saulteaux mission. Saint Peter was also an Indian settlement (Stobie 1967–1968: 73), and there was a small Indian colony set up by the Protestant missionary W. Cochrane in the north.

There were also differences among the various Catholic French parishes. A parish like Saint François Xavier was basically a community of buffalo hunters, whereas Sainte Agathe was mainly agricultural (St.-Onge 1985). As already mentioned, there were also linguistic differences between the different classes. The elite spoke mostly French, whereas the hunters of Saint François Xavier spoke Native languages and, possibly, Michif. Sainte Agathe was basically francophone.

That these class differences still play a role in this century is clear from St.-Onge's (1992) study of Saint Laurent, a French-speaking Métis community on the southeastern shore of Lake Manitoba. There used to be a community adjacent to the village whose inhabitants were considered dirty and uncouth by the farmers and fishermen of Saint Laurent. In this community, Fort Rouge, the people "still spoke Cree or Saulteaux to each other . . . in the 1940s" (St.-Onge 1990: 82). The people in Saint Laurent denied having any relatives in that community, although the Métis mostly know exactly who is a relative—often most of the community. The Saint Laurent Métis had only a few social contacts with the Fort Rouge people. The origin of this other community is nebulous. Apart from fishing, they made a living from trapping, berry picking, seneca root digging, frog harvesting, and seasonal wage labor. As St.-Onge (1990: 82) claims, "Several Métis villages had such small communities at their outskirts. These seem to have been given different names to emphasize their separateness."

Historical Events after 1821

There were regular migrations from and to the Red River (Giraud 1945: 766, 779, 839, 841, 1084), some of them caused by drought or flooding in the Red River settlement. In other cases people were looking for better hunting grounds. There were movements to and from the Pembina district in Minnesota, the Turtle Mountains in North Dakota, the Northwest (Saskatchewan and Alberta), and the Parklands. Thus there were numerous family ties with these areas (Giraud 1945: 1085). Apart from the many families who left the community for the regular bison hunts, there were also the *hivernants* "winterers," who were the poorest of the Métis. They spent the winters in the hills of the Parklands, which were rich in game, such as the Turtle Mountains, Duck Mountains, Riding Mountains, Wood Mountain, Cypress Hills, and Moose Mountains (Giraud 1945: 818, 819, 820). There it was possible to survive by living off the land. It is striking that many of the migrations, before as well as after the events of 1867 (see Chapter Nine), had these territories as their destinations. Hunters from the Red River had also traveled there in the hunting seasons, so the areas must have been familiar.

In the meantime, the population of Red River increased. White settlers began to arrive in the area, although the French Métis and English-Scottish half-breeds remained by far the most numerous population groups in the Red River settlement. At the first Manitoba census of 1870, there were 12,000 inhabitants in the newly formed province. No fewer than 6,000 were French-speaking Métis; 4,000 were English-speaking Scottish-Cree mixed bloods, 1,500 were white, and 600 were Indians

(Joseph Howard 1952: 147). The French Métis had been by far the most important group in the Red River area at least since the 1840s (Brown 1980: 210, 218; Boisvert and Turnbull 1985). The Métis intermarried and often had big families. The proportion of Métis and Scottish mixed bloods increased over time (Giraud 1945: 761).

There were more and more disagreements between the Métis and the authorities of the HBC (Giraud 1945: 902–904) after 1821. Despite their numerical strength, the Métis were initially not consulted in 1836 in the Assiniboia Council of the HBC, although later they were granted a small parcel of land by the authorities (Giraud 1945: 905, 943). Neither did the Métis accept that the lands they considered theirs could be sold to the Canadian confederation by the HBC. This discontent culminated in the occupation of Lower Fort Garry by a group of Métis in 1869, under the leadership of Louis Riel, in the name of all the inhabitants of the Northwest. They formulated a bill of rights and elected a provisional government. They wanted a land settlement and compensation for the loss of hunting grounds. The laws and institutions of this government were based on those used at the buffalo hunt (Barkwell 1991), where the leaders had also been called "provisional government."

After the execution in 1870 of Thomas Scott (one of the Protestant, anglophone prisoners of the Métis), the Canadian army, who came from Upper Canada to keep order after Riel left, defeated the Métis. Nevertheless, some of their demands were included in the Manitoba Act of 1870 (Sealey and Lussier 1975: 86–87), by which Manitoba became part of the Canadian Confederation. The rights of the francophone Métis were recognized. A bilingual French-English school system was established, and a land settlement with the Métis was promised in the Manitoba Act. The Métis would receive land scrips, papers issued by the government that ensured rights for money or land. They were worth either 240 acres (approximately 100 hectares), later augmented to 300 acres (120 hectares), or $240 ($300). More than 1 million acres (400,000 hectares) of land were reserved for the Métis.

However, because of speculation, bribing, the ignorance of the people involved, and purposeful manipulations by the authorities (Pelletier 1975; Sealey and Lussier 1975; St.-Onge 1985), these lands never really materialized. Some of the people, especially the hunters, lost the land because they were not able to make it fit for agriculture within the time demanded by the authorities. The land scrips are still the subject of court cases between the Manitoba Metis Federation and the government. The loss of their lands forced many Métis to leave the Red River area. Great numbers, often in family-based groups, moved to Saskatchewan and even further north and west (see map 3; Slobodin 1966). They hoped they could continue their way of life—hunting, fishing, and berry picking—where they would not be hindered by the growing numbers of white settlers.

In 1885 an armed conflict again took place when the Métis and their Cree allies around Batoche (near Duck Lake, Saskatchewan) felt threatened by white land surveyors. Batoche was one of the places to which a number of the Red River Métis had migrated after they realized that they would never receive their land in Manitoba. Here, too, there was a conflict about ownership and use of the land. The Métis felt threatened because of the arrival of white settlers on the Canadian Pacific Railway, which was completed in 1885, and because they had witnessed the near extinction of the bison around the same time. A confrontation of the 6000-man army and 600 armed

Métis occurred in 1885. It was called the "Battle of Batoche" by the army and "massacre" by the Métis. Again the Métis (and their allies, the Crees) were defeated. Their leader, Louis Riel, who is still a hero and a martyr for the Métis, was hanged for high treason later that year.

These events led to new waves of migrations. Many Métis fled to Montana and the Turtle Mountains in the United States and elsewhere. Some of the Métis found refuge among relatives on Indian reserves; they are now assimilated among the Cree Indians. Others started new villages, often on land hardly fit for living, sometimes in places formerly used by the "winterers." Today the descendants of the Red River Métis can be found in almost any province of Canada and in many places in the United States. The most important groups are still located in Manitoba, Saskatchewan, Alberta, and the Northwest Territories in Canada, and Montana, North Dakota, and Minnesota in the United States. Some of them, however, hide their real identity and say that they are French Canadians (Giraud 1945: 1234).

Their two rebellions (so described by the victors) or resistances (according to the defeated) hindered their assimilation into white society; their actions had greatly worsened their relationships with the English and even with the French Canadians (Giraud 1945: 1232). Life for the Métis became even harder in the 1890s, when the hunting of certain animals on which they depended for their living was forbidden (Giraud 1945: 1219). Many of them have lived in utter poverty since then in small communities scattered throughout the prairies and the woods. They have had to stick together in isolated communities, without the support of the government or the sympathy of society as a whole.

In the 1990s there are more than 98,000 descendants of the Red River Métis in Canada, most of them in the prairie provinces. They live in scattered villages and in big cities, in what we could call a "diaspora." By federal law, the Métis are not allowed to live on Indian reserves, unless they marry an Indian. Nor do they have any of the financial advantages that Indians have, such as free schooling, free medicine, subsidized housing, and exemption from taxes. The Indians and the Métis are usually the poorest inhabitants of these provinces, but the Métis, who do not have government support, are the worse off. Most of them can be found on the lowest economic levels. They form a minority of less than 5 percent among the roughly 3 million inhabitants of Alberta, Saskatchewan, and Manitoba.

The Métis as an Ethnic Group

In the previous section, the Métis were depicted as a separate ethnic group, which was formed by specific historical circumstances and whose members went through roughly the same historical events. As this situation is perhaps difficult to understand, it may be useful to deal with Métis identity and the Métis as an ethnic group or nation in more detail. Before that, we need to make an important distinction between the pan-Métis and the historical Métis (Krosenbrink-Gelissen 1989; see also the following section).

Since the late 1960s or early 1970s the term "Métis" gained general acceptance. Before that time, the term used by the Métis themselves and by the general population and officials was "half-breed," but this disappeared from official use because of its negative connotations. The term "Métis" was used for the descendants of the Red River Métis, but its use was also extended to include all people of partial aboriginal descent, such as those with an Icelandic father and an Ojibwe mother or a Chipewyan father and a Dutch mother. These people of Euro-Canadian and Indian descent can be called "pan-Métis," in distinction to the "historical Métis" (see figure 3.1). The pan-Métis are usually individuals who do not form an ethnic group and who have no group identity as such. The historical Métis used to marry within their group and within their class, whereas a pan-Métis could choose an Indian or Euro-Canadian, as well as a pan-Métis or historical Métis. In this book, only the historical Métis are discussed; when I use the term "Métis," it refers only to this group. In 1982 "Métis" was recognized officially when it was made a legal category in the Canadian Constitution Act, which recognized the aboriginal status of the Métis.

The Métis do not consider themselves as white (French or otherwise) or as Indians (Cree or otherwise). Perhaps this is one of the main ethnic traits of these people: their common wish to be neither Indian nor white. For the Canadian Métis who have lived in the United States for many generations, the situation is slightly different. South of the border, they are allowed to live on Indian reserves. When they do, they still remain distinct from the Indians who live there. Everybody knows who is Métis and who is so-called "full blood." As they are legally Indian, they sometimes use that word for themselves. A Métis from North Dakota told me the following story:

> I was invited to speak at a meeting in Winnipeg in 1985. They were all Michifs who came to listen. Somebody asked: "Are there any Indians where you are?" I said: "Well, I am an Indian." Then everybody was silent. You could have heard a pin drop. I thought: "O God, I must have said something wrong!" Later I realized that they do not want to be Indians.

It is also clear that "Métis" does not have a biological meaning, nor does its colloquial counterpart "half-breed." Most, if not all, Canadian Indians have European ancestors, too. Many treaty Indian families are aware of one or more Scottish or French traders among their ancestors, but they do not consider themselves Métis. Even the most acculturated of the Métis, those living in big cities, usually socialize with members of their group alone.

French ancestry seems to be a condition for Métis identity. I met a man in northern Manitoba who said that he was not a real Métis because he also had Irish and Scottish ancestors. Almost all of the Métis have French surnames, such as Bouvier, Blondeau, Desjarlais, Larocque, Lavallee, Ledoux, and so on (Havard 1879). A few Scottish names are Métis names, too, such as McDougall, Bruce, Fisher, and Fidler. The number of Métis family names in the West is fairly limited. It is usually possible to tell by the name whether a person is Métis or French Canadian.

Despite this diversity, I here attempt to sketch Métis culture in general. Before this, it may be useful to give the terms used for the Métis by themselves and others and the ethnic names used by the Métis for others. This also points to the distinctiveness of their group.

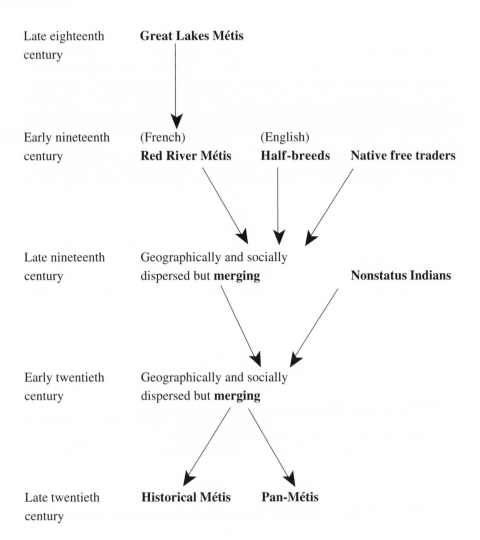

FIGURE 3.1 Who Are the Métis?
From L. E. Krosenbrink-Gelissen, The Métis National Council: Continuity and change among the Canadian Métis, *ERNAS. European Reviw of Native American Studies* 3.1 (1989): 33–42.

Synonymy

A wide variety of names is in use for the group whose language I am dealing with here. The word "Métis," which is most common now both among whites and Métis when dealing with outsiders, came into wide use only fairly recently, that is, the second half of the twentieth century (Goddard 1981). The word "Métis" is now pronounced as [meti] or [mɛtIs] by speakers of English, both incorrect imitations of French [metis]. Among the Métis themselves, the French word "Métis" is not often used, whether they are speaking English or French.

In the 1810s in the Red River settlement, three words were most commonly used for the mixed Indian-French group: "Métif," "half breed," and *Bois Brulé* and its abbreviation *Brulé* (see, e.g., *Statement* 1817: 17, 98). The English word used was "half breed," which at the time did not have the undesirable connotations it has today and was said by both Métis and whites. In the 1810s, some letters were signed with names and "chiefs of the Halfbreeds" (see, e.g., MacLeod and Morton 1963: 30). Even today it is used by the Métis when speaking English, although it is not always appreciated when outsiders use the term. The word "breed" is also used by English-speaking Métis. People of mixed Scottish and Amerindian descent often dislike the word "Métis" for their people; they prefer "half breed" for their ethnic affiliation.

The French word *Métif* and its old Canadian French form *Mitif* are etymologically related to *Métis*, and Spanish words like *Mestizo*, meaning "mixed," denote the fact that these people are of mixed ancestry. In standard French this archaic word is pronounced [metif], but the Métis themselves pronounce it [mIčIf]. This follows the older Canadian French pronounciation since older sources give the word as "Mitif" (see Trudel 1960: 83, who quotes from documents referring to "Mitif" slaves). This word is still used universally by the Métis themselves, both for the people and for some of the languages they speak. It is not often used with outsiders, however.

The French name *Bois Brulé*, which means "burnt wood," is usually related to the skin color of the Métis, who are often of lighter complexion than the Indians (e.g., Sealey and Lussier 1975: 14). This may be a translation of an Ojibwe word. The Ojibwe language specialist Baraga (1878–1880: 2:4, 421; cited in Goddard 1981) stated that the Indians "call the half-breeds so, because they are half-dark, half-white, like a half-burnt piece of wood, burnt black on one end, and left white on the other." Sealey and Lussier (1975: 14) use the Ojibwe term *wi:ssakkote:w-inini*, meaning "half-burnt woodmen" (*wi:ssakkote:* "half-burnt wood"), which would be the source for *bois brulé*. The Chipewyan term *bèpa rédhkkpayṇ* also has this meaning (Goddard 1981). In fact, most of the other terms used for the Métis are of any of these three types. They stress that the Métis are "half (like us)," they denote some type of "mixing," or they relate to the skin color (i.e., if the interpretations are correct; see the following).

A fourth group of terms stresses the freedom of the people. In the earliest period many of the Métis and Canadians were not bound to fur-trading companies, and a number of terms relate to this: *gens libres* "free people," *hommes libres* "free men," and "freemen." These terms, however, do not necessarily refer to Métis alone; they include French Canadians, too. A Cree term *otipemisiwak* is given by Payment (1991), meaning literally *otipêyimisowak* "those who command themselves," but I have never heard this term and I suspect it has been made up as a translation of "freemen."

The Cree term for Métis is *âpihtawikosisân*, from *âpihtaw* "half" and *-kosis-* "son." In the Odawa dialect of Ojibwe it is *aayaabtawzid* or *aya:pittawisit* "one who is half," which also contains the root "half."

The word *chicot*, like *bois brulé*, is also of French origin. It literally means "stump of a tree." This was also a self-assigned designation in the nineteenth century. A contemporary observer translated it with "half-burnt stump," and it was, like *bois brulé*, related to skin color by observers. According to Peterson (1978: 62, n. 3), however, *chicot* was already used for the French *coureurs de bois* as early as the seventeenth century, when the settlers would strip land of its timber and then abandon the land, leaving "chicots"—which suggests that it had nothing to do with skin color.

According to Peterson (1978: 54) various other words were common in the nineteenth century, more specifically after 1812, when the Métis became a separate group. Some of the Green Bay, Michigan, mixed people called themselves *creole*, meaning "locally born." Some of the HBC records mention "French Indians" in the eighteenth century.

A totally different term is the one used in Plains Indian sign language. It combines the sign for "wagon" and "man." This is perhaps the consequence of the long caravans of Red River carts, which ventured south for trade on the prairies in the nineteenth century. This was undoubtedly the way the Métis became known in the central Plains, where this sign language was in use.

As I said, the most common self-designation now and in the past has always been *Métif*, both in French and in Michif, pronounced by them as *Michif* [mIčIf]. The term is used both for the Métis people and the languages that they speak. This can lead to confusion. The Métis dialect of the French language as used by the Métis is called Métif, as is the mixture of Cree and French. The Manitoba Metis Federation usually speaks of Michif French and Michif Cree to distinguish between the two languages (and Michif Saulteaux, for that matter). To make the terminology even more complex, not only does the term *Michif* refer to two or more different languages but the mixed language Michif is also called Cree by its speakers. However, most of its speakers are aware that their Cree, in having many French words, differs from the Cree as spoken by the Indians, although a few who have never met Cree speakers seem to be unaware of the distinction.

It may also be useful to mention briefly the terms used for Indians by the Métis. The general term is *les sauvages*, pronounced /li: šava:ž/. Some of the most important Indian nations for the Métis are the Crees, *les Cree* [li: kri:]; the Ojibwes, *les Saulteaux* [li: su:ty:] or [su:tu:]; and the Sioux, *les Sioux* [li: sju:]. White people in general, except French Canadians, are called *les blancs* [*li: blā*] or, more commonly, *les Anglais* [*li: zãglɛ*]. Some people also know the Cree word *mu:nija:s* "white person" (< Montreal). French Canadians are called *les Canadiens* [*li: kanayæ̃*]. This word never refers to English Canadians. Ukrainians are called *les Galiciens* [*li: galisjæ̃*], and Americans are called *les Américains* [*li: zamɪričæ̃*].

This discussion of Michif ethnonymy shows once more that the Métis consider themselves to be a group distinct from Europeans and Indians. The Métis also have distinct cultures and traditions.

Métis Culture

This is not the place to give a thorough description of Métis culture. Culture captures so many aspects of human life that it is impossible to provide a complete picture. Furthermore, Métis culture is especially heterogeneous, as communities can be found in very different environments—prairies or forests, isolated farms and villages or cities. Many Métis no longer live according to traditional values. Some even hide their identity to procure a better place in a society in which they are victims of discrimination. This diversity also shows in the number of different languages spoken by people who consider themselves as belonging to the same ethnic group or nation.

Métis culture can be distinguished from both Indian and French culture in several ways, and a number of traditional Métis cultural aspects may be considered typical. The following description is based mainly on my personal experiences and interviews with Métis elders conducted mostly in 1990 in Manitoba, North Dakota, and Saskatchewan. Similar descriptions can be found in Sealey and Lussier (1975), Dusenberry (1985), Harrison (1985), and other sources. There is also a growing body of Métis writing on their own people, of which Campbell (1973) is the most successful. I deal with only some aspects of the culture.

FOOD

Obviously, since the introduction of jobs or, more often, social security, most of the Métis foods are bought in stores. Nevertheless, some still keep gardens, where they grow mainly potatoes, turnips, and carrots. There are a number of traditional Métis recipes, like [*lagalɛt*], unleavened bread, or bannock, usually served with lard; [*rababu*], rabbit soup; [*li:bulɛ*], meatballs; and others. Wild meat—mostly rabbit, deer, and moose—is still popular and is sometimes obtained by hunting off-season. In the late summer and fall, quite a few Métis women venture into the woods to pick different kinds of berries. These traditional foods are still praised as unequaled by any white man's food.

CLOTHING

Although today the Métis wear clothing bought in stores, as do all other Canadians, in the past they wore a distinctive type. Long dresses were considered appropriate for women. Poverty, however, often prevented Métis families from purchasing clothing, and some elders remember being dressed in clothes made out of flour bags when they were children. Their moccasins (*les souliers moux*), similar or identical to those of the Indians, are still worn. The "sash" (*ceinture flechée*), a colorful shawl worn around the waist, came to the Métis from Quebec via the *voyageurs*, who used it to support loads across portages and to hang their pipe bags and tobacco pouches. The sash is now worn only on special celebrations.

Many of the garments are embellished with beadwork with flower motifs, said to have originated with the French missionaries. This motif is now commonly seen on Indian (notably Ojibwe) beadwork, too, and the Métis may very well have been its source. Feathers, as far as I am aware, were never a part of Métis clothing, a variation from the Indian tradition. Harrison (1985: 31; following Ewers) states that the Indians took over braiding from the Métis, but I have found no confirmation of this.

ARCHITECTURE, DESIGN, AND IMPLEMENTS

The Métis had a special way of building houses, too. During buffalo-hunting parties, some of the Métis used tipis, as did Indians, but their farmhouses were different from those built by white farmers (Burley and Horsfall 1989). Both eastern Canadian techniques and apparently new technologies were used. The Red River cart—an all-wood vehicle on two wheels, drawn by oxen or horses—was intensively used from the early 1800s or perhaps earlier for freighting and transportation and is claimed to be a Métis invention. It is still one of the symbols of Métis identity; the Manitoba Metis Federation have it in their logo, along with a bison and rifles. Today, knowledge of automobile technology is widespread among Métis men.

ECONOMY

The economic system in the Métis communities today is not significantly different from that in white communities, although the unemployment rate is higher among the Métis. In the first half of the nineteenth century, the Métis economy could be seen as a combination of Indian and French subsistence: keeping small gardens in the summer, as did the Ojibwes (Giraud 1945: 51); fishing in the winter; picking berries in the fall; and hunting bison in the summer and fall. Harvesting frogs and digging seneca roots—both of which were sold for food and medicine—also took place. Seasonal labor like clearing bush and picking up stones for farmers and helping them in harvesting, threshing, stoking, and other farm activities became more common with the influx of farmers.

Many Métis today live off welfare, but some hold salaried jobs, for example, in offices, politics, Métis organizations, RCMP (Royal Canadian Mounted Police), building companies, social work, stores, and so on. Some are professional or semiprofessional musicians. Others have farms. Traditional occupations are still common in the northern woods, such as trapping and fishing. The most important job for most of the nineteenth century used to be the buffalo hunt, but as these animals are now virtually extinct, no Métis living today ever witnessed this hunt.

MUSIC AND DANCE

Métis music is significantly different from Indian music. Traditional Indian music in the northern prairies mainly involves two musical instruments: drums (in many varieties, according to the type of celebration) and flutes (a few varieties). The Métis traditionally use neither. Their most important musical instrument is the violin, on which they often play Scottish tunes that originated in Quebec. Lederman (1988: 209–211) argues that there are a number of underlying Indian patterns in Métis fiddle music, such as a musical signature before starting the tune, variations in phrase lengths, and descending musical contours. There are also similarities with Quebec fiddle music, so that the label "syncretic" as used by Lederman seems appropriate.

Other instruments played until recently in Métis communities are the accordion and the mouth harp. In some places, a guitar has been used since the period between the two world wars. There is also a long tradition of songs in French, often ballads dating from any period between the late Middle Ages and the first decades of the nineteenth century. It is well known that the *voyageurs* also had an important singing culture, and one tends to relate the two, although I am not aware of any study linking these traditions. Métis songs are almost always sung in French, even in communities where little or no French is spoken. There are also songs in Michif, Cree, Ojibwe, and English or in mixtures of two of these languages (one of these mixed songs is discussed in Chapter Nine). Songs associated with drinking are usually in Michif. This singing culture, however, is in fact extinct. Some of the older people remember parts of songs, but it is no longer traditional to sing songs like "Les jeunes mariés" at weddings or ballads at funerals or wakes or other important events.

In some communities there are still house parties during the weekends, when people gather to have fun, sing, make music (with the traditional fiddle and guitar, as well as country and western style), drink, and dance. These often take place after weddings and dances in the local halls, where now the bigger parties are held. In all Métis communities people remember the house parties in the 1930s, when there would be a party in a different home every weekend. In a few communities this tradition persists. Usually a group of fiddle players played music continuously, sometimes for several days. As these parties were already described by people like Paul Kane ([1859] 1968: 261–263) in the first half of the nineteenth century, this must be a long, continuous tradition. The tradition of "calling," in which one person yelled commands about the way people had to move and switch partners, is virtually extinct among the Métis today (Bear et al. 1992).

There was, and sometimes still is, a fiddle dance at Indian weddings, but not in the way these occurred among the Métis. In a number of Indian communities in Manitoba and Saskatchewan, the square dances, jigs, and reels are part of their heritage and traditions.

Mythology

Among the Métis there are still many excellent storytellers. This tradition combines Indian oratory with the tall stories of the *voyageurs*. The Métis distinguish *les contes* and *les histoires* (Rhodes 1987), following the Cree distinction between *âtayôhkêwina* and *âcimowina* (Ellis 1990).

The *âcimowin* or *l'histoire* deals with real events, or events considered real, either from the teller's experience or from the experience of others. They may contain aspects that would be considered supernatural by outsiders but they are told as real stories. These are usually local stories, although some of them describe events that took place 100 or more years ago. *Les contes*, or *âtayôhkêwina*, are the traditional sacred stories of the Crees and Ojibwes, to which other stories are added, many of them from European traditions. They often describe a world before ours, in which animals and other natural beings were able to talk. Supernatural events are common, often explaining certain facts in the environment or in nature. Among the Crees these narratives are surrounded by a number of supernatural beliefs: they cannot be told during daylight, and one has to offer tobacco or other gifts before telling an *âtayôhkêwin*. Among the Red River Métis, there are no such taboos concerning these stories. Although considered "sacred stories" by the Indians, the listeners usually laugh at the events in the narration, Métis and Indians alike.

The *âtayôhkêwina* as narrated by the Crees deal with Wisâhkêcâhk, the Cree trickster, whereas Ojibwe stories deal with Nanabozho. One can hear similar stories among other Algonquian peoples, although the tricksters have different names.

Métis mythology is an amalgam of the Indian and European traditions. In all Métis communities, stories are told about the Cree trickster, Wisâhkêcâhk; the trickster Nenabush (the Michif equivalent of the local Ojibwe trickster, Nanabozho); and the French (perhaps French Canadian) trickster, Ti-Jean. Métis people often say that these three are one and the same. Sometimes the same story is told with different actors. An example is the story "The Shut-eyed Dancers," of Cree and Ojibwe origin, which I recorded in three different versions. The versions are strikingly similar in that they combine events that originally constituted different stories in the Indian tradition. In southern Saskatchewan I recorded a version with Wisâhkêcâhk as the main actor; in eastern Manitoba it was told about Nenabush, and in North Dakota it was told in French with Ti-Jean as the hero.

There are also a number of other characters in the stories, such as the *rugaru* (*rou garou*). This is the Michif version of the *loup garou*, the werewolf. These stories are sometimes told to scare children when they do not want to obey their elders, but there is still a rather widespread belief among the old people that the *rugaru* is a real being. The name of the werewolf is consistently *rugaru* among the Métis, which is a distortion of the French word *loup garou*, as French has both the phonemes /r/ and /l/. The *rugaru* stories are a French tradition. The name was originally Spanish, according to one of the Métis elders I interviewed. Among the Métis, I have never heard stories about the Indian creature that is roughly equivalent to the *rugaru*; there is fear among the people for this being, which is seldom if ever sighted: the Wihtiko (*wîhtikôw*) in Cree, Windigo in Ojibwe. The Wihtikos are cannibals, often humans transformed into cannibals. It is possible that the Métis have this tradition, but I am unaware of it. Stories in which *le diable* "the devil" *[lɪ dʒaːb]* figures are also widespread.

Another popular kind of story is the traditional fairy tale, often identical to European fairy tales. Stories like "Cinderella" ("La petite cendrieuse,")[2] "The Three Bears," and others are commonly known among the Métis. It is not known whether these were learned through nursery books or mission schools or whether some were originally transmitted orally. There are arguments for the latter. There are many other stories that are more or less widespread among the Métis—like Bible stories, unrecognizably transformed and adapted to the local situation—perhaps even stories from *A Thousand and One Nights* (Wolfart 1990a)[3] and tall stories about hunting and fishing.

In short, the Métis mythology (a subject of the Métis culture that is most urgently in need of research) is a mixture of Cree, Ojibwe, and French traditions, the last drawing on several European traditions. Unfortunately the stories are rapidly disappearing.

RELIGION

The Métis are traditionally Catholics. Few, if any, take part in traditional Amerindian religious practices, such as sweat baths, shaking tents, round dances, and sun dances. In some communities people have joined the Pentecostal church in the last decade or so.

NICKNAMES

In all Métis communities, there is a strong tradition of nicknames, and some people's real names are not known. These nicknames can be distortions of names (/naplul/ for Napoleon), the name of an animal ("Weasel"; /ku:ku:s/ "Pig" for a boy who is a big eater; "Chickadee"), or refer to some physical feature (*les jeux croches* or "the blind man"), or they can be of mysterious origin (/bulakai/ has no meaning; /cepakuhp/ refers to "little seven"). There are names in Cree, English, and French. This practice is probably not connected with the Indian tradition of giving names and contemporary nicknaming. In the latter, names are usually given in a more ceremonial way and are connected to dreams. Dreams generally do not have the special value among the Métis that they do among Indians. In at least one Métis community, Indian names and nicknames exist side by side, together with the European names. One Métis told me that this tradition of nicknaming originates with the Scottish fur traders, but this information needs to be confirmed.

INTERPERSONAL CONTACTS

Joking, especially leg pulling, is one of the most striking features of Métis communication. Jokes are very important, as they are among Indians. Sharing food is a habit that is not as common today as it was in the past. In other respects, the Métis differ from Indians in being less reserved and quiet. Maria Campbell (1973), herself a Métis who grew up near a Plains Cree reserve in Saskatchewan, described the differences between Indians and Métis and the rather ambiguous relationships between Métis and treaty Indians as follows:

> There was never much love lost between Indians and Halfbreeds. They were completely different from us—quiet when we were noisy, dignified even at dances and get-togethers. Indians were very passive—they would get angry at things done to them but would never fight back, whereas Halfbreeds were quick-tempered—quick to fight, but quick to forgive and forget.
>
> The Indians' religion was very precious to them and to the Halfbreeds, but we never took it as seriously. We all went to the Indians' sun dances and special gatherings, but somehow we never fitted in. We were always the poor relatives, the *awp-pee-tow-koosons*.[4] They laughed and scorned us. They had land and security, we had nothing. As Daddy put it, "No pot to piss in or a window to throw it out." They would tolerate us unless they were drinking and then they would try to fight, but received many sound beatings from us. However, their old people, our "Mushooms" (grandfathers) and "Kokums" (grandmothers) were good. They were prejudiced, but because we were kin they came to visit and our people treated them with respect. . . . Treaty women don't express their opinions, Halfbreed women do. Even though I liked visiting them, I was always glad to get back to the noise and disorder of my own people.

There are important similarities between the cultures of the *voyageurs* and the Métis, such as the French-Amerindian bilingualism (Lang 1990), some of the food resources (*les boulets*; *la galette*), the sashes and other items of clothing, the use of beadwork, the long narratives, the French songs, and the loudness and gaiety. A logical, almost unavoidable, conclusion would be that Métis culture is in part a continuation of the culture of the *voyageurs* and that the *voyageurs* were among the ancestors of the Métis—a statement that is supported by the documentation available.

In summary, even today the Métis are a distinct ethnic group in Canada. Their culture is partly a mixture of French Canadian and Scottish, partly Amerindian, and partly original to the Métis; it emerged to fill up gaps that could not be filled by any of the ancestors' cultures. The people consider themselves Métis, a nation different from both whites (French or English) and Indians. This shows itself in the language. They call themselves *les Métifs*, Indians *les sauvages*, French Canadians *les Canadiens*, and other white people *les blancs* or *les Anglais*. In the next section I discuss some legal differences between the Métis and Indians.

Métis versus Treaty Indians and Nonstatus Indians

Both the Métis and Indians clearly distinguish themselves from each other, and members of both groups do not like to be confused with the other (Giraud 1945: 879). They are also distinct according to the law. The most important difference is that between treaty Indians and the rest. Treaty Indians are *legally* Indians. They are the descendants of those Natives who signed treaties with the British Crown between 1871 and 1921. On the basis of these treaties, numbered from 1 to 11, these Indians have so-called "treaty rights": they pay no taxes, they have free education, they are allowed in principle to hunt year-round (outside of the regular hunting season), they have access to free medicine and hospitalization, and they have the right to live on reserves. It is financially and morally advantageous to be a treaty Indian, but the Métis do not belong to this group.

Apart from the treaty Indians and the Métis, there are others, termed "nonstatus Indians." This is not really a legal category since it refers to those people who consider themselves Indians or part Indians but who are not recognized as such by the law. Either they or their parents lost their treaty status (e.g., by marriage to nontreaty Indians), or their ancestors never had treaty status because they were absent when the treaties were signed. Also some Métis who stress their Indian heritage consider themselves to be nontreaty Indians. Many reserves in the West have Métis communities near or at the edge of the reserve, sometimes called "satellite" communities. The people living here are often Métis or Indians who lost their status in the past. Sometimes there is significant intermarriage between the two communities.

Since the late 1980s, some people were able to regain their treaty status, according to Bill C-31. By this law, some Métis also gained treaty status. A Métis friend once remarked to me when his Métis wife received treaty status according to Bill C-31: "Suddenly, from one day to the other, you are no longer a Métis but an Indian. What do you do now? Throw your fiddle away and learn drumming and powwow dancing and quit dancing jigs and reels? From one day to another, you are supposed to be a different person."

There were also Métis who signed treaties together with the local Indians. Now they often live on reserves. For this reason some Michif speakers can be found on reserves, for instance, on the Peepeekisis Reserve in southeastern Saskatchewan. There were also Indians who accepted half-breed scrips (see the previous discussion). In other cases, Métis families were accepted by the treaty Indians and allowed to live on reserves (see, e.g., Campbell 1973: 22).

Many Indian families mention Europeans among their ancestors. In oral history these Europeans are reported to have been fluent in the Native language and they followed the Native way of life, apparently assimilated into the Native community. So it is partly a matter of chance whether a person today has Indian rights or not.

In short, it is clear that the difference between Indians and Métis is more cultural and legal than biological. The Métis are a group that is distinct from both French Canadian and Indian groups, including the Plains Cree and Ojibwe, whose languages they traditionally speak. The Métis also differ from the Scottish "half-breeds." The Métis believe themselves to be distinct, and other groups find the Métis different from themselves. As Giraud (1945: 1277) says: "The Métis is isolated from White society as well as the indigenous society."[5]

The legal differences between Indians and Métis and nonstatus Indians as of 1975 were summarized by Sealey and Lussier (1975: 174–176). They mention tax freedom, hunting rights, free medicine, a land base, and free education as advantages for Indians. Nevertheless, both groups suffer racial discrimination and are confronted with a negative image in history.

Métis Languages

The Métis and other inhabitants of the Red River settlement have spoken distinct languages from the earliest period of their existence. Here I summarize these languages briefly and present some figures about their actual use.[6] Five languages are spoken by the descendants of the Red River Métis: Michif, French, Cree, Saulteaux, and English.

Michif

Michif is mentioned here as a language of the Métis only for the sake of completeness. I confine myself to a very short characterization of the language since it is dealt with on almost every page of this book. It is a mixed language, in which the verbs, question words, demonstratives, personal pronouns, and postpositions are Cree, and the nouns, numerals, articles, almost all adjectives, most conjunctions, and most prepositions are French. Adverbs and quantifiers are about equally Cree and French. A detailed grammatical sketch is given in the next chapter.

Métis French

Métis French is the dialect of French as it is still spoken by the Métis. Phonologically, it stands apart from all other French dialects in that the standard French /e/ and /o/

are systematically raised to [i] and [u]. The raising of /ø/ to [y] is much more variable. Mid-vowel raising could in principle also have been influenced by northern Plains Cree, in which /i/ and /u/ are phonemes, whereas /o/ is not. In addition, Métis French does not distinguish [s] and [š]. In French words like *chasseur* "hunter," *chaise* "chair," or *sauvage* "Indian," usually both sibilants are either [s] or [š]. A further phonological, or rather phonetic, distinction is the palatalization of dental plosives before high front vowels: Métis French /pči/ "little"; Canadian French /pt^{s}i/.

The syntactic differences between Métis French and Canadian French dialects are perhaps less pervasive, but they nevertheless exist. For example, possession is expressed syntactically as *l'homme son livre* in Métis French, whereas other dialects have *le livre de l'homme* or *le livre à l'homme*. This looks like a direct copy of the Cree construction *nâpêw o-masinahikan*, literally "man his-book," although it might be an independent development since this construction is also found in other languages, including those resulting from contact situations (e.g., Indian Ocean French Creoles). The third-person pronoun, particularly the plural form, is usually *ça* for referring to persons, as well as to objects, perhaps to avoid possible confusion between masculine /i/ (*il*) and feminine /a/ (*elle*). Both the masculine and the feminine forms can be used to denote persons of either sex in Métis French (see, e.g., Douaud 1985) and in French and English spoken by Crees and Métis. It must be remembered that in Cree, gender distinctions are based on an animacy-inanimacy distinction instead of a masculine-feminine distinction. Other differences between Métis French and Canadian French can be found in Papen (1984a and b) and Douaud (1985); see also Préfontaine (1980) and Lussier (1980). I deal with some of the differences between Métis French and Canadian French in Chapter Nine.

Métis Cree

Cree as it is spoken by the Métis also seems to differ in some ways from Cree as spoken on the reserves, although it is not evident that this has always been the case. Nevertheless, these differences are readily acknowledged by the Métis. Douaud (1985: 85), for instance, cites one of his Métis informants about his language: "It's not good Cree, not like on the reserves."

At this stage of our knowledge of Cree dialects, it is not possible to say with any degree of certainty which features should be considered typical of Métis Cree. It might be that Métis Cree tends to be more analytical than Indian Cree. A sentence like "He takes it for him," which on the reserve would be

(1a)   otin-am-aw-êw
        take-TI-BEN-3→3'
        take-it-for.him-he

would be rendered in Métis Cree as

(1b)   utin-am wIja kIčI
        take-TA-1→4 him namely
        take-it-(he) him for

where a postpositional phrase (the postposition is derived from an adverb meaning "namely") replaces a benefactive verb morpheme (see also Chapter Five). Similar changes have also been noted elsewhere in the Cree as used by Métis.

Apart from the more analytic character of Métis Cree, there may also be some phonological and morphological differences between this language and Indian Cree. In any case, the Cree part of Michif differs in a number of respects from Cree, but there are no data available about whether these are also present in Métis varieties of Cree that are not mixed with French. Not much published material is available. A Métis Cree vocabulary was published in Andrews (1985), and that is about all there is. As I discuss the differences between Cree and the Cree component of Michif in more detail in Chapter Nine, I do not deal with them here. In any case, my recordings of eight Métis speakers of Cree from Manitoba, Saskatchewan, and Alberta do not show these phonological and morphological features of the Cree part of Michif. The differences between Cree as spoken by the Métis and Cree as spoken by the Crees themselves remains to be studied.

Métis Saulteaux

My information about Métis Saulteaux (Canadian Ojibwe) and Indian Saulteaux is both thin and contradictory. In Manitoba, a significant number of Métis speak Saulteaux as their aboriginal language. Some Saulteaux speakers claim that the Indian version of the language and the Métis version are recognizably different. My knowledge of the language is negligible, so I had to rely on the judgment of others. I tested it with one Saulteaux-speaking Indian from central Manitoba who had a lot of Saulteaux-speaking Métis and Saulteaux friends and acquaintances. I had him listen to tape recordings of Métis who spoke Saulteaux, and he correctly identified the speakers as Métis without any hesitation. A linguist with a good knowledge of Ojibwe could not discern any difference. In Camperville, a Métis community that borders on the Saulteaux reserve Pine Creek, Saulteaux is spoken in addition to Michif. Local people remark that the Saulteaux of the reserve does not differ from the Saulteaux spoken in the Métis community. However, as there is considerable intermarriage, it is very likely that in the latter community the indigenous language Michif was ousted by the Saulteaux language from the reserve, so that it is indeed the same language in both communities.

In 1985 the Manitoba Metis Federation organized a meeting on the languages of the Métis. In this meeting Métis Saulteaux was one of the Métis languages discussed as a distinct language (Michif Languages Committee 1985).

In short, the conjecture that Métis Saulteaux is different in some marked ways from Indian Saulteaux could not be confirmed nor disconfirmed because of lack of information. More research on this subject is necessary.

Métis English

English should be mentioned here, too. Virtually all speakers of Michif are also fluent in English. In fact, today most of them speak English as their only everyday language. Many Canadian Métis and Cree have a particular accent in English.

Numbers of Speakers of Métis Languages

No specific study has been undertaken by Canadian government agencies concerning the languages of the Métis (personal communication to author from Indian and Northern Affairs, 1987). Documents relating to the data collected for the 1981 census in Canada show that for the whole of Canada almost 14 percent of the Métis spoke an Amerindian language. Almost all of these were speakers of Cree (10.3 percent) and Ojibwe (2.3 percent). Almost 9 percent of the Métis reported French as a mother tongue, but the vast majority (75 percent) learned English as their first language (Statistics Canada 1984). These are the figures for all of Canada; the ambiguity of the term "Métis" outside the prairie provinces makes it hard to evaluate these data.

Fortunately some information about the prairie provinces is also available. According to the same census of 1981, about three-quarters of the Métis there spoke English as their mother tongue. Fewer than 20 percent spoke an aboriginal language as a first language, and 3 percent reported French as a mother tongue (Priest 1985: 15). The aboriginal languages are not specified. The figures for Native languages are higher for the prairies than for Canada as a whole, and the figures for French are lower.

In 1983 the Manitoba Metis Federation (MMF) made inquiries about the Métis' knowledge of indigenous languages at the 1983 Annual Assembly. The figures are given in table 3.1. I do not know whether this was the result of an inquiry among all the members or just those who came to the meeting. Unfortunately Michif was not mentioned specifically, but because it is also called Cree, it may be among these numbers.

A 1989 survey by the University of Manitoba had a sample of 1011 members of the MMF. No more than 16 percent reported speaking French, Cree, or Saulteaux at home. Some regional variation was reported, as shown in table 3.2. It is not clear how many Michif speakers are in this survey either.

A survey in the Northwest Territories in 1993–1994 showed that only 136 out of 3353 Métis speak Métis French, only 4.6 percent of the Métis population, according to an article in the *Métis Voice*, fall 1994.

TABLE 3.1 Manitoba Métis Knowledge of Indigenous Languages

Languages	Percentage of Speakers
French	8.25 %
Cree (Algonquian)	26.58
Saulteaux (= Ojibwe, Algonquian)	19.40
Dakota (Siouan)	0.20
Chipewyan (Athapaskan)	0.10
	Total: 54.53

Lawrence J. Barkwell, David N. Gray, David N. Chartrand, and Lyle Longclaws, Languages spoken by the Métis, Manitoba Métis Federation Inc.—Submission to the Aboriginal Justice Inquiry. Research and analysis of the Impact of the Justice System on the Métis (Winnipeg: MMF, 1989), app. 4.

From these figures we learn that only a minority of the Métis today speak languages other than English at home. This is, of course, in line with other observations on Métis language use. It is not a very encouraging result for the future of these languages. Unfortunately the Métis are massively shifting toward all-encroaching English.

Number of Speakers of Michif

As for the number of Michif speakers, only an educated guess is possible, although for the communities I visited I have a reasonable insight into that number. We know that there are, or were, speakers in some other communities. Considering the fact that most speakers moved away (many to Saskatoon, Regina, Brandon, and Winnipeg), I estimate their number to be between 200 and 1000 in the early 1990s, almost all of them older than 60. They were born mostly in the Fort Qu'Appelle Valley, Camperville and Duck Bay, Turtle Mountain, and Boggy Creek and San Clara. Most speakers probably live in the cities, and it is likely that there are some other pockets in Manitoba, Saskatchewan, North Dakota, and Montana and possibly also in Alberta and Minnesota (see Bakker and Papen, 1996). Some Métis in Saskatchewan have much higher estimates: at least 3000 speakers in Saskatchewan alone.

Summary and Conclusions

It is clear that the Métis have identified themselves as a separate and new nation at least since 1810. Although the Métis were still living far apart, they knew where to find each other. Their central point was the area of the Red River settlement, where they emerged as a nation and regularly gathered for buffalo-hunting expeditions to the west and southwest. Some of the Métis stayed on the hunting grounds and wintering areas. It was also here that their problems started: the upheavals of 1867 and 1885 forced many of the Métis to move, especially the poorer hunters, because they had not been able to prepare their land for agriculture as demanded by the authorities.

The Métis clearly have been a distinct society and a separate people from around 1810. Their culture and lifestyle differed, and still do, both from the Indians and the Europeans. Their ancestors on the European side are French-speaking fur traders and *voyageurs*. Some of these must have been independent traders; others were employees of the North West Company. On the Amerindian side, their ancestors are mostly Ojibwe and Cree women. From an early date there were differences among the Métis, much like class differences, in lifestyle, economic activities, and languages.

TABLE 3.2 Regional Variation in Manitoba Métis Language Skills

	Winnipeg	Southern Manitoba	Northern Manitoba
French	14.0 %	21.0 %	6.4 %
Cree	3.6 %	3.6 %	14.3 %
Saulteaux	12.7 %	6.5 %	12.1 %

Especially after the fusion of the North West Company with its competitor, Hudson's Bay Company, in 1821, the Métis were a distinct people. They were renowned for their abilities in the bison hunt, which was organized twice a year from the Red River settlement from 1820 until around 1870 and in which whole families were involved. The hunters were closer to the Indians in a number of ways, not only in the hunting lifestyle and dress, but also in language. The hunters, who had the closest contacts with the Indians, must have spoken Cree, Saulteaux, and Michif. The other main activities of the Métis were freighting and trading. Trails and cart routes were established throughout the West by Métis pioneers.

Both of these main activities demanded much mobility and geographical knowledge. From the 1820s small Métis settlements were established in increasing numbers along the ox-cart routes and in buffalo-hunting country (mainly Montana and North Dakota). This was the beginning of the Métis diaspora. Especially after the Riel resistance of 1867, named after its leader Louis Riel, and the defeat of the Métis in 1885, many more Métis were forced to find a new home elsewhere. Despite their geographical spread and despite (or thanks to) misperceptions and hostility by both white Canadians and Indians, they cherish their past and their Métis identity.

The Métis, who form an ethnic group with its own identity, do not have some of the legal rights of the Indians. Their culture is different from both groups from which they are the offspring. They speak a number of languages, of which Michif is the most remarkable. Its grammatical structure, focusing on the mixed nature of the language, is discussed in the next chapter.

Grammatical Sketch of Michif

This chapter contains a grammatical sketch of Michif. Unfortunately it is impossible to explain in a brief survey all the intricacies of this language, and many formal terms must be used to describe the grammar. Without this terminology it is not possible to describe the language, and without mastering these terms it may be difficult to understand the grammatical sketch. Thus the sketch of Michif is a rather technical discussion, which readers not versed in linguistics may find difficult and which they may want to skip. These readers may go directly to the summary at the end of the chapter. For the arguments concerning the origins of the Michif language, this sketch is perhaps less important. It is necessary for linguists, however, because much more information about Michif has been gathered since Rhodes's pioneering and insightful grammatical sketch of Michif in 1977.

To refresh the reader's memory, I again first start with a short story in Michif, in which the intricate mixture of French and Cree appears (with Cree elements in italics). This story is part of a longer narrative recorded in 1990 in Brandon, Manitoba. The speaker is Madeleine Prescott-Tanner from Sainte Madeleine, to whom I express my gratitude.

(1) *Pemmican*

    kaja:š ma:na li: šava:ž *ki:pe:kIjoke:wak ni:gIna:hk.*
    long.time.ago usually the Indians they.came.to.visit in.our.house

    wIjawa:w ušta:čIk li: suji: mũ.
    they they.make the shoes soft

    pi la vjãd *ki:pa:šamwak*
    and the meat they-dry-by-heat

    e:gwanIgi li: sava:z *ki:pa:šamwak* la vjãd.
    they the Indians dried the meat

la vjãd ɔrIja:l, la vjãdi šovrø, tut *ki:pa:šamwak.*
the meat moose the meat.of deer all they.dried it

e:gwanIma e:gwa ki:šIkwahamwak
that now they.mash.it

da:dɪbčca:k *ki:a:šta:wak ma:na.*
in.little.bags they.put.it usually

egwanIma pɛmik∂n *ka:šnIhka:tahkIk.*
that pemmican we.call.it

li: sava:z *gi:kanawa:pama:nIk e:ušIta:čIk ma:na.*
the Indians we-watched.them them.making.it usually.

"*Long time ago* the Indians *used to visit us at our house. They made* moccasins and *they dried* meat. *These* Indians *dried* the meat. Moose meat, deer meat, they *dried it* all. *This then they mashed.* They *used to put it* in little bags. *We called it* pemmican. *We used to watch* the Indians *when they made it.*"

In this story, the verbs, discourse particles, personal pronouns, and demonstratives are all derived from Cree. Nouns, articles, prepositions, coordinators, and quantifiers are derived from French. The sound systems for the two languages are clearly different.

As a basis for the following grammatical sketch, I rely mostly on the wealth of data provided in Laverdure and Allard (1983). I take the dialects of these two speakers, from Turtle Mountain, North Dakota, as a point of departure. In the dictionary, they provide several example sentences with every entry. Elsewhere (Chapter Five) I show that Canadian dialects are virtually identical, so this can be taken as valid, except for minor details, for all true Michif dialects.

In this chapter, every sentence used as an example is Michif, unless stated otherwise. For Michif I use a broad phonetic transcription, whereas for Cree and French I use the standard orthographies. Thus for Cree long vowels are indicated with a circumflex over the vowel, and for Michif with a colon after the vowel. In this way, Cree and Michif can be generally distinguished. The abbreviations used in the glosses are explained in the beginning of this book.

For Michif, the sound system (phonology), noun and verb endings (morphology), and word order (syntax) are partly Cree and partly French. There appear to be, for instance, two different sound systems, one for the French and another for the Cree. The Cree part and the French part also have separate morphologies. The sentential syntax is probably closer to Cree, but the noun phrase syntax is mostly French.

I discuss the sound system first. The two different phonological systems for the Cree and the French components are discussed separately. There is no influence from either component on the other. Then I discuss Michif structural features, that is, the structure of the simple clause. I present some sentence types as well, to give an impression of the language. I then describe the grammatical categories and the language from which each is taken, as there seems to be a categorial dichotomy in Michif (nouns French, verbs Cree, etc.). After I consider some morphological aspects of the language, the chapter ends with a summary.

The Two Phonological Systems

In Michif, there are two separate phonological systems, one for French elements and one for Cree elements. This is clear from the phoneme inventories (see table 4.1). The Cree part has seven oral vowels (or four if one does not distinguish length) and three nasal vowels, and the French has ten oral and four nasal vowels. Cree nasal vowels are rather marginal. The French component has twenty-three consonants and Cree only ten. This means that a considerable number of phonemes exist only in either of the components of Michif. For instance, the phonemes /y/, /l/, /r/, and /f/ exist only in French words, whereas only the Cree part has clusters (or preaspirated stops) such as /ht/ and /hk/. It is obvious that the language has two different phoneme inventories, one for each component. A few other arguments support the claim of two separate phonological systems in Michif: the nature of the allophones, assimilation, and the nonexistence of liaison. Only in the stress system is there some Cree influence on French words.

Allophones

The different values of Cree and French allophones were shown by Rhodes. For instance, French /a/ has the allophones [a] and [æ], whereas Cree /a/ has the allophones

TABLE 4.1 Cree and French Phoneme Inventories in Michif

Vowels			Consonants				
			French Part of Michif				
Oral			p	t	č	k	
i	y	u	b	d	ǰ	g	
ɩ			f	s	š		h
ɛ	œ	ɔ	v	z	ž		
æ			m	n	ñ	ŋ	
	a	ɑ			r		
					l		
Nasal			*Glides*				
		ũ	w		j		
æ̃		ø̃					
	ã						
			Cree Part of Michif				
Long							
			p	t	č	k	
i:		u:			š		h
e:			m	n			
	a:						
			Glides				
Short							
i		u	w		j		
	a						
Nasal							
ĩ		ũ					
æ̃							

[ʌ] and [ɑ]. Also, in unstressed syllables French phonemes are more or less central-
ized in value, which is not the case in the Cree part (see Rhodes 1986 for details).

Vowel Assimilation

Another feature in the French part of Michif is that a form of vowel assimilation seems
to have developed (Rhodes 1986). The place of articulation of one vowel is often
adjusted to the value of other vowels in the same word. This is valid only for the
French component. Rhodes[1] gives the following examples:

(2) *Orthography* *Standard* *Michif*

    pouilleux   [pujø]   [pujy] ~ [pyjy]
    mesure   [mɘzyr]   [myzyr]
    chevreuil   [šɘvrœj]   [šuvry]
    fusil   [fyzij]   [fizi]
    musique   [myzik]   [myzyk]

Vowels tend to get raised and/or rounded under the influence of fronted or rounded
vowels in the word. I suspect that such a system also exists in Métis French (the source
dialect of the French component), but this has not been studied.

Fossilized Liaison Consonants

The Cree and French component also differ in phonology in the way in which two
adjacent vowels are treated. French normally has "liaison" consonants, which are
placed between the two vowels and which display underlying consonants. For example, the French plural article *les* is normally pronounced [le] or [lɛ], but before a
vowel-initial noun the underlying *s* shows up, for example, in *les artistes* "the artists," pronounced [lezartist] in standard French. In Michif, this kind of liaison does
not exist. Liaison processes, very productive in all French dialects, are not so in the
French part of Michif for the vast majority of speakers. In Michif, there seem to be
numerous examples of these consonants—for example, *æ̃-n-ãfã* "a child"; *li-z-ãfã*
"the children"—in which the normally mute final consonants of the article seem to
be pronounced. In fact, these are not due to a productive liaison rule in Michif. It
would be better to consider these consonants as being part of the noun, which thus
becomes a consonant initial word.

There are three arguments against a liaison analysis. First, many nouns have initial
consonants different from those predicted by the liaison rule, for example, æ *za:br*
"a tree," lι *l-u:r* "the bear," æ *gru n-ιtwɛl* "a big star," and so on. This means that
originally vowel-initial nouns have alternants starting with /n-/, /l-/, and /z-/ and sometimes /t-/. In fact, in my fieldwork all of the following were heard:

(3) /æ lu:r, æ̃ nu:r, æ̃ zu:r/   (F. /œ̃nurs/)   "un ours"
    /lu:r, lι lu:r, lι nu:r, lι zu:r/   (F. /lurs/)   "l'ours"
    /li: lu:r, li: nu:r, li: zu:r/   (F. lezurs/)   "les ours"

Second, non-French nouns do not show any liaison consonants, although English words are normally adjusted at least partly to French phonology, for example, *ã ɛnikũs* "ant" (not *ãn-ɛnikũs*); *ã a:mũ* or *ã ja:mũ* "bee" (not *ã n-amu* or *ã l-amu*); *li ɛlðvetð* "elevators" (not *li-z ɛlðvetð*).

Third, some French nouns etymologically starting with *n-* have been reanalyzed and also have alternates in *z-*. Speakers do not know whether this *n-* or *z-* was originally part of the word. So we find forms like *li zɔmbr* "(the) numbers" (F. *les nombres*) and *ã narvedžɪn* or *li zarvedžɪn* "Norwegian" (F. *un Norvégien, les Norvégiens*).

In short, it is best to regard this question as follows: some nouns in the French part of Michif have several variants (*n-, z-, l-*) for the initial consonants. Mostly these words start with *n-* in indefinite singular nouns, *l-* in definite singular nouns and *z-* in plurals. Liaison rules do not exist. Rather, nothing is inserted or there is a weak glottal stop or a glide, /w/ or /j/ or /h/. The variation in this point has not been studied, so it is not known what factors play a role. Liaison rules provide only historical explanations for the origins of the variable consonants of the different nominal stem forms.

In Plains Cree, adjacent vowels are either merged, if one of them is short, or a /j/ (written *y* in standard Cree) is inserted between the two vowels if both are long (Wolfart 1973b: 79–83; see also Wolfart 1989). For the Cree part of Michif, this seems to be true as well.

Stress

Stress assignment in French and Cree are similar, but in a few instances there appears to be Cree stress in French words. Both source languages have stress on the last syllable. In Cree, all odd syllables (final, antepenultimate, etc.) have stress, whereas French stress seems to be lexically governed. The syllable between these stressed syllables is either extremely short or extremely long, depending on whether this vowel is phonologically short or long. Some examples follow to show the variable stress position (´ indicates primary and ` secondary stress, e.g., English "cònsolátion"):

(4a)   máskisìn "shoe"

(4b)   maskísinà "shoes"

(4c)   maskisínihkèèw "S/he makes shoes."

Some standard French examples follow:

(5a)   vàriatión "variation"

(5b)   còmbinaisón "combination"

(5c)   dèjeunér "lunch"

The Cree and French stress systems are close enough to merge in most words. Only French words longer than three syllables are stressed differently from the French, and only in these French words is it clear that the stress systems differ.

(6)   /lɪ dížœnì/ "breakfast"

(7)   /la kɔmbínæ:zǜ/ "longjohns, long underwear for men"

In these words, primary stress is on the antepenultimate syllable and not
one, as in French. Also, the /œ/ in (6) is extremely short and the /æ/ in (7) is extremely
long, as would occur in Cree words. It appears that French nouns have Cree stress
patterns in words of three syllables and longer. In shorter words, the stress patterns
for Cree and French are indistinguishable. This is the only point of Cree influence
on the phonology of the French component.

Many English words are used in Michif, whether by code mixing or by borrowing, and they partly preserve their own phonology and are partly adapted toward French
(Rhodes 1986: 295). For instance, they have French stress, as in these examples:

(8)   pi:tə́r "Peter"

(9)   kawbój "cowboy"

The question now is, are the French and Cree components indeed so compart-
mentalized or is there phonological convergence between the components?

Phonological Convergence

There has been some discussion in the literature about whether or not there is convergence of the two sound systems in the Michif language. Evans (1982: 171) stated:
"(1) There is a definite distinction between the two components of the language,
syntactically and phonologically; (2) there is some phonological convergence
occurring."

After careful study, however, I can only conclude that there is no solid evidence
for phonological convergence: the two systems have remained completely separate
throughout the existence of Michif. In a discussion of convergence, one has to point
to phonological features in the French part of the language that do not exist in the
source language but do exist in Cree, and vice versa. Therefore we have to compare
the phonology of the Cree component with that of the source dialect, Plains Cree,
and the French component with that of the source dialect, French—Métis French,
that is, not standard French or even Canadian French (as some of the other researchers did). This would enable us to see how the French component may have changed
before it was mixed with Cree in the Michif language.

Evans (1982) mentions the following four possible points of convergence.

Aspirated Consonants

There are aspirated consonants in the Cree and the French components in Michif.
Evans (1982: 166) gives the following French examples:

(10)   /thæb/ "table"; /sɪ thuth/ "it's all" (F. *c'est tout*)

Furthermore, it was already noted by Rhodes (1977: 23) that stops in the Cree component of Michif are also optionally aspirated. Neither in Plains Cree nor in standard French are there aspirated consonants. Canadian French dialects, however, especially those in the prairie provinces (where all French speakers also know English), do have optionally aspirated consonants. It is not possible to ascertain whether the aspiration in either component of Michif is due to influence from the other component since in both cases it is more likely to have come from English. There is no convergence, but there is parallel influence from a third source—English. Evans actually suggests that aspiration entered Michif under the influence of English, which is spoken by all modern Michif speakers. If anything, the source of this phenomenon is ultimately English rather than Michif internal convergence.

Nasal Vowels in the Cree Component

Plains Cree does not have nasal vowels (Evans 1982: 167), whereas nasal vowels are prominent in French. In the Cree component of Michif, however, there appear to be nasal vowels. Some examples follow:

(11) *Cree*   *Michif*

ôhi /o:hi/   /ũhĩ/   "those"
cî /ci:/   /čĩ:/, /či:/   (question marker)
mêkwat /me:kwat/ /mãẽkwat/   "while, in the meantime"

It seems logical to ascribe the presence of these nasal vowels to French influence, although this is probably not the case. Some of the eastern Saskatchewan Plains Cree dialects do indeed have nasal vowels, apparently in some of the same words as in Michif. In the Cree component of Michif, nasal vowels are not pervasive: they show up only in a limited number of words and endings. In any case, the nonlinguist Mandelbaum ([1940] 1979: 11) states that the eastern dialects of Plains Cree differ from the western dialects in "degrees of nasalization."[2] Since this dialect is spoken adjacent to the Michif area and in the area of the Métis buffalo hunt, it may have been an important source for Michif. These dialect differences, however, need to be checked. An additional argument against French influence could be given: the Michif nasal /ĩ/ exists in the Cree component of Michif but not in French. This makes French influence unlikely. It exists in Ojibwe, though, so that one could consider Ojibwe influence on Michif (see Chapter Nine for discussion of Ojibwe features in Michif). The eastern Plains Cree dialects are spoken near Ojibwe territory.

Sibilant Leveling in the French Component

In the French component of Michif, sibilants are either all palatal (/š/, /ž/) or all alveolar (/s/, /z/), creating a kind of "consonant assimilation" (Evans 1982: 168), for example:

(12) /šeš/ "dry" (F. *sec, sèche*); /šava:ž/ "Indian" (F. *sauvage*); /sa:si:/ "window" (F. *chassis*)

In Plains Cree, there is no phonological distinction between the two sibilants, so they are in principle in free variation. In a single word, only one variant of the two is used. It is obviously a case of Plains Cree and/or Ojibwe influence in Michif, but both Douaud (1980, 1985) and Papen (e.g., 1984b) have shown that the French dialect source of Michif, Métis French, displays exactly the same phenomenon. Speakers of Métis French today generally do not know Cree or Ojibwe, so it must be an old phenomenon in Métis French. It is also a feature of the Cree-influenced English dialect called Bungee (Blain 1987, 1989), spoken by the descendants of the Scottish-Indian couples. Therefore, sibilant leveling came into the language with the French component and not from the influence of the Cree component. Ultimately, of course, it is a Cree influence, but there is no convergence here between the two parts of Michif proper since it was already present in the source language, Métis French.

Vowel Length in the French Component

Vowel reanalysis is the fourth possible area of convergence in Michif, according to Evans (1982: 169). Standard French does not have distinctive vowel length, whereas Cree does distinguish /i/ and /i:/, /a/ and /a:/, and /u/ and /u:/ (or /o/ and /o:/). In Cree, the distinction is actually not only in length but also in vowel quality. In the French component of Michif, vowel length is phonologically distinctive. Some minimal pairs follow:

(13) /li: šu/ "the cabbages" (F. *les choux*); /li: šu:/ "warm bed" (F. *lit chaud*)
      /sa:si:/ "window" (F. *chassis*); /sasœr/ "hunter" (F. *chasseur*)

Here, too, there is only apparent convergence. In fact, Canadian French also has conspicuous, distinctive vowel length (see, e.g., Hewson 1989), and one may speculate about a possible influence from Algonquian languages in Quebec and Acadia. In this, too, the difference between long vowels and their short counterparts is not only in length but also in quality. Vowel length differences are typical of all Canadian French dialects. Vowel length in the French component of Michif appears to be an inheritance from Canadian French, not an innovation in Michif.

One can see on closer scrutiny that in none of these areas discussed by Evans is convergence plausible. However, there are a number of additional points in which Michif differs phonologically from its source languages, which may be cases of convergence. These are the loss of liaison in the French component, the development of vowel assimilation in the French component (Rhodes, 1986), the voiced-voiceless contrast in the Cree component, and the nature of the fricatives and palatalization in both components.

Other Possible Points of Convergence

The loss of liaison cannot be directly ascribed to Cree influence since nothing similar exists in Cree. The absence of anything like it in Cree, however, may be partly responsible for the loss of this feature in the French part of Michif. Furthermore, vowel-initial nouns are common in Cree, so it does not seem to be a way to adjust to Cree phonotactic patterns.

Vowel assimilation in French, as in the examples in (2), exists in the French and not in the Cree part. It is an innovation in the French that cannot be ascribed to Cree influence since nothing similar exists in Cree.

In the Cree component, there is a voiced-voiceless contrast, whereas this does not exist in the Cree language. This contrast exists only in initial consonants (stops and /š/), for example, in these items:

(14)   *Michif*   *Cree*

      gi:wa:n   ni-ki:wa:n   "I go home."
      ki:wa:n   ki-ki:wa:n   "You go home."

This is probably an independent development since other Algonquian languages also display it (Rhodes and Todd 1981; see also Chapter Nine for more detail). There is no reason to assume that it is influenced by French since it is clearly an independent development in the other Algonquian languages. Furthermore, it is limited to initial consonants.

Michif differs from both Canadian French and Plains Cree in that the affricates are alveolar in the latter but alveopalatal in Michif itself. Plains Cree has /c/ and /s/ (phonetically ranging from [s] to [š]); Canadian French has /c/, /š/, and /s/. Michif has /č/ and /š/ in both components and /s/ only in the French component. Here, Michif differs from both source languages, and again it is not possible to state whether either component took this over from the other.

In conclusion, we are on safe grounds when we decide that Michif has two separate phonological components. These components must have coexisted in the language since its inception, perhaps 150 years ago. It is all the more remarkable that there is no phonological influence at all from either of the components on the other. The only point of influence is the Cree stress system in French words. For the rest, the phonologies of the two source languages, Métis French and Eastern Plains Cree, in Michif have remained immune from influence from the coexisting language. In this, Michif may very well be unique among the languages of the world, having two separate phonological systems in one language. The rest of this chapter is devoted to nonphonological features of Michif.

Morphology and Syntax

In this section, I deal only briefly with Michif grammar. The Michif examples are given in a broad phonetic transcription. All Cree morphemes are in italics in the example sentences, so it is clear which element is from which language.

Plains Cree and Michif have two main orders (also called "modes"; the term has nothing to do with word order), the independent and the conjunct, as in all Algonquian languages. These are different verb forms. The independent order is used in main clauses, the conjunct order in embedded clauses and in question-word sentences. In some Cree dialects (those spoken in the western woodlands), the conjunct mode is used frequently in main clauses, but this occurs rarely, if ever, in Michif. These orders have specific negators: *e:ka:wIja* (usually shortened *e:ka*) for conjunct order clauses, *namo:ja* for independent order clauses. In the conjunct order, person agreement is exclusively suffixing. In the independent order, it is both prefixing and suffixing. A prefixed marker *či-/ši-* (future), *e:-* (contemporaneous nonindividuated), or *ka:-* (contemporaneous individuated) is required on conjunct order verbs.

Algonquianist grammarians also distinguish a third mode or order, the subjunctive. This order, which occurs in "if" clauses, is marginal and derived from the conjunct order by the addition of the suffix *-i / -u* to the conjunct verb form. Further there are two imperatives, the immediate and the delayed imperative, for first- and second-person singular and plural. Imperatives have the negator *ka:ja*.

The Structure of the Simple Clause

Word order in the clause is rather free in Michif, following the typological characteristics of Cree. The nature of the grammatical relations in the sentence is marked on the verb, except for one nominal marker called obviative. This grammatical element is therefore also discussed in connection with constituent order.

Standard French is characterized by a rather rigid word order. Spoken French, however, is somewhat less rigid and often diverges from this pattern. It is a subject of debate whether or not Cree and Ojibwe have an unmarked word order and, if so, which one that would be (Proulx 1991). Michif syntax is basically that of Cree—that is, word order is relatively free in Michif. The more French elements are used, however, the closer the syntax seems to conform to norms of spoken French. Some examples of different constituent orders follow:

(15) SVO: la žyma: *ki:-aja:w-e:w* æ̃ pči pulæ̃
DAFS mare PST-have-TA.3→3' IAMS little foal
"The mare had a foal."

(16) SOV: *kahkIja:w* awIjak la pwi *dawe:stam-wak*
all somebody the rain want.it-3PL→4
"All the people want rain."

(17) VSO: *ki:-wanIst-a:w* lι žwal su lιku
PST-lose.it-3→4 the horse his halter
"The horse lost its halter."

(18) OVS: la kurɔn *ka-kIškaw-e:w* Prince Charles
DAFS crown-AN FUT-wear-TA3→3' P.C.
"Prince Charles will wear the crown."

(19) VOS: *ki:-učIpIt-am* sa tεt la tɔrčy
PST-pull-TI3→4 his head-INAN DAFS turtle
"The turtle pulled back his head."

(20) OSV: æ̃ be:bi la præ̃ses *ki:-aja:w-e:w*
IAMS baby DAFS princess PST-have.him-TA3→3'
"The princess had a baby."

Sentences that consist mostly or only of French elements, which are rare, normally follow colloquial French word order:

(21) žɪ rɪspɛk mu nuk
      1SG respect my uncle
      "I respect my uncle."

(22) lɪ žardǽ d čwɪzɪn i furni tut li: žardinaž
      DAMS garden of kitchen 3.SUBJ furnish all DAP vegetable
      "The kitchen garden furnishes all the vegetables."

Word Order in the Noun Phrase

Whereas sentential word order is free, word order within the Michif noun phrase is rather fixed. The internal order of the noun phrase is

(23) *REL – DEM* – NUM – ART – ADJ – N – ADJ – *DEM* – REL

The categories in italics are always Cree derived. Some French-derived adjectives precede nouns; others follow, as in French. Cree-based relative clauses can precede and follow the noun phrase; French-based relative clauses can only follow it. There are two points in which the order of the noun phrase differs from French. The first is the position of the numeral. In French, the numeral follows the article, but in Michif it precedes the article.

Possessives also differ. Michif possessives have the order possessor → possessive pronoun → possessed, whereas French has the order possessed → preposition → possessor. A sample phrase with two possessives follows:

(24) mũ pči garsũ sũ pči žwal
      POSS.1S. little boy POSS.3SG. little horse
      "my son's pony"

Here French would have *le petit cheval de/à mon petit garçon/fils*, whereas Cree would have *ni-kosis o-têm-a* (my-son his-horse-OBV). Notice that the possessed noun requires the obviative marker if possessed by a third person in Cree. In Michif, if the possessed noun happens to be Cree, it will be marked for obviation, but French nouns are not. Furthermore, quantifiers, including numerals, can be separated from the noun phrase in Michif (as in Cree, but not as in French), as in this example:

(25) kat vǽ džɪs *gi:-aja:w-ak* lɪ mu:d la prɔmji žurni dɪ l-ã
      ninety 1.PST-have-3PL DAMS people the first day of the-year
      "I had 90 people (over) the first day of New Year."

Obviation

Obviation in Cree is marked on the verb as well as on the noun. Its function is to distinguish two or more third persons within a sentence or stretch of discourse. The third-person noun not mentioned previously is marked obviative (*-a* and its allomorph *-wa*); the known third person (topic) remains unmarked and is called proximate. Number is not marked in obviative nouns, which are neutral in number. Obviative endings must be used in third-person possessive phrases and in sentences with two animate third persons.

Cree obviation marking is reduced in Michif (Weaver 1982, 1983; for Cree see Wolfart 1978 and Dahlstrom 1991). The first mentioned use (with possessive noun phrases) does not exist for French-derived nouns in Michif, only in the few Cree nouns in the language.

(26)   *o-ma:ma:-wa* (* *o-ma:ma:*)   (Cree and Michif)
       his-mother-OBV
       "his mother"

The other use of Cree obviation occurs when two third persons can be found in the same sentence but not in the same noun phrase, for instance, as coarguments to a given verb or in the same stretch of discourse.

(27)   John *ki:wa:pame:w* Irene-*a*   (Cree and Michif)
       John PST-see-3→3' Irene-OBV
       "John saw Irene."

This use of what we could call syntactic obviation is reduced more than in Plains Cree, in which an obviation marker is obligatory for animate nouns. With respect to French nouns in Michif, personal names are always marked for obviation, as in (28); humans often; animals sometimes, as in (29); and inanimate entities never:

(28)   æ̃ nɔm dã lɪ bãd dɪ mu:d *ki:-nIpa-h-e:w* Bobby Kennedy-*wa* (*Bobby Kennedy)
       IAMS man in DAMS crowd of people PST-die-CAUS-3→3' B.K.-OBV
       "A man in the crowd killed Bobby Kennedy."

(29)   John *ki:-wa:pam-e:w* æ̃ šæ̃-*wa* (also: æ̃ šæ̃) (Cree: *atim-wa*, *atim)
       John PST-see-3→3' DAMS dog-OBV
       "John saw a dog."

It must be stressed, though, that even when French forms are not overtly marked for obviation, an obviative (or possessed noun) agreement marker in the Cree verb is nevertheless often present, as in this example:

(30)   bæčɪs[3] su: frɛ:r *nIpa:-jI-w*
       John his brother sleep-OBV.SUBJ-3S
       "John's brother is sleeping."

Finally, when a third-person possessed noun is the object of a sentence, it has an agreement marker *-Im-* on the verb in Cree. This is very uncommon in Michif.

In short, obviative marking is present in Michif but more reduced than in Cree.

Sentence Types

Here I deal only with some sentence types: copula constructions, question sentences, negative sentences, relative clauses, and "modality" clauses.

COPULA CONSTRUCTIONS

There are five kinds of copula constructions in Michif: (a) a Cree-based predicative construction that uses verbal adjectives or nouns, (b) a Cree-based identifying construction that uses the Cree demonstrative determiner, (c) a Cree verb suffix, (d) an innovative equative construction without any verb or copula, and (e) a French-based equative clause construction that uses the French copula.

(a) Cree has no copula as such. In Michif, the equivalents of copulas in European languages are expressed by a noun phrase and a verbal adjective or by noun constructions. Order in the clause is free. What is usually expressed by predicative adjective constructions in European languages is expressed by a stative verb in Michif, for example:

(31) *papIkwa:-w* lι læ̌ž
      be rough.AI-3 the cloth
      "The cloth is rough."

(32) la bwɛt *mIša:-w*
      DAFS box be.big.II-3
      "The box is big."

(33) lι za:br *mIšIkItI-w*
      DAMS tree be.big.AI-3
      "The tree is big."

(b) Identifying constructions use Cree demonstratives along with a nominal predicate as a subject. The predicate always precedes the demonstrative.

(34) æ̃ za:br *ana*
      IAMS tree DEM.AN.S
      "That is a tree."

(35) æ̃ narabjæ̃ *ana* lι žwal
      IAMS Arabian DEM.AN.S DAMS horse
      "That horse is an Arabian."

In emphatic sentences the construction is slightly different (Rhodes 1977: 13). A personal pronoun is followed by the noun phrase, which is preceded by a demonstrative:

(36) *nIja u:ma* mũ: papji
      1S DEM.INAN.S my.M.S paper
      "This is my paper."

(c) The Cree verb can also be a verbalized noun in Cree, with a copulalike suffix,-*lwl*-. The Cree verb agrees in animacy with the noun, in Cree and in Michif. A Michif example follows:

(37)   la-pusjɛ:r-*lw-an* lι pɔrtmãtũ
        DAFS-dust-BE-II3 DAMS suitcase
        "The suitcase is dusty."

The -*lwl*- suffix does not seem to be used with Cree elements in Michif, strangely enough, although it is quite common in Cree. In Michif it is used productively with French nouns and adjectives, always preceded by the French definite article.

(d) In Michif the noun and its nominal predicate may simply be juxtaposed in any order, giving *equative* sentences, but these are relatively rare in the data:

(38)   ɛn krɛm la žymã
        IAFS cream DAFS mare
        "The mare is a buckskin."

(e) Some constructions involve a French copula, derived from the inflected forms of the French verb *être*, with cliticized pronouns. A list of these forms can be found in a subsequent section. They can appear in the order predicate-subject or subject-predicate (as in colloquial French).

(39)   *e:wako* la rɔb ιlι kwarɛk
        that the dress COP correct
        "That dress is appropriate."

(40)   sι žali larãžmã d flœr
        COP nice arrangement of flower
        "The flower arrangement is nice."

YES-NO QUESTIONS

Yes-no questions in Michif differ from declarative sentences in having a question element *čī* or *či*, either after the first major constituent that is questioned, as in (41), or at the end of a sentence (42), as in Cree. There are also some cases in which the question elements do not appear, as in (43). It is not known which factors are responsible for this variation.

(41)   la munιsjũ: *čī klt-aja:-na:n šI-papa:m-ma:či:-jahk*
        DAFS ammunition Q 2-have-21 COMP-about-hunt.AI-21
        "Do we (INCL) have ammunition for hunting?"

(42)   *ki:-ki:mu:čI-natustaw-a:w-ak* ti: zami: *čī*
        2.PST-secretly-listen-3.OBJ-P your-P friend Q
        "Did you eavesdrop on your friends?"

(43)   *ki:-kašt-æ:n ke:kwaj ka:-wi:-ušta:-jɛn*
       2.PST-be.able-4 what COMP-VOL-do-2SG
       "Were you able to do what you wanted to do?"

QUESTION-WORD QUESTIONS

Interrogative pronouns are derived from Cree, and they are fronted as in Cree:

(44)   awi:na, awe:na, auna   "who"
       ki:kwe:, ke:kwaj   "what"
       ta:nde   "where"
       ta:ne:hkI, tā:næhkI   "why"
       ta:nšI, tā:šI, tā:šIšI   "how"
       ta:nšpi: "when"

(45)   ta:na   (AN S)   "which"
       ta:nIma   (INAN S)
       ta:nIhI   (INAN P/AN OBV)

(46)   *ta:na lɔm ka:-naškwe:ht-ahk*
       which man COMP-answer-TI3→4
       "Which man answered?"

(47)   *ta:nIhI li livr ka:-utInam-a:n*
       which-PL DAP book COMP-take.it-TI.1→4
       "Which books shall I take?"

Very few French forms are in use. These are fixed expressions.

(48)   kɪl a:ž kɪta
       which age that.you.have
       "How old are you?"

(49)   kũbjæ̃ d fwɛ *ka:-wa:pastam-an* la ni:ž
       how.many of time COMP-see.it-2 DAFS snow
       "How many times did you see the snow?" (i.e., "How old are you?")

(50)   kɪl sɔrt dɪ flœr *anIma*
       which kind of flower that
       "What kind of flower is that?"

NEGATIVE SENTENCES

The most common negative particle in Michif is *nu*, presumably from the French
non. This particle is typically used with nonimperative Cree verbs. It usually occurs
immediately before the verb in independent or main clauses, as in (51) and (52), but
it immediately precedes the complementizer in negative embedded clauses, as in (53).
In the latter case, Cree would use *êka*. If there is an adverb, *nu* immediately precedes
it to indicate scope over the adverb, as in (54).

(51) nu *ka-pakItIn-Ika:šu-w čI-Ituhte:-t*
NEG FUT-allow-PASS-3 COMP-go-3
"She will not be allowed to go."

(52) nu *kI-tIpe:jIm-a:w* lɪ mɪnuš
NEG 2–own.TA-3→3' DAMS cat
"The cat does not belong to you."

(53) li nasjũ ǣ trǣti *aja:-w-ak* nu *šI-nu:tIn-Ito-čIk*
PA nation IAMS treaty have.TI-3–P NEG COMP-fight-REC-3P
"Nations have treaties not to fight each other."

(54) nu tultã *aja:-w* a lɪkɔl
NEG always be.AI-3 in the school
"S/he is not always at school."

In Michif, nouns are usually negated by the French particle *pat* (< F. *pas de*), whereas *pa* is used to negate adjectives. French verbs are sometimes negated with *pa*, but these may all be fixed expressions (*žɪpãspa* < F. *je ne pense pas*). Here, negation follows French syntax: it precedes the noun and adjective but follows the verb:

(55) lɔm pat barb *ana*
man NEG beard DEM-AN.PROX.
"That's the man without a beard."

(56) pat *wicIhIwe:wIn*
no help
"no help"

(57) žɪ pãs pa *šI-Ituhte:-t*[4]
I think NEG COMP-go-3
"I do not think he will go."

The most common negator derived from Cree in Michif is *namu(:)*. It occurs in Michif with an identical distribution to that of *nu*, except before conjunct clauses. It precedes the verb, the noun, or adverb that it negates:

(58) *namu nI-wi:-Ituhta:-n*
NEG 1–VOL-go-non3
"I will not go; I do not want to go."

(59) *mIsče:t* laržã *aj-aw-e:w ma:ka namu:* ǣfãtas
much money have.TA-3→3' but NEG IAMS braggart
"He has a lot of money but he is no braggart."

(60) *namu: wa:hjaw d-aja:-na:n* a Bismarck *uhčI*
NEG far 1–be-AI.11 to B. from
"We are not far from Bismarck."

There are also instances of the use of the Cree-derived negation *e:ka*, always before Cree conjunct forms, as required in Cree or sometimes French subordinate sentences).

(61)   *ahkIkI-n* la mus *ita* lı salεj *e:ka: e:-wa:še:n-Ike:-t*
       grow-4 DAFS moss where DAMS sun NEG COMP-shine-DETR-3
       "Moss grows where the sun does not shine."

Imperatives are negated with the Cree form *ka:ja*.

(62)   *ka:ja napač-Im-In*
       NEG bother-with.words-IMP.TA.2→1
       "Do not hassle me."

   It should also be mentioned that some Cree negative plus noun-adverb constructions are copied in Michif as well. In Cree and Michif these form a phonological unit,
for example, Cree *namôya nânitâw* "nowhere, nothing," Michif *nama na:nda:w* or
nu: na:nda:w; Cree *namôya kîkwê:*, often *nama ki:kwe:* or *maki:kwe:* "nothing, not
at all," Michif also *namake:kwaj* or *no ke:kwaj*; Cree *namawiyêk* "nobody," Michif
nu awijak; and so on. These combinations can function as negators, too. They seem
to have scope only over nouns instead of over verbs or sentences.

COMPLEX CLAUSES

Most relative clauses that modify nominals are based on Cree constructions. These
are typically embedded clauses with conjunct order verbs, introduced by the
complementizer prefix *ka:-*.

(63)   *bakwat-a:w-ak* lı mu:d *ka:-kImutI-čIk*
       1.hate.TA-3–PL DAMS people COMP-steal-3P
       "I hate people who steal."

(64)   *ke:kwaj ka:-Itwe:-ja:hk*
       something COMP-say-AI.11
       "something that we said"

A few occurrences of French relative forms, possibly only in fixed formula constructions, have also been noted, with the shapes *kıla* (< F. *qu'il a*) and *kılı* (< F. *qu'il
est*); these are almost always followed by French predicates (adjectives or nouns).

(65)   *dılu kılı bū*
       water REL-s/he-is good
       "fresh water"

(66)   *awIjak kılı drul*
       someone REL-s/he-is funny
       "someone funny"

   There are locative relative forms *Ite:* and *Ita* "where" (*Ite:* is directional and *Ita*
is locative) and a temporal relative pronoun *Išpi:*. These are sometimes combined
with a French relative clause.

(67) *ka-mi:ču-na:n Išpl* tut *e:-aj-ahk-u*
      FUT-eat-11 when all COMP-be-11–COND
      "We will eat when we are all there."

(68) *bakwat-æ:n či-tuhte:-ja:n* d-æ̃ nɪkɔl *Ita* kɪlɪ strɪk
      1.hate-TI.3→4 COMP-go-AI.1 in-a school where REL.3S.be strict
      "I do not like to go to a school where they are strict."

Adverbial Relative Clauses

Most adverbial conjunctions are from French; they control either a Cree conjunct
clause or a French clause, with the *k-ɪl-a* or *k-ɪl-ɪ* element just mentioned.

(69) no *pe:ht-am* akuz *e:-pa:kI-pajIn-IjI-k* su zaraj
      NEG hear.TI-3→4 because COMP-thick-become-OBV-II.4 his.M.S ear
      "S/he does not hear it because of an ear infection."

(70) *pe:hta:w* zyskatã *či-takušInI-ja:n*
      wait until COMP-arrive.AI-1
      "Wait until I arrive."

(71) sitæ̃[5] bræv la fij aprɛ k-ɪl-a su:vi lɪ bebi
      3.be.IAMS brave DAFS girl after COMP.3.have save-INFL DAMS baby
      "She is a heroine after she saved the baby."

A peculiar type, which uses French lexical material but is nonexistent in French, is
used as a manner or degree adverbial:

(72) pa mwajæ̃ lœz aržã *šI-akIm-Im-Iht* k-ɪ-sũ riš
      no means their money COMP-count-PO-IMPERS that-3–be.PL. rich
      "They cannot count their money, they're so rich."

(73) *ki:-tu:hka:pI-w* kɪlɪtɛ syrpri
      PST-have.eyes.open-AI.3 COMP-3–was surprised
      "S/he was open-eyed, so surprised was she."

(74) nu *mIhče:t* mɛri *čI-lɪ-budæ̃-Ihke:-t* kɪlɪ tužur budœz
      NEG much Mary COMP-DAMS-pout-make-AI.3 COMP.3.is always moody
      "It does not take a lot for Mary to pout, she's so moody."

Embedded Questions

Embedded polar questions sometimes use the Cree particle *ki:špIn* "if" in Michif.
Its Cree equivalent *kîspin* introduces only conditional sentences. Cree has no embedded questions; direct questions are used instead. This use seems to be due to
French influence. In most cases embedded question-word questions are identical
to nonembedded sentences, with the exception of the use of *Išpi:* instead of *tãšpi:*
and *ita* or *ite:* instead of *ta:nde:* as an indirect question markers; see (67) and (68).
These are the forms that would be required in Cree also. The Michif relativizer
ta:nšI, for instance, is the independent and embedded question word "how" in Cree
and Michif:

(75) *nI-nIšItuht-æ:n ta:nšI Itwe:-jan*
      1s-understandTI-4 how speak-AI.2
      "I understand the way you speak."

FRENCH PARTICLE-BASED MODALITY CLAUSES

Modality is the only area where Michif departs significantly from French and Cree.
It is not clear why it is the modality system that is the locus of so much innovation.
A French adverb or phrasal expression is used to introduce a Cree clause, which
is in the conjunct mode (also, rarely, a French infinitive or complement clause).
The semantic relation between the French source word and the Michif word is
not always clear, as in example (76), where French *encore* "still, again" is the
source for the Michif way to express a wish. See also (72) for another such phrasal
expression.

(76) æ̃ šæ̃ āku:r *e:-aja:w-ak*
      a dog WISH COMP-have-TA.1→3
      "I wish I had a dog."

(77) saprã tɪ ãdžyr lɪ træ̃
      NECESSITY you endure the noise
      "You have to endure the noise."

Following is a list, probably not exhaustive, of the modality markers found in
the data:

(78) āku:r   (< F. *encore* "again")   "I wish."
      pa mwajæ̃   (< F. *pas moyen* "no means")   "It is impossible."
      magre   (< F. *malgré* "in spite of")   "oblige, coerce"
      fu(lɛ)-bæ̃   (< F. *fallait/faut bien*)   "It is/was necessary."
      sa-prã   (< F. *ça prend* "it takes")   "It is necessary."
      sa-s-pura-bæ̃   (< F. *ça se pourra(it) bien*)   "It is possible."
      sa-sɛr-da-rjæ̃ (< F. *ça sert de/à rien*)   "It is useless."
      sɪ-pa-si   (< F. *je ne sais pas si*)   "It is doubtful."

Several French and some English adjectives and, more rarely, adverbs or nouns
occur with the impersonal French expression *sɪ* (< F. *c'est* "it is") or *sɪtɛ* in the past
tense.

(79) sɪ-d-valœr   (F. *c'est de valeur*)   "It's too bad."
      sɪ-tɛrib   (F. *c'est terrible*)   "It's awful."
      sɪ-bæ̃-ra:r   (F. *c'est bien rare*)   "It's rare."
      sɪ-bæ̃-n-a-swɛti   (F. *c'est bien a souhaiter*)   "It's to be hoped."
      sɪtɛ-pa-nɪsɪsɛr   (F. *ç'était pas nécessaire*)   "It was unnecessary."
      sɪ-pa-fær   (F./E. *c'est pas fair*)   "It's not fair."
      sɪ-t-izi   (F./E. *c'est easy*)   "It's easy."

Cree also has impersonal constructions, which may have served as a model for the reanalysis of the French forms. These Cree constructions are used in Michif, too. They are followed by a conjunct verb form, but this does not seem to be obligatory.

(80) *ki:ja:m čɪ-pe:htwa:-hk uta*   (Cree and Michif)
      all.right COMP-smoke-IMPERS here
      "It is all right to smoke here."

(81) *pɪko ta-šlpwe:hte:-ja:n*   (Cree and Michif)
      NECESSITY COMP-leave-AI.1
      "I must go."

(82) *ma:škut ka-Išpajɪ-n*   (Cree and Michif)
      MAYBE FUT-happen-II.4
      "It will probably happen."

In short, these Michif constructions look very similar to Cree constructions, despite the French source of the lexicon in a number of them—(76) to (79).

Grammatical Categories

In this section I discuss the different grammatical categories and their source languages. It is perhaps most convenient to deal with the grammatical categories one by one since those in Michif have a source in either French or Cree.

Verb Phrase

Almost all verbs in Michif are Cree, although a few are French. These are discussed separately, as are mixed verbs subsequently.

The Cree Verb Phrase

This is not the place to give a full account of the Cree verb phrase. Since a very simplified overview is given here, for descriptions and analyses I refer to Wolfart (1973b), Wolfart and Carroll (1981), Dahlstrom (1991), and Ahenakew (1987a).

The Michif verb phrase is basically that of Plains Cree (but see the following for some differences). Michif and Cree verb paradigms can be found in Rhodes (1977). Compared with Plains Cree, there is little reduction of the paradigms. Michif does not have dubitative or preterite verb forms; at least, there are only a very few such forms in our data. These are rare, defective, or nonexistent in most contemporary dialects of Plains Cree as well (Wolfart 1973b and pers. comm.).

A Cree verb can be infinitely long in theory since it can contain a great number of formatives. Many things that are expressed in the noun phrase in European languages are expressed in the verb in Cree, and therefore also in Michif. The verb is the central element in Algonquian languages. An English translation of many Cree verbs would show a whole sentence. Cree has inflectional morphemes, derivational morphemes, and stem-formational morphemes. In theory verbs can contain twenty morphemes or more. Normally verbs are not that long, but they contain minimally three morphemes: two stem morphemes and one or two inflectional morphemes. All Cree verbs are inflected; infinitival forms do not exist in Cree. The morphemes appear in a particular order in the verb, which can be summarized as follows:

(83)   *Prefixes*

Conjunct marker *or* person agreement – tense – mood – modality – preverb – aspect (reduplication) –

Stem

Root – medial – final

Suffixes

Quantitative valency – direct/inverse – obviative – agreement – plural – conditional

A Cree or Michif verb starts either with a conjunct marker (*ka:-*, *e:-*, or *či-*), which indicates that the verb is the core of a subordinate clause, or with first- or second-person prefixes (*ni-* or *ki-*) if the verb is in the independent order in a main clause. In conjunct verbs, all the person agreement markers are suffixed to the verb; in independent order verbs there are additional prefixes. Tense and mood prefixes can indicate past (*ki:*), future (*ka*), or volitional (*wi:*). There are a great number of "modality" prefixes, such as *ka:kwe:-* "to try" and *pu:nI-* "to quit," and many of these can also be used in combination. Preverbs can be adverbial-like elements with such meanings as "strongly," "loudly," and so on. There are a great number of these preverbs. Two types of reduplication adjacent to the stem mark durative and iterative aspect.

Cree stems are also complex. They contain minimally an element that indicates a state or configuration (final) and an indication of how this was caused (initial). Medials (incorporated nouns or noun classifiers) can be added in between. These stem formatives can in themselves be complex. Stems also contain a so-called abstract final that indicates the gender of the arguments, traditionally called "theme."

The morphemes that follow the stems are several derivational suffixes, which indicate changes in the number of arguments of the verb (quantitative valency). They either extend the number of arguments (causative *-h-*, benefactive *-aw-*, applicative *-aw-*, and some other morphemes), or they reduce it (passive *-Ika:šo-* and *-Ika:te:*; reflexive *-Iso-*; reciprocal *-Ito-*; detransitivizer *-Ike:*). Some of them can be used in combination. These morphemes are followed by what is called a "direction" morpheme, which is fairly typical for Algonquian languages like Cree.

Cree has a hierarchy of arguments, which is 2 > 1 > 3 > 3'. If a subject is lower in the hierarchy than the object, the verb has an "inverse" marker; otherwise it has a "direct" marker. Thus a verb with a first-person subject and a second-person object will have the inverse marker *-ItI-*, third-person subject on first- or second-person object *-ik(u)-*, and obviative subject on proximate object *-ik(u)-*. The corresponding direct markers are, respectively, *-I-* (you-me), *-a:-* (I-him/her or you-him/her), and *-e:-* (he/she-him/her). These can be considered inflectional morphemes. If the subject is a possessed third person (e.g., "her mother"), an obviative morpheme *-jI-* can be added here. After this, the person agreement suffixes follow (not described here). These are different according to the animacy or inanimacy and the transitivity or intransitivity of the verb. Transitive verbs show both object and subject agreement, often in fused morphemes. The direct or inverse marker indicates which of the arguments is the subject and which is the object. The third-person plural object agreement morpheme *-Ik* or *-ak* can follow the person inflection morphemes. Finally, a morpheme *-i* or its allomorph *-u* can be added to change conjunct verbs into an "if" clause.

This is the structure of the Michif verb in a nutshell, which, as I said, differs only minimally from the Cree verb. The potential complexity of Michif and Cree verbs is clear. A few facts that are of special importance to Michif must be mentioned.

First, consider gender assignment. Remember that verbs agree in animate or inanimate gender with their objects or subjects. In Cree, all nouns are either animate or inanimate. Although Michif has virtually only French nouns, the Cree verb agrees in gender with the noun, showing the same gender idiosyncrasies as in Cree. For example, in Cree, all means of transportation are animate; some trees are animate, others inanimate; some household items are animate. Michif appears to follow Cree gender assignment closely, as in the examples (84a) and (84b):

(84a)   *ki:-mIčImIn-e:w a:tIht* laržã
        PST-hold-TA.3→3' some money
        "He kept part of the money."

(84b)   *ki:-mIčImIn-am a:tIht* la pɛj
        PST-hold-TI.3→4 the pay
        "He kept part of the payment."

In this example French *laržã* "money" is animate because Cree *sôniyâs* "money" is animate; see also (59); *la pej* is inanimate, presumably following Cree verbalized nominals in *-win*, such as *tipahamâkêwin* "payment," which are inanimate. This is visible in the person agreement suffixes and demonstratives, if present. Similarly, cars and bicycles trigger animate verb agreement markers and animate stems in the Cree verb.

Second, some morphemes are shortened forms of the Cree equivalents. For example, whereas Cree has the finals *-tisah(w)-* "send" and *-êyi-* "think," Michif has *-ča-* and *-e:-*, respectively.

(85)   *Michif*   *Cree*

       Ite:htam   it-êyi-ht-am
       "S/he thinks so."   thus-think-TI-(s)he.it

       kiške:htam   kisk-êyi-ht-am
       "S/he knows it."   remember-think-TI-(s)he.it

       šipwe:-čah-uk   sipwê-tisah-ok
       "Send them away."   away.-send.IMP-PL

Third, the person agreement prefixes *nI-* and *kI-* merge with verb stems or prefixes that start with a stop or a sibilant. In fact *kI-* disappears before stems or prefixes that start with *k-*. The first-person prefix *nI-* causes the following voiceless stop to become voiced, and the *nI-* element disappears; see also (14). In this way the verb form **nI-še:kIh-Iku-n* (Cree equivalent *ni-sêkih-ik*) becomes *že:kIhIkun*, as in (86):

(86) nI-še:kI-h-Iku-n   →
      1S-fright-CAUS-INV-NON3
      nI-že:kIhIkun   →
      n-že:kIhIkun   →
      že:kIhIkun
      "I am alarmed."

This phonological process is obligatory in Michif (see also Chapter Nine), whereas it does not exist in Cree, or at most as an option in some dialects.

Fourth, Michif appears to use analytic constructions (where possible) more often than Cree does. The presence of French nominal constructions probably makes this possible. The average Michif verb will therefore contain fewer morphemes than the Cree verb. The following examples may illustrate this pattern:

(87a) George *ušIpe:hIke:-stamaw-e:w*
       G. write-BEN-3→3'
       "George writes on his behalf."

(87b) George *ušIpe:hIke:-w* pur *wIja*
       G. write-3
       "George writes on his behalf."

Example (87a) shows the normal Cree synthetic form, and (b) is an analytic form used by many Michif speakers (see Chapter Five).

By way of closure, a rather long Cree-Michif verb form with a series of "modality" prefixes follows as an example:

(88) ni-nôhtê-mâci-kakwê-pôni-pîhtwâ-n   (Cree)
      nI-nuhte:-ma:čI-ka:kwe:-pu:nI-pi:stwa:n   (Michif)
      I-want-start-try-quit-smoke-I
      "I want to start to try to quit smoking."

The French Verb Phrase

Apart from the commonly used Cree verbs, Michif also uses some French verbs, albeit rather marginally. It is necessary to distinguish between French verbs conjugated as they would be in French and French or English verbal lexical forms integrated into Cree verbal morphology. The first group is discussed here, the latter group in a subsequent section.

All Michif speakers use at least some French verbs, often frozen expressions such as *allons* "let's go"; *ça prend*, literally "it takes" meaning "one has to"; and the French copula. Although speakers who know French could, in principle, use any French verb in their Michif, this occurs relatively infrequently (see Chapter Five). In fact, the speaker in my sample who used French verbs most frequently in his spontaneous Michif was not able to speak or understand French. Speakers sometimes use forms that should not be used in French, for example, participle forms instead of infinitives, or vice versa. This points to the marginality of the French verb forms. In examples (89) and (90), the verb is ambiguous between the French infinitive form in *-er* and the participle form in *-é(e)*. In examples (91) and (92), a participle is used, whereas an infinitive would be expected in French:

(89) ɪ va paːs-i
      "It will pass."

(90) ɪ va bɔk-i
      "He will buck."

(91) ɪ va ufɛr sa plas
      "He will offer his seat." (F. *il va offrir/il a offert*)

(92) ɪ va dispary
      "He will disappear." (F. *il va disparaître/il est disparu*)

Some Michif imperatives are in French; see (62) for an example of a Cree imperative. They can be derived from the French singular or plural imperatives. There does not seem to be a plural-singular distinction between these forms. They are sometimes used in combination, as in (93):

(93) taːš-i ãdžyr lɪ pwæ̃
      attempt-INFL endure the pain
      "Try to endure the pain."

In the data there are a few examples of French verbs with cliticized pronouns, but most of them seem to be more or less fixed expressions or are remembered as a whole. In any case, they are rare. In fact, they are so few that generalizations are impossible:

(94) ɪ-m-a-ufɛr   "he offered me"
      ɪ-l-a-nɔz-amyzi   "He amused us."
      sa-s-akɔrd pa   "They do not get along."
      ɪ-vœ-s-marji   "He wants to get married."

Sentences with French verbs are unusual (see Chapter Five for some quantitative data), and it is not known what factors (style, competence, or the interlocutor) trigger their use. If a French verb is used, all nominal subjects require cliticized pronouns on the verb. These forms are always based on the French singular masculine forms:

(95) Delia ɪl-a fɛ sãblã eː-jaːhkošI-t
      Delia (s)he-has made seeming COMP-be.sick.3
      "Delia pretended to be sick." (F. *Delia elle a fait semblant*)

(96) žyl ɪl-a ãfarži lɪ žwal
      Jules (s)he-has hobble(d) DAMS horse
      "Jules hobbled the horse."

There is a special place for the verbs "to be" and "to have"; these are the only French-derived verbs that have rather elaborate paradigms. Second-person plural forms are lacking in the data taken from Laverdure and Allard (1983):

(97) "to be"

	Present	*Past*
1	žι /žι swι	žιtε
2	tι	tιtε
3	ιlι / sι	ιlιtε / s(ι)tε
1P	ūlι	ūlιtε
2P	—	—
3P	ιsū:	isūtε

Infinitive

(pur) jεt

(98) "to have"

	Present	*Past*	*Future*
1	ža	žave	(not attested)
2	ta	tavε	
3	ιla, sala	ιlavε	
1P	ū:la	ūlavε	
2P	—	—	
3P	ι/salū	i/salūvε	

The use of both verbs is rather limited. The forms derived from the French *être* "to be" are often used as a copula (beside other copulalike constructions). The inflected forms of the French verb *avoir* "to have" are used in a variety of fossilized verbal expressions such as *avoir besoin* "need," *il y a* "there are," and so on. It is also used as an auxiliary, even when French would use the auxiliary *être*, for example, in *ιla vny* "he came" and *ιla arivi* "he arrived" (F. *il est venu*; *il est arrivé*).

THE NOUN PHRASE

The noun phrase in Michif is fundamentally French, regardless of its syntactic function. Nouns are always accompanied by a French determiner or a possessive. Cree demonstratives, animate or inanimate, can be added to the French noun phrase, which also has the French definite article. Apart from the French nouns, a limited number of Cree, Ojibwe, and English nouns are also used. Most Michif French nouns are identical to those found in archaic dialects of Canadian French, except for phonological differences caused by the processes discussed earlier in this chapter. All French nouns belong to one of two gender classes, masculine and feminine. Gender is not marked on the noun itself, but it surfaces in the singular article (M *le* or *un*; F *la* or *une*) or in the possessive pronouns (M *son* "his, her"; F *sa* "his, her"). It also surfaces in the shape of modifying prenominal adjectives, for example, M *gros*; F *grosse* "big, fat."

French Nouns

Normally Michif nouns are identical to Canadian French nouns, but some of them have been reanalyzed phonetically in Michif. The French vowel-initial nouns are reanalyzed as starting with a variable consonant, which comes either from the agglutination of a liaison consonant segment taken from the most typical French determiner (99) or through the truncation of the initial syllable (100). In Cree, by the way, there are numerous vowel-initial nouns. That these initial consonants are part of the noun (and not the result of a liaison rule, as in French) is argued previously, and it is shown that these initial consonants are variable (e.g., *na:br* and *la:br* in addition to *za:br* "tree").

(99) *Agglutination*

zafɛr	"business"	(< *les affaires*)
zavœgl	"blind person"	(< *les aveugles* "the blind ones")
za:br	"tree"	(< *les arbres* "the trees")
lamur	"love"	(< *l'amour* "(the) love")
nɪvrɔñ	"drunkard"	(< *un ivrogne*)
nɪl	"island"	(< *une île* "an island")

(100) *Truncation*

æ̃ spjũ	"spy"	(F. *espion*)
la lɛksjũ	"election"	(F. *élection*)
la sjɛt; ɛn sjɛt	"plate"	(F. *assiette*)
la pɪtal, ɛn pɪtal	"hospital"	(F. *hôpital*)

The gender assigned to these truncated nouns seems to be identical to the gender of the original French noun.

In general, the gender assigned to the noun in Michif is not necessarily typical of European or even of Canadian French, when the latter differs from the former. In the vast majority, however, the genders are the same. Some examples of gender dissimilarities are the following:

(101) *Masculine in Michif; feminine in French*

   šɛvr, šɛv "goat"
   grɪf "claw"

(102) *Feminine in Michif; masculine in French*

   batũ "stick"
   bɔl "bowl"

Articles

Articles in Michif are derived from French. Cree does not have articles. Both the French definite and indefinite article forms are used in Michif, except for the plural indefinite article *des*, which is rare or nonexistent. The etymologically definite form *li:* is used instead for both definite and indefinite plural nouns. Both masculine and feminine articles are used, and the nouns generally have the same gender as in French.

The liaison rules prevailing in French do not exist in Michif (see the beginning of this Chapter). The forms of the article are as follows:

(103)   *Definite*   *Indefinite*

M S   lι (F. *le*)   æ̃ (F. *un*)
F S   la (F *la*)   ɛn (F *une*)
PL   li (F *les*)   li (rarely di) (F *des*)

Personal Pronouns

Personal pronouns are used only for emphasis since person agreement markers attached to the verb mark subject and object. Independent personal pronouns are always derived from Cree.

(104)   nIja   "I"   nIjana:n   "we (EXCL)"
        kIja   "you"   kIjana:n   "we (INCL)"
        wIja   "he, she" kIjawa:w   "you (PL)"
                          wIjawa:w   "they"

There are also forms meaning "me, you (etc.) too." These have *-št-* instead of *-j-*—for example, *ni:šta* "me too"—and the first vowel is long.

Non-French Nouns: Ojibwe and Cree

A very few Cree nouns are also used in Michif. Usually these have Cree nominal morphology (Cree plural, obviative, and locative suffixes) if required, for example, *ni-mušum-ak* "my grandfather-s" *tahkwahami:n-a* "chokecherries," with, respectively, the animate plural suffix *-ak* and the inanimate plural suffix *-a*. Some Ojibwe nouns are also used in Michif, such as *jamũ* "bee" (Ojibwe *aamoo /a:mõ:/*; Cree *amu:*), *ɛnikũs* "ant" (Ojibwe *enigoons*; Plains Cree *e:yikos*), and *kašahkæ̃s* "cat" (Ojibwe *gaazhagens*). Most of the Algonquian nouns used in Michif turn out to be Ojibwe rather than Cree. I return to this topic in Chapter Nine.

Only historical borrowings from Cree into Canadian French—for example, *le pichou* "bobcat" (Canadian French "woolly shoes"), *moccasin* "moccasin," and *mitasse* "leggings"—are totally adapted to French phonology. The Cree nouns *mušum* "grandfather" and *kuhkum*, literally "(your) grandmother," are used by Métis and Cree alike, even when speaking English or French, and can also be considered Cree borrowings into Métis French or English.

In Michif, as in Cree, any verb can be nominalized by using one of four nominalizing suffixes: *-kan* ("instrument"), *-win* (abstract nouns), *-sk/-hk* ("repetitive V-er"), and *-hk* ("action by unspecified actors"). French determiners are commonly used with these Cree nominalizations. Cree nouns in *-wIn* are always inanimate, and all examples found have French masculine gender. Nominalizations of Cree verbs are productive for all Michif speakers, although they are perhaps more marginal in Michif than for Cree.

(105)   lι *pakamahI-kan* "the striker"   (Cree *pakamahw-e:-w* "S/he beats him/her.")
        lι *mǣtawa:-kan* "the toy"   (Cree *me:tawe:-w* "S/he is playing.")

lɪ *we:pɪn-Ike:-wIn* "the garbage"   (Cree *we:pɪn-Ike:-w* "S/he throws things.")

ɛn *pu:ju:-sk* "a (female) quitter"   (Cree *pu:ju:-w* "S/he quits.")

æ̃ *dutama:ke:hk* "a panhandling"   (Cree *nItutama:-ke:-w* "S/he asks people for things.")

Cree conjunct verb forms are like relative clauses in themselves and can be considered nominalized forms, too. These can take French determiners.

(106)   (æ̃) *ka:-ata:we:-t* "one who buys; a buyer"
IAMS COMP-buy-3S

(æ̃) *ka:-pe:hkIsčI-ke:-t* "one who cleans; a custodian"
IAMS COMP-clean-DETRANS-3S

All in all, Cree and Ojibwe nouns remain a marginal part of Michif (see Chapter Five for quantitative data).

Non-French Nouns: Some English Nouns

A significant number of English nouns are used by Michif speakers: between 4 percent and 24 percent, depending on the speaker (see Chapter Five). These may be phonologically adapted to French or not. Stress is often assigned according to Cree or French stress assignment rules. As noted, the English influence on Michif is pervasive now. In fact, any English noun can be used in Michif, and so it is difficult to distinguish between code mixing and borrowing. Gender assignment of English nouns is not understood very well; it often seems to follow the gender of the French noun.[6]

(107)   la light "(electrical) light"   (F. *la lumière, une ampoule*)

lɪ base   (F. *le but, le coussin*)

Note the possible exceptions:

(108)   la fun   (F. *le plaisir*; Canadian French *le fun*)

la dam   (F. *le barrage*)

ɛn mouthharp   (F. *un harmonica*, but *une harpe?*)

æ̃ binder   (F. *une moissonneuse*)

It should also be remarked that English nouns have French masculine or feminine determiners and that they agree in animacy or inanimacy with Cree demonstratives and verbs. So the English nouns have both Cree animate or inanimate gender and French masculine or feminine gender, for example:

(109)   *wIja* lɪ trɔk *pamIn-e:w* pur la me:l
3 DAMS truck drive.TA-3→3' for DAFS mail
"He drives the mail truck."

(110)   lɪ æ:rple:n *awa a:še:-pajI-w*
DAMS airplane this.AN back-move-3.AN
"This airplane goes back."

In (109), the English word "mail" is feminine because *la poste* and Métis French *la malle* are feminine, and "truck" is masculine because *le char* is masculine. The verb *pamin-e:w* refers to an animate object because all means of transportation are animate in Cree and therefore in Michif. In (110), English "airplane" is animate and has an animate Cree demonstrative *awa*, and it agrees with an animate verb.

Plurality is marked only in the French article, not in the English noun—*li stepsister* "the stepsisters" and *li drug* "drugs"—with occasional exceptions like *li binz* "beans." It should also be mentioned here that some French words that are plural in English take a plural French article: *li polčık* "politics" (F. *la politique*); *li polıs* "police" (also *la polis*) (F. *la police*). The latter word, even with a singular article, always has a plural agreement marker on the verb, as in English.

NOUN MODIFIERS

French nouns can be modified in several ways. They can have determiners of different kinds (articles, demonstratives, possessives), they can be marked for number, and they can be modified by several elements. These modifiers include quantifiers, numerals, and adjectives. Some categories within the noun phrase are always French, some always Cree, and most are sometimes French and sometimes Cree.

Adjectives

Adjectives are always French since Cree does not have adjectives. In Cree, noun modifiers are expressed by verbal constructions, that is, relative clauses, or by prefixation to the noun. All "real" adjectives in Michif are of French origin. Most French adjectives are typically either pre- or postnominal. In Michif they have the same position as they would have in French. There is an important difference, though. In French, adjectives agree in gender (and, in written French, also in number) with the nouns they modify. In Michif, a curious thing happens: postnominal adjectives do not agree in gender and number (111, 112, 113) with the noun, whereas prenominal adjectives do (114, 115).

(111)   la mæ̃zũ blã
         DAFS house-*F* white-*M* (F. *la maison blanche* [blãš])
         "the white house"

(112)   ɛn fam nœ
         IAFS wife-*F* new-*M* (F. *une femme neuve*)
         "a new wife"

(113)   lı bwa šɛš
         DAMS wood-*M* dry-*F* (F. *le bois sec*)
         "the dry wood"

(114)   æ̃ gru sarpã
         IAMS big-*M* snake
         "a big snake"

(115)   la grus tãt
        DA*F*S big-*F* tent
        "the big tent"

French adjectives may be reinforced with *vre* [< F. *vrai(e)* "real"] or by reduplication. Both these reinforcements are also known in Canadian French dialects (R. Papen,
personal communication).

(116)   ɛn vrɛ žali rɔb
        IAFS real nice dress
        "a real(ly) pretty dress"

(117)   lι vjœ-vjœ *kI-mušum-Ina:n*
        DAMS old-old 21-grandfather-21
        "our (INCL) very old grandfather"

Comparatives and superlatives can be French (118) or Cree (119) or mixtures
of both systems.

(118)   lι ste:k sι la ply mιjœr vjãd (F. *la meilleure viande*)
        the steak it-is DAFS more best meat
        "Steak is the best meat."

(119)   æ̃ tũ *nawat mIšIkItI-w ašpIcI* ɛn muš
        DAMS horsefly more big-AI.3 than IAFS fly
        "A horsefly is bigger than a fly."

Cree relative clauses are common in Michif. These clauses are also used to express adjectival functions.

(120)   dilu *ka:-wi:hkašI-hk*
        water COMP-taste.good-3
        "fresh water"

(121)   ɛn mɔrsu-d-vjãd *ka:-mIša:-k*
        IAFS piece-of-meat COMP-big.II-3
        "a big piece of meat"

It also happens, more or less rarely, in seemingly all dialects of Michif that Cree
"adjectivelike" elements are prefixed to French nouns.

(122)   *napakI*-lι-pwɛsũ
        flat-DAMS-fish
        "flatfish" (Cree *napakaw* "it is flat"; compare *napaki-tâpânâsk* "a flat sled")

Possessives

Possessive markers for French nouns in Michif are French. The paradigm is virtually
identical to French, but see the preceding discussion of prevocalic forms and liaison.

(123) *Singular*   *Plural*

	masculine	*feminine*	
1S	mu/mũ	ma	mi
2S	tu/tũ	ta	ti
3S	su/sũ	sa	si
1P	nɔt/nut	nɔt/nut	nu
[2P	vɔt/vut	vɔt/vut	vu][7]
3P	lœ	lœ	lœ:/ly

Cree nouns, however, usually have Cree possessive prefixes and suffixes (124), except for Cree borrowings in French. A few exceptions, such as *mušum* "grandfather" and *kuhkum* "grandmother," can also have French possessive determiners. In some cases there are possessed nouns with Cree suffixes and French prenominal possessive markers—for example, *sa tãt-Iwa:w* "their aunt," in which -*Iwa:w* is a morpheme that refers to a plural possessor. Notice that the obviative ending -*a* does not seem to be present here, but it is present in ordinary Cree and in Cree words in Michif. The normal paradigm for Cree nouns in Michif is seen in (124).

(124) *Singular*   *Plural*

nI-mušum (1)   nI-mušum-Ina:n (11)
kI-mušum (2)   kI-mušum-Ina:n (12) (Cree -*Inaw*)
                     kI-mušum-Iwa:w (2PL)
u-mušum-a (3)   u-muSum-Iwa:w-a (3PL)

Both the Cree component and the French component distinguish between alienable and inalienable possession (mostly kinship and body parts). Cree inalienable possessions have an obligatory possession marker. In the rare case of nonpossession ("someone's head"), the Cree noun is marked by the prefix *mi-*, which cannot be used for alienable possessions. This prefix does not seem to be used in Michif. French inalienable possessions always have a possessive element.

(125a) Cree inalienable and alienable possession

Inalienable		*Alienable*	
ni-stês	"my brother"	ni-paskisikan	"my gun"
? mi-stês	"someone's brother"	paskisikan	"a, the, someone's gun"
*stês	"brother"	*mi-paskisikan	"someone's gun"

(125b) Michif inalienable possession
mũ frɛ:r "my brother"
*frɛ:r "a brother"
? æ frɛ:r "a brother"

Demonstratives

Demonstratives are almost always Cree. This has a number of interesting consequences since Cree distinguishes animate and inanimate gender for nouns, and demonstratives must agree in gender and number with the noun. Moreover, in Michif, whenever a Cree demonstrative is used, it must be accompanied by a form of the French definite article or by a possessive. This must agree in French gender (masculine or feminine) and number with the noun. The Cree verb also agrees in animacy or inanimacy with the French or Cree subject and/or object. This means that nominal forms must carry both French and Cree gender. Michif uses the following demonstratives, with some of the variants noted:

(126)

	Proximal	Intermediate	Distant
AN S	awa	ana	naha
AN PL	ū:kIk/u:kIk	anīkī/anIkIk/ɛnɛkIk	ne:kIk
INAN S	u:ma	anIma	ne:ma
INAN PL	ū:hī:/ū:hi	anIhI/anīhī/ɛnɛhī	ne:hī, nɛhi

Demonstratives are mostly placed before the noun, although they are also frequently found after. Some typical examples follow:

(127)

awa la fij	"this girl"	(proximal, animate, feminine, singular, preposed)
awa lɪ garsū	"this boy"	(proximal, animate, masculine, singular, preposed)
lom *awa*	"this man"	(proximal, animate, masculine, singular, postposed)
la fæm *ana*	"that woman"	(intermediate, animate, feminine, singular, postposed)
ana lɪ nur	"that bear"	(intermediate, animate, masculine, singular, preposed)
u:ma lɪ papji	"this paper"	(proximal, inanimate, masculine, singular, preposed)
u:ma la bwɛt	"this box"	(proximal, inanimate, feminine, singular, preposed)
anIma la mǣzū	"that house"	(intermediate, inanimate, feminine, singular, preposed)
ne:ma lɪ šã	"that field"	(distal, inanimate, feminine, singular, preposed)
ū:hī lɪ zafɛr	"those businesses"	(proximal, inanimate, feminine, plural, preposed)

French demonstratives are used only marginally and in a limited number of contexts, that is, only in some fixed temporal expressions. They do not seem to be productive. The form of the French demonstrative varies: [ɪstɪ, stɪ, st, ɪs, s, ɪst] (from popular F. *c'te*). These may be fossilized forms in most, if not all, cases.

(128) la sãdr *ki:-mIšI-pahkIstI-n* ɪs prǣtã
        the ash PST-much-fall.II-4 DEM spring
        "We had an ash fallout this spring."

(129) *wi:-wi:wI-w* st-atɔn
        VOL-marry-AI.3 DEM-fall
        "She'll get married this fall."

Numerals and Quantifiers

Numerals are always French, except that occasionally the Cree numeral *pe:jak* "one" is used. They do not differ from other quantifiers, which may be either French or Cree. Most quantifiers (including numerals), whether French or Cree, require the French article between the quantifier and the noun, as in these examples:

(130)   džɪs li žɛn dǣd
        ten DAP young turkey
        "ten young turkeys"

(131)   plys kɪ hɛn lɪ sɔkl
        more than one DAMS blade
        "more than one blade"

(132)   ǣ pči brǣ la sup
        a little bit DAFS soup
        "a bit of soup"

(133)   jǣk *pe:jak* ǣ narãž *dawe:jIm-a:w*
        only one IAMS orange want-TA.1→3'
        "I want only one orange."

Michif quantifiers are subject to a syntactic rule not present in French. Algonquian languages in general allow the preposing of certain elements of the noun phrase, often numeral quantifiers, thus creating discontinuous constituents (see Dahlstrom 1987 for the Fox language). This is also possible in Michif, as in example (134), even with French quantifiers; see also (25) and (137).

(134)   *ka:ja mIštahI ašta* lɪ sɛl
        NEG much put.IMP.TI.2→4 DAMS salt
        "Do not put in (too) much salt."

Prepositions and Postpositions

All Michif speakers use both French prepositions and Cree postpositions and prepositions. Some speakers use more Cree adpositions (as in some Manitoba communities), others more French (such as those of Turtle Mountain and southern Saskatchewan). For some discussion of the variation, see Chapter Five. Cree also has a locative nominal suffix, *-Ihk/-uhk*, which is added to Cree nouns. Yet even for those speakers who use French forms, some of these suffixes typically express Cree functions. For example the Michif preposition *dal/dã* (< F. *dans* "in")[8] no longer denotes "in(side)" uniquely, as it does in French. Rather, it has become a general locative marker, which is also obligatory with some locative adpositions, as the following examples make clear:

(135)   *šnikun-a* lɪ sæv da: tu: bra:
        rub-TI.IMP.2 DAMS salve LOC your-M arm
        "Rub the salve on your arm."

(136)   dã lɪ frɪdž *uhčI*
        LOC the fridge from
        "out of the fridge"

(137)   *a:tIht manIša* li brãš da lɪ za:br *uhčI*
        some cut-off-IMP.TI2 DAP branch LOC DAMS tree from
        "Cut off some of the branches from the tree."

In Cree, the locatives of examples (135) and (136) would be as follows:

(135')   ki-spiton-ihk
          2–arm-LOC
          "in, on, at your arm"

(136')   tahkascikan-ihk ohci
          fridge-LOC from

The prepositions *da/da:/dã* (dans) and *dι* (de) both merge with the articles æ and *εn* to /dæ̃/ in Michif. Merging in Michif occurs in a somewhat different way than in French.

(138)   *French*   *Michif*

          de + le →   *du*   *dlι* (*dy* in some fossilized expressions)
          de + les →   *des*   *li* (*di* in some fossilized expressions)
          à + le →   *au*   not attested (*u* in some fossilized expressions)
          à + les →   *aux*   not attested
          dans + un   *dans un*   *dæ̃*
          de + un   *d'un*   *dæ̃*

Furthermore, the preposition *da* is often also *sa* in a possessive construction, for example, *sa sa mæ̃zũ* "in his/her house." The preposition *dι* is not always used in Michif as it is in French. The French semantic distinction between partitive and nonpartitive forms does not exist in Michif. The partitive forms, marked with *de* (singular) or *des* (plural) in French, are not used in Michif. There are some fossilized forms of partitives, for example, *dιlu* "water" (from F. *de l'eau* "water"). The word *dιlu* has both partitive-indefinite and definite meaning, as does the rarer form *lu*. There are instances of *dι* in Michif, in which it occurs as an optional complement to a French adjective:

(139)   la šaye:r ιlι plæ lι sa:b
          DAFS pail it.is full the sand
          "The pail is full of sand." (F.: pleine *de* sable)

(140)   mi suyi sũ plæ d sa:b
          my.PL shoes 3PL.are full of sand
          "My shoes are full of sand."

(141)   æ̃ žyp dι rɔb plæ li pli d akɔrdžιjũ
          DAMS skirt of dress full DAP ruck of accordion
          "a skirt full of accordion rucks" (F. plein *de* plis)

A remarkable element in the prepositions from French in Michif is that some of them have the shape of the French adverb (used independently or as verb modifiers in that language) instead of the corresponding French preposition (modifying nouns). This is also typical of Canadian French and older stages of European French.

(142) | *French preposition* | *French "adverb"* | *Michif preposition* | *Meaning* |
|---|---|---|---|
| sur | dessus, en dessus | dɛsy, ãdsy or dã/da | "on" |
| derrière | en arrière, derrière | ãnarjɛr, darjɛr | "behind" |

A final aspect to be mentioned is the possibility of preposition stranding in Michif with some prepositions (143), just as in Canadian French. French prepositions used as postpositions, as in (144), are rare:

(143) la mɪčɪn *e:-nIpe:-h-Iwe:-hk* avɛk
       DAFS drug COMP-sleep-CAUS-INDFZR-IMPERS with
       "the drug people are put to sleep with"

(144) ãẽ gru: *nawat,* aku:z lɪ bi:bi: pur
       IAMS big more because DAMS baby for
       "a bigger one, for the baby"

FURTHER CATEGORIES: ADVERBIAL PARTICLES, CONJUNCTIONS, AND DISCOURSE MARKERS

Some categories that are neither strictly part of the verb phrase nor of the noun phrase are discussed here.

Adverbs

Ideas expressed by verb-modifying adverbs in other languages can be expressed in Cree by preverbal modifiers. In Michif these modifiers are also common:

(145) *mIyu-atuške:-w*
       well-work-AI.3
       "He works well."

(146) li bɔn mark a lɪkɔl *mIšI-mIjæstam-Ih-Iko-w*
       DAP good.F mark at school big-be.glad-CAUS-INV-3
       "Good marks in school make him very happy."

There are also some Cree adverbial particles that have the same function as adverbs in other languages, such as *ki:htwa:m* "again" and *mItunI* "much." These adverbial particles are also commonly used in Michif. Furthermore there are also many indeclinable particles from French, such as *a pi pre* "approximately," *dɪ kučym* "usually," *surtu* "especially," and so on. Cree adverbs are more than twice as common as French adverbs (see Chapter Five). Some types are more commonly used in either language.

In French, manner adverbs can be formed productively from adjectives by the addition of the suffix *-ement*, but this does not exist in Michif. Michif often uses the Cree preverbal modifiers, but adjectives are also made into adverbs by the addition of the preposition *ã* (F. *en*) in front of the adjective. We have only a few rare examples, as in the following:

(147) *či:stast-am* si parɔl ã grus
       pick-TI.3→4 POSS-3P word in big
       "She speaks in an affected way."

(148) ã rɔf *pi:klškwe:-w*
       in rough speak.AI-3
       "He speaks in a rough way."

Coordinating Conjunctions

The Cree word *ma:ka* is used for "but"; rarely is the French-derived *mɛ* used. In Michif two noun phrases can be connected by *pi* "and" (from F. *puis* "and then") and rarely *avik* (F. *avec* "with"). Sometimes the Cree forms *e:kwa* or *mi:na* are used for this construction. French *et* does not occur in the data. Michif *ubǽ* or *ubǽdũ* is used for "or," from the French *ou bien/ou bien donc* "or" (these are emphatic forms in French; the normal form is *ou*). Sentences can also be connected by the Cree *e:kwa* "and" and French *pi*, and probably *ubǽdũ* as well. Cree and French verbs are sometimes connected by *pi*.

(149) pi:kupIč-Ika:t-e:-wa *pi dɪsk-i*
       fallow-PASS-DIR-4.PL and disk-INFL
       "They (INAN) are fallowed and disked."

Discourse Particles

Many discourse particles are used in Michif, most of them from Cree, such as *e:ša* ("it is said"; used in fairy tales), *ma:na* "usually," and the hesitation element *aji* "ehm." In narratives, English elements also appear, such as "but" and "well."

Morphology

Some morphological aspects have been mentioned in passing, such as Cree verb morphology and nominalized verbs in *-hk*, *-wIn*, and *-kan*. Other suffixes added to nouns are the diminutive *-Is* (perhaps not used in Michif) and *-Ipan*, which is added to nouns that denote persons who have died. The latter is sometimes added to French and Cree nouns in Michif, for example, *mũ vjæ-Ipan* "my deceased husband."

In this section I discuss French derivational and compositional noun morphology and the combination of French and Cree, as well as English, elements within the boundaries of one word.

FRENCH NOMINAL DERIVATION

French compositional and derivational morphology is severely reduced in Michif. New concepts seem to be expressed by circumlocution rather than by composition or derivation. Only a few of the many French derivational suffixes are used productively in Michif. These can be added to French and sometimes English stems. They show that the French component of Michif is not all fossilized but is still subject to productive word-formation rules (Papen 1987b, 1988). In table 4.2 there are some

TABLE 4.2 French Derivational Morphology in Michif

Michif	Morphemes	Standard French
lı vɔl-æž "theft"	(F. *vol-* "steal" + F. *-age*)	(F. *le vol* "theft")
sykr-æž "a sweet"	(F. *sucre* "sugar" + F. *-age*)	(F. *bonbon*)
trɔst-ab "trustworthy"	(E. *trust* + F. *-able*)	(F. *fiable*)
bɛg-œr, bɛg-œz "beggar"	(E. *beg* + F. *-eur/euse*)	[F. *mendiant(e)*]
avarısœ "miser"	(F. *avare* + F. *-isseux, -isseuse*)	(F. *avare*)
ažãsri "office"	(F. *agence* + F. *-erie*)	(F. *agence*)
kũtãtri "happiness"	(F. *content* "happy" + F. *-erie*)	(F. *bonheur*)
lãtũ, lãtɔn "slowpoke"	(F. *lent* "slow" + F. *-on, -onne*)	[F. *lambin(e)*]
kũfidasjũ "confidence"	[F. *confid(ence)* + F. *-ation*]	(F. *confidence*)
pwɛsũnjĩ "fisherman"	(F. *poisson* "fish" + F. *-ier*)	(F. *pêcheur*)
pruvas "proof"	[F. *prouv(er)* + F. *-asse*]	(F. *preuve*)

examples of lexical elements in which these mostly nominalizing suffixes have formed words that do not exist in French dialects.

The pattern most often used for extending the lexicon is circumlocution, which creates analytic constructions rather than compounds (usually N Prep N; often N ã N, N dı N). This is a common pattern in French. In the following examples Michif has a circumlocution where French has a separate word:

(150)   ɛn butaj ã vıtr
        DAFS bottle in glass
        "a carafe" (F. *une carafe*)

(151)   ɛn mæ̃zũ d lɔg
        a house of log
        "a log house" (F. *une cabane*)

(152)   æ̃ pči pwɛsũ d-ɔr
        DAMS little fish of-gold
        "a goldfish" (F. *poisson rouge*)

MIXTURE OF FRENCH AND CREE WITHIN WORDS

Usually French and Cree are not mixed within word boundaries. In my questionnaire data, the mixed forms account for less than 1 percent of the verbs. There are a number of ways, however, in which French and Cree elements can co-occur in one word. In all these cases, a French stem appears with Cree inflection. These are separated by what seem to be dummy elements.

In all Michif dialects it is possible to convert French and English nouns and adjectives into Cree verbs that have the approximate meaning "to be X-y" by means of the Cree suffix *-Iwl-* "to be," to which the appropriate inflectional endings are suffixed. This is a productive process. The suffix does not seem to be used with Cree stems, however (see the preceding section on copulas and Chapter Eight).

(153) *kIja:pIt* lı bœr dılɛt-*Iw-an*
       still DAMS butter milk-BE-4
       "The butter is still milky."

(154) *ki:*-lı-fu-*IwI-w e:*-lı-pči-*IwI-t*
       PST-DAMS-crazy-BE-3S.AN COMP-DAMS-little-BE-3S.AN
       "He was crazy when he was small."

(155) *ma:ma: gi:-It-Iko-na:n e:ka:* la-tɛt-džyr-*IwI-ja:hk*
       mother 1.PST-speak-INV-TA.3→1P NEG DAFS-head-hard-BE-1PL
       "Mother told us not to be boneheads."

Most of these examples are nouns with French definite articles. Some are adjectives accompanied by the article. This article seems to be a dummy element used to indicate a non-Cree form integrated into a Cree word.

Another productive Cree verbal suffix that may be added to French, and presumably English, adjectives and nouns is *-Ihke:* "to make" (see also example 74). Again, the French article is required:

(156) lı-žalı-*Ihke:-w*
       DAMS-pretty-MAKE-TA.3→3'
       "S/he is decorating him/her."

Finally, a small set of French and English verbal lexical items may perhaps take the full set of Cree verb inflectional affixes. Many of these verbs seem to refer to nontraditional actions, such as *bénir* "to bless," *témoigner* "to witness in court," and *bousiller* "to plaster." Others, however, cannot be considered as such: for example, *astiner* "to argue" (< F. *obstiner*?), *broder* "to embroider," *arranger* "to fix," and so on. The way in which these verbs are integrated into the Cree verb pattern is rather unusual: it is always the inflected form of the French verb (infinitive and participle) that is used, and the French masculine definite article is prefixed to it. The French verb retains its original phonological structure.

(157) lı pɛr *ki:*-lı-bın-i-*w* lı mu:d
       DAMS priest PST-DAMS-bless-INF-TA.3→3' DAMS people
       "The priest blessed the people."

(158) *kIškejIm-e:w* džan su mɛtr *ka:*-l-asčın-i-*čIk*
       know.TA-TA.3→3' John his master COMP-DAMS-argue-INF-3P
       "John knows who his master is when they argue."

Some English verbs (such as "to celebrate," "to haul," "to settle," "to deal," "to can," "to rob," "to box," and "to gamble," many of which denote nontraditional activities) can be used in the same way: these retain English phonemes but require the French masculine definite article, as well as the French ending *-er/é* [i:]. These have Cree person marking and can also have Cree tense and mood marking and preverbs, but apparently not inverse and causative markers.

(159)   lɪ kat dɪ žyjɛt *gi:*-lɪ-sɛlibre:t-i-*na:n*
         DAMS four of July 1PST-DAMS-celebrate-INF-AI.1P
         "We celebrated the Fourth of July."

(160)   nu *ki:-kIške:ht-am* la bãk *e:-ki:*-lɪ-rab-i-*hk*
         NEG PST-know.TI-TI3→4 DAFS bank COMP-PST-DAMS-rob-INF-IMPERS.
         "He did not know about the bank being robbed."

These morphological aspects will be discussed in more detail in Chapter Eight.

Summary

A grammatical sketch of Michif is given in this chapter. Michif is mixed in all respects except one—its phonological system. Its phonology consists of two completely separate systems, one for the Cree part and one for the French part. These systems do not influence each other at all. English elements are phonologically adjusted toward the French component, never toward the Cree. This has a parallel in Basque dialects, in which French borrowings are adapted to Gascon (the former prestige language) rather than Basque (Haase 1992).

There is a striking categorial dichotomy in Michif. Verbs are virtually always Cree, and nouns are almost always French. There are a few French and English verbs with Cree affixes. French nouns are accompanied by French articles—distinct according to gender and definiteness, exactly as in French—but French demonstratives are rarely, if ever, used. Instead, the Cree demonstratives display gender agreement with the noun according to the Cree system; that is, the form of the demonstrative differs according to the animate or inanimate gender of the nouns. Cree or Ojibwe nouns sometimes have French articles and sometimes Cree affixes attached. Numerals are French. Usually only the Cree numeral "one" is known. Question words are virtually always from Cree. Function words (question words, discourse particles, etc.) are mostly Cree, except for the French articles, prepositions, and a reasonable number of adjectives. Most of the other categories (adjectives, pre- and postpositions, adverbs, negation, and conjunctions) are drawn from both languages, with some regional variation. The differences are summarized in table 4.3.

It is not possible to make definitive statements about constituent order. Word order in the clause seems to be free, as in Cree, but French definitely has an influence. The word order in the noun phrase is close to French word order, with three differences: quantifiers can be separated from the noun phrases (as in Cree but quite unlike French); numerals precede articles, whereas in French articles precede numerals; possessors precede the possessed in Michif, whereas the order is the opposite in French.

Overall, the structure of the language seems closer to Cree than to French. That the verbs are Cree is in line with the observation that in Algonquian languages like Cree, the verb is the basic element of the sentence. It often gives a summary of the action in one word, whereas English would use many words to express the same content. It could be argued that Michif is Cree with massive French intrusion, whereas intrusion in the opposite direction would be much more difficult to defend. In the

TABLE 4.3 Approximate Proportion of Language Source for Each Grammatical Category

Category	Language(s)
Nouns	83–94% French; rest Cree or Ojibwe, English
Verbs	88–99% Cree; few French verbs; some mixed Cree and French
Question words	Almost all Cree
Personal pronouns	Almost all Cree
Adverbial particles	70% Cree; 30% French
Postpositions	Almost all Cree
Coordinate conjunctions	55% Cree; 40% French; 5% English
Prepositions	70–100% French; rest Cree
Numerals	Almost all French
Demonstratives	Almost all Cree
Negation	Roughly 70% French; 30% Cree

first study of Michif (Rhodes 1977), the French elements were considered to be "a case of borrowing." Michif is the only language in the world with such a mixture of languages across categories.

The sketch in this chapter is based on the dialects of Patline Laverdure and Ida Rose Allard (1983), the two authors of the Michif dictionary from Turtle Mountain, North Dakota. In the next chapter I show that the Michif dialects spoken in Canadian Métis communities are in fact identical to this dialect, although there is some regional variation.

Variation in Michif

Introduction

One may wonder whether the description in Chapter Four of the Michif language as spoken in Turtle Mountain, North Dakota, holds true for the varieties of the language spoken in scattered locations in Canada as well. In this chapter I show that Michif as spoken in a number of Métis communities in the Canadian prairie provinces is virtually identical to the Michif of Turtle Mountain. However, there are also villages where the local mixture of Cree and French differs significantly from the Turtle Mountain dialect.

Variation in Michif has been described by researchers in completely contradictory terms. On the one hand, Papen (1987b: 248) states that there is great variability among Michif speakers: "A realistic way of looking at Métif [Michif] is to consider that it represents a continuum with French and Cree at the opposite poles," which would imply an almost infinitely variable language or even a spectrum of different languages (see Papen 1986a and b, 1987a). Rhodes (1986: 288), on the other hand, writes: "Where Michif exists, it is as uniform as any Algonquian language," adding that Algonquian languages are more variable than linguists tend to think. Crawford (1983a: viii) takes an intermediate position: "It is true that there is quite a lot of dialect variation shown by speakers of Michif . . ."; however, "this dialect variation, although appreciable, is not greater than that shown within many language groups." And he adds: "Much more remarkable than the dialect differences that exist on the [Turtle Mountain] reservation is the consistency that Michif shows in a variety of locales" Crawford (1985b) already suggested that Michif dialect (i.e., variation) research was needed urgently, and I hope that this chapter will not remain the only study on the subject.

There is indeed little variation among Michif dialects spoken in Saskatchewan, Manitoba, and North Dakota, that is, no more than in other comparable languages.

Despite the geographical spread, the language is remarkably uniform among the settlements. There are no problems of comprehension whatsoever among Michif speakers of different communities. There can be no doubt that it is one and the same language.

These villages are between 100 and almost 170 years old, which suggests that the Michif language was already crystallized before these communities were populated. The people had taken the language with them to their present locations, and they have coexisted more or less separated from one another for more than a century. Michif's situation is, therefore, rather unusual among the languages of the world: the speakers do not live in a contiguous area. Furthermore, the social circumstances are different in all these communities, and other languages are spoken by non-Métis in the same villages. Many Michif speakers use other languages in addition to Michif and English, and some of their fellow nationals speak entirely different languages again. Therefore it would be interesting to study both intercommunity and intracommunity variations.

There are minor differences in the speech of the diverse Michif communities. Although it is clearly the same language, with the same verb-noun dichotomy, some communities appear to be oriented more toward French, having mostly French prepositions, adverbs, and so on; others draw mainly on Cree for some of the less central grammatical categories.

I do not describe the variation as a subject in its own right but with the goal of learning how the Michif language emerged. Although the variability may be interesting in itself, I use the data in this study only to determine whether there is one Michif language with a normal range of dialectal variation or a number of independent mixtures of Cree and French. If there were independent mixtures that happened to show striking similarities, that fact would have to be explained. Indeed, it becomes clear in the course of this chapter that not all mixtures of French and Cree stem from this source. In fact, three types of mixtures appear in the data. Apart from Michif, a mixture of Cree and French, which is basically Cree with relatively few French words, is spoken in a region in Saskatchewan. At several essential points it differs from Michif. It is clear that this dialect came into being independently of the other dialects. These two groups of dialects are spoken by people who do not necessarily know both French and Cree; in fact, only a very small minority knows both. In addition to these two Cree-French mixtures, there are also fluent speakers of both French and Cree who mix the two languages in ways different from the others. They make up a third type.

The study of the nature of these three variations can lead to several insights concerning the origin of Michif. First, the fact that there are three different types of mixtures of Cree and French is indicative of the different processes that were at work in these cases. In this chapter I indeed propose different processes as responsible for the three types of mixtures. Second, the homogeneity of the Michif language (as one of the three different types of mixtures) across the different communities shows that the language must have crystallized into a separate language before these communities were settled. Third, the linguistic variations among the different Michif-speaking communities indicate some of the changes the local dialects have undergone under the influence of diverse social circumstances and, in particular, different situations of multilingualism. Does knowledge of French or an Amerindian language, for instance, influence the form of Michif spoken by bilinguals?

To answer this type of questions, I studied variations in diverse communities where Michif or Cree and French are spoken. In 1990 I conducted a survey among speakers of Michif and some Métis speakers of other languages, plus some Indian speakers of Cree and Ojibwe. I visited a number of Métis and Indian communities in Manitoba, Saskatchewan, Alberta, and North Dakota. The objective of my visits was to see whether the mixtures of Cree and French spoken in these communities are identical or different. If there were differences among these communities, what had caused them? Was it an independent mixture of the two languages that had emerged in all or some of these communities, or did the mixtures stem from a common source? In more concrete terms, did these community languages already exist when the Métis were still living together in the Red River settlement or when they regularly met during the period of buffalo hunts, or did they create their mixture of Cree and French only after they had settled in the communities where they live now? Or is the language an incidental mixture made up on the spot?

When people mix languages, in this case French and Cree, there are in principle a limited number of possibilities:

(1) It could be *spontaneous language mixture* (*code mixing*), in which case one would expect much variation and fluent knowledge of both French and Cree.

(2) There could also be a number of *different mixed languages*, all based on French and Cree but which emerged locally among French-Cree bilinguals. In that case one would expect more or less different mixtures of the two languages in the different communities, especially where people do not necessarily speak Cree or French today. There will be common features in the mixture of the languages, but one can expect significant differences as well, especially in the less central grammatical categories. One would expect little intracommunity but considerable intercommunity variation. In these communities, the people are not spontaneously mixing languages, but they have a fixed code of mixture locally.

(3) Finally, it is possible that exactly the *same mixture* of French and Cree is spoken in all communities, with only little interpersonal and intercommunity variation. In this case, we can be certain that the language existed prior to the settlement of these communities and therefore prior to the dispersion(s) of the Métis.

I begin with a brief outline of the method I used to obtain roughly comparable data from almost thirty speakers. Then, to give an impression of the diverse social circumstances, I introduce the communities where I carried out my research on the French-Cree mixture, after which I present the results. I measure the proportion in which the different source languages contributed to a number of grammatical categories from some twenty-two speakers. Then I show that one of the mixtures of French and Cree is definitely not the same as the Michif language of the other communities. I also measure how close the language of my subjects is to the source dialects of French and Cree. All speakers appear to diverge from the source languages. Finally, I briefly review the three types of mixtures that surfaced through the questionnaire. In the end I summarize the results.

Method

I made a questionnaire to obtain comparable data from different speakers. As Michif is spoken only by older people, often only a handful in a community, it did not appear possible to obtain data from a representative sample of different age groups, social classes, both sexes, and so on. I worked with all the people who spoke the language and who were willing and able to work with me. As my goal was to obtain data about dialect differences, to see whether these dialects arose from a common source or developed independently, possible social differences in speech were less central to the goal of this study. Only the data of the people who completed the whole questionnaire are presented in this chapter.

I also conducted interviews to obtain samples of spontaneously spoken language. It depended on a number of factors whether particular persons would translate the questionnaire or would be interviewed. In principle I left it up to the people themselves, who often had a preference.

The questionnaire consisted of a list of some 200 sentences and a few phrases, which I read aloud in English. Michif speakers then translated this orally into Michif. This took between forty-five minutes and one-and-a-half hours per person. All the results of these questionnaires were tape-recorded in the homes of the consultants. If anything was unclear, I asked my informants to repeat what they had just said. Later I completely transcribed these tapes. Before starting, I told the consultants that they could speak in any way they wanted, that I was interested in French and Cree mixed ("the Michif language"), and that the use of English words was allowed whenever they felt it was natural. The questionnaire also contained questions about language use in the community, both in the past and present, and data about the interviewees' genealogy and the languages used by their ancestors, as far back as they could remember. These questions were asked after the translation task and as informally as possible. In not all cases did it appear to be possible to obtain these data. The material produced with the questionnaire was used in order to have data available that could be compared directly, to reveal the differences within a community and among the communities. In the questionnaire I used words, phrases, and syntactic constructions that I expected, on the basis of my earlier fieldwork, to yield diagnostic words or grammatical structures with interesting variations.

Complete questionnaire data were obtained from a total of twenty-nine people, most of them speakers of French and Cree mixed and also some speakers of nonmixed Native languages or Métis French for comparison. The Michif speakers were all born between 1904 and 1933 (ages at the time of the interview ranged from 57 to 86). The oldest Michif speaker that I met, by the way, was born around 1894, but because of his health problems he was not consulted on the questionnaire. He was about 96 years old when I interviewed him. All of these people spoke English in addition to the language about which they were interviewed (Michif, French, or a Native language). I have not encountered monolingual Michif speakers. Some of them could also speak French; only one could speak Cree. For virtually all of them Michif was their first language, and they had learned English only later, at school age or even older. For an overview, see table 5.1. on page 131.

Apart from the people who speak mixed French and Cree, the questionnaire was recorded with three speakers of Plains Cree[1] (Manitoba, Saskatchewan, and Alberta), one speaker of Swampy Cree, two speakers of Ojibwe (one Chippewa from North Dakota and one Saulteaux from central Manitoba), and one speaker of Métis French from North Dakota—all of them for the purpose of comparison.

For the speakers of a mixture of Cree and French, data from five communities or regions were used: Camperville (central Manitoba), Saint Lazare (southeastern Manitoba), Turtle Mountain (northern North Dakota), Fort Qu'Appelle Valley (southeastern Saskatchewan), and Ile-a-la-Crosse (northeastern Saskatchewan). Also some data were obtained from Métis in Lac La Biche, Alberta. The latter two dialects are the most divergent, as I show subsequently.

It appeared impossible to group the speakers clearly according to these communities since some of them were not originally from those places. For instance, in Camperville I interviewed people who were originally from Sainte Madeleine, not far from Saint Lazare. A brother and a sister in Camperville have grandparents on one side who were originally from Turtle Mountain. One man interviewed in the Fort Qu'Appelle Valley was originally from Willowbunch near the Wood Mountain in southwestern Saskatchewan. For the statistics, these people were counted as belonging to the community where they had spent most of their lives. There is apparently some contact between different Michif-speaking communities. Nevertheless, I encountered Michif speakers who were quite surprised to hear that their language was also spoken outside of their village, province, or state.

The Michif-speaking Communities

The communities from which questionnaire data were obtained are discussed individually. Their location can be found on map 3.

Turtle Mountain, North Dakota

Turtle Mountain is the only Michif-speaking community I visited in the United States. It is different from the Canadian communities in several ways. The number of speakers of Michif residing in and around the Turtle Mountain Chippewa Reservation in North Dakota is estimated at several hundred (Rhodes 1977). It is undoubtedly the most thriving Michif-speaking area and the largest single group anywhere. This is probably due to the considerably large size of the community throughout its existence; the fact that it is an Indian reserve; and subsequently the fact that the Métis people here were not discriminated against as much as in Canada, where the Métis were legally no different from whites but where Indians and Métis alike are still looked down on by large segments of the white population. Giraud has a similar analysis:

> The population [of the Turtle Mountain Reservation], which is in essence formed of Canadian Métis who were recruited from the Pembina winterers and from Saint-François-Xavier and Wood Mountain . . . owes to advantages of all kinds assured to them, the fact that they could avoid the material deprivation of the prairie groups.

They did not undergo the demoralizing effects of hostility or contempt of the Whites, nor the repercussions of a competition they could not sustain. (1945: 1281)[2]

Speakers of Michif can also be found in communities like Walhalla and Grand Forks in North Dakota, with whom Turtle Mountain people have regular contacts. The Michif language of Turtle Mountain was the subject of a number of articles, such as Rhodes (1977) and Crawford (1973a and b, 1976, 1983b, 1985a and b).

The Turtle Mountain area differs from the Canadian communities in a number of important respects. First, the largest part, where the Michif speakers live, is an Indian reservation ("reservation" is the American term; "reserve" is Canadian). The American reservation policy is different from the Canadian policy for reserves. Some of these differences are discussed in Chapter Three. They can be summarized as follows:

- In the United States, everybody with at least "one-quarter" of Indian "blood" (sometimes other proportions apply) can claim Indian status. In Canada, however, one is an Indian only if one ancestor is on a list of people who signed a treaty with the government in the nineteenth century.

- In Canada, non-Indians are in principle not allowed to live on reserves, but in the United States anyone can live on reservation land, although non-Indians would not receive certain services there such as medical care.

- On Canadian reserves, stores and businesses of any importance can rarely be found (especially on the prairies), whereas in North Dakota there may be complete shopping malls on the reservation, with businesses often owned by Natives. This, at least, is the case on the Turtle Mountain Reservation.

- Since Canadian Métis are by definition not allowed to live on Indian reserves, they have always lived in communities with at least some whites. As it does not fit into traditional Native values to ask payment for food and services, only a few Métis have started businesses, so that they are almost always economically and numerically dominated by whites. This, however, has never been the case for the Métis at the Turtle Mountain Reservation, where they have had many more opportunities to continue their traditions independently of white people.

On the Turtle Mountain Reservation, in fact, two distinct population groups (ethnic groups) are living side by side (apart from a few white people): on the one hand, those who are called "full bloods" and, on the other hand, the Métis (Gourneau 1980: 9). They are different culturally, linguistically, and historically. The group of full bloods is, and always has been, much smaller than the group of Métis. The Métis are the most important group, both in numbers and in prestige, on the reservation.

Culturally, the full bloods follow many Indian traditions, such as offering tobacco before telling sacred stories, the use of "bad medicine" (magic), playing drums,

and until recently the organization of sun dances (Turtle Mountain Indian Reservation 1985: 91). The Métis, however, have no restrictions on telling the Amerindian
sacred stories (*les contes*), they do not use "bad medicine," they do not make music
with drums (they sing and play the fiddle), nor do they ordinarily participate in sun
dances (see also Chapter Three).

Linguistically, the full bloods (also called Chippewas on the reservation, as
opposed to Métis) speak an Amerindian language. For most of them this is a dialect
of Ojibwe, locally called Chippewa. It seems that two dialects of Ojibwe coexist,
namely, a Chippewa dialect from Minnesota and a Plains Ojibwe dialect closer to
Saulteaux, that is, Canadian Ojibwe (Richard Rhodes, pers. comm., 1990). Less than
a handful of Chippewa people speak Cree, as well as Ojibwe. The Métis speak Michif,
the mixture of French and Cree. Most, if not all, of the older Chippewas also speak
Michif—until fairly recently the dominant tongue on the reservation—but few, if any,
Métis also speak Chippewa or Cree. Very few speak French, that is, the Métis variety of this language. Many of the Métis also use the name Chippewa for the Cree
language (Rhodes 1982:7) because Cree is used as an alternative name for Michif,
as in Canada. For them, "Chippewa" means an Indian language (Cree or Ojibwe)
without French. In both ethnic groups, a language shift is taking place toward English. Probably few people under 40 are able to speak either Michif or Chippewa.
Cree is already virtually extinct on the reservation. Michif is taught at the local community college but not Cree or Chippewa.

Historically, the two ethnic groups are also different. For the Métis of the Plains,
the Turtle Mountains were hunting grounds from the early 1800s onward, where they
came seasonally. Some Métis families stayed there more or less permanently from
an early date, possibly around 1840 (Giraud 1945: 779, 809, 818). The Chippewas
of the Turtle Mountain Reservation are descendants of Ojibwe hunters of the Plains,
in particular those of the band who stayed around the fur traders' fort at Pembina,
almost 200 kilometers east of the reservation. They had come originally from the
Minnesota woodlands (Gourneau 1980). The official name later became Turtle
Mountain–Pembina Band. They signed a treaty in 1863, when they had fewer than
300 members. In December 1882 this band was granted a reservation in the Turtle
Mountains. When two of the chiefs settled on the reservation immediately after its
creation, a number of Métis were already living on the grounds reserved for the Turtle
Mountain Reservation. They stayed there, and new groups of Métis associated with
the Turtle Mountain–Pembina Band (Turtle Mountain Indian Reservation 1985: 89)
also arrived in the subsequent decades. Some of these Métis were Canadian refu-
gees, who had fled to the United States after the defeat of the Métis at the 1869 Riel
resistance in Manitoba (see Chapter Three).

The Métis must have been the largest ethnic group from the beginning of the
reservation. In 1892, a state commission counted 1759 members, 1476 "mixed bloods"
and 283 "full-bloods." Although these probably biological measurements cannot be
equated with differences between the two ethnic groups, they can be taken to be
indicative of the numerical dominance of the Métis at the reservation. Later cen-
suses—using different methods with growing degrees of flexibility and therefore
not directly comparable with one another—show similar tendencies. In 1904, 201
full bloods and 1,893 mixed bloods were counted, and in 1940, 7,317 reservation

members were counted, 160 of which were full bloods. In 1964, over 23,000 members were counted, with fewer than 100 full bloods (Turtle Mountain Indian Reservation 1985: 93). Today the band has approximately 10,000 members, many of which live outside the reservation.

Both the Chippewas and the Métis distinguish the two coexisting ethnic groups. The Métis call the Chippewas *les sauvages* (which for them does not have the deprecatory sense that it has for us), best translated as "Indians." The government does not make this distinction: as long as the Métis have one-quarter of "Indian blood," they fall under the responsibility of the Bureau of Indian Affairs and are legally Indians. This means they have certain treaty rights with regard to medicine and other public services, which are free for Indians. For this reason, the Métis may call themselves Indians in a general sense, something that Canadian Métis would never do. In Canada, Métis rarely participate in powwow dances (in the Indian tradition), whereas this is quite common on the Turtle Mountain Reservation. Nevertheless, the members of the Turtle Mountain Band know very well to which of the two ethnic groups they themselves and others belong. And for the vast majority, this is the Métis group.

Both groups are spread over the reservation. In the adjacent towns (especially Dunseith and Saint John) and in the rural area, there are also Chippewas and especially Métis. Dances are regularly held on the reservation and in the adjacent villages, where local Métis fiddlers provide the music (Vrooman 1984). Singing in French in public places, once common in all Michif-speaking communities, is no longer practiced.

Saint Lazare, Manitoba

Saint Lazare, Manitoba, is a Métis community that arose on the forks of the Assiniboine and Qu'Appelle rivers, where a fur-trading post, Fort Ellice, was established before 1840. In 1880 twenty families from Saint François Xavier (Red River settlement) settled here (Giraud 1945: 1138). I estimate the number of inhabitants today at around 400.

One of the most striking features of this community is the large number of French-speaking immigrant families, most of which seem to have emigrated from France around the turn of this century. I do not know whether they came directly from France. Despite the European origin of these French speakers, their French is Canadian French, for reasons unclear to me. French is still spoken widely, although it is losing ground to English. Among the older people, it is still commonly used on a daily basis, but young people speak only English. The Métis in Saint Lazare still form a significant proportion of the population (I estimate almost half). The community is dominated by the French Canadians, especially by one family clan. There are regular contacts between the two groups, but most of the Métis marry other Métis (Giraud 1945: 1272–1273). The Métis also tend to live near the fringes of the community. Some of the people who say that they are French Canadians are said to be Métis, too.

Michif is spoken only by people older than 60. I estimate the number of speakers between ten and twenty in Saint Lazare. As far as I know, all of them speak French and English, too. Nevertheless, the Métis say that they "speak French different from the way the [French families] do" (Louis of Saint Lazare in 1990).

Qu'Appelle Valley, Saskatchewan

The Qu'Appelle Valley is not really one community but rather a series of towns and villages along the Qu'Appelle River east of Fort Qu'Appelle (including this town, which is a regional center) and some towns nearby. Métis winterers stayed here as early as the 1840s (Giraud 1945: 1259). A large number of families settled in the valley in the 1870s, arriving from Saint François Xavier in the Red River settlement (Giraud 1945: 1137). In the past, some Métis families lived in isolated coulees in the valley; but today, having moved to the towns, they form a minority among the white people in all of the towns in the valley. However, in the 1930s the Métis were still the largest ethnic group in, for example, Lebret (Giraud 1945: 1273). I have personally met Michif speakers in Fort Qu'Appelle, Lebret, Katepwa, Balcarres, and Lestock, and I also heard about some in Indian Head, Abernethy, Marieval, and on some of the Cree reserves in the area, notably Peepeekisis (Fredeen 1991: 102–10) and Crooked Lake (Giraud 1945: 1138).

I estimate the number of Michif speakers in this area to be between fifty and one hundred. A significant number have moved away, especially to the big cities of the province, Saskatoon and Regina. Many of the Métis in the area married non-Métis, and some speakers here deny being able to speak the language at all, although others claim that this is not true. Some of the Michif speakers also know French, but many of the younger Métis speak only English. Until several decades ago, French was still used in the church in Lebret. There may also be speakers who know Cree, as there are Cree reserves in the area.

Camperville, Manitoba

Camperville was described to me by a Métis employee of the Manitoba Metis Federation as "the last 100 percent Métis community that we have." There are indeed very few whites living in the community of about 500 people (mostly teachers), so almost everybody is Métis. A description from an economic viewpoint can be found in Woodley (1978). The village is adjacent to the Pine Creek Reserve, where Saulteaux, the local name for Ojibwe, is spoken. North of the Pine Creek Reserve is the Métis community of Duck Bay.

The relationship between the Métis of Camperville and the Indians of Pine Creek is ambivalent. On the one hand, there is some animosity between them. For example, if wedding parties or dances, which are held almost every weekend either on the reserve or in Camperville, become too wild, the fight that results is usually between one person from the reserve and one from the Métis community. The custom is that other people watch but do not join in.

Despite these skirmishes, marriages between Métis and people from Pine Creek are common. Most of the people of Camperville have relatives in Pine Creek and vice versa. In fact, these marriages have been common for such a long time that the Camperville people shifted away from Michif, still the colloquial language of the community in the 1930s (de Mishaegen 1946: 106), to Saulteaux. Many of the people who learned Michif as a first language now speak Saulteaux with their partners, and often to their fellow Métis. Probably all the people who speak Michif also speak

Saulteaux (Barkwell et al. 1989: 141). In Camperville, most people in their 40s and some in their 30s can speak Saulteaux, which is said to be identical to the Saulteaux as spoken on the Pine Creek Reserve. Some Duck Bay people speak Cree or Michif, and a few people in Camperville speak French. All, except for a handful, speak English, which is the only language many of the young people speak. On the Pine Creek Reserve, there is a similar move away from the aboriginal language toward English.

I estimate the number of Michif speakers in Camperville to be between twenty and fifty, so they form a small minority here. Some of them are immigrants or descendants of immigrants from other communities, such as Sainte Madeleine, which was a Métis community until the 1930s. At that time the people were evicted and the houses burned to make the land available for cattle breeding by changing it into community pasture (Zeilig and Zeilig 1987). The community is described in miserable terms by Giraud (1945: 1259, 1266–1269). The people who settled here were winterers and bison hunters, originally from Saint François Xavier and some from Baie Saint Paul, in the Red River settlement. Until eviction, it must have been a predominantly Michif-speaking community (with some French), where all the inhabitants were Métis. Today, the people from Saint Madeleine live all over the prairies, for instance, in Binscarth, Birtle, Brandon, and Camperville. One of my consultants for the questionnaire, Robert from Camperville, was born in Sainte Madeleine, but his speech appears not to differ in any significant way from the other Michif speakers from Camperville.

Ile-a-la-Crosse, Saskatchewan

Ile-a-la-Crosse is a community of approximately 1200 people, about 90 percent of whom are Métis, in northern Saskatchewan. It is one of the most important Métis communities in Saskatchewan, providing some of the leaders of provincial Métis organizations. It is relatively isolated, as it is situated at the end of a 20-kilometer-long peninsula. It is surrounded by the lakes and the woods of the Canadian shield. Fur-trading posts were established here, at the confluence of important rivers, at the end of the eighteenth century. The people who visited the posts were Chipewyans and Crees. It has been an important regional center for a long time; a mission center was established here in 1846 and a hospital early in this century. There is also a convent, to which a school was connected, where French was the obligatory language. Many of the Métis families from this town have French family names, only some of which are also Red River names.

Despite two local history books (Lesage 1946; Longpré 1977), it is still not clear to me when the Chipewyans disappeared from the community, when it became a Cree-speaking community, and when it evolved into a Métis community. Until a few decades ago, most families were still living off the land in the woodlands, but the obligations of school for the children forced them to move to town.

The language spoken in Ile-a-la-Crosse is a mixture of Cree and French but so different from the other communities that it has to have a different origin (as argued subsequently). It is more a dialect of Cree with some French borrowings than a truly mixed language. Most, if not all, of the older inhabitants are also fluent in Cree. Many of them also speak French, although not the young people. Cree and English, and until recently also French, are the languages used in the local Roman Catholic church. People under 20 speak only English (Fredeen 1991).

Of the four people from Ile-a-la-Crosse who responded to the questionnaire, three of them speak in a very similar way, probably close to the ordinary speech of the community. It is basically Cree with some French nouns. One woman (Beatrice) tried to mix as much French and English as she could, in a way that does not seem to reflect the natural form of speech of the village. Her speech diverges strikingly from the others, probably because of my pressure, in her case, to mix French and Cree. Nevertheless, all four are represented in the results discussed later in this chapter.

Lac La Biche Mission, Alberta

Lac La Biche is an essentially white community of about 2200 inhabitants. It is situated on a lake in the woods north of the prairie. The Cree Indian reserve of Beaver Lake lies close to the town. There are also two Métis settlements in Lac La Biche. One is a kind of permanent trailer camp 8 kilometers south of Lac La Biche and adjacent to the Indian reserve. The other Métis community is Lac La Biche Mission. Several Métis families live around the church and mission, 10 kilometers northwest of the town. Patrick Douaud (1980, 1982, 1985, 1989) described and analyzed this community, focusing on its sociolinguistic features. Most of the background information here comes from these sources.

The lake had been an Indian settlement for centuries, and a fur-trading post was established in 1798. A Catholic mission was established in 1853. According to Douaud, Métis families arrived from the Red River area between 1853 and 1872. Their descendants are the core of the fourteen Métis households at Lac La Biche Mission. White people arrived massively in Lac La Biche around the turn of the century, so that today the Métis are a minority.

The oldest people are trilingual in French, Cree, and English; some of the middle generation speak French and/or Cree in addition to English, and the young people speak only English. In Douaud's work, no mention is made of Michif or even of some more or less fixed mixture of Cree and French. According to Rhodes (1986: 22), Michif is spoken here, but I have not been able to find any speakers of it and I personally do not believe Michif exists here. All the people I taped whom I had asked to "mix French and Cree" spoke either all French or all Cree. I taped one man who did mix French and Cree, but it does not show similarities with Michif at all, nor does it seem to be a very natural mixture of the two languages—an observation independently made by my French-Cree bilingual companion, a Métis. Michif may have been spoken here in the past, as some people appeared to understand at least some of the Michif recordings I brought, but I was unable to record a single phrase that could be Michif. Nevertheless, the mixture of Cree and French as spoken by one of my consultants (François) was recorded in the questionnaire. It becomes clear that his speech differs significantly from that of others. The second respondent from Lac La Biche Mission used Cree without French or English, although he said that normally he would use some French words in his everyday speech.

A Comparison

It is clear that these communities differ in a number of ways that may affect the language use of the Métis (Crawford 1983b). First, the knowledge in the communities of languages other than Michif and English can be expected to be a big influence on the local variety of Michif. French is generally used in Saint Lazare, especially by the older people. The community of Sainte Madeleine was somewhat more isolated, but there were regular contacts with the Métis and the French people of Sainte Lazare. The four Michif speakers from Saint Lazare (Ivan, Jeanne, Katinka and Louis) all reported speaking French, too (and three of the four were observed doing so). The people of Camperville all speak Ojibwe in addition to Michif, but they do not speak French. English is usually the only other language known in Turtle Mountain and the Fort Qu'Appelle Valley. One of my respondents from Turtle Mountain is renowned for her singing in French, but even she claimed to understand "only some" French. In Ile-a-la-Crosse and Lac La Biche Mission, both French and Cree are spoken widely by older people, although Cree is more commonly used.

The second important factor is the number of white people in the community and the degree to which they exert economic dominance. In all communities there are white people. In some, as in Camperville and Ile-a-la-Crosse, the only whites are shopkeepers, teachers, and those who married Métis from the community. In Saint Lazare, the whites are dominant, both economically and numerically. In the Fort Qu'Appelle Valley, they are dominant in all sectors and look down on the Métis. This made it more difficult to find Michif speakers who were willing to cooperate.

A third factor is whether or not there are Indian reserves with Cree speakers in the area. This is the case in Lac La Biche, where there is a Cree reserve less than 30 kilometers away, and in Ile-a-la-Crosse, where a Cree reserve (Canoe Lake) can be found about 40 kilometers away as the bird flies but 100 kilometers by road in the summer. This can be connected with the fact that Cree is spoken so widely in these communities. Other neighboring Métis communities, such as Green Lake, Beauval, and Pinehouse Lake, are also predominantly inhabited by Cree speakers, and there are more than ten reserves (Sioux, Assiniboine, and Cree) in the Fort Qu'Appelle Valley. It is not known what influence this has on the knowledge of Cree of the Michif speakers in the Fort Qu'Appelle area. None of the Michif speakers I met there (in total about ten) was able to speak Cree, but some of them knew some Cree words not known in other communities. Only in Camperville do the Michif speakers appear to know a Native language, but that is the Saulteaux dialect of Ojibwe, not Cree.

The Michif speech in Camperville is characterized by, at least, a heavy phonological influence from Saulteaux. For instance, many intervocal stops and fricatives are voiced in the Camperville dialect (e.g., /š/ > [ž]; /p/ > [b]; /k/ > [g]), which puts Camperville apart from all other Michif dialects. Undoubtedly it is the influence of the dominant language, Saulteaux. There are also a number of Saulteaux particles in common use in Camperville, such as *ke:ma* for "or" instead of the more common *ubã̃ed͡ʒ* (< F. *ou bien donc*). The Plains Cree equivalent, *ahpo*, is not to my knowledge used anywhere. A number of other points in which the Camperville dialect deviates from those of the other communities is discussed later in this chapter.

A fourth factor is the status of Michif vis-à-vis the other languages in the community. In all communities there is a strong tendency to shift toward English. Before this shift, there was a tendency to shift toward Michif by Ojibwe speakers in the Turtle Mountain area, whereas Michif speakers shifted to Ojibwe in Camperville. In both areas this may be expected to have some influence on the language.

The Michif Speakers: Their Knowledge of Cree and French

It is perhaps useful to list the people who provided data for this questionnaire. All names are fictitious and have been arranged alphabetically in such a way that they reflect their geographic origin, as shown in table 5.1.

Of the twenty-nine people recorded in the questionnaire, twenty-six identify themselves as Métis. The other three are Indians. Annette is a Chippewa (Ojibwe) from the Turtle Mountain Reservation. Bernadette is a Saulteaux (Ojibwe), originally from the Pine Creek Reserve but residing in the neighboring Métis community, Camperville, with her husband (who is Métis). Craig is a Plains Cree from a reserve near Prince Albert, central Saskatchewan. All of them, and virtually all other Métis and Indians, also speak English. In the following survey of language knowledge, English is therefore left out of consideration.

Among the twenty-six who are Métis, not all speak mixed French and Cree. Debora, from the central Manitoba woodlands, speaks Swampy Cree (mixed with some English); Ellen, from Duck Bay, speaks Plains Cree (mixed extensively with English); Françoise, from Turtle Mountain, speaks French; and Ernest, from Lac La Biche Mission, speaks Plains Cree. All the other Métis, twenty-two in all, mix Cree and French. These numbers are, of course, not representative for the languages known by the Métis population as a whole (see Chapter Three) or for the Native population in any area. My primary focus was to work with those Métis who mix Cree and French, which the sample is weighted to reflect. The others were selected only for comparison.

Of the twenty-two people who speak a mixture of French and Cree, only nine claimed to be able to speak French, that is, to carry on a conversation in French of whatever variety; no normative values were applied. Most of these French-speaking people come from three of the communities surveyed: Lac La Biche Mission, Ile-a-la-Crosse, and Saint Lazare. In the first two communities, apparently not all people who mix French and Cree are actually able to speak French; André and Delia in Ile-a-la-Crosse and Ernest in Lac La Biche Mission, for instance, do not speak French. In these two communities, by the way, all the elders, including some of my consultants, are fluent in Cree.

The other French-speaking Métis are Catherine and Beatrice from Ile-a-la-Crosse. Both were raised by the French-speaking nuns in the local convent. In this community, the schools used the French language. Many people in Ile-a-la-Crosse say that the French-speaking Oblate mission is responsible for the influence of the French language.[3] (This claim is investigated later.) In Lac La Biche Mission, the French language may have been present since the mission arrived and the first Métis families settled there from 1853 onward. At least some of those people came from French-

TABLE 5.1 The Consultants, Their Communities and Their Age

Name	Year of Birth	Languages Spoken
Saskatchewan, Ile-a-la-Crosse		
André	ca. 1921	Cree, English
Beatrice	ca. 1916	Cree, French, English
Catherine	ca. 1917	Cree, French, English
Delia	ca. 1930	Cree, English
Alberta, Lac La Biche Mission		
Ernest	ca. 1950	Cree, English
François	ca. 1930	Cree, French, English
Saskatchewan, Lebret		
Gerard	1911	Michif, French, English
Saskatchewan, Lestock		
Hilaire	1919	Michif, English
Manitoba, Saint Lazare		
Ivan	ca. 1920	Michif, French, English
Jeanne	ca. 1926	Michif, French, English
Katinka	1925	Michif, French, English
Louis	1924	Michif, French, English
Manitoba, Camperville		
Nora	1934	Michif, Saulteaux, English
Olivia	1931	Michif, Saulteaux, English
Pierre	1929	Michif, Saulteaux, English
Kevin	1919	Michif, Saulteaux (?), English
Robert	1910	Cree, Michif, Saulteaux, English
Suzanne	1933	Michif, Saulteaux, English
North Dakota, Turtle Mountain		
Tina	1913	Michif, English
Ursula	1908	Michif, English
Victoria	1916	Michif, English
Valerie	1912	Michif, French, English
Zachariah	1904	Michif, English
Additional Data		
Turtle Mountain, N.D. (Chippewa/Saulteaux)		
Annette	ca. 1920	Chippewa/Saulteaux, Michif, English
Pine Creek, Manitoba (Saulteaux)		
Bernadette	ca. 1932	Saulteaux, English
Sturgeon Lake, Saskatchewan (Indian Plains Cree)		
Craig	ca. 1958	Plains Cree, English
Thicket Portage, Manitoba (Métis Swampy Cree)		
Debora	ca. 1940	Swampy Cree, English
Duck Bay, Manitoba (Métis Plains Cree)		
Ellen	ca. 1931	Plains Cree, English, Saulteaux (?)
Turtle Mountain, N.D. (Métis French)		
Françoise	ca. 1925	French, Michif (?), English

speaking parishes in the Red River settlement, so it can be assumed that they arrived with a knowledge of French.

All four of the people from Saint Lazare are speakers of French, as well as Michif. This must be related to the fact that Saint Lazare is a French-speaking community, and much of the social life among the elderly is conducted in French. Gerard, from the Fort Qu'Appelle Valley, also speaks French. He is originally from Willowbunch, however, which is also basically a francophone community (Jackson 1974). Here again, the presence of francophones must have stimulated the continued use of French by these Métis. Apparently all of the Michif speakers from the other communities (fifteen out of twenty-two people, or 68 percent) do not speak French, which is a considerable majority. If we disallow the six people from Ile-a-la-Crosse and Lac La Biche (and it becomes clear later in this chapter why it is reasonable to do so) and only count the sixteen Michif speakers from the other communities, eleven of them, or 65 percent do not speak French. Only one-third of the Michif speakers in my sample are able to speak French. Even if Ile-a-la-Crosse and Lac La Biche are included, only a minority of roughly one-third of the Michif speakers are able to speak French.

Of the twenty-two people who mix French and Cree, only seven claim to be able to speak "pure Cree," that is, a variety not mixed with French (many of the Michif speakers also call their language Cree). Two of them come from Lac La Biche Mission, four from Ile-a-la-Crosse, and one from Camperville. The first two are Cree-speaking communities, with French as a minor language and a source language for borrowings into Cree. The people speak a mixture of French and Cree that arose independently. Even if we count all the informants who speak mixed French and Cree, only a minority of 30 percent appears to speak Cree. If we leave these two communities out of consideration, there is only one person who claims to speak Cree—Robert, from Camperville (originally Sainte Madeleine). He is the only Michif speaker among my consultants who also speaks Cree. He had learned it, he said, "from our people." He is a generation older than my other Manitoba Michif informants, which may be a contributing factor. Also, his grandparents came from Crooked Lake, Saskatchewan, in the Qu'Appelle Valley, an area with a number of Cree reserves. Nevertheless, his grandparents were reportedly also speakers of Michif. All other Michif speakers claim to speak "no Cree at all" or "a little"; they say they understand "a fair bit" or "a bit." So if we disregard the two communities mentioned, only one out of seventeen Michif speakers speaks Cree, which is only 6 percent.

If we consider these Michif speakers as a kind of "random selection" (whereby every Michif speaker who was willing and able to work on the questionnaire was automatically selected), we arrive at the striking result that the great bulk of the Métis people who speak the mixture of Cree and French called Michif actually do not speak either of these languages in a nonmixed form. Virtually none of them speaks Cree, and only one in three speaks French.

This is very strong evidence that Michif is not an ad hoc mixture because its speakers do not know the languages they are supposed to mix. It is not code switching or code mixing since one must be bilingual to switch between languages. What it is is a mixed language, with two clearly separate components. This mixture of Cree and French is not haphazard but very systematic.

In the next sections I discuss the relative frequencies of French and Cree words that my subjects use in their speech, as well as what grammatical categories these words belong to.

Language Variation across Linguistic Categories

In this section I consider variations in the language of origin of the diverse linguistic categories (nouns, verbs, etc.) for all consultants who responded to the questionnaire. To give an impression of the rather limited range of variation displayed, I first present two example sentences from the questionnaire, with the results from all speakers quoted in full. Then I discuss verbs and nouns, as it is known from earlier research that verbs tend to be Cree in Michif and nouns to be French. I end with a discussion of some minor categories such as prepositions and adverbs and particles. These two categories can be either in Cree or in French. Where I give quantitative data I count tokens, not types. As I tried to use as varied a lexicon in the questionnaire as possible, the figures for types would not differ much.

In the next section I show that the language spoken in Ile-a-la-Crosse is linguistically too different from Michif to be historically connected. Next, I measure a number of points in which the Cree component of Michif differs from its equivalents in the Cree language, as well as a number of points in which the French component of Michif differs from its equivalents in the most closely related French dialect. I conclude that there are three different types of mixture displayed in the questionnaire: Cree with French borrowing (Ile-a-la-Crosse), Cree-French code mixing (Lac La Biche and Ile-a-la-Crosse), and Michif (the others).

Examples from the Questionnaire

As an illustration of the results of the questionnaire, I present two example sentences in a broad phonetic transcription from all speakers. I could not in all instances understand all the phonetic details and sometimes I had to make rather arbitrary decisions about whether to classify a sound as, for example, [č] or [c]. Nevertheless, I hope these sentences will illustrate some of the statements made in this chapter.

For both example sentences, I first give equivalent translations in Plains Cree and colloquial Canadian French. In the resulting sentences, all Cree elements are italicized. It is striking in both examples (and in fact in all of the results of the questionnaire) how close the results are for most of the speakers—except for those from Ile-a-la-Crosse and Lac La Biche, who use hardly any French.

EXAMPLE 1

"Jesus died for us."
Jesus (or *manito* "God") ki-ki:-nipo-stama:-ko-naw.   (Cree)
2–PST-die-for.him-INV-11
Jésus il est mort (*or* il a mouru) pour nous autres.   (spoken Canadian French)

Ile-a-la-Crosse

André   *mantu: gi:-nIpu-stama:-gu-naw.*
Beatrice   dži:zƏs *ki: . . . i:nipo:stama:gojahk.*
Cathérine *mantuw ki:nIpow kijanaw kIcI.*
Delia   *manituw nki:nipustama:gunaw. manituw i:ki:nipustama:gunaw.*

Lac La Biche Mission

Ernest   *kse:manto ki:nipo:stIma:gujah.*
François   II bɔ̃ dži ijamo:r pur nuzot. (with more Cree?) *kise:manituw e:gi:nipIstama:gwija:.*

Fort Qu'Appelle

Gerard   *kše:manitu ki:nIpuštama:guna:n.* that's Cree. II bɔ̃ dži ija mori:, ija . . . ija mɔ:r
           pur nuzɔt.
Hilaire   *ana ka:pma:čiwe:t ki:nIpuw* pur *kijana:n.*

Saint Lazare

Ivan   II bɔ̃ džø *nIpuw* pur *kijana:n.*
Jeanne   II bɔ̃ džø *ki:nIpuw* pur *kijana:n.*
Katinka   II bɔ̃ džø *ki:nIpu:w* pur *kijana:n.*
Louis   l bo džø *ki:nIpuw* pur *kijana:n.*

Camperville

Kevin   II bɔ̃ džø *ki:nipuw kijana:n uhčI.*
Nora   II bɔ̃ dži *ki:nipuw kijana:n uhčI.*
Olivia   II bɔ̃ džy *ki:nIpuw kija:na:n uhčI.*
Pierre   II bɔ̃ džy *ki:nIpuw kija:na:n uhčI.*
Robert   II bɔ̃ džø *ki:nipuw kijana:n uhčIh.*
Suzanne   II bɔ̃ džø *ki:nipuw kijana:n uhčIh.*

Turtle Mountain

Tina   II bɔ̃ džy *ki:nIpøw* pur *kijana:n.*
Ursula   II bɔ̃ džy *ki:nIpow* pur, you know, *kijana:n.*
Valerie   II bɔ̃ džy *ki:nIpøw* pur *nijana:n . . . kijana:n.*
Victoria   II bɔ̃ džy or zi:zy *kInIpu:w* pɔr kijana:n. II b . . . II ze:zy *kInIpuw* pɔr *kijana:n.*
Zachariah II bɔ̃ džy *ki:nIpow* pur *kijana:n.*

Turtle Mountain Chippewa

Annette   *a gišemanitu kinipuhtama:guna:n.*

Manitoba Saulteaux

Bernadette dži:zƏs *ki:nipuw kinajIn tIndžI.*

Indian Plains Cree

Craig ci:sas *ki:nipostamagunɔ.*

Métis Swampy Cree

Debora dži:zƏs *ki:nipu kina:naw usčI.*

Métis Plains Cree

Ellen   dži:z∂s *ki:nipuw kijana:n uhčI.*

Métis French

Françoise   l∂ Z∂zy. . . . II zezy krila mo:r pur nɔzɔt.

EXAMPLE 2

"The girl and the boy see a skinny horse."
iskwêsis êkwa nâpêsis ê-sîhkâci-yi-t misatim-wa kî-wâpam-êw-ak   (Cree)
girl and boy COMP-be.lean-OBV-3 horse-OBV PST-see-3→3'-P
La fille puis le garçon ils ont vu un cheval maigre.   (spoken Canadian French)

Ile-a-la-Crosse

André   *Iskwe:sIs ekwa na:pe:sis i:sahkIčijIk mIstatImwa wa:pami:wak.*
Beatrice   *napi:sIs ana gwe:sIs wa:pama:t æ̃ šval mɛ:gr. či:katIm. šihkati:w mIstatIm*
Catherine   *Iskwe:sIs ascI na:pe:sis wa:pami:wak i:si:hkačijIt mIstatImwa.*
Debora   *Iskwi:sIs ɛkwa napi:sIs wa:pami:w i:sIhkacijim mIstatImwa.*

Lac La Biche Mission

Ernest   *ušInigIkwɔw egwa ušini wa:pame;w išigačik mIstatImwa.*
François   la fij i le garsɔ̃ ijɔ̃ vø ∂̃ *šeniwatImwa.*

Fort Qu'Appelle Valley

Gerard   l garsɔ̃ *ekwa* la fij *ki:wa:pame:wak* æ̃ žval mɛ:gr.
Hilaire   l garsõ pi la fij *ki:wa:pame:wak* æ̃ š∂val mɛg.

Saint Lazare

Ivan   II pči garsū pi la pčit fij *ki:wa:pame:wak* æ̃ šval mɛg.
Jeanne   la fij pi la . . . l∂ garsɔ̃ *ki:wa:pame:wak* æ̃ žwal mɛgr.
Katinka   la pčit fij pi l∂ pči garsū *ki:wa:pame:wak* æ̃ žwal mɛ:gr.
Louis   l∂ pči ga pi la fij *ki:wa:pame:wak* æ̃ žwal mɛ:g.

Camperville

Nora   la pčit fij či garsɔ̃ *gi:wa:pame:w∂* æ̃ pči . . . æ̃ pči žwal.
Olivia   la pčit fij *egwa* pči garsɔ̃ *ki:wa:pame:wak e:kawak* æ̃ žwal *e:kawak katahkasowijIt.*
Pierre   la pčit fij *egwa* l pči gars *wa:pame:wak* æ̃ žval *e:kawa:kitasojIt.*
Kevin   ɛn fij *egwa* æ̃ garsū   *gi:wa:pame:wak* æ̃ žwal ɛ: . . . *ka:kawa:kɔtɔšut.*
Robert   *ki:wa:pame:w∂* la fij *egwa* la garsɔ̃ *ki:wa:pame:wak e:ka:wa:patIsujIt* æ̃ žval.
Suzanne   li garsū *egwa* la fij *gi:wa:pame:wak* æ̃ žwal *e:ga:wa:gatɔšejIt.*

Turtle Mountain

Valerie   la fij *kwa* II garsɔ̃ æ̃ žwal mɛs *ki:wa:pame:wak.*
Victoria   l∂ pči garsɔ̃ pi la fij *ki:wa:pame:wak* æ̃ žwal mæ̃gr.
Ursula   la fij *ekwa* l garsɔ̃ *wa:pame:wak* æ̃ žval mɛgr.
Tina   II garsɔ̃ pi la fij *wa:pame:wak* æ̃ žwal mɛ:g.
Zachariah   l garsɔ̃ pi la fij *ki:wa:pame:wak* æ̃ žwal mɛg.

Turtle Mountain Chippewa

Annette   kwi:wzẽs awɛ ogwa:bama:n mIstatimo:n gawahdadzozInIk.

Manitoba Saulteaux

Bernadette   skIni:gwawɛt egwa that boy obiwa:bama:n mIstatIm ø̃pakate:dIt mIstadImu:n

Indian Plains Cree

Craig   Iskwi:sIs e:gwa na:pi:sIs wa:pame:wak gi:pa:wni:t mIsatImwah.

Manitoba Métis Swampy Cree

Debora   iskwe:sIs ekwa na:pe:sIs ki:wa:pame:wak utI e:pawani:nIt mIsta:tImwa.

Métis Plains Cree

Ellen   ɔškani:kIškwe:w eta gušklnigu wa:pame:wak e:pa:kahde:t o:rs.

Métis French

Françoise   ll garsõ pi la pčit fij ijavy (. . .) hors, so pči žwal.

The first example sentence from the questionnaire is "Jesus died for us," chosen for the possibility of expressing it in a synthetic or analytic way. For example, most of the speakers from Ile-a-la-Crosse use a synthetic verb in which the benefactive is morphologically expressed. André, for instance, says, in standardized spelling, *manitow ni-kî-nipo-stamaw-iko-naw*, equating Jesus with God (*manitow*). Instead of this transitive inverse verb, the speakers from Saint Lazare and Turtle Mountain use the intransitive verb *nipiw* "s/he dies" and express the benefactive in a prepositional phrase with a French preposition. The people from Camperville do exactly the same, only they use the Cree postposition *ohci* instead of a French preposition. All people from Saint Lazare, Camperville, and Turtle Mountain use *le bon Dieu* "the good God" for Jesus, although they are aware that the two are not the same, whereas most of the speakers who do not speak Michif use the English word "Jesus." Notice the variation in pronunciation of the word *Dieu*. Two speakers, François and Gerard, give both French and Cree translations.

The second sentence is "The girl and the boy saw a skinny horse," which can illustrate how different speakers express an adjective, conjunction, and word order variants. There is also some phonetic variation. The speakers from Ile-a-la-Crosse use the Cree conjunctions *êkwa* "and, now" and *asici* "with." In the other communities some speakers use Cree *êkwa*, others French *puis*. The speakers from Ile-a-la-Crosse do not use any French, except Beatrice who gives one noun phrase in both French and Cree. Ernest, from Lac La Biche, does not use French either. The adjective "skinny" is given as a Cree relative clause (e.g., *ê-sîhkaci-yi-t* "the other who is lean") by the speakers from Ile-a-la-Crosse (of course) and most people from Camperville, whereas almost all the people from Saint Lazare and Turtle Mountain use the French adjective *maigre*. Almost all who use the Cree relative clause, use the obviative and possessive agreement marker *-yi-*. The Cree word for "horse," *mistatim*, is followed by the obviative suffix *-wa*, but none of the French nouns is followed by this suffix. All speakers use the order subject – verb – object, except for André, from

Ile-a-la-Crosse, and Valerie, from Turtle Mountain, who use subject – object – verb order. Almost all speakers outside Ile-a-la-Crosse use Cree verbs and French nouns. Only François from Lac La Biche uses a French verb phrase, *ils ont vu*, and a Cree noun, *atim* (with suffix *-wa*).

These two examples show the kind of data obtained by the questionnaire. On the one hand, there is remarkable homogeneity both within and between some communities. On the other hand, the communities of Ile-a-la-Crosse and Lac La Biche stand apart from the rest. Readers may also notice other tendencies from these examples.

Nouns and Verbs in French and Cree

I have tabulated in table 5.2 the verbs used by the speakers throughout the whole questionnaire according to language of origin. It is very clear from this table that the verb is predominantly the domain of Cree for all Michif speakers. Speakers who know a Native language (those from Camperville) tend to use somewhat more Cree verbs (97 percent on the average) than those who do not (92 percent). For all but two speakers (Beatrice, from Ile-a-la-Crosse, and François, from Lac La Biche), between 86 percent and 100 percent of the verbs come from Cree. Beatrice and François stand out, having "only" 72 percent and 60 percent Cree verbs, respectively. Not surprisingly, they also have a much higher percentage of French verbs. The use of French verbs by most of the other speakers is less than 4 percent, with the exception of Louis, who uses 10 percent, and the Michif speakers from Turtle Mountain, who use between 14 percent and 20 percent. For all of these Michif speakers, those instances are mostly French copulas, so even for them the number of French content verbs is lower than the figures suggest.

Beatrice and François, however, use French verbs freely. They use Cree and French words in roughly equal numbers. These two speak both French and Cree fluently, and in this they differ from the others. Some of their phrases are all in Cree, others are all in French, and some are mixed. It was my strong impression that they mixed Cree and French much more than they are accustomed to do in ordinary conversation. François's remarks, such as "I have to put that in French and Cree mixed; huh, how can I do that?" are indicative of his way of responding. Also my Métis companion and his friend afterward remarked in private that François never speaks like that. For Beatrice, from Ile-a-la-Crosse, there were also indications that it is not her daily way of speaking. The speech of André, Catherine, and Delia is fairly similar, for example, in its low rate of French nouns, and can therefore be taken as much more representative of the community than Beatrice's speech. This was clear in my other interviews, in which people spoke Cree with some French and English borrowings or plain French, and also from local radio broadcasts in Cree, in which more English was mixed than French. Also, Wes Hogman's unpublished texts, recorded from a score of speakers from Ile-a-la-Crosse and neighboring Buffalo Narrows, all show a consistently low rate of French nouns and a complete absence of French verbs; so we can safely assume that this is the natural speech of Ile-a-la-Crosse.

In short, François and Beatrice use only 60 percent and 72 percent of Cree verbs, respectively, versus an average of 94 percent for the others. The speaker with the

TABLE 5.2 Source Language of Verbs

Speaker	Total Verbs	Cree (%)	French (%)	English (%)	Remainder (%)
		Ile-a-la-Crosse			
André	212	99	0	0	1
Beatrice F	196	72	27	0	1
Catherine F	211	98	1	0	1
Delia	198	100	0	0	0
		Lac La Biche Mission			
Ernest	189	100	0	0	0
François F	207	60	39	1	0
		Qu'Appelle Valley			
Gerard F	181	93	6	0	1
Hilaire	185	96	4	0	0
		St. Lazare			
Ivan F	182	93	4	1	2
Jeanne F	187	95	3	0	0
Katinka F	199	95	4	0	0
Louis F	179	89	10	0	0
		Camperville			
Nora	193	98	1	1	1
Olivia	182	97	1	1	3
Pierre	200	95	1	0	5
Kevin	205	99	1	0	0
Robert	202	99	1	0	1
Suzanne	190	97	1	1	2
		Turtle Mountain			
Tina	184	91	8	2	0
Ursula	178	88	11	0	1
Victoria	203	86	12	0	2
Valerie F	188	92	7	0	1
Zachariah	173	95	5	0	1
		Indian Plains Cree			
Craig	224	100	0	0	0
		Métis Plains Cree			
Debora	222	99	0	0	1
Ellen	204	96	0	3	1

The first column indicates the absolute number of verbs used (tokens); the other numbers denote percentages.

"F" after a name in this and all subsequent tables means that this person speaks French, as well as Michif.

The "Remainder" column in this and subsequent tables includes mixed forms and Ojibwe items.

Bernadette and Annette have not been counted here since they do not show variation in the use of verbs (both use 100 percent Ojibwe). Françoise was omitted because she uses only French verbs.

lowest score still uses 86 percent Cree verbs. Therefore, based on the origin of the language used in the verbs, it is useful to keep Beatrice and François apart from the rest. They are Cree-French bilinguals who speak differently from others in their communities. Table 5.2 confirms what all previous researchers of Michif have noted: the verb in Michif is almost exclusively the domain of Cree. There is some variation in the number of French verbs used, a number significantly higher for the Turtle Mountain speakers. I have no idea why.

I now consider for these same people the language of origin for nouns. Nouns appear to be almost always French—89 percent in Michif on the average. People who speak French, as well as Michif, tend to use a few more French nouns than those who do not (94 percent versus 87 percent). In table 5.3 we can see that the source languages for the nouns are somewhat more variable than those for the verbs. The three Cree speakers at the bottom of the table use no French at all, as we would expect, but they use a considerable number of English nouns, between 7 percent and 56 percent. We are not concerned with these speakers, however, as we are mainly interested in mixtures of French and Cree.

For those Michif speakers who do use French nouns, we can clearly set Ile-a-la-Crosse and Lac La Biche apart from the rest: whereas the other speakers use between 67 percent and 88 percent French nouns, in these two communities it ranges from 0 percent up to 48 percent, which is significantly less than for all the other speakers. Furthermore, in addition to their use of French verbs, Beatrice and François also appear to diverge from other speakers in the community in their use of nouns. For the others the percentage of French nouns does not exceed 21, whereas Beatrice has a percentage of 43 and François one of 48. Ernest does not use any French nouns at all in the questionnaire, although in colloquial speech he uses some, such as *la table* "table" and *le cheval* "horse," as do others in the Lac La Biche Mission community. However, most of them do know the Cree equivalents. Therefore, it seems useful to keep Lac La Biche and Ile-a-la-Crosse separate, as the percentage of French nouns in their language is less than one-third of that in the other communities.

Michif is considered to be a mixture of French and Cree. The English words may very well be later borrowings, and if one accepts that, it would be useful to discount them. If we disregard the English nouns, we of course get higher proportions of French nouns. The English nouns do seem needed and part of the language, however, since the speakers of "pure Cree" also use English nouns at a rate of 7 percent, 33 percent, and even 56 percent. I put some words in the questionnaire for which I suspected that most people would not readily know a Cree or French equivalent, to challenge my consultants' creativity: "outlaw," "(grain) elevator," "gallbladder," and "unicorn." Some other words, such as "screw" and "gopher," were also regularly left untranslated.

The differences between Ile-a-la-Crosse and Lac La Biche and the rest are even clearer if we do not count the English, Ojibwe, and mixed nouns but only the French and Cree. For the former, the percentage of French nouns ranges from 0 to 51, whereas for the other communities there is a narrow range between 83 percent and 94 percent (with the exception of Pierre, who has "only" 71 percent). This is a clear quantitative difference.

For the communities of Saint Lazare, Camperville, and Turtle Mountain, there are also some observations to be made in table 5.3. One can observe clear regional

Table 5.3 Source Language of Nouns

Speaker	Total Nouns	French (%)	Cree (%)	English (%)	Remainder (%)	French/Cree (%)
			Ile-a-la-Crosse			
André	183	16	81	3	0	16
Beatrice F	202	43	54	3	0	44
Catherine F	185	21	73	6	0	22
Delia	180	5	85	10	0	6
			Lac La Biche Mission			
Ernest	188	0	98	2	0	0
François F	202	48	46	7	0	51
			Qu'Appelle Valley			
Gerard F	220	90	5	5	0	94
Hilaire	211	84	8	8	0	91
			St. Lazare			
Ivan F	197	83	5	11	1	94
Jeanne F	213	85	5	9	1	94
Katinka F	213	87	6	7	0	94
Louis F	218	83	6	10	0	93
			Camperville			
Nora	193	67	7	24	2	90
Olivia	186	74	10	16	1	88
Pierre	171	77	23	17	3	71
Kevin	197	72	15	12	1	83
Robert	213	76	14	9	0	84
Suzanne	211	73	14	13	0	84
			Turtle Mountain			
Tina	227	78	9	11	1	89
Ursula	222	86	10	4	1	90
Victoria	237	86	8	5	2	92
Valerie F	229	86	7	6	1	92
Zachariah	176	83	11	6	0	88
			Indian Plains Cree			
Craig	174	0	93	7	0	0
			Métis Plains Cree			
Debora	191	0	63	33	4	0
Ellen	197	0	43	56	2	0

The first column indicates the absolute number of nouns used, and the other numbers denote percentages.

The last column indicates the percentage of French nouns in comparison with Cree nouns (thus not including English, Ojibwe, or mixed nouns).

tendencies in the number of French nouns used. The numbers used in Saint Lazare and Turtle Mountain are roughly equal, between 81 percent and 87 percent (or 89 and 94, counting only French and Cree). This is, by the way, a surprisingly narrow range. For the speakers from Camperville, however, it ranges from 67 percent to 77 percent (or 83 to 90, counting only French and Cree). In Camperville, there is a tendency to use both more Cree nouns (ranging from 7 percent to 23 percent in Camperville and from 5 percent to 11 percent elsewhere) and more English nouns (from 9 percent to 24 percent in Camperville and from 4 percent to 12 percent elsewhere). I do not want to venture an explanation here, but it seems to relate to the fact that all Camperville people are also speakers of a closely related Native language, which may have stimulated the tendency to use more Cree. This does not explain the relatively greater number of English borrowings, however. The figures show that there is a clear regional variation in the origin of the nouns in Michif. The proportion of French nouns correlates with the community of origin of the speaker.

It can also be assumed that the number of Cree nouns is lower in normal conversation than it is in this questionnaire. From other sources and from my earlier fieldwork, I know that a few Cree nouns are commonly, if not universally, used in Michif. I have used all of these nouns in my questionnaire, to see whether they would be treated morphologically and phonologically as French words or as Cree words. These are *n-uhkum* "(my) grandmother"; *ni-mušum* "(my) grandfather" (these two words are also universally used in Métis and Indian English and French); *ba:pa:* "(my) father"; *nI-ma:ma:* "(my) mother"; and *takwahImIna:na* "cranberries." There are only a few others in common use, as well as some Ojibwe nouns (see chapters Four and Nine). If these words had not been used in the questionnaire, the figures for French nouns would have been closer to 95 percent of the total.

Most of the nouns mentioned in the "Remainder" column are Ojibwe nouns; a few are mixed nouns, for example, French nouns with a Cree modifying prefix (see Chapter Four, example 122). Here, too, there is a striking difference between Ile-a-la-Crosse and the other communities. In Ile-a-la-Crosse, no Ojibwe is used at all, whereas most others do use a few Ojibwe nouns (almost all have *ɛnIkū:s* "ant" and *jāmū* "bee," and some have *kwezǣs* "girl"). This is, of course, not surprising for the Camperville Métis, who are all fluent in Ojibwe, but it is striking that the others also use these Ojibwe nouns even though they have not been in contact with Ojibwe speakers within living memory. The reasons for this are discussed in chapters Eight and Nine, where it is suggested that there is an Ojibwe substrate in Michif.

In summarizing the results based on the origin of the nouns, we can divide the Michif speakers who use French nouns with Cree verbs into three groups. First, there are those who use relatively few French nouns (up to 21 percent), which is the case only in the communities of Ile-a-la-Crosse and Lac La Biche. Second, there are those whose use of French nouns is between 43 percent and 48 percent. This group has only two speakers, François and Beatrice, from the same two communities, who also used verbs differently from the others. Third, all other speakers use between 72 percent and 88 percent French nouns (83 percent or 90 percent if we count only Cree and French nouns). This finding corroborates earlier research, which suggests that almost the total nominal lexicon is derived from French in the Michif language. The proportion of French nouns is even higher in conversational Michif since the questionnaire was weighted toward Cree nouns.

Some Further Categories

Several features of Michif show that some of the linguistic categories that have partly a grammatical function and partly a lexical function can derive from either French or Cree. Some categories are virtually always derived from either one or the other language for all speakers (see Chapter Four), and thus it makes no sense to study these categories from the viewpoint of variability of the source languages. It is perhaps useful to restate here the categories that are always in either of the two languages:

- Question words are virtually always Cree. Only very few French question words have been encountered.
- Personal pronouns ("we," "it," etc.), too, are virtually always Cree. Some French forms were attested to, but they form a tiny minority.
- Demonstratives are always Cree, although a few (perhaps fossilized) French demonstratives have also been encountered.
- Numerals are always French. Few Michif speakers can count beyond three in Cree.
- Articles are always French. Cree does not have articles or anything similar.

Other categories, such as quantifiers, adverbial particles, adpositions, and conjunctions can be in either of the two languages. For some other categories familiar from Indo-European languages, Cree does not have a strictly comparable equivalent. For instance, the notions expressed by European adjectives are either noun prefixes or inflected verbs in Cree. The European copula can be expressed as a verb suffix in Cree. These categories, too, can be expressed variably in either language. In this section I survey a number of categories that can be both French and Cree in Michif. By counting these, I hope I can determine whether the choice of a particular language is due to knowledge of other languages, to chance, to regionalisms, or to some other factor. I have chosen two categories in which variation appears to be considerable and amenable to survey questionnaire methodology: prepositions and adverbial particles.

Prepositions

French is a language with only prepositions; Cree has both prepositions and postpositions. Therefore, postpositions are always Cree derived, except for a few instances, for example, when a French preposition is used as a postposition: *dans le car en arrière* "behind the car." Thus I focus here on the more variable category, prepositions. In table 5.4 I list the number of prepositions and postpositions (tokens) used from both languages.

TABLE 5.4 Source Language of Prepositions and Postpositions

Speaker	Postpositions Cree	Prepositions				
		French	French (*dans*)	Cree	English	French (%)
Ile-a-la-Crosse						
André	12	2	—	15	2	12
Beatrice F	13	18	—	8	1	67
Catherine F	12	4	—	4	1	20
Delia	13	0	—	14	6	0
Lac La Biche Mission						
Ernest	All	0	—	All	0	0
François F	5	22	—	3	2	81
Qu'Appelle						
Gerard F	5	43	(28)	1	0	98
Hilaire	6	45	(3)	0	0	100
St. Lazare						
Ivan F	4	48	(21)	0	0	100
Jeanne F	5	40	(20)	0	0	100
Katinka F	6	44	(18)	0	0	100
Louis F	8	48	(18)	0	0	100
Camperville						
Nora	3	25	(18)	4	9	66
Olivia	7	38	(20)	3	0	93
Pierre	6	19	(16)	7	0	73
Kevin	12	22	(17)	7	1	73
Robert	10/1	35	(23)	5	1	85
Suzanne	9	31	(17)	6	0	84
Turtle Mountain						
Tina	2	44	(17)	3	3	88
Ursula		53	(24)	0	2	98
Victoria	5	45	(15)	2	0	96
Valerie F	5	50	(20)	1	1	96
Zachariah	7	34	(13)	0	1	97

The first column shows the absolute number of postpositions. All postpositions (except one by Robert) are Cree derived, so the result is 100 percent Cree for all respondents. The percentage is therefore not given in a separate column. The second column shows the total number of French prepositions and, in parentheses, how many of them are variants of *dans* (see chapters Four and Nine). The next two columns give absolute numbers for the Cree and English prepositions. The last column shows the percentage of French prepositions used of the total number of prepositions.

From this table, a few things are evident. First, the speakers from Ile-a-la-Crosse and Lac La Biche stand apart from the rest. They use very few French prepositions, between zero and 20 percent; this percentage is very close to the percentage of French nouns used there, which varies from 5 percent to 21 percent. Here again we have to isolate Beatrice and François, who use 67 percent and 88 percent, respectively. The speakers outside Ile-a-la-Crosse and Lac La Biche use between 66 percent and 100 percent. There are some regional differences: Saint Lazare and the Fort Qu'Appelle Valley are most extreme, as all of the speakers there use only French prepositions (no Cree prepositions at all, but they do use Cree postpositions); speakers from Turtle Mountain also use many prepositions from French (between 88 percent and 96 percent); and Camperville speakers use between 66 percent and 85 percent. Again, the Camperville dialect appears to differ from the other Michif dialects in being more oriented toward Cree.

In short, there is a similar grouping of the speakers: Lac La Biche and Ile-a-la-Crosse have few or no French prepositions; Beatrice and François again stand apart in these communities because they use many more French prepositions. The other speakers use mostly or exclusively French prepositions.

ADVERBS

I counted only particlelike adverbs and adverbial expressions, such as "again," "soon," "yesterday," "a little," and so on, not the adverbial prefixes on Cree verbs. In table 5.5, it can be seen that the people from Ile-a-la-Crosse and Lac La Biche do not use any French adverbs, except again for Beatrice and François. It confirms the separate position of these two communities, which was indicated by the other quantitative data.

Another fact that is clear from these data is that the Turtle Mountain people and the Saint Lazare people use roughly the same percentage of Cree adverbs (between 63 percent and 75 percent and between 56 percent and 70 percent respectively), whereas the Camperville people use between 86 percent and 92 percent. This is in line with what we have noted previously: the Camperville people use somewhat more Cree in their Michif than people in the other communities.

In short, Ile-a-la-Crosse and Lac La Biche Mission appear to be almost completely Cree oriented. Beatrice and Françoise use both Cree and French. The Camperville speakers appear to use more Cree prepositions and adverbs than the other communities, as well as more Cree in other variable categories that are not reported here (see the example sentence from the questionnaire with respect to the coordinator "and" and the translation of the adjective "skinny"). Still, Camperville speakers do not differ sensationally from those from Turtle Mountain or Saint Lazare, for example. It makes sense to classify these speakers with those in Fort Qu'Appelle, Saint Lazare, and Turtle Mountain. Beatrice and François are in a category apart, and Ile-a-la-Crosse differs strikingly from the others in having very few French function words.

Ile-a-la-Crosse French-Cree versus Michif

Important quantitative differences show up between the mixture of Cree and French as spoken in Ile-a-la-Crosse and Lac La Biche, on the one hand, and the mixtures spoken in Camperville, Turtle Mountain, Saint Lazare, and the Fort Qu'Appelle Valley, on the other hand (as well as minor differences among the communities).

In fact, the language spoken in Ile-a-la-Crosse (or actually all of northwestern Saskatchewan) and perhaps Lac La Biche (and I suspect other parts of Alberta, too) is a mixture of Cree and French, like Michif, but it is so different that it seems to be

TABLE 5.5 Source Language of Adverbs

Speaker	Number of Adverbs	Percentage of French Adverbs
Ile-a-la-Crosse		
André	66	0
Beatrice F	70	16
Catherine F	62	0
Delia	59	0
Lac La Biche Mission		
Ernest		0
François	67	31
Qu'Appelle		
Gerard F	55	45
Hilaire	53	38
Saint Lazare		
Ivan F	62	39
Jeanne F	57	30
Katinka F	56	29
Louis F	65	44
Camperville		
Nora	72	8
Olivia	64	12
Pierre	87	7
Kevin	65	8
Robert	70	11
Suzanne	64	14
Turtle Mountain		
Tina	73	17
Ursula	67	27
Victoria		
Valerie F	59	29
Zachariah	60	25

a different language altogether. I focus here on Ile-a-la-Crosse, as I consulted four speakers from there and only two from Lac La Biche, one of whom filtered out all French from his speech. Except for Beatrice, the results from Ile-a-la-Crosse are fairly consistent.

Some of the linguistic differences in Ile-a-la-Crosse that involve the source languages are discussed subsequently: the complete absence of French adverbs or prepositions, the consistent rule-predicted use of liaison and French irregular plurals, the low use of French nouns, the virtually complete absence of French verbs, and the consistent source for function words (Cree). There is also one important sociolinguistic difference: the knowledge of Cree in Ile-a-la-Crosse and Lac La Biche as opposed to the other communities. Actually there is abundant evidence that the Ile-a-la-Crosse variety of mixed Cree and French really has nothing to do with Michif as spoken in, for instance, Saint Lazare, Turtle Mountain, Camperville, or the Qu'Appelle Valley.

There are linguistic and historical arguments for this assertion. I take the Ile-a-la-Crosse dialect as the sample dialect of the area, as it seems to be the one most influenced by French in that region, but the speech of some speakers from Beauval and Buffalo Narrows is similar in this respect. Apart from the quantitative differences already discussed, there are also structural and dialectal differences between the language of Ile-a-la-Crosse and the Michif language that is spoken in the other communities.

First, the varieties of Cree and French used in Ile-a-la-Crosse differ from those in the source dialects of Michif. In Michif, southern Plains Cree and probably the eastern variety of this language (see Chapter Nine) are evident. This eastern dialect seems to have some nasal vowels and palatal consonants, as does Michif. The Cree component, though not the French component, of Michif has a phonological distinction between /e:/ and /i:/, like all *southern* Plains Cree dialects. In Ile-a-la-Crosse, however, these two vowels merge into /i:/ in the Cree part, as in all *northern* Plains Cree dialects (Wolfart 1973b: 11; Pentland 1978a: 111). In other words, the Cree components are different.

A second phonological difference is the nature of the sibilants. In Ile-a-la-Crosse, they are almost exclusively /s/ and /c/—as in all other known present-day dialects of Plains Cree—whereas the other communities surveyed have /š/ and /č/ instead.

A third phonological difference is that in Ile-a-la-Crosse, as in other dialects of Cree, /k/ between vowels is usually voiced. In Michif, /k/ is never voiced in this environment (see Chapter Nine).

In the final phonological difference, most Michif speakers do not know that the voiced initial stops in Michif verbs are derived from the underlying prefix *ni-* (e.g., Cree *ni-kîwân*; Michif *gi:wa:n* "I go home"), which disappeared and made the initial voiceless stop voiced (see Chapter Four). In Ile-a-la-Crosse, the prefix is usually present in its full form; reduced forms were also encountered but not as consistently as in Michif.

There are also differences of a morphological nature. Some of these are subtle but pervasive. The first-person inclusive is *kijana:w* for all people from Ile-a-la-Crosse, as in almost all Cree dialects, whereas all the Michif varieties have *kIjana:n*, a form not used in Ile-a-la-Crosse (see the example sentences). The first-person plural used with a transitive verb with the third-person plural object is *-na:nak* in Ile-a-la-Crosse (and all known varieties of Cree) and *-na:nik* in Michif. There are also less subtle differences. All Michif speakers have certain fixed ways of verbalizing French nouns and French or English verbs into Cree, like *labu-Iwan* "it is muddy" or *ka:-li-sɛlɪbret-i:-cIk* "when they celebrate" (see Chapter Four for a discussion of these constructions). Only in Ile-a-la-Crosse are these mixed forms not used and not understood.

Moreover, a few features of language change not present in Ile-a-la-Crosse (or in Cree) can be found in all other communities, although not all speakers use them. One of these is the change of the French-derived *da* "in" to *sa*, apparently only in possessive constructions, for example, *sa sa mæzū* "in his/her house." Similarly, in all communities there are some Michif speakers who use /st/ for the Cree-aspirated /ht/, for example, *niwa:pastæn* for *niwa:pahtæn* "I see it," but nobody in Ile-a-la-

Crosse or Lac La Biche does so. Another difference between the Cree components of Michif and Ile-a-la Crosse Cree is the frequent use of conjunct order verbs in main clauses in the latter. This is only exceptionally possible in Michif or in the Plains Cree of the prairies.

A difference between the French components is the fact that the preposition and article *dans un* are merged to *dã* in Michif but not in Ile-a-la-Crosse. This sequence of words occurs rarely in the questionnaire data from that community. Beatrice and François use *dans un* and not *dã*. Ordinarily people from Ile-a-la-Crosse do not use indefinite articles from French (see also Hogman 1981 for the closely related Buffalo Narrows dialect), whereas Michif speakers use both definite and indefinite articles.

There are also lexical differences, both in Cree and in French. In Ile-a-la-Crosse, *masinahikam* is the common word for "he writes it," whereas the others say, with one or two exceptions, *ušipehikam*. Both are Cree words but made from different formatives. Also, all Michif speakers use a few Ojibwe nouns, including those speakers who do not know Ojibwe, but Ile-a-la-Crosse people do not. For example, the Cree word for "ant" is *i:li:kus* in Ile-a-la-Crosse (ordinary Plains Cree has *êyikôs*) and *ɛnikū:s*, the Ojibwe word, in Michif. For some of the typical French-derived words in Michif, more standard forms are used in Ile-a-la-Crosse. Whereas Ile-a-la-Crosse people know /furmi/ (F. *fourmi*), Michif speakers use /frɪmij/, with metathesis. Another difference is that Michif speakers count in French and Ile-a-la-Crosse people count in Cree.

I used a few Michif tapes to test intelligibility in other communities. Cree-French bilinguals in Ile-a-la-Crosse were able to understand most of what was said in Michif, though with some difficulty, but they considered the language different from theirs. They pointed out some of the same differences I note here.

Among the Michif communities, the dialects that diverge most in purely linguistic and quantitative terms are those in Camperville and Turtle Mountain. The Camperville dialect is heavily influenced by Ojibwe in its phonology and contains more Cree than the dialects of the other communities. Turtle Mountain is most French oriented: the people there use on the average more French verbs and prepositions than the other communities. Nevertheless, when people in Camperville listened to a Turtle Mountain Michif tape, one woman remarked amazedly: "She speaks as if she is from here." Apparently despite the divergences, there were no problems at all in understanding her, which points to the fact that the same language is spoken in the two communities.

From a linguistic viewpoint, we can conclude that the mixture of Cree and French as spoken in Ile-a-la-Crosse has nothing to do with Michif. They must have developed independently. The former dialect must be considered Cree, with some borrowings from French, whereas Michif is a mixed language. It seems that the French elements in Ile-a-la-Crosse were introduced by the French-speaking missionaries and the school system. This is what the Ile-a-la-Crosse elders also say. At least one of them, who is known in the community for his excellent knowledge of pure Cree, claims that he uses no French in his Cree because, as he said: "I went to school only one day." People like him blame the church and the school for the introduction of French words into the language.

In addition to the linguistic evidence just given, there are also a number of historical (see Chapter Six) and ethnological arguments in favor of an independent development. The French element in Ile-a-la-Crosse must be relatively recent since the French mission was established here in 1846.

Further, the names given to the languages differ. In the Michif communities, the labels "Cree" and "Michif" are both used for the mixed language that is spoken. In Ile-a-la-Crosse, however, the language is called Cree. Only a few people know the word "Michif," and they use it to refer to the people, not to a language—although the publication of the dictionary (Laverdure and Allard 1983; Fredeen 1991), as well as some other factors, led to the use of this word in Ile-a-la-Crosse, too, since the late 1980s (Community of Ile-a-la-Crosse 1990).

As a final argument I can mention here the important fact that some Michif elders make the same distinction between the two varieties—one that they call Michif and one that they call French-Cree. Only Michif is the language of the Red River Métis. French-Cree is a more recent development.[4]

In short, linguistic, ethnological, and historical arguments make it clear that the mixture of French and Cree as spoken in Ile-a-la-Crosse is different in almost all respects from the language spoken in the other communities because of a different origin. An overview of the most important differences is given in table 5.6.

The Ile-a-la-Crosse language seems to be the regional variety of Plains Cree (the northern dialect), into which French nouns were borrowed. This vocabulary was mostly introduced through the Catholic school system, which used standard Canadian French as the language of instruction.

TABLE 5.6 Summary of Linguistic Differences between the French-Cree Mixture of Ile-a-la-Crosse and Michif

Item	Ile-a-la-Crosse	Michif
Cree part		
s/š contrast	No	Yes
hC/sC variation	No	Yes
Ojibwe influence	No	Yes
Mixed verbs	No	Yes
e/i contrast	No	Yes
Voiced initial stops	No	Yes
Voiced intervocal stops	Yes	No
3p INV verb -*ik*	Yes	No
TRANS we-them verb -*ak*	Yes	No
F/C mixed verbs	No	Yes
Count in Cree	Yes	No
Conjunct order in main clauses	Yes	No
French part		
INDF + DEF articles	No	Yes
da > sa	No	Yes
Standard French frequent	Yes(?)	No
Liaison	Yes	No

Influence from Cree and French on Michif

One can hypothesize that among the speakers of Michif, those who speak French will tend to use more French words and those who also speak a Native language will use more Cree or Ojibwe words. These hypotheses were tested in different ways. One method, discussed in this chapter, counted lexical categories (nouns and verbs) and some functional categories (prepositions and particles and adverbs), specifically how many of these are French and how many Cree for each individual speaker. This yielded different results for both groups of bilinguals (French-Michif and Amerindian-Michif) and for the Michif speakers who do not know French or Cree.

One can also test this hypothesis by measuring the degree in which the French and the Cree components deviate from the more standard varieties of these languages. How far do the individual speakers differ in their deviations from the norms in the source languages? I relate these data with whether or not these individuals are also speakers of other languages, in addition to Michif, notably Cree, Ojibwe, or French. If Michif is a fixed code, which differs at some points from the source languages, it would be possible that those Michif speakers who also speak French would be influenced by standard French in their Michif. Likewise, the Cree part would be more "conservative" for speakers who also know Cree or French.

How "French" Is the French Component?

In discussing the French component, I consider the position of the numeral and the article (a syntactical difference between Michif and French), some irregular plurals (morphological), and liaison (phonological).

NUMERALS

Michif differs from standard French in the position of the numeral in relation to the article and the noun. Michif also seems to differ from Métis French; neither Papen (1984a, 1984b) nor Douaud (1985) mentions the deviant order of numeral and noun as a feature of Métis French, and I do not have sufficient data myself to confirm the correctness of this supposition. My only consultant for Métis French, Françoise, uses the Michif construction in her response in the questionnaire.

In all varieties of French, the order of noun (N), article (A), and numeral (Num) can be either A – Num – N (*les trois femmes* "the three women") or Num – N (*trois femmes* "three women"). The first is definite, the second indefinite. In Michif, the order is always Num – A – N [*trwa: li: fam* "(the) three women," literally, "three the women"] for both definite and indefinite nouns. In short, in Michif the definite article is obligatory and the numeral always precedes the article, whereas in French the article precedes the numeral or is entirely omitted.

One can hypothesize, however, that Michif speakers who know French would place the numeral in the position it has in French. That is, they could try to make the French part as French as possible. In the questionnaire there is only one sentence— "He shot three moose there"—with a numeral and an indefinite object. All of the speakers from Ile-a-la-Crosse and one from Lac La Biche used a Cree numeral. The other speaker from Lac-La-Biche (François) used the standard French expression (/trwaz oriño/). Only one of the Michif speakers used a Cree numeral; the other sixteen used a French numeral. Of the latter, only three used the standard French method. So thirteen out of sixteen (81 percent) used a non-French numeral construction. Among the three who used the French order, two are also speakers of French and one is not. Of the six French speakers, three used the Michif construction and three used the standard French construction.

This construction, therefore, seems to be independent of the knowledge of French: both speakers of French and nonspeakers of French use the typically Michif construction.

FRENCH IRREGULAR PLURALS

In all varieties of French, the plural ending -s is written but not pronounced. In fact, plurality is marked in the article: *le, la, un*, and *une* in the singular and *les* and *des* in the plural; in Michif /lɪ/, /la/, /æ /, and /ɛn/ for singular nouns and /li:/ for plurals. Nouns cannot be used without an article or possessive in French. The articles seem to be somewhat more intimately connected to the nouns than, for example, English articles. In French, for instance, only a few adjectives can appear between the article and the noun, whereas in English all adjectives appear in that position. In general, French nouns in themselves are not marked for plurality. Nevertheless, a few words in French have different forms for plural nouns, such as *l'animal, les animaux* "animals" and *le cheval, les chevaux* "horses." These two words and the Canadian French *orignal, les orignaux* "moose," recurred a number of times in the questionnaire, nine times if French plural nouns were used whenever possible. I counted the plural forms of those words ending in *-al* or *-aux* (phonetically /u:/ in Michif) and tabulated the scores in table 5.7.

Although the total sample is not very large, a few tentative conclusions may be drawn. Most of the speakers do use the irregular French plural form in the majority of cases, except Louis from Saint Lazare and Robert from Camperville. The French-Michif bilinguals score exactly the same on the average (67 percent) as those who do not speak French. There are also several non-French speakers who score higher than some of the bilinguals (in particular Suzanne, Tina, and Ursula). Only five of the nineteen Michif speakers have the correct (at least from the viewpoint of French) plural forms in all cases, two of whom are bilingual in French.

Although we could expect those who are bilingual in French to score higher than the non-French speakers, this does not appear to be true. It is possible that they only use "correct" forms when they speak French. Unfortunately this hypothesis has not been tested for these speakers. In any case, Françoise, a speaker of Métis French, also uses incorrect plural forms in her French. Here again, knowledge of French does not appear to obviate the Michif forms, which would be incorrect in any form of French.

In short, using normatively correct French forms in Michif tends to be independent of the knowledge of French, as with the numerals. The language is not adjusted toward "correct" French by those who also speak French.

TABLE 5.7 Irregular Plurals for Michif Speakers

Speaker	Total absolute	-*u* plural (%)
Qu'Appelle		
Gerard F	3	100
Hilaire	5	60
St. Lazare		
Ivan F	6	83
Jeanne F	7	71
Katinka F	4	50
Louis F	5	20
Camperville		
Nora	3	67
Olivia	3	67
Pierre	2	50
Kevin	7	57
Robert	5	40
Suzanne	2	100
Turtle Mountain		
Tina	5	80
Ursula	5	80
Victoria	7	71
Valerie F	6	83
Zachariah	3	67
Turtle Mountain French		
Françoise	5	80

LIAISON

In French, the term *liaison* is used to describe the addition of a consonant between the final vowel of a word and the first vowel of the following word. For example, *petit* "little," normally pronounced /pəti/, becomes /pətit/ if followed by a vowel-initial word like *oreille* "ear": /pətit orɛj/. It is argued in Chapter Four that liaison is not a productive process in Michif. Any liaison consonant /n/, /l/, or /z/ can be used in principle in any position.

In my questionnaire, there are sixteen places where liaison would be possible in French. Four of these are English words ("elevator," "outlaw," "Expos," and "Oilers") and twelve are French words (*arbre* "tree," *aigle* "eagle," *oreille* "ear," *homme* "man," *étalon* "stallion," and *ours* "bear"), some of which could be used more than once. In principle, there are four possible solutions to these cases. First, people could use liaison as in French, by adding the right underlying consonant. Second, they could add the wrong underlying consonant, as for instance in [li: na:rb] "the trees" instead of [li: za:rb]. Third, they could not add an intervening consonant at all, saying, for instance, [li: autlɔ:] "outlaws." Fourth, the liaison may not surface because the respondents could use a different word or not give a translation. The results for the

Michif speakers are tabulated in table 5.8. Some speakers from Ile-a-la-Crosse and Lac La Biche are omitted because four of them did not use these French words at all. The two speakers from these communities (Beatrice and François) who did use French both used liaison according to the standard French rule.

There are a few striking facts in this table. First, most speakers do use consonants that are the same as the expected French liaison consonants in most of the cases. Only two speakers (Nora and Pierre, from Camperville) use more liaison consonants that are not the productive ones expected in French. Second, only one speaker (Louis, from Saint Lazare) never uses an "incorrect" consonant and never omits one where it would be required. It is not surprising that Louis is a Michif-French bilingual. Third, only three of the seventeen Michif speakers never use a liaison consonant that is "incorrect" from the point of view of French. All of them are bilingual in French. The three remaining bilinguals still use a few (between 7 percent and 15 percent) "incorrect" liaison consonants. On the average the French-Michif bilinguals have higher scores, 84 percent "as in French," than the non-French speakers, 54 percent. The overall average is 65 percent.

TABLE 5.8 Liaison for Michif Speakers

Speaker	As in French (%)	Different consonant (%)	No liaison consonant (%)	Total potential
		Qu'Appelle		
Gerard F	93	0	7	15
Hilaire	82	0	18	17
		Saint Lazare		
Ivan F	77	8	15	13
Jeanne F	77	15	8	13
Katinka F	91	0	9	11
Louis F	100	0	0	12
		Camperville		
Nora	38	46	15	13
Olivia	50	20	30	10
Pierre	33	50	17	6
Kevin	67	17	17	6
Robert	71	14	14	7
Suzanne	63	13	25	8
		Turtle Mountain		
Tina	67	20	13	15
Ursula	73	7	20	15
Victoria	73	19	7	26
Valerie F	74	16	11	19
Zachariah	47	29	24	17
		Métis French		
Françoise	73	27	0	26

In this study no scores for liaison are recorded for these bilinguals when they are speaking French. One would expect them to apply the liaison rules correctly, but without evidence this cannot be taken for granted. Indeed, our sole Métis French consultant, Françoise, did use "incorrect" liaison consonants, as did the Michif speakers.

In conclusion, we can state that liaison is not productive for the vast majority of speakers. People speaking French, as well as Michif, on the average use liaison "correctly" more often (84 percent to 54 percent), but some people who speak no French at all score better with French than some of the bilinguals (e.g., Hilaire).

Concerning the overall difference between French and Michif French, all three points studied here lead to the same conclusion: people who speak French in addition to Michif on the average use forms closer to non-Michif French, but it is not at all the same as in French. Some non-French speakers are more "correct" in French than some bilinguals. This suggests that they use the French component of Michif independently from their knowledge of French, showing that Michif and French are separate languages.

How "Cree" Is the Cree Component?

To what degree does the Cree part of Michif differ from Cree as spoken by non-Michif speakers? Does it differ significantly among individual Michif speakers? If so, does this correlate with the knowledge of Cree or Ojibwe, which these individuals may have? To study this subject, I counted two Cree verbal morphological features that appeared to show variability in Michif (see table 5.9). These are "prepositional" items, which are normally expressed with a bound morpheme in the Cree verb but which are sometimes expressed with a prepositional phrase in Michif (Weaver 1983; Weston 1983). This can also be considered as the use of synthetic forms (morphologically expressed) versus analytic forms (expressed in independent words). The morphemes studied are as follows.

- *wi:či-V-m-* "do something together with." What is expressed by the preposition "with" in a language like English is often expressed by the verb prefix *wi:či-* "together" plus the suffix *-m* (related with the animate possessive marker *-m*?) in Cree. The resulting verb is transitive, for example:

  (1a) wi:či-me:tawe:-m-e:w   (Cree, Michif)
  with-play-?-3-e:3'
  "He/she plays with him/her."

  This can also be expressed with a postposition in Métis Cree:

  (1b) me:taw-e:w wija asiči   (analytic alternative)
  play-3 him/her with
  "He/she plays with him/her."

- *V-stamaw-* "do something for/on behalf of someone." This, too, is expressed by a preposition in French or English but generally by a verb

TABLE 5.9 Relative Syntheticity of Cree Verbs

Speaker	"with," "for" S A X	Percentage of Synthetic Forms
Ile-a-la-Crosse	*Average*	**48**
André N	4 3 0	57
Beatrice N F	4 3 0	57
Catherine N F	4 3 0	57
Delia N	3 4 0	43
Lac La Biche Mission	*Average*	**100**
Ernest	5 0 2	100
François	4 0 3	100
Qu'Appelle	*Average*	**46**
Gerard F	4 3 0	57
Hilaire	2 4 1	33
Saint Lazare	*Average*	**14**
Ivan F	1 6 0	14
Jeanne F	3 4 0	43
Katinka F	0 7 0	0
Louis F	0 7 0	0
Camperville	*Average*	**71**
Nora	3 2 2	60
Olivia	6 1 0	86
Pierre	4 2 1	67
Kevin	4 2 1	67
Robert	6 1 0	86
Suzanne	4 3 0	57
Turtle Mountain	*Average*	**15**
Tina	1 5 1	17
Ursula	0 7 0	0
Victoria	2 5 0	29
Valerie F	2 5 0	29
Zachariah	0 7 0	0
Unmixed	*Average*	**87**
Annette N	6 0 1	100
Bernadette N	5 1 1	83
Craig N	7 0 0	100
Debora N	4 1 2	80
Ellen N	5 2 0	71

Numbers printed in bold represent community averages.

A = analytic form + number of occurrences.

F = speaker knows French.

N = speaker knows Cree and/or Ojibwe.

S = synthetic form.

X = other, irrelevant alternative (not counted in the total score).

suffix in Cree and, in some varieties, also by a postposition, for
example:

(2a)   masinahike:-stamaw-e:w   (Cree, Michif)
       write-for-3→31
       "He/she writes for him/her."

(2b)   masinahik-e:w wija kici   (analytic alternative Ile-a-la-Crosse)
       write-3→3' him namely
       "He/she writes for him/her."

A verbal morpheme would be obligatory in Cree. Here, the synthetic forms are
taken as "norms" and the analytic forms as "deviations." What I did here can be seen
as a way to measure whether the verb in Michif is more simplified than the verb in
its source language, Cree.

The results have been tabulated in table 5.9, where the analyticity and syntheticity
of the two items were counted for each individual speaker, as were those instances
when the synthetic form was actually used. The morphological (synthetic) expression scored one point and the analytic form zero. The use of a totally different expression or the omission of the sentence scored zero as well, but these are not included in the totals. By dividing the total number of synthetic plus analytic realizations,
by the number of synthetic actualizations I arrived at a rate of "syntheticity": the more
synthetic forms used, the higher the rate. The results are organized according to the
region of origin of the speakers. I give not only the results for each individual but
also the average scores per community (in boldface). Michif speakers who also know
French, as well as those who know Cree or Ojibwe, can be found in areas with higher,
middle, and lower syntheticity indices. Some clear regional patterns emerge. For
instance, the Turtle Mountain and Saint Lazare people use almost exclusively analytic forms (only 15 percent and 14 percent synthetic forms, respectively), whereas
the Camperville people, the nonmixed speakers, and the Lac La Biche people use
mostly synthetic forms (71 percent, 87 percent, and 100 percent, respectively). The
Ile-a-la-Crosse and the Fort Qu'Appelle people fall in between, with an average of
48 percent and 46 percent synthetic forms. Generally, the people who speak unmixed
Cree or Ojibwe, either in addition to Michif or as their only language, clearly use
mostly synthetic forms. This indicates that knowledge of a Native language can influence the nature of the Cree component, in this case the Cree verb morphology.

I also counted a number of other items that are normally expressed with a verb
morpheme in Cree: the delayed imperative versus an ordinary imperative, an adverbial prefix versus a prepositional phrase expressing "by accident," the conditional
suffix versus an "if" conjunction, and a morpheme meaning "to come." For these
items, however, the results did not show regional or other tendencies so they are not
reported here in detail.

The tentative conclusion (since it is based on relatively few instances) to be drawn
from these results is that the rate of analyticity or syntheticity in the prepositional
verb affixes correlates positively with the knowledge of a Native language in addition to Michif. In general, however, the use of more complex or simpler verb forms
seems independent of the knowledge of a Native language because some people who

do not know a Native language score better than some who do; moreover, morphological or analytical expression does not appear to correlate with a region or a knowledge of other languages.

CONCLUSIONS

It appears that the use of French irregular plurals, liaison, and the position of the numerals is independent of the knowledge of French. Also, knowledge of a Native language does not necessarily lead to more complex verb forms.

French and Cree in Contact: The Three Types

In most of the quantitative data presented in this chapter, there is a natural distribution into three groups of speakers. First, there are the two individuals, Beatrice and François, who use roughly as much Cree as they do French in most categories. Second, there are the speakers from Ile-a-la-Crosse, who use much Cree and some French, almost exclusively nouns. Third, there are those who use a mixture of Cree verbs and French nouns called Michif. I argue that three different processes are responsible for the three mixtures. To show this more clearly, I present table 5.10, in which the differences are immediately clear.

The differences are clear: Beatrice and François use a considerable number of French verbs, whereas the other two groups use hardly any. In Ile-a-la-Crosse hardly any French nouns are used, Beatrice and François use French for almost half, and the others use three-quarters to nine-tenths. Again, Beatrice and François differ from the Ile-a-la-Crosse speakers, who do not use any French adverbs. They also show a correct use of liaison and irregular plurals, whereas only a few speakers in the third column show this characteristic.

I propose to classify these groups as follows: Beatrice and François, who belong to the select group of fluent Cree-French bilinguals, are code mixing. The people in Ile-a-la-Crosse speak Cree with nominal borrowings from French. Only the third column includes speakers of Michif, which are neither code mixing nor

TABLE 5.10 Quantitative Comparison of the Three Groups of Speakers

	Ile-a-la-Crosse	Beatrice & François	Others (Michif)
		% in French	
Verbs	0–1	27–39	1–12
Nouns (without English)	6–22	44–51	71–94
Prepositions	0–20	67–81	73–100
Adverbs	0	16–21	11–45
Irregular plurals as in French	N.a.	100	40–100
Liaison as in French	N.a.	100	33–100

N.a. = not attested.

borrowing. (For what Michif is see chapters Seven and Eight.) The difference among the three groups becomes more clear if we look at some texts representative of these three mixtures of Cree and French. The non-Cree elements are italicized both in the text and in the translation. The first two texts and the last are given in standard orthography.

- Speaker 1, male, Ile-a-la-Crosse, 75 years old in 1990. Does not speak French and did not go to school:

  (3) Nimâmâ êka pimâtisit, êyâko êkwa piko tâskôc nimâmâ. nama kîkwê *brothers* nitâyâwak, nama kîkwê *sisters*. pêyak piko awâsis nimâmâ kî-ayâwât, êyâko niya. mêkwâ *seventy-five* nitahtopiponwân *last birthday, November thirty* awa êkwa *I will be seventy-six*. êkwa mâka kâ-kî-wâpahtam-ân ôma kâ-awâsisîwiyân.

  Since my mother passed away, this one [pointing to a 93-year-old woman visiting] is now like my mother. I have no *brothers* or *sisters*. My mother had only one child, and that was me. I am now *75* years old, on my *last birthday*. On *November 30 I will* then *be 76*. And this is what I saw when I was a child [followed by childhood memories].

- Speaker 2, female, Ile-a-la-Crosse, around 50 years old in 1988. Went to school. Does not know French:

  (4) Kayâs ayîsiyiniwak atimwa êkwa mistatimwa poko ê-kî-pimohtahocik. ê-kî-maskisin-ihkawâcik atimwa, maskwamiy kâ-mâyâtisit ekâ ta-pîkosinisicik ositiwawa. *le padla*[5] ohci êkî-osîhtâcik maskisina atimwa kici. ê-tahkopitahkwaw *le padla* atimwa ositihk êkwa *la corde* asici ê-sôhkahpitahkwaw.

  A long time ago people used to travel with dogs and horses only. They made moccasins for the dogs when the ice was bad, so that they would not hurt their paws. Out of *canvas* they made the shoes for the dogs. They tied *the canvas* to the dogs' paws and they would tie it with *a rope*.

- Speaker 3, female, about 75 years old in 1988. Went to school. Is fluent and literate in French, Cree, and English.

  (5) *Quand les poires* ka-atihtîki, kahkiyaw mâna ni-kî-wî-kakwî-mawisonân. nikîspônân. *une femme* ni-kîwîsamanân *pour garder les enfants* kapî-kîsik. *toute la journée* kî-kanawîyimawisow îkwa *on lui donnait les poires* mîskuc kâ-kanawîyîmât *les enfants*. makîkwê sôniyâw. *Des fois a [elle] gardait les enfants* niyânan *cinq differents familles* uhci awâsisak. î-nakatamawayakwaw *le grub* êkosi taki-asamîw awâsisak, kanakî *la galette* asicî pimîy. *yaenk* [rien que] *les femmes ça allait au grains, ramasser les poires*. nâpîwak *ça travaillait*. î-natonahkwaw kîkwê t-ohcî *pour nourrir leurs enfants*.

  When the berries are ripe, we all used to go to try to pick berries in the bush. We had our fill. We hired *a woman to take care of the kids* all day. *All day* she was looking after the kids and *we gave her berries* for looking after *the kids*. No money. *Sometimes she looked after the kids* from *five families*. We brought *the food* so that she could feed the kids, especially *bannock* with lard. *Only the women went to pick berries.* The men *they worked.* They were trying to find things *to feed the children.*

- Speaker 4, male, about 69 in 1988. Retired steam engineer. Michif is his mother tongue. He was born and raised in southern Saskatchewan.

(6) *Les scrips* nânitâw kâ-kî-miyi-cik *les Métif. And un Blanc* ka-pê-itohtêw, ka-wayêsimêw. âtiht ka-masinahikêw. âtiht ka-nakatam. *"ton nom* asta." *les Métif no* kaskihtâw ta-osipêhikêcik, *so le croix.* "Marquez *ta croix. ça, c'est ton nom." puis un témoin signed his name.* êkosi *le Métif* kî-wayêsimâw *leur terrain, leur homestead, you see.* êkosi kî-ispayin. *C'est la vérité* ôma kâ-wîhtamâtin.

The Métis were given *(land) scrips* somewhere. *And a Whiteman* would come and he would cheat them. He would write something. He would leave something. "Put *your name." The Métis* could not write, *therefore a cross. "Mark your cross. That's your name." And then a witness signed his name.* In that way *the Métis* were cheated off *their land, their homestead, you see.* That's how it happened. *It is the truth* that I am telling you.

The differences are obvious: speaker 1 uses some English borrowings in a Cree discourse (although he knows the Cree words for numbers and kinship). This is Cree-English code mixing, with Cree as the base or matrix language. He does not use French here. Speaker 2 uses Cree, with a few French borrowings for items introduced by the French and probably learned in the French school. Speaker 3 shows a more or less arbitrary distribution of French and Cree: for all French words she knows the Cree equivalents, and vice versa. Sometimes she uses equivalent words from both languages (*awâsisak, les enfants* "children"; *kapî-kîsik, toute la journée* "all day"). Speaker 2 also uses French definite articles for indefinite nouns, whereas speaker 3 uses all kinds of French articles. Speaker 3 shows code mixing as often reported from the literature (see Chapter Six for some other cases of Algonquian code mixing with French and English). Speaker 4 is a Michif speaker. Apart from the English he mixes in, the patterns are the same as those we saw before: verbs, demonstratives, and adverbial particles are Cree; nouns, possessives, and articles are French. One French verb is also used (*marquer*). Speaker 4's text looks very different from the others. It is clearly different from code mixing and from the borrowing in Ile-a-la-Crosse. I call this third process "language intertwining," which is discussed in detail in Chapters Seven and Eight.

Conclusions

This chapter confirms the observation made repeatedly that verbs in Michif come from Cree and nouns generally from French. In the French-Cree mixed language of Ile-a-la-Crosse, no French verbs are used and a much smaller number of French nouns. It also shows explicitly that some two-thirds of the Michif speakers I interviewed do not speak or understand either Cree or French, which confirms the status of Michif as a separate language.

The considerable quantitative and structural linguistic differences between the language of Ile-a-la-Crosse and that of the other communities make it crystal clear that the Ile-a-la-Crosse language is unrelated to Michif, despite some remarkable similarities (such as the use of French nouns and no French verbs). It is better to distinguish Michif from the Ile-a-la-Crosse mixture by using the term "French-Cree" (following Hogman 1981) for the Cree language with a French admixture used in Ile-a-la-Crosse and the neighboring communities, reserving the term "Michif" for the mixture of French and Cree spoken in the other communities. Apart from these two languages, there are two speakers who differ from both. Their language use is classified as code mixing. They are fluent bilinguals (in contrast to the others), and their Cree and French show the same arbitrary mixture of two languages as reported from other cases of code mixing. So there are Michif, the French-Cree dialect, and French-Cree code mixing, which represent what I tentatively call language mixture, borrowing, and code mixing, respectively.

I have also shown two types of variation in Michif proper. There is variability from community to community, such as the tendency to use slightly fewer French nouns in Camperville, the complete absence of Cree prepositions in Saint Lazare, or the tendency to use Cree adpositions in Camperville and French adpositions in Saint Lazare. There is also variability within the various communities, and it is striking that many of the points of variation recur in several communities. For a more complete picture, more research would be needed, but a few striking differences are already clearly visible. For example, in all of the communities there are speakers who use /st/, as well as people who use the Cree-aspirated /ht/ (e.g., *wa:paht-* "see it" or *wa:past-*). Also, in all of the communities there are people who use *sa* as a locative preposition with certain possessive phrases instead of *da*. As it is very unlikely that these forms of variation arose independently in all these communities, it is highly likely that this variation was already present in the language before the dispersion of the Métis. As some of the communities were already settled by Métis in the first half of the nineteenth century (such as Turtle Mountain), this is an indication that Michif had already crystallized at that time as a language one learned (as already surmised in Rhodes 1992). Already before 1850 one could not create the language ad hoc by mixing Cree and French. The fact that some forms of variation are limited to one community (such as the use of Ojibwe *ke:ma* for "or" in Camperville) is, of course, not at all surprising after more than a century of separation.

There is variability within all Michif-speaking communities. Some of this is specific to one community, such as the use of voiced intervocal stops in Camperville, which is no doubt an influence of the locally dominant Saulteaux language. This makes the Camperville dialect readily distinguishable from the others. There are fewer differences among the other communities. Indeed, it is remarkable how many similarities the dialects of the Qu'Appelle Valley, Saint Lazare, and Turtle Mountain show, considering their relative isolation from the other speakers and the pressures from different languages.

It seems that the knowledge of French and/or a Native language has some influence on the variety of Michif spoken. People who know French tend to use more French elements (especially the function words), and people who know Ojibwe tend to use more Cree words in their Michif. With only a few exceptions, no Ojibwe function words are used by these people. Apparently the use of Ojibwe in addition to Michif has stimulated the survival of the Cree elements, but there is little or no tendency to use Ojibwe lexical elements, except for those present in all dialects (see Chapter Four and especially Chapter Nine for examples). This is another indication that these Cree function words have been preserved from the past and not borrowed locally. Apparently Michif was rather variable before the Métis people dispersed and started living in their current communities. In the formative period of Michif and also afterward, the choice for either a French or a Cree function word has been variable. These were derived from both languages, perhaps with individual preferences. The Cree words must still have been known at the time of the settlement of the modern communities; otherwise one could expect Ojibwe words instead.

It has been shown that both the French and the Cree elements deviate from the source languages in a number of respects. Strikingly, however, people who also speak French do not always use a form that is closer to standard French than those who do not know this language. Similarly, those who also know a Native language do not conform more to the Cree norm. In short, knowledge of Cree and French influences the amount of French and Cree used in Michif to a certain extent, especially in the number of lexical items, but it does not influence the quality or the nature of the Cree and French elements. This shows again that Michif must be seen as a separate language, independent of both source languages. Speakers are often aware of some differences between Michif and Cree or Michif and French.

Apart from these two types of variation, there is one other form that could not be studied—the way in which the same person speaks to different interlocutors. It is very possible that Michif speakers vary their speech according to the person they are talking to. One of my consultants was very clear on this point:

SUZANNE: You know what, Peter, it really depends where you are and who you're with. Honest. I just noticed that too, you know. For instance, *sa prā čI-šIpwe:hte:ja:n*[6] for "I have to go." I'll say that to some of the people here. But with some people I will say, *pigo čI-šIpwe:hte:ja:n.*[7] You know, something like that.

PB: Is it then the family, how much French they use or what?

SUZANNE: It doesn't matter. You know what kind of language they use, and how it fits in. You do it just automatically, you know. They're all Métis, but they talk different, you know.

Apparently Michif speakers are at some level aware of different types of speech in their community, to which they automatically adjust. It is, of course, very hard and time consuming to study this phenomenon. Actually it must be common in most communities, but it is more clearly noticeable and identifiable here because two languages of completely different stocks are involved, not just different dialects or registers.

As the final conclusion of this chapter, the variation shows that Michif must have crystallized before the dispersal of the Métis from the Red River settlement. Michif must have been a separate language, not just an ad hoc mixture of Cree and French, at least before the 1860s and probably the 1840s.

6

Cree-French Language Mixture

Types and Origin

One of the conclusions reached in Chapter Five is that there are three types of mixtures of Cree and French as represented in the data: code mixing (Beatrice and François in the questionnaire), Cree with French borrowings (the speakers from Ile-a-la-Crosse), and Michif (the other speakers of mixed Cree and French). In this chapter I put the three types into a broader perspective.

The most substantial part is devoted to the historical documentation of Métis language use in the past. As noted in Chapter Five, dialectal similarities suggest that Michif must have crystallized roughly before 1850. To learn when Michif may have emerged, I discuss a number of contemporary documents that relate to Métis language use in the nineteenth century, focusing especially on the Red River area. I also bring forward some Métis oral history sources. Further, I present some historical data on the French-Cree dialect of Ile-a-la-Crosse and its possible implications for the genesis of Michif. I conclude the chapter by comparing the French-Cree code mixing as I recorded it with other cases of code mixing that involve Algonquian languages: would these have identical or different features, and if different, would they perhaps be similar to Michif in its mixture of languages? Remember that in Chapter One, I mentioned that fossilization or nativization of code mixing seems to be a possible means toward a mixed language.

Red River Métis Language Use in the Past

It cannot be ascertained precisely when Michif came into existence, but different historical and linguistic facts make it possible to make an educated guess. Written sources of the language only go as far back as 1971. In that year Bette Boteler finished her master's thesis in anthropology on the ethnobotanical knowledge of the inhabitants of the Turtle Mountain Reservation in North Dakota. She was the first to

161

cite a few phrases in Michif that she had collected from residents, which she identified as showing a significant French influence. Of course, this year cannot be taken as the birth date of Michif, as many elderly people born long before 1971 speak it as their first language.

Still, there are very few explicit references to Michif before the 1970s, such as this quotation from Joseph Kinsey Howard in his book *Strange Empire*, which is devoted to the history of the Métis;

> They [the Métis] were, however, exceptionally apt linguists. Most of them spoke at least two languages, French and Cree, and many quickly added other Indian tongues and English. Some even learned German while they were in contact with Selkirk's DeMeuron veterans. Their own patois, still spoken by them throughout the West, is a mixture of French and Cree or Chippewa with some English words. The base is an obsolete French of a type said to be still heard in Normandy and Picardy, and a large vocabulary of terms applying to the prairie has been added. Words French in origin have been given new meanings. French was the "official" language, used in letters and documents. It was also favored over English for spoken intercourse with whites and is still preferred by the elder Métis and widely used by them in Canada and the United States. As used in their own homes, however, the patois is more Cree than French. (1952: 52–53)

It is clear that if one wants to know when Michif emerged as a language, one cannot count on written sources. Neither can one rely on the memory of living speakers since the crystallization of Michif must have occurred long before their birth. One has to rely on other types of information: scattered bits and pieces written on Métis language use in the past, historical and geographical data on the spread of the Métis, some cultural information, genealogical data on present-day speakers, and linguistic information entrenched in the language itself.

The published sources about the early Métis say something about Michif indirectly, at best. The existence of the Michif language was never mentioned as such, not by fur traders, travelers, missionaries, nor anyone. Still, it is known for a fact that Michif was already spoken around 1900. The oldest speakers of Michif now living, who spoke it as their only language at least until school age, were born just after the turn of the century. Were these Métis the first speakers, or have there been generations of speakers before them, as suggested previously?

In this section I first discuss a number of historical sources that deal with the Métis from the early 1800s until the 1880s. I hope these enable me to discover which languages were spoken by the Métis before 1880. I also present some data from oral history.

Languages Spoken by the Métis According to Early Written Sources

The first phrases cited in print in Michif date from 1971 (Boteler 1971),[1] but the language is undoubtedly much older. Perhaps Michif was hardly ever noticed by outsiders (at least those who could write) partly because it was an in-group language. Strangely enough, in *Le Métis Canadien*, Marcel Giraud's 1400-page monograph on the Métis and still a standard work, Giraud nowhere refers to the Michif language. Some Métis speak French (Giraud 1945: 800, 1113, 1272), and some Métis speak a "Native language," which is never specified (e.g., Giraud 1945: 826, 834, 848, 855, 1003, 1070–1071, 1145, 1261). Many Métis, of course, must have known both French and Amerindian languages (Cree or Ojibwe), as acknowledged by Giraud (e.g., 846, n. 2, 987, 1006, 1014, 1061). Giraud went through an enormous number of documents of diverse sources (fur traders' reports, missionaries' and travelers' accounts, historical works, etc.) in his studies. Because he does not know about this mixed language, we can assume that these source documents do not mention, at least explicitly, the existence of anything like the Michif language among the Métis. Nor did he himself remark on its existence in his reports of his visits in 1935 and 1936 to Métis communities such as Lebret, Sainte Madeleine, and Turtle Mountain, where Michif is spoken today and must have been spoken then. Either he did not speak with its inhabitants, or all Métis preferred to, and were able to, speak to him in languages other than Michif (e.g., French or English).

In this section I try to establish the approximate date at which Michif was first spoken, and I rely in part on written historical sources: documents produced by contemporaries, who mention languages used by the Métis and the *voyageurs*. These can be travel accounts, missionary reports, fur traders' memories, and published letters. I cite printed sources only published before 1900 and then mostly from eyewitnesses. The twentieth-century historians of the fur trade and exploration sometimes mention Métis language use, but this information may be unreliable because many of their remarks appear to be just assumptions.

First, a cautionary note on the method used here is required. This section is not the result of exhaustive historical research. A complete survey of the sources would be too time consuming and not particularly rewarding. It might yield interesting results but probably not very different from mine. Furthermore, I make no critical evaluation of the reliability of the sources. Thus, one should read the following quotations with these remarks in mind.

Basically, I collected the quotations as follows. During my travels through Canada, I visited university libraries whenever I had the opportunity (Montreal, Toronto, Winnipeg, Saskatoon, and Regina), and there I went through their books on the fur trade, the Red River settlement, travel in the old Northwest, and similar publications to see whether they contain any remarks about the language use of the Métis. The number of the primary sources thus located, all dating from the nineteenth century, is about forty. References to the Métis from the period before 1800 are rare, as they did not exist as a separate group yet, and no special remarks are made about their language. My sources are thus completely arbitrary and limited to those published. Although I am aware that this does not stand up to any standard of historical research, a number of general tendencies can be extracted.

Multilingualism, Code Mixing, Interpreting

The frequent remarks about the language use of the Métis in the sources indicate that it was already in some way different. The language was already distinct around 1815, when Giraud refers to "the colloquial and picturesque language that already distinguished the Métis" (Giraud 1945: 548).[2] Three general trends can be noticed in the sources: there was widespread bilingualism among the Métis, many were interpreters, and there was frequent language mixing.

MULTILINGUALISM

Many of the sources mention the ability of most Métis to converse in more than one language. The languages most often mentioned are Cree, French, and English but also Gaelic, Blackfoot, and others. An American reporter described the Métis in 1877 as a "large favorable intermediate class, *speaking both the Indian and the civilized language*" (Dowse 1877:11; my emphasis). The painter Paul Kane visited Fort Edmonton in December 1847, where a party at the fort

> was early filled by the gaily dressed guests. Indians, whose chief ornament consisted in the paint on their faces, voyageurs with bright sashes and neatly ornamented moccasins, half-breeds glittering in every ornament they could lay their hands on; whether civilized or savage, all were laughing, and *jabbering in as many different languages* as there were styles of dress. English, however, was little used, as none could speak it but those who sat at the dinner-table. (Kane [1859] 1968: 263; my emphasis)

James Hargrave, a clerk at Hudson's Bay Company (HBC), makes the following remark about a Métis ferryman (Sprague and Frye 1983, tables 1 and 4) at the Red River forks, by the name of McDougall: "The name of the ferryman is Duncan McDougall. He is a linguist, being competent to speak English, French, Cree and Gaelic, and in consequence of his abilities and usefulness as an interpreter, ought long before his present time of life to have occupied a good position" (Hargrave 1871: 184).

In March 1858 the Palliser expedition ran into a group of Métis "travelling in a style hardly different from Indians. There were about 200 men, women, and children in the band, with forty tents, which were merely Indian wigwams of buffalo skins sewn together and stretched over poles." (Spry 1963: 109–110). They spoke at least two languages: "They wore clothes of European manufacture, but even those of the men who could speak French preferred to speak Cree."[3]

INTERPRETERS

It is not surprising that many of these Métis were interpreters, like the ferryman McDougall. Many of the expeditions and many of the so-called "discoverers" and "explorers" into the Northwest and beyond used Métis guides and interpreters. Although this fact has not, to my knowledge, been studied in detail, many sources mention it. Captain G. L. Huyshe, for instance, who was with one of the expeditions to the Red River area, used a Métis interpreter in Fort Frances at the Ontario-Minnesota border, about whom he remarked: "We had a half-breed to interpret for us, who translated the Chippewa into French, and very bad French too" (1871: 145).

LANGUAGE MIXING

In addition to the multilingualism of the Métis and the occasional reports of their interpreting, a third theme is found in many contemporary sources. This is the most interesting for us, as it concerns language mixing. Anne De Mishaegen, a Flemish hunter-adventurer who visited western Canada in the 1930s, spoke both French and Cree, and she recognized this mixture as a separate language: "The Métis do not live in the middle of the woods like the Indians. They settle on the outskirts of the towns of the Whites, or they form true colonies, a separate little world, like, for example in Camperville on Lake Winnipegosis, where an extraordinary language is spoken consisting of Cree and French" (Mishaegen 1946: 106).[4] This is the oldest reference I have been able to locate that points unambiguously to the existence of Michif. It refers to one of the communities where the language is still spoken. The nineteenth-century sources, however, are much more ambiguous. Typical is the following description: "Vital, our buffalo hunter, alone spoke very bad English. He succeeded in intermixing French, English and Cree to a degree unequalled by any person of my acquaintance" (Erasmus [about 1850s] 1976: 67, cited in Douaud 1985: 30).

An extreme example of language mixing is given by John McDougall, a Methodist missionary who had learned Cree. He found it "easier . . . to speak in Cree than in English" in the 1860s (McDougall 1903: xxvi). He remembers a meeting with a Métis at the Assiniboine River around 1870. When asked for directions, this man "began his reply in Cree, then went into broken English, and was bringing in some French when I quietly interjected an inquiry if he could speak Cree. He laughingly apologised and then became intelligible" (McDougall 1903: 271–272). From this meeting McDougall seems to predict the emergence of a mixed language like Michif: "I thought as I shook the snow from my beard and rode after my wife that this was how languages had been formed. Here was a people who, if left to themselves long enough, would construct a distinct language out of a fusion of English, French, Cree and Saulteaux." In fact, exactly this may have occurred already when he made this remark, but apparently he did not know about the existence of Michif.

These citations seem to point to extensive language mixing by the Métis in the nineteenth century. Would this be code switching, or must these citations be interpreted as references to the Michif language? An argument for spontaneous mixture is that English is included in all of these cases. Although there are some English words in contemporary Michif, they mostly seem to be recent borrowings. It is possible that because these accounts were written by speakers of English, English elements were overemphasized. Also the presence of an English interlocutor may have stimulated the use of English words by the Métis (as observed by Adrienne Bruyn, pers. comm. 1992).

Another argument for spontaneous mixture is the fact that there are also a few accounts about non-Métis groups who mixed French, Cree, and English, although it is unlikely that they spoke Michif. For example, when the Palliser expedition arrived in the Columbia Valley in British Columbia in the late 1850s, the following occurred:

> Then, suddenly, after they had camped, they heard someone calling out down by the river. It was Capôt Blanc (White Coat) with his son. He was the chief of the Shuswaps, who had for a long time been the Jasper House guide for crossing the mountains. . . . In a mixture of French, Cree, and English, Capôt Blanc explained

that it would take three days to go downstream in a canoe to the Boat encampment. (Spry 1963: 253)

It is more likely that this Indian used his knowledge of the three important languages of the fur trade and not the one mixed language of the Métis. A final argument for spontaneous mixture is that none of these sources mentions people who are able to speak only a mixed language. They all may have been able to speak the languages separately as well.

Thus I am hesitant to call these language mixtures Michif, although one can also raise arguments in favor of this possibility. If these Métis could speak the three languages without mixing, why would they otherwise mix them in conversations with people who are not bilingual or even trilingual, as they are themselves? It would have been more likely that they would speak an unmixed language—if they were actually able to. This is the observer's paradox in code-mixing research: code switching and code mixing are in-group phenomena; code switchers do not switch in the presence of outsiders. The people mentioned may have spoken French and Cree in addition to Michif at that time but still have felt more comfortable using a mixture.

Another argument in favor of Michif is the observation that some inhabitants of the Red River settlement could express themselves only by mixing languages. The reporter James Ross, son of Alexander Ross and an Indian woman (see Van Kirk 1985), commented in his Red River newspaper, the *Nor'wester*, about the multilingual situation in the settlement in the 1860s: "As to languages, we have English, French, Gaelic, Chippewa and Cree, and we do not enumerate all, but only those spoken by large sections of the community" (cited in Stobie 1967–1968: 73). He continues with an interesting comment on language mixing: "There are some who cannot speak one or other tongue solely. In order to express themselves to their satisfaction, they must be allowed the free use of their own exquisite jargon—half this, half that—a "composite tongue." Unfortunately, it is not specified which languages are mixed. This may be interpreted as the use of Michif in the Red River settlement in the 1860s.

The references about Métis language mixture go back to the 1830s and even the 1810s. James Ross's father, Alexander Ross, an inhabitant of the Red River settlement himself, who married an Indian woman and who must have known the Red River people intimately, remarks in his 1856 book that "the vernacular of both Canadians [i.e., French Canadians] and halfbreeds [at Red River] is a provincial jargon of French and Indian mixed up together" (Ross [1856] 1962: 200). That this language mixture is also associated with the *voyageurs* is suggested elsewhere by Ross; referring to the 1820s, he writes that the *voyageurs'* narratives "are made up of an almost unintelligible jargon of the English, French and Indian languages" (Ross [1856] 1962: 79).

Alexander Ross also describes a skirmish between a group of Métis and a group of the newly arrived Selkirk settlers in 1812, in which the Métis apparently used a mixture of French and "Indian": "The settlement of this contract between parties ignorant of each other's language, furnished a scene as curious as it was interesting; the language employed on one side being Gaelic and broken English, on the other, an Indian jargon and mongrel French, with a mixture of signs and gestures, wry faces, and grim countenances" (Ross 1856: 21). As it occurred so long ago, it is not possible that Ross witnessed this conflict himself, and it is not clear what his sources were for this remark. In any case it is echoed in other sources, too, such as Joseph Howard (1952) and L. A. Wood (1915: 54). Could these remarks by Ross on the mixtures of "French and Indian" be references to Michif? I do not want to exclude this possibility.

If Michif was a common language in the Red River settlement in the first half of the nineteenth century, why is it that so many contemporaries do not even mention it—the missionaries, for instance, who worked in the Red River area, or other travelers? I now discuss the languages used in the Red River settlement in more detail.

Language in the Red River Settlement

It is sometimes assumed that Michif arose as a language in the Red River settlement (e.g., Rhodes 1992). Missionaries who worked there, however, never mention the existence of such a mixed language, although there is some contradiction about which languages were spoken by the Métis in the area. Sometimes French is mentioned, sometimes Cree, and sometimes Saulteaux, but the workers for the church rarely mention bilingualism and never language mixture. On the contrary, they sometimes state explicitly that the Red River Métis spoke only one language. As an illustration, I quote a number of missionary sources.

In trying to reconstruct which languages were spoken by the Native people, both Indians and mixed bloods, in the Red River area, we are confronted by a number of problems. Most important, the evidence is contradictory. The earliest reference to Native groups in the area dates from 1738. In that year the French explorer La Vérendrye met Cree-Assiniboines at the forks of the Red and Assiniboine rivers, the center of the later Red River settlement (Greenberg and Morrison 1982: 94). Fewer than fifty years later, Ojibwes (Saulteaux) were living at the same site. Alexander Ross ([1856] 1962: 12; cited in Stobie 1967–1968: 68) mentions oral traditions that state that the Saulteaux arrived at the forks around 1780. This is confirmed by documentary sources (Hickerson 1956).

Confusion about which languages were spoken here begins after 1800, as can be seen from the writings of missionaries who worked with the Natives of the area. In August 1818 the French Catholic priest Sév. Dumoulin wrote from the Red River settlement that Saulteaux was the important language to learn for the local missionaries there: "Our priority will be the Indians, but we would have to follow them from camp to camp in order to preach to them, which is not possible before we know their languages. *I have been partly busy until now with learning Saulteux* [Ojibwe]" (Nute 1942: 134–135[5]; my emphasis). In a letter written a month later that same year, Dumoulin suggests that different languages were spoken by the Métis: "There are quite a few obstacles to their immediate education [of the Métis]; and these are the main ones: their different languages which we do not understand . . ." (Nute 1942: 155).[6]

From remarks like these, one would think that French was not spoken by the Indians in 1818, as this was the language of the Catholic missionaries. If the Indians did speak French, the missionaries would not have had to learn the Indian languages. English was also spoken in the area, if one can interpret Vicar-General Provencher's letter in 1819 as such: "It would be very desirable that the priest and seminarian who come up next year *be able to speak English*, a language that we all three understand a little, but which we can scarcely speak" (Nute 1942: 242; my emphasis). He also asked for someone to study the Native language, presumably Ojibwe: "Another thing even more desirable would be that one of the two spend the winter at Lake of Two Mountains,[7] to study the Indian language and transcribe many things we shall not easily procure here. He would learn more there in three or four months than here in two years, for we have nothing concerning this language" (Nute 1942: 242).

The Métis women apparently understood a little bit of French:

> It is there [Saint François Xavier] where it would be easiest for me to study the Indian language that I want to learn, but which I am afraid not to succeed in by lack of sufficient means. Nevertheless I understand how necessary it is to know it; for it is not to say that only with Métis women and several children who know very little French that one can make progress in God's work. For most part, the French Canadians and the old Métis are unfortunately quite poor Christians.[8] (Nute 1942: 282)

In the years 1812–1816, the Métis who resisted Selkirk's settlement were reported to speak French (e.g., *Statement* 1817: 75, appendices).

Sarah Tucker discusses the work of the Wesleyan Protestant mission school for "Native Indians" in the 1820s in Image Plains, about 20 kilometers downstream from the forks of the Red and Assiniboine rivers (Giraud 1945: 599). Some of the children have made progress in English and the Reverend Mr. Jones "hoped it would not be long before he should be able to avail himself of their assistance in the arrangement of a grammar of their own language—the Cree" (Tucker 1851: 30). Still, the missionaries wanted to stimulate the use of English and French as much as possible among the Métis and Scottish-Cree families (Brown 1980: 203). Knowledge of the Indian languages was a means toward that goal.

Relying on these sources, I cannot definitely assert which languages were spoken by the Red River Métis in the 1810s. It seems that Saulteaux (Ojibwe) was the prevalent language, then Cree and then French. The Saulteaux Indians were also the first people toward whom the missionaries turned their attention: "Father Provencher brought from Quebec in 1831 Mr. Belcourt, an intelligent and energetic man who wished to dedicate himself to the conversion of the Indians. Naturally they started with the ones close by. The Sauteux were the goal of the first attempts at evangelisation" (*Annales de la Propagation de la Foi* 1868: 237).[9]

Other sources concerning the Red River Settlement relate to the 1840s, when there seems to have been extensive multilingualism, as well as code mixing. The HBC Governor George Simpson claimed around that time that four-fifths of the population of Rupert's land, whether white or Métis, spoke French (Giraud 1945: 906). It is not clear whether he includes the Indians. Paul Kane visited the Red River Settlement in June 1846. He mentions general French-Cree bilingualism among the Métis: "The half-breeds are more numerous than the whites, and now amount to 6,000. . . . They all speak the Cree language and the Lower Canadian patois [French]" (Kane 1859: 51). In 1849 the French Catholic priest G. A. Belcourt mentions Chippewa, Cree, and French, but French is spoken less than the Indian languages: "I have already opened two schools for the instruction of the half-breeds; *one in French and the other in Chippewa,* for *these tongues, conjointly with the Cree, are the only ones now in use here,* and even the French is not much spoken" (Wood 1850: 43; my emphasis).

According to Alexander Ross, the different languages of the community were mixed together by both Métis and French Canadians in the 1840s (see the preceding quotation). I have already cited sources from the Palliser expedition, where Métis were reportedly Cree-French bilinguals. Apparently there was extensive multilingualism among the Métis, at least from the 1840s, as well as language mixture. Nevertheless, some sources mention only one language. Captain G. L. Huyshe said in 1871 about the Manitoba Métis: "The French half-breeds are by far the most numerous, and the *French language is spoken throughout the Territory*" (Huyshe 1871: 219; my emphasis).

Two decades before, another military officer had also stated that French was the language spoken by the Red River Métis: "The greater part of these people ["half-breeds" residing in Pembina] are descendants of the Canadian French. *They speak the French language*" (Major Wood 1850: 27; my emphasis). Probably because of their lack of close contact and because of their own use of French, the military officers failed to notice the apparent knowledge of any indigenous languages by the Métis. Also, Lewis Henry Morgan visited a Cree family from Pembina Mountain (30 miles west of Pembina); the wives were Métis and were bilingual: "The women are half-breed Crees and talk French and Cree" (Morgan 1993: 125, 133), but the Cree vocabulary he obtained from them contains no French elements.[10]

In short, there are no unambiguous references to Michif in the early written sources, but there are numerous references to the use of the Ojibwe (Saulteaux), Cree, and French languages in the Red River settlement, and these languages were also mixed.

Oral History

Métis oral history is another source of historical data. Many people with whom I have worked have an incredible memory and also a great knowledge of oral accounts of former days. These people have given me valuable information about Métis language use before 1900. This oral history makes it plausible that Michif was indeed spoken in the first half of the nineteenth century.

The first and foremost form of oral history is, of course, the fact that the oldest speakers who are now alive—and in their 70s, 80's, and even 90's—state that they had learned the language as their first (and sometimes only) language from their parents or grandparents (it is common in Indian and Métis families for grandparents to raise small children). If we calculate back, there must have been speakers of Michif before 1900, perhaps even before the 1880s.

The Métis themselves have traditions about the origin of the language, as in the following history, which a Michif speaker from the Qu'Appelle Valley had learned from her grandfather (I use standardized spelling; the Cree elements are italicized).

Michif

Les Canadiens come across, les Sauvagesses *mâci-wîsamêwak* and then puis *êkwa* les enfants *ê-ayâwâcik*. La Sauvagesse *namôya kaskihtâw* en français *ta-kitotât* ses enfants. Le Français *namôya kaskihtâw* ses enfants *ta-kitotât* en cri.

En français *êkwa kitotêw. êkwa* quelques les deux *kiskinôhamahk kîkway. ê-ohci-pîkiskwê-yâhk* rien que en cris *êkwa* en français.
(Margaret Desjarlais, Fort Qu'Appelle Valley 1988)

An English translation follows:

When the French Canadians came here, they *started to marry* Indian women and then they had children. The Indian woman *couldn't speak* French to the children. The Frenchman *couldn't speak* Cree to their kids, *so he spoke to them* in French. Then some of them *learned to speak* both. *Since then we speak* only French *and* Cree.

This story does not tell us when and where this occurred, however, so we have to resort to other means.

Cultural items may reveal facts about the origin of Michif. The songs in Michif are an example. If they describe historical events that can be approximately dated, it is obvious that the language was already spoken at the time. For instance, an account of the Battle of Seven Oaks in 1816, in which a group of Métis killed white immigrants they considered to be intruders, is preserved in a song in the French language. French has always been the language in which formal and official songs were sung and must therefore have been so already in the 1810s. However, I was able to record only a very few songs in Michif since they often seem to involve more private or delicate subjects like sex and drinking, and people are reluctant to sing them. Some of these songs seem to deal with the Métis way of life. One song I recorded follows (in standard spelling, with Cree elements italicized):

Michif Song

La Montagne Tortue *ka-itohtânân*
en charette *kawîtapasonân*
les souliers moux *kakiskênân*
la viande pilée *kamîcinân*

[repeat first three lines]
l'écorce de boulot *kamisâhonân*

We are going to Turtle Mountain
We will be traveling in a Red River cart
We are wearing moccasins
We will eat pemmican

We will wipe our behind with birch bark
(Modeste Gosselin, Fort Qu'Appelle Valley 1988)

The content of this song refers to the overland trips in Red River carts, which were frequent in the buffalo-hunting period between the 1820s and 1870s (Gilman, Gilman, and Stultz 1979). This song therefore must predate the 1870s.

There is additional evidence for an early origin of Michif in the oral history of the Métis. I asked about twenty Métis elders whom I interviewed in 1990 about the languages spoken by their parents, grandparents, and so on, as far back as they could remember. Some people were able to give a lot of information about their ancestors, which I then tried to relate to the archival and genealogical data about the Red River settlement as published in Sprague and Frye (1983). In two cases I managed to obtain names and birth dates of individuals who were Michif speakers according to people who remember them. One was Gregoire Ledoux, who was born in the Red River settlement (Saint François Xavier) in 1845, according to the Métis oral historian I consulted (Louison Ledoux, Camperville, Manitoba). Sprague and Frye give 1847 as his approximate birth date. This is undoubtedly the same individual. His grandmother was probably a Saulteaux woman. The other person who was reported to be a speaker of Michif was Andrew Allery, who was born in the Red River settlement in 1825. He, too, was a speaker of Michif, the language he most commonly spoke (Elizabeth Keplin, Turtle Mountain).

Thus, according to these data, Michif must have already been spoken in the 1840s and even the 1820s. It is not known whether these people had learned the language from their parents or whether they were among those who created the language from the languages they had learned from their parents and/or peers.

In short, the oral history of the Métis brings us back to the late 1880s (the approximate birth date of the teachers of current speakers), to the first half of the nineteenth century (activities described in songs, such as traveling by Red River cart), or to the 1820s (stories about language knowledge of the ancestors), depending on what one accepts as evidence. To me, the 1820s seems to be a reasonable estimate.

Geographical Data

There are also geographical arguments, based on spread of the language, for an early existence of Michif. In Chapter Five I have shown that Michif is quite uniform in all communities where it is spoken. There can be no doubt that Michif must stem from a common source, a single language community. Therefore the language must have crystallized before the Métis people had settled in these communities. In Chapter Three, I discuss the exodus of the Métis people from the Red River settlement. This had already started in the early 1800s. The largest migration took place in the 1860s and, especially, the 1870s, when most of the people left the Red River area for various reasons, mainly the manipulation of their land. The second dispersal occurred when the Métis lost the battle near Batoche in Saskatchewan in 1885, whereupon many Métis moved west or north or fled south to the United States. The people must have taken the Michif language with them during these migrations since it is spoken in all the communities they traveled to. So the language must predate 1860, when some of these communities were settled, but a closer study of the data on Métis migration and buffalo hunting suggests an earlier origin.

EARLY EIGHTEENTH-CENTURY MÉTIS WINTERERS AND PRESENT-DAY MICHIF-SPEAKING COMMUNITIES

Some of the communities where Michif is spoken were already settled before the 1860s. In fact, most of the places to which the Métis trekked were known to them from their biannual bison hunts, which took place from the 1820s until the 1870s, some even in the 1880s (Giraud 1945: 1165). At some of the locations, there were permanent Métis settlers (*hivernants*, "winterers"), and many of the dispersed Métis settled there, sometimes joining the resident families. It is a misconception that the Métis diaspora was caused solely by the flight after the Métis resistances of 1869 and 1885 or the manipulations of their land in Manitoba from about 1870.

To support this assertion, I present data from Giraud, who had meticulously studied the relevant documentation on these migrations. In doing so, I focus on the communities that are now Michif speaking, which I have discussed in Chapter Five: the Fort Qu'Appelle Valley in Saskatchewan, the Saint Lazare and Sainte Madeleine area and Camperville and Duck Bay in Manitoba, and the Turtle Mountains in North Dakota. This is, of course, not a complete list of Michif-speaking communities today or in the past (see Chapter Three). To these I add one more location where Michif was spoken: the Wood Mountain and Cypress Hills area.

One of my Michif-speaking consultants was from Willowbunch, close to Wood Mountain in southeastern Saskatchewan, where Michif was one of the languages of the Métis communities. The presence of Michif speakers in the Cypress Hills near Wood Mountain is confirmed by Louise Moine's autobiography: "As a descendant of Indian, French and Scots ancestry, my life was more or less guided by a mixture of these three nationalities. Since my parents were both Métis, it was only natural that my Indian blood predominated. Our first language was a mixture of Cree and French" (Moine 1979: unpaged). Moine grew up near Val Marie, close to Lac Pelletier, about 40 kilometers south from Swift Current, close to Wood Mountain and Cypress Hills. In this area, there were apparently Michif speakers in the past, but it is not known whether any are still there.

The places where Michif is spoken today all appear to be past sites of Métis winterers, who lived off the buffalo hunts and other natural resources. They visited the area between the 1820s and 1860s (see Chapter Three). As the presence of food and water was important for survival, the wintering grounds were often close to water (rivers or lakes) for fishing and drinking, forests for game and firewood, and prairies for the buffalo hunt for food and supplies (Giraud 1945: 820). The wintering places of these hunters' families surely played a role in the choice of a permanent place to live when the Métis were more or less forced to leave the Red River area. These communities were sometimes described as simple dwellings, consisting of tipis covered with buffalo hides, but often the Métis built log houses as well (Giraud 1945: 821). The villages could lodge as many as 200 families at a time, and some of these communities grew into flourishing towns (Giraud 1945: 1170–1171). For example, Saint Joseph, today Walhalla, in North Dakota in the Pembina district, already had a population of up to 1500 people in the 1850s (Gilman, Gilman, and Stultz 1979: 38).

Several preferred locations for the winterers in the 1840s and 1850s had the right environmental conditions: the area around Pembina, the Qu'Appelle Valley, Turtle Mountain, Wood Mountain, Touchwood Hills, Cypress Hills, and the Souris River area near Turtle Mountain (Giraud 1945: 817, 818, 820). These are the only places mentioned by Giraud for these decades, and they are exactly the places where Michif is spoken. There was much movement between these locations, especially Pembina, and the Red River forks, where many of the hunters spent the summers (Giraud 1945:

817; Gilman, Gilman, and Stultz 1979: chap. 1). Nevertheless, sometimes Métis winterers who had not visited Red River for ten years were encountered in the prairies. Often the Métis buffalo hunters would gather for their hunts in Saint François Xavier (Red River settlement) and Pembina. From there they would travel into Montana, Saskatchewan, and the Dakotas, searching for bison.

Strikingly, all of these wintering places mentioned by Giraud are also where people living today grew up speaking Michif as their mother tongue: Walhalla, North Dakota, is in the Pembina district, although most of the Métis moved to Turtle Mountain (Giraud 1945: 1281). The Turtle Mountain Chippewa Reservation is where Michif is still most widely spoken, as we have seen in Chapter Five. Willowbunch, on the slopes of the Wood Mountain, was once a prospering Michif-speaking community. Val Marie, Ponteix, and other places close to the Cypress Hills also had Michif speakers until recently. Lestock and Punnichy, on the south side of the Touchwood Hills, were communities with Michif speakers, although most of them have moved away. In Lebret, Fort Qu'Appelle, and other villages in the Fort Qu'Appelle Valley, Michif speakers can still be found.

Another important factor concerning these wintering places is Métis and Indian cooperation (Giraud 1945: 819). Here, Indians and Métis often lived and hunted together: "In these improvised villages, which could gather close to 200 families, the Indians and the Métis lived in good harmony" (Giraud 1945: 821). Saint Joseph, for example, had French-Canadian, Cree, Ojibwe, Assiniboine, and Métis inhabitants (Gilman, Gilman, and Stultz 1979: 38) around 1850.

Later, from the 1860s onward, Saint Laurent and Oak Point, on the southeast shore of Lake Winnipegosis; Duck Bay, on the west shore of the same lake; and the banks of Lake Manitoba were also mentioned as wintering places. No Michif has been reported from these places, however. Saint Laurent is mainly French speaking, and some elderly residents also speak Saulteaux (see also Lavallee 1988, 1990). I have no data on Oak Point.

These geographical data tell us that speakers of Michif in the late twentieth century can be found at the wintering places of the Métis buffalo hunters of around 1850. Although occasionally the farming Métis of the Red River settlement joined the winterers (Giraud 1945: 820), this was not common and the nomadic hunters predominated. It is not certain, on the one hand, that these places were continuously (or at least, say, every winter) inhabited by the Métis from the 1840s until the twentieth century. On the other hand, it is certain that at least some of the Métis who moved into these communities between 1870 and 1900 (Sprague and Frye 1983: table 6) were Michif speakers. The Fleury family clan of Saint Lazare and Sainte Madeleine, for instance, moved there from Saint François Xavier in 1886.

Nevertheless, whether or not there was a continuous occupation of these sites, and whether or not Michif speakers moved there before or after the great exodus from the Red River settlement, it is beyond doubt that these locations were chosen because the people were familiar with them from the bison hunts. This suggests a connection of the Michif language with the Métis bison hunt. It also suggests that Michif was a fixed code in the 1840s since the communities were already inhabited by Métis by that date and the languages in all of them are virtually identical, even today.

THE RED RIVER MÉTIS BISON HUNT

Although the Red River settlement is often described as a more or less homogeneous community, it was actually "an amalgamation of several different communities divided by language and religion" (Gilman, Gilman, and Stultz 1979: 28). I have already discussed this point in Chapter Three. In fact, many of the parishes had different populations, religions, and languages (see map 4).

It may be useful to summarize here some of these diversities (Giraud 1945: 773–774). Saint Boniface and Saint Norbert were inhabited by Roman Catholic, French-speaking Canadians and Métis, some of whom were farmers. Gaelic-speaking farmers from the Scottish highlands, mostly Presbyterians, were living in the Kildonan parish. Retired HBC employees and their families spoke English, belonged to the Church of England, and lived north of the forks. The former HBC people in Saint Andrew parish may have spoken Bungee[11] (Stobie 1967–1968: 69). Closer to Lake Winnipeg, there were Saulteaux Indians around a Protestant mission. Baie Saint Paul and Saint François Xavier were mostly inhabited by Roman Catholic "Indian"-speaking Métis buffalo hunters, who spent long periods outside their community following the herds. The latter community was a main center for the hunt, which although called the Red River hunt, in fact was attended by only a small group from the settlement. The Métis from the parish of Saint François Xavier spent most of their time outside of the community, traveling for buffalo hunts or living off the land in the wintering places. These hunts took place from the 1820s until the early 1880s, when the bison were effectively annihilated.

These were the years of prosperity for the Métis, who succeeded in hunting a surplus of animals. What they did not use themselves for food, for housing, or in other ways, was given to the starving European settlers, traded, or sold to the Hudson's Bay Company. Thus, the fur traders and settlers could survive in areas where food was scarce. The Métis were the most important suppliers of pemmican. In the beginning this trade was not allowed by the HBC, but after a court case against a Métis petty trader, its monopoly was successfully challenged in the 1850s. Long caravans of Métis traders and hunters in Red River carts traveled overland through the prairies and south into the United States to trade mainly bison products (Giraud 1945: 801–808; Gilman, Gilman, and Stultz 1979). During these travels the Michif song quoted previously must have been sung.

Hunting trips generally brought the Métis into new areas. They became thoroughly familiar with the prairie landscape and developed or ameliorated all kinds of techniques for hunting (shooting bison from horseback), transportation (Red River cart), food preservation (pemmican), and so on. They partly intruded on Sioux territory, which sometimes led to skirmishes between these two groups, but the Métis in general related well to the bison-hunting Crees, Plains Ojibwes, and Assiniboines, with whom they regularly engaged in common hunts (Giraud 1945: 658, 802, 817, 819, 823; Sharrock 1974: 112). There are also reports of conflicts, however, so relations may not always have been friendly.

The Métis who dispersed from the Red River settlement included not only the lower class of the bison hunters but also (and somewhat later) the farming elite of, for example, Sainte Agathe (St.-Onge 1985). When looking at the 1870–1900 migrations of the Red River Métis as presented in Sprague and Frye (1983), one gains the impression that their destinations depended on whether they were farmers or hunters. The elite, French-speaking Métis farmers often moved to towns like Prince Albert or farming communities like Lindsay, whereas the people from Saint François Xavier often moved to the locations discussed above. Non-Métis—Scottish or mixed Indian-Scottish families—moved to different places again. The Métis bison hunters and former bison hunters of Saint François Xavier with French surnames moved to the sites where Métis hunters used to winter—and these are the places where Michif is spoken today.

Summary and Conclusions

In trying to summarize the data, we can tentatively state that the Native languages were strongest among the Métis in the Red River settlement in the 1810s, probably especially Ojibwe and then Cree. French was also spoken widely. English was, of course, also used, in any case by the Orkney and Scottish (Selkirk) settlers and probably also Gaelic. The Red River settlement was undoubtedly a multilingual community from the 1800s on, but it is hard to say whether there were many bilingual or multilingual individuals at that time. The only data I have on bilingual individuals are two sources (published long after the event), which state that some of the Métis mixed French and "Indian" languages. In 1812 the Métis tried to chase away the Selkirk settlers from the area they considered theirs. The events are described (much later) as follows: "But when the riders came into close range, shouting and gesticulating, it was seen that they wore borrowed apparel, and that *their speech was a medley of French and Indian dialects*. They were a troop of Bois Brûlés, Métis, or half-breeds of French and Indian blood" (L. A. Wood 1915: 54; see also Ross 1856: 21; my emphasis).

I have not been able to find a contemporary source that confirms this assertion. If this indeed refers back to sources dating from that time, there were bilingual individuals who already mixed "French and Indian" in 1812. It is certain that this language mixing was common from the 1840s onward; independent and presumably reliable sources contain similar comments, and most important, oral history of the existence of Michif also goes back to the decades between 1825 and 1845.

In table 6.1 I summarize some of the contemporary comments on language use in the Red River settlement in chronological order. The table suggests that Saulteaux, Cree, and French were spoken in the settlement in the beginning of the nineteenth century. There may have been a shift from Saulteaux to Cree after the 1820s. There is no direct evidence for the existence of Michif, although several people mentioned the extensive mixture of "French and Indian" as the "vernacular" of the French Canadians and the Métis of the Red River settlement in the 1820s and 1840s. This is likely to be Michif, although it is not definitely proven.

Geographical data suggest that most of the communities that are now Michif speaking were already in existence around 1840 as the winter settlements of the Métis. As they lived off the land, they lived like, and often with, local Indians. This also suggests the existence of Michif prior to the permanent settlement of these communities, and hence, prior to 1840.

TABLE 6.1 Language in the Red River Settlement—Chronology

Year	Ethnicity	Language	Source
1738	Cree-Assiniboines	Unknown	La Vérendrye (Greenberg and Morrison 1982)
1800	Saulteaux	Saulteaux(?)	Hickerson 1956
1812–1816	Métis	French	*Statement* 1817
1818	Indians	Saulteaux	Dumoulin (Nute 1942)
1818	Métis	"Indian"	Dumoulin (Nute 1942)
1818	Unknown	Saulteaux	Provencher (Nute 1942)
1819	Unknown	English	Provencher (Nute 1942)
1820s	Indians	Cree	Tucker 1851
1831	Indians	Saulteaux	Provencher (Nute 1942)
1830s	Métis women	Indian	*Annales de la Propagation de la foi* 1868
1840s	All	French	Simpson [in Giraud 1945]
1840s	Métis, French	French, Cree	Ross [1856] 1962
1846	Métis	Cree, French	Kane [1859] 1968
1849	All	Cree, French, Saulteaux	Belcourt [in Major Wood 1850]
1850	Métis	French	Major Wood 1850 (Pembina)
1871	Métis(?)	French	Huyshe 1871

The Origin of the Northwest Saskatchewan Dialect of French-Cree (Ile-a-la-Crosse)

In Chapter Five, I show that the contemporary Cree-French dialects of the northwestern Saskatchewan Métis in and around Ile-a-la-Crosse are unrelated to Michif. Both the Cree part and the French part appear to be based on different dialects of these languages. Culturally there are also many differences between the people of Ile-a-la-Crosse and the Métis of Red River. In this section I make an educated guess about the origin of this language.

Today, the Cree spoken in the area is northern Plains Cree (in which /e/ merges with /i/; see Chapter Nine). The dialects as spoken in the nonreserve communities have some French borrowings (see Chapter Five). The amount of French used differs from community to community, according to my own observations and conversations with local Natives, probably as follows (from many French borrowings to few borrowings):

(1) Ile-a-la-Crosse > Beauval > Buffalo Narrows > Pinehouse > Meadow Lake > Green Lake

The dialect of the Métis and nonstatus Indians of northwestern Saskatchewan, in particular the dialect spoken in Ile-a-la-Crosse, is known among Saskatchewan Métis and linguists alike to be "a mixture of Cree and French." In Chapter Five I propose to consider it as Cree with French borrowings.

The question one has to ask is, where do these French words come from? I have two kinds of data, which make an educated guess possible. On the one hand, there are historical sources on Ile-a-la-Crosse language use; on the other hand, there are the beliefs of the people themselves.

Although this matter has not been researched systematically, there are some indications that the Cree dialects of Ile-a-la-Crosse and surroundings have undergone considerable changes in the nineteenth century. Today a *y*-dialect of Cree is spoken (meaning that it has a /j/, written "y" as the reflex of proto-Algonquian */l/), but in the middle of the nineteenth century an *r*-dialect was spoken here. A. A. Taché, who lived in Ile-a-la-Crosse at that time, wrote in 1869 that the Crees at Lac Ile-a-La-Crosse said *nira* "I" and *iriniw* "person" (see also Pentland 1978a: 107), whereas they now say */nija/* and */ijiniw/*—the ordinary Plains Cree forms. Additional evidence comes from Michel (1866: 83) in a book about the missionary Henry Faraud, who learned his Cree in Ile-a-la-Crosse: "The Crees have three different R's, the most frequent is somewhat like the fat R of the people of the Provence."[12] In any case he says nothing about any French used by the Cree, although he mentions French speakers among the neighboring Chipewyans (not to be confused with the Chippewas).

There is also other evidence for the existence of an *r*-dialect in Ile-a-la-Crosse. A few years later Lacombe (1874a: xv; cited in Wolfart 1973b: 8) also stated that an *r*-dialect was spoken by the Crees of the Athabasca district. The only *r*-dialect word I recorded in Ile-a-la-Crosse was /karačɛ/ or /okaračɛ/ for "spider," a word that does not seem to be a Cree word, and I have not been able to find out where it comes from. None of the living Cree speakers remembers this *r*-dialect being spoken, although Keith Goulet (pers. comm. 1988) informed me that he had met people in northern Saskatchewan who remembered that their late relatives had spoken an *r*-dialect.

According to Taché (1869: 82), apart from the speakers of an *r*-dialect, some Crees in Ile-a-la-Crosse ("certain Cris de l'Isle à la Crosse") spoke an *l*-dialect in the 1860s, for which he cites *nila*, *kila*, and *wila* for "I," "you," and "me." Today there is, as far as I could find out, only one Cree word in general use in Ile-a-la-Crosse that has an /l/. The word for "ant" is /iːliku:s/ for all speakers; see Plains Cree *êyikos* and Saulteaux and Michif /ɛnikūs/. This *l*-dialect is now completely gone, and I am unaware of any other indication of an *l*-dialect of Cree in Ile-a-la-Crosse. Pentland (1978a) mentions only the existence of *l*-dialects of Cree around James Bay. The Ile-a-la-Crosse *l*-dialect seems to have disappeared completely. In any case, 100 years ago there was a different Cree dialect spoken in Ile-a-la-Crosse.

The past of the Ile-a-la-Crosse speakers, however, is unclear. The earliest historical sources report mostly or only Dene (locally called Chipewyan or Chip) speakers in the area, the Crees arriving later. The Denes speak an Athabaskan language, unrelated to Cree. In 1776 a fur-trading post was opened in Ile-a-la-Crosse (Longpré 1977), soon followed by other posts of competing fur traders close by. There must have been English-speaking and French-speaking fur traders in the area around 1800 (Johnson 1967: 217, n. 6, lxxxii). All the oldest sources mention Dene Indians, who are called by the name derived from Cree, Chipewyans, meaning "hide stretchers" *ocipwayânîwak*, or according to Helm, *oči:pwaya:ni:w* "[he who was] pointed skins or hides" (see Helm 1981: 283). For instance, a letter written in 1799 says: "I brought three boats and one canoe to the Isle le Cross Lake. Mr Linklater accompanied me to the above

lake where I left him with the Ochipoyans and proceeded hither with two boats"
(Johnson 1967: 217).

Crees were also mentioned in that area at that time. Daniel Harmon (1820: 168),
for instance, reports in August 1807 from "Isle la Cross Fort": "The Indians who come
to this establishment, are Chipewyans, in considerable numbers, and a few Crees." In
the nineteenth century more and more Crees are mentioned. Today, Ile-a-la-Crosse is
the northernmost Cree-speaking community in the area. Of the two neighboring communities in the north, Buffalo Narrows is partly Chipewyan and partly Cree, and Patuanak
is Chipewyan, with Cree as a second language. Historically, it seems that the Crees moved
north into Chipewyan territory in the late eighteenth or early nineteenth century.

There are also numerous cultural differences between the Ile-a-la-Crosse Métis
and the Michif-speaking Métis of the prairies (see Chapter Five), although old-time
Métis traditions are found in Ile-a-la-Crosse as well, such as fiddle music, dances,
and Catholicism. Quite a few of the inhabitants have no objection to being considered "Indian," whereas Michif speakers generally do not like this designation. The
Ile-a-la-Crosse inhabitants seem more like Indians, many of them nonstatus, with some
French cultural influences.

Although the French lexicon has not been studied in detail, it is my firm impression that in some cases in Ile-a-la-Crosse, standard French words are used where
Michif typically uses Métis words. It seems that the French element is partly derived
from Quebec French and partly from Métis French. It is very possible that the French
element was introduced through the mission and the school system. Many Quebecois words, some of them rather archaic, are also in use in Ile-a-la-Crosse (see Community of Ile-a-la-Crosse 1990, which lists more than 200 French words generally
known in the community).[13] It seems that there are two sources of the French lexicon: traders and/or Métis French, on the one hand, and a more standard form of
Canadian French through the mission and its school, on the other hand. Certainly,
the French element in Ile-a-la-Crosse differs at some crucial points from the French
element in Michif (see Chapter Five).

Some of the elders are still fluent in Cree without an admixture from French.
For those who are not fluent in Cree, the use of French elements seems to be limited
mostly to cultural innovations. The community itself (Community of Ile-a-la-Crosse
1990) ascribes the French influence to the activities of the French traders and the
school system.

As a tentative conclusion, it seems that the Ile-a-la-Crosse mixture of Cree and
French is of fairly recent origin. In the early contact period, Chipewyan was spoken
in the area; in the nineteenth century, an *r*-dialect of Cree (as well as an *l*-dialect),
apparently without French admixture. Sometime in the decades around 1900, the
r-dialect shifted into a *y*-dialect, and around the same time the French elements seem
to have entered the language. Although some typically Métis words are known there,
the standard Quebecois word is often used in Ile-a-la-Crosse. The elders in the community say that they learned French in the schools. The lifestyle is also closer to the
traditional Native way of life than in many other communities. More research is
needed, however, to confirm these suggestions. In short, it seems that the mission
school and the activities of French-speaking traders were responsible for the presence of French elements in Ile-a-la-Crosse.

Code Mixing with Algonquian Languages

So far in this chapter, I have discussed some historical data on the genesis of Michif and Ile-a-la-Crosse French-Cree. In this final section, I focus my attention on code mixing, not from a historical perspective, but from a comparative perspective. Code-mixing studies take more and more language pairs into consideration, and many proposals have been made to account for the similarities and differences in the diverse situations. There is little theoretical consensus among the people who are studying this phenomenon. The first language pairs studied were often typologically similar, both being Indo-European languages, like Spanish-English and French-English. Universal constraints were formulated on the basis of these pairs only, such as the "equivalence constraint" and the "free morpheme constraint." In simplified terms, the first phrase means that in code mixing the grammatical structures of both languages cannot be violated at the point of switching. The second means that there can be no stems with affixes from the other language in code mixing, as opposed to borrowing (Poplack 1980).

In studies of other language pairs, however, these constraints appear not to hold. For instance, in code mixing in which one of the languages is an agglutinative language, it is common to have stems from one language and affixes from the other. Thus the free morpheme constraint does not hold for these language pairs. Agglutinative languages have clear boundaries between stems and affixes by definition, as well as between the affixes themselves. Furthermore, they often have long words with affixes that convey a range of meanings. In pairs that involve an agglutinative language, we very commonly find that code mixing violates the free morpheme constraint.

Not surprisingly, people studying code mixing that involves languages of this sort propose completely different constraints and models. Sentence (2) is an example of Finnish-English code mixing (English elements italicized) (from Boeschoten 1991; after Sankoff and Poplack 1987), and (3) is an example of Turkish-Dutch code mixing (Dutch elements italicized) (from Backus 1992; see also Boeschoten 1991).

(2) Mutta ne oli *fridg*-i alla   (Finnish-English)
     But they sat fridge-the under
     "But they sat under the fridge."

(3) *Cassetterecorder*-nan *friettent*-e gidelim lan   (Turkish-Dutch)
     Tape recorder-WITH cafeteria-TO let's.go hey
     "Let's go to the cafeteria with the tape recorder, hey."

Apparently there is a clear typological dimension in code mixing: no or very little word-internal mixing that involves two fusional languages and massive word-internal mixing in pairs with one agglutinative language. Myers-Scotton (1993, and elsewhere) proposes a matrix language frame model (MLF) to account for this type (or actually any type) of code mixing. Very briefly, this model states that there is one matrix language, in which foreign elements can be employed. That is, the matrix language provides the grammatical framework of the code-mixing utterance. The other language is called the embedded language. If the embedded elements are longer than one word, they should follow the grammatical system of the embedded language. Anything else should follow the grammatical system of the matrix language, including bound and free grammatical morphemes (called "system morphemes" by Myers-Scotton). This works neatly for many language pairs with different typological characteristics.

More recent work by Muysken (1997) and Van Hout and Muysken (1995) shows a step forward. As a lot of material from different language pairs has become available lately, a truly comparative study has become possible. Not only isolated sentences or selected switches are classified but also entire corpora. Based on this comparative approach, Muysken distinguishes three types of code switching and code mixing: alternation, insertion, and congruent lexicalization, which he also wants to link with different social situations. Alternation is the type of switching in which bilinguals start a sentence in one language and end in another. Both languages keep to their grammatical characteristics. This type can be linked to some of the language pairs on which Poplack (1980) based her conclusions. In the insertional type, one language provides the grammatical framework, into which elements from another language are placed. The embedded elements are limited mostly to stems or phrases. This type can be associated with most of the language pairs that Myers-Scotton studied (1993). The congruent lexicalization type is the most complex. It shows an inextricable mixture of the two languages, whereby one cannot identify a matrix language and whereby the grammatical systems do not remain separate but have considerably converged. This type may be rarer than the other two types.

It appears that all cases of code mixing that involve Algonquian languages are of the insertional type. Moreover, it is an overwhelmingly constituent insertion: whole noun phrases (including determiners and possessive pronouns) and prepositional phrases from English and French are inserted into the Algonquian framework. Verbs are much rarer or totally absent; the only instances are Attikamek and Betsiamites Montagnais both of which show a construction with the French verb in the infinitive form with a *do*-support verb from the Algonquian language, which has all the inflections.

Several pairs of other typological combinations have not yet been studied. In all cases reported in the literature, at least one of the languages is Indo-European, so there is always at least one language of the fusional or inflectional type. No cases that involve two agglutinative languages have been studied, for instance, nor those with two isolating languages. Furthermore, only very little research has been done on code mixing that involves polysynthetic languages. As Cree is a polysynthetic language, this is of course the most relevant type.

To my knowledge, the only case of code mixing studied that involves a polysynthetic language that is not Algonquian is reported in a short note on Navaho-English mixing (Canfield 1980). Navaho is an Athapaskan language spoken in Arizona. Unfortunately, Canfield discusses only the use of English verbs in Navaho since he does not consider "lexical items and phrases used in the midst of a predominantly Navaho discourse" (Canfield 1980: 218). What remains are two ways of using English verbs in Navaho. The most common type is the use of English stems with Navaho helping verbs meaning "to do" or "to make"; the other, much rarer type is the use of English verbs that are embedded in Navaho morphology, which is restricted to "playful speech." Apparently only with a creative and conscious mind, the polysynthetic verb of Navaho is "invaded" by foreign elements. Normally, the inflection of the verb is separated from the English stem by placing the inflectional elements in helping verbs. The English stem is given in an infinitival form. This type of code mixing differs considerably from Michif. They have one important point in common, however: the verbs must be left intact, except in special circumstances. In both cases, verbal inflection is *not* combined with foreign stems (unlike in agglutinative languages).

In the rest of this section I discuss code mixing with Algonquian languages.

Ojibwe-English Code Mixing

Rhodes (1985: xxv) devotes a short discussion to English borrowings in Ojibwe in the introduction to his Ojibwe dictionary. Some speakers of Ojibwe cannot converse with only Ojibwe words; they have to use at least some English. His three examples suggest that no English articles (or perhaps other function words) are used:

(4) *accident* ngii-yaa-naa
     accident 1–PAST-have-11
     "We had an accident."

(5) *diet* ngii-igoo
     diet 1–PST-(tell)-INV
     "I was told (to go on a) diet."

(6) *two clock*
     "two o'clock"

These examples are perhaps borrowings rather than code mixing, but as Rhodes says, the borderline between the two is not strict. In both cases, the function words of the English noun phrase seem to be omitted. This phenomenon is found in a variety of language pairs. Functional elements (system morphemes) not existing in the matrix language are omitted, even though the same speakers do use them when they are not code switching (see Myers-Scotton 1993, chap. 4, for an analysis of what she calls "bare forms").

Lisa Philips Valentine considers Severn Ojibwe–English code mixing. She analyzed the English elements in an hour's radio broadcast in Severn Ojibwe. Apart from a few longer stretches of discourse in English, the fifty-one tokens of English embeddings all show constituent insertion. Some are place names, others are noun phrases ("Toronto regional director"; "radio station"), and a few are prepositional phrases ("across Canada"; "for one week") (Lisa Valentine 1995: chapter 4). It is clearly of the type constituent insertion, and the inserted constituents are never verbal.

Plains Cree–English Code Mixing

Nothing has been published, to my knowledge, about Cree-English code mixing. There seem to be two types. Some speakers use the bare nouns, exactly as in the preceding Ojibwe-English examples. There is an example in Chapter Five: the first speaker in (3) says, "last birthday" with no preposition or possessive element. In this type of code mixing, too, English nouns do not have definite or indefinite articles. Other examples from my recordings in Saskatchewan are as follows:

(7)   *school* ni-kî-wâpam-âw-ak   (Cree-English)
      school 1–PST-see-3–PL
      "I saw them in the school."

(8)   otina *hood*   (Cree-English)
      take hood
      "Open the hood."

In the other type of Cree-English code mixing, the pattern is the same as in Michif: the English nouns are used with the articles, possessives, and prepositions from English, as in the following examples:

(9)   namoya nêhiyawak *in hell* ayâwak   (Cree-English)
      NEG Crees in hell they-are
      "There are no Crees in hell."

(10) ê-âyimôskito-cik tântê ê-wî-nitawi-ayâ-cik *their holidays*   (Cree-English)
      COMP-discuss-3PL where COMP-want-go-have-3P their holidays
      "They were discussing where they would have their holidays."

Cree is the main language of the discourse (the "matrix language" in the terminology of Myers-Scotton 1992, 1993) in all these examples. In both types, the use of English verbs is rare. This is strikingly similar to Michif. This pattern is also clearly visible in some of the recent published recordings of Plains Cree texts by Ahenakew (Bear et al. 1992). Although there are quite a few complete sentences in English, there are no English verbs (except in those longer stretches of English) nor constructions with a Cree helping verb for "to do"; there is a considerable number of bare nouns, noun phrases, and prepositional phrases.

(11) môy êkw ânohc, tâpiskôc, â, *hospital*, âskaw ê-pêyakocik kêhtê-ayak, nam âwiya ê-wa-wîtapimikocik *in their final hours.*

      "Not like today, sometimes, *in, ah, the hospital*, where old people are alone and nobody sits with them *in their final hours.*" (Alpha Lafond, in Bear et al. 1992: 248)

(12) katisk ôm ê-waniskâyân, môy âhpô *my glasses.*

      "I woke up just now; I don't even have *my glasses.*" (Rosa Longneck, in Bear et al. 1992: 252)

(13) êwako mâka mîna nitôtinên pêyakwâw, *about a year ago* êtikwê, «îwahikanak niwî-osîhâwak,» nititâwak awâsisak. nitôtinên êkwa ôhi, kâ-sêkwâpiskinamân êkwa, mêtoni nikâspihkasên, *you know*; ê-kî-tahkâk êkwa aya, êkwa aya, *canvas* anihi mâna . . .

      "I bought that once, *about a year ago*, I guess, "I'm going to make pounded meat," I told my children. I bought it and put it in the oven until it was really crisp, *you know*; and when it had cooled, well then, ah, that *canvas* . . ." (Alpha Lafond, in Bear et al. 1992: 274)

Here we see either constituent insertion with all articles, prepositions, and so on or (more rarely) deletion of function words, as *hospital* in the first example, which has neither article nor preposition.

In short, in both Ojibwe-English and Cree-English code mixing, there is a type of mixture that integrates English bare nouns (and some uninflected elements, but no verbs) in an Ojibwe or Cree context. There is also a type of code mixing in which English nouns trigger English articles, prepositions, and possessives, so that it seems similar to Michif in that verbs are Algonquian and nouns are non-Algonquian. It is not yet clear what factors play a role in this choice. Perhaps the words without modifiers are borrowings and the words with modifiers are more like code mixing.

Naskapi-English Code Mixing

Naskapi is an Algonquian language spoken in Labrador and Quebec. It shows similarities to both James Bay Cree and Montagnais, but it is a separate language. In about one hour of Naskapi dialogue that I recorded in Montreal in 1993, the following forty-four English words and phrases were used:

(14)   address, after, apartment (twice), appointment, April, August, ball, bar (three times), cabin (three times), cassette, Christmas (twice), church, Cosby show, December (twice), dee-jays (twice), dentist appointment, every day, fifteen, fifty dollars, fifty-five, free trip, Friday (twice), green, Guy, metro, happy new year, hours, in the morning (twice), jogging, meetings, my ticket, next year (twice), once a week (twice), plastic, protest, quarter to three, right now, room, roommates, somewhere Montreal, Spanish, squash, tape recorder, tent, what time (twice).

Here we see the same patterns as in all other cases: only noun phrases and prepositional phrases, including possessive elements, are taken from English. English elements also have English plural markers. In some cases the functional elements are omitted, certainly in "somewhere Montreal," where "in" is omitted.

Micmac/Maliseet-English Code Mixing

There is also code mixing of Micmac or Maliseet with English. These are eastern Algonquian languages, not closely related to Cree but still typologically similar. They are spoken in the Atlantic provinces of Canada. Robert Leavitt informs me that "one frequently hears English nouns and verbs with native-language prefixes (these are person-markers: I, you, they, etc.) and endings (these are abstract roots plus inflectional endings)." The examples he gives in a publication (Leavitt 1985) are as follows:

(15)   *culture*-em-atigw
       culture-DO-21
       "We are (going to be) doing culture."

(16)   *correct*-ewatu
       correct-IMPER
       "You correct them!"

(17)   g-*papers*-m-l
       2–papers-POSS-INAN.PL
       "your papers"

Recordings made by me in Gesgapegiag (Quebec) in 1996 also show English stems with Micmac affixes. Micmac linguist Bernie Francis told me in 1995 that this usage (English stems, both verbal and nominal, with Micmac suffixes) is a common pattern in Micmac when English words are used. I do not know how representative this is for Micmac-Maliseet borrowing or code mixing. It resembles borrowing or nonce borrowing more than code mixing, as it seems to be limited to cultural innovations. In contrast with the language mixture just discussed, the English elements have Algonquian affixes. I do not know whether this occurs because the social situation is different or because Micmac shows more similarities toward agglutination in its morphology.

Montagnais-French Code Mixing and Borrowing

The best documented case of code mixing with an Algonquian language occurs in the Montagnais community of Betsiamites, Quebec. There is extensive code mixing there, indeed to such an extent that one could speak of the current emergence of a mixed language of French and Montagnais, according to Lynn Drapeau. Montagnais is closely related to Cree, although the two are not mutually intelligible. Algonquianists classify Cree and Montagnais as parts of a dialect continuum. The language pairs French-Montagnais and French-Cree are therefore highly comparable cases of language contact. As the language mixture is taking place at this very moment in Betsiamites, it is very useful to discuss this case in relation to Michif. The data come from Drapeau (1980, 1991; several personal communications in 1991 and 1993). A few examples are also given in Mailhot (1985).

Betsiamites is a community of about 2000 people, all Montagnais, except for a handful of French-speaking whites (Oudin and Drapeau 1993). It is located on the north shore of the Saint Lawrence River, almost 400 kilometers northeast of Quebec. Montagnais is spoken on the local radio station, but other media are in French only. Virtually all people are bilingual in Montagnais and French, except for a handful of elderly Montagnais monolinguals and a significant number (perhaps most) of the children under school age, who speak "Montagnais" as their first language. It can be disputed, however, whether it is really Montagnais these children are learning from their parents. The elderly monolingual Montagnais speakers cannot understand them because of the number of French borrowings. Montagnais-French code mixing is so extensive in this community that the children hear only parts of the Montagnais language. The way in which this code mixing is structured is similar to that in Michif. In fact, Drapeau (1991) considers the emergence of this mixed language in Betsiamites as a replication of Michif.

In French-Montagnais code mixing, the base language is Montagnais. The French elements include the following, according to Drapeau (1991):

(18)   greetings, calendrical reckonings (days of the week, months, etc.), time expressions, numerals, expressions of quantity and measures, conjunctions, exclamatives and interjections, adverbs, discourse particles

These are all parts of speech commonly taken from other languages (for instance, from Spanish in South American Indian languages; see Brody 1987) in comparable situations of language contact. Chamorro, the Austronesian language of Guam in the Pacific Ocean, shows *exactly* the same borrowed elements from Spanish as those that Montagnais is borrowing now from French,[14] but one cannot reasonably claim Chamorro as a mixed language. The basic vocabularies of Montagnais and Chamorro remain almost untouched. Most of the elements mentioned are French derived in Michif, too. In Michif, however, the use of French is not limited to these semantic categories. There is another important qualitative difference between Michif, on the one hand, and Betsiamites Montagnais and Chamorro, on the other hand: the use of French verbs. Drapeau (1991) says that French verbs are ordinarily used in Montagnais-French code mixing, and I have shown in chapters Four and Five that French verbs are virtually nonexistent in Michif. In Betsiamites they are used in an apparently infinitival form with a Montagnais helping verb that means "to do." This, by the way, is a common pattern for borrowing verbs in the languages of the world, and it is also used in code mixing. Moravcsik (1975: 14–15) mentions Korean and Japanese and a number of Indic and Dravidian languages from India, and we can add Australian Aboriginal languages and others (P. McConvell and A. Backus, pers. comm., 1996). As I have said, it is also reported from Navaho-English code mixing (Canfield 1980). For Montagnais examples, see the short text (19) that follows; the French words are italicized, and the Montagnais verb *tut-* "to do" is printed in boldface (from Drapeau 1991; Drapeau and Bakker 1994).

(19)   mukw ekwe peikuan *engager* **nitutakuti** utehe, tshissin-a. nana tshashtaian *le CÉGEP* tshia, ekue nutepalipan miam *un professeur*, auen ne ka nutepalt, *remplacer* ne **nitutuau** *pour un an*. Ekue *engager* mipua **tutakuian**. Ekuan, *depuis ce-temps-là* tshissin-a, nanitam *ré-engager* ekue **tutakuian** tshia, mukw *une condition* nimilikutait, tshetshi *suivre* **tutamuk** *des cours* nanitam utin-a? *à tous les ans*-a? *pour avoir six crédits au moins par année* tshissin-a?

But then they **did** *hire* me anyway here, you know. When I finished *the CÉGEP* see?, *a teacher* was missing just at the time, the person who was missing, I **did** *replace* her *for a year*. So of course they **did** *hire* me. That's it, *ever since then*, you know, they always **did** *rehire* me, yes? But they put *one condition* on it, that I **do** *take some courses* always, say, *each year*?, *to get at least six credits a year*, you know?

Apart from the elements mentioned in (18) and the verbs, many nominal constituents are derived from French in Betsiamites French–Montagnais code mixing. The nouns are used with the articles, possessives, and prepositions. Drapeau cites sentences that have French nouns like *un cyste* "a cyst," *le foyer d'accueil* "the foster home," *son talon* "his heel," and *dans ma chambre* "in my room." Apparently this use of French nouns occurs to such an extent that young Montagnais-speaking children hardly ever hear the Montagnais forms of some of these nouns. In a naming test conducted among seventeen 4-year-old speakers of Montagnais, it appeared that none of them knew the Montagnais words for "apple" and "milk," sixteen used the French word for "horse," twelve used the French word for "soap," and ten used the French word for "bird" (Drapeau 1995). This shows the extent to which these French words are used by their parents in speaking Montagnais. As in Michif, the French nouns are used with French definite or indefinite articles, possessive pronouns, and even partitives (unlike Michif), which all have the appropriate gender. French prepositions are also used. Both in Michif and Betsiamites Montagnais, Cree and/or Montagnais demonstratives are used with the French nominal constituents.

In short, the way Montagnais and French are being mixed in Betsiamites is similar to the way in which Cree and French are mixed in Michif. Some of the Betsiamites sentences can be transferred almost syllable by syllable into Michif (see also the example in Chapter One). The way in which French nominals are used in otherwise Montagnais contexts is identical to the way in which this occurs in Michif. The preponderance of nominals may be the consequence of the relative ease in borrowing nouns in Cree and Montagnais. Still, the text also makes clear one important difference: the quantity, both of French verbs and of French items in general. In Michif, virtually no French verbs are used, whereas this is common in Montagnais-French, with the helping-verb construction. Nevertheless, the totality of the polysynthetic verb is not violated: no foreign stems are used with Montagnais affixes.

Another important difference is in the extent of borrowing from French. In Montagnais it is much more limited, as shown in (18). Whereas all nominal items are French in Michif, in Montagnais they would be limited to what Myers-Scotton (1993) calls "cultural borrowings." The Montagnais corpus also shows long stretches of discourse without any French items, whereas it would be close to impossible to have even a single sentence without any French items in Michif. The Montagnais material also shows core vocabulary, but most French items constitute cultural innovations and words associated with or learned in formal education. It seems to be more a case of incipient borrowing—although of an unusual pattern and to a rather considerable extent—than code mixing.

Attikamek-French Code Mixing

Attikamek is a Cree dialect spoken in Quebec. The social situation in the three Attikamek communities is similar to that of Betsiamites. Montagnais and Attikamek are not mutually intelligible, and there is very little contact between the two language groups.

The results of Lynn Drapeau's study of Attikamek-French code mixing, from two hours of transcribed recordings of oral speech, is tantalizingly similar to the Betsiamites case. In both cases, around 80 percent of the switches are intersentential. Among the intrasentential switches, around 75 percent are multiword switches. Less than 5 percent of the single-word switches are bare nouns. The exact figures (from Drapeau and Bakker 1994) are given in table 6.2. These figures indicate that similar social situations with typologically almost identical language pairs lead to very similar types of mixtures.

Ojibwe-Cree Code Mixing

The code mixing between Ojibwe and Cree shows totally different patterns from that of either of these languages with English or French. Ojibwe and Cree are, of course, closely related languages, and many people in Kingfisher Lake, Ontario, know both. This section is based on the studies of Lisa Valentine (1995: chap. 4; 1994) on the

TABLE 6.2 Statistical Comparison of Montagnais and Attikamek Code Mixing

Betsiamites Montagnais (30 hours, 8500 switches)	Percent	Manuan Attikamek (2 hours, 921 switches)	Percent
Intersentential	16	Intersentential	22
Intrasentential	84	Intrasentential	78
Intrasententials (= code mixing)			
Multiword	76	Multiword	73
Single words	24	Single words	27
Multiword switches			
Noun phrases	76	NP/PPs	73
prepositional phrases			
Single word switches			
Single nouns	< 5	single nouns	< 5
Conjunctions, discourse markers	10		
single V, ADJ	5		

use of language in this community. Severn Ojibwe, the main language, is an Ojibwe dialect influenced by Cree. Cree has been the prestige language for a long time, perhaps centuries. It is still used in the local church, and thus its influence is most significant in religious discourse.

This influence can be seen in phonological, morphological, and lexical levels. On the phonological level, Cree preaspirated consonants are used instead of the equivalent nasal-plus-stop clusters of Ojibwe. On the morphological level, one finds the deletion of the negative verb suffix (nonexistent in Cree but obligatory in Ojibwe) or the use of Cree verb suffixes instead of Ojibwe suffixes. A few Cree words are also used in addition to or instead of their Ojibwe equivalents. Of course, phonological and morphological "borrowing," as in this case, are possible only when the languages involved are closely related.

Algonquian Code Mixing

There are a few types of Algonquian code mixing. The Micmac-English mixture, however, seems to imply borrowing rather than code mixing, although there is no absolute criterion to distinguish the two (Myers-Scotton 1993) since the English words used are much like cultural innovations, as far as one can judge from the examples. They also show the use of Algonquian affixes with English stems. The other cases do seem to involve code mixing.

Some cases of Algonquian code mixing with English are different from those with French. Sometimes when English words are used in an Algonquian context, all function words are dropped (articles and prepositions), whereas French words are always used with their prepositions and articles. In most cases, however, the mix of Cree and English is similar to Michif: predominantly English nouns, which trigger the use of articles and other noun modifiers, and no verbs. This suggests that Michif could in principle have emerged as a form of code mixing or that it was influenced by code mixing. Strangely enough, the cases of French-Cree code mixing that I recorded in the questionnaire and in a number of stories look very different from the other cases that involve Algonquian languages.

The following text fragment illustrates this type of code mixing. It was recorded in 1988 in Ile-a-la-Crosse; the narrator is Elizabeth Bouvier. All Cree (northern Plains) elements are italicized, and French verbs are in boldface.

Le Sirop de Bouleau

tânisi ça **faisait** le sirop de bouleau
how people made the syrup of birch

î-manisw-at apisîs le bouleau
you cut a little bit the birch

îkut-uhci îkwa les tubes *ki-tamuhtâw*
there-from now the tubes you-stick-there

îkusi kwayes pour que il **coule** le saf dans la chaière.
thus right for that it-flows the juice in the pail

le saf il **coule** dans la chaière *iskuhk ta-sakaskinîpayik.*
the juice it-flows in the pail until it-will-become-full

îkwaspi sîkînam nawac î-misikiti-t le chaudron.
after pour it more big the kettle

îkwaspi pûnam un grand feu.
then make.fire a big fire

pîyâhtik piku ta-uhtîk le sirop de bouleau.
slowly one-must make boil the birch syrup

îka ta-pîhkahtîk osâm ta-wîsakam.
do not burn it, because it will be bitter

îkwa sukaw[15] *apisîs asici* **met** ça dans le sirop.
and sugar a little with it, put that in the syrup

d'une chaudière la moitié *piko pîyak* la chaière *uhci ta-utsisu.*
from one kettle the half only one pail from will-be left

le sirop de bouleau *îyako ûma kâ-ayimutamân*
the syrup of birch this I am telling you about

tânisi comment ça **faisait** leur sirop la place dans le bois
how how that made their syrup the place in the woods

English Translation

How they **made** birch syrup. Cut a birch a little bit and then put tubes in it, so that the tree's juice will **flow** into a pail. The "juice" **flows** into a pail until it fills up. After that pour it into a bigger kettle. Then make a big fire. Make the birch syrup boil slowly. Do not burn it, because it will be bitter. And also a little bit of sugar, **put** that in the syrup. From one kettle only half of it will be left, for one pail. This birch syrup, I am telling you how they **made** their syrup in the old days on the place in the woods.

If this is representative for Cree-French code mixing, it is clear that it is rather different from that in the Betsiamites community and the cases with Ojibwe and Cree just discussed. In fact, texts such as these look more like the code mixing that is known from studies about European languages than the mix of French with Cree or Montagnais: that is, it looks like a spontaneous mixture of two languages, whereby in principle any element can be used in any language, as long as certain constraints on the mixture are not violated. The pattern is alternating rather than insertional. For instance, French verbs are used here. The difference may be caused by the situation: in this case dictation rather than spontaneous speech, which was written down after some pressure by me to mix the two languages (see Chapter Five). I suspect that this is not representative for any form of spontaneous code mixing with Cree and French.

The evidence for a possible link between code mixing and Michif is contradictory. In some cases, the mixture of Michif seems to be replicated in one type of code mixing that involves English nominals. In other cases it is different. Is there some diagnostic feature that distinguishes code mixing from a language mixture such as Michif? It has been argued that the latter has distinctive properties.

In code mixing, the different elements seem to keep the features they have. For example, in Montagnais-French mixing, French words mean the same as in French and they function in the same way. Each component from each language keeps its integrity and is a grammatical phrase or constituent in the source language.

In the type of language mixture called relexification, however, a word from the lexifier language used in the language of the grammatical system would have the grammatical properties (meaning, argument structure, selection restrictions, etc.) of the word with the closest meaning that was replaced (Muysken 1981, 1988a and b). In Media Lengua, for instance, the language with Spanish lexemes and a Quechua grammatical framework, an adposition derived from the Spanish preposition *despwesitu* "after" ended up in a postnominal position to replace the Quechua postposition *k'ipa*, which has the same meaning. Furthermore, a new verb stem *nuway* (< Sp. *no hay*) was formed to replace the Quechua stem *illa-* "there is not." There are some more examples, too, such as the semantic system of the Media Lengua demonstratives, which are derived from Spanish but also have semantic properties from Quechua (Muysken 1988a).

If this is correct, there is a diagnostic difference between language mixture and code mixing. The question therefore is, are there French elements that clearly have the properties of the Cree element they replaced? The answer is yes. Some have been mentioned in chapters Four and Five, and I mention some again here: the French preposition *dans* functions exactly like the Cree locative suffix *-ihk* (see Chapter Four); the French distinction between definite and indefinite plural noun phrases was lost in Michif (see Chapter Four); the French possessive markers function like obligatory possession markers with inalienable possessions, as in Cree; obviation agreement markers are present in the verb even where obviation is not overtly marked on the French noun; the partitives in Michif are lost; and all French nouns show agreement in gender with the verb following the animate or inanimate gender of the original Cree noun. Other features may be present, too, but they are harder to recover.

If this argument is correct, it suggests that Michif is not a case of fossilized code mixing. French elements have properties of the Cree items that were replaced by the French nouns. Nevertheless, Cree-French code mixing of the Cree-English type (nouns with their modifiers, except demonstratives) may have influenced the outcome of the Cree-French language mixture. We cannot exclude the fact that the predominance of French nouns in French-Cree code mixing led to the overall disappearance of Cree nouns, as a way of regularizing the system. For the time being, however, code mixing alone is clearly insufficient as an explanation for the genesis of Michif. In chapters Seven and Eight, I propose a model for the genesis of mixed languages called "language intertwining."

Conclusions

In this chapter I discuss the different mixtures of French and Cree shown in Chapter Five: code mixing, Cree with French borrowings, and Michif.

As for the origin of Michif, diverse sources point to the same two decades of the nineteenth century when the language must have been already established. First, the communities where Michif is spoken today were established camps of Métis winterers in the 1840s. Second, people born in 1825 and around 1845 are remembered as primarily Michif speakers by their descendants. Third, there is a strong Ojibwe element in Michif (see Chapter Nine). In the early 1800s many Métis may have spoken French, Ojibwe, and Cree. Fourth, there are some references to the use of a French-Cree-Ojibwe language mixture by Métis in the 1840s, perhaps even in the 1810s. The *voyageurs* were depicted as using a mixed language of Indian and French in the 1820s.

Although none of these points can be taken as proof by itself, they all roughly coincide and we can safely assume that Michif must have been an established language by 1840. It probably originated between 1812 and 1821, dates that mark two important historical events for the Métis: the genesis of the ethnic identity of the Métis as a "new nation" and the beginning of the massive, organized bison hunts. As Michif speakers are descendants of these hunters, Michif must have been the language of the "poorer" Métis, whereas most of the elite spoke French. The main centers of the bison hunt were Pembina in Minnesota and Saint François Xavier in the Red River settlement, Manitoba. These were also the centers of the Michif language. Finally, the striking absence of any mention of Michif in written sources indicates that it must have been an in-group language of the Métis. Their political representatives were French speakers. Many of the Michif speakers must have known other languages as well (notably French), in order to communicate with outsiders. As Michif was a language used only in the home, that is, a private, internal language of the Métis, outsiders failed to notice its existence.

I have concluded that Ile-a-la-Crosse French-Cree is indeed an independent development that has nothing to do with Michif. The French part of the language is less extensive than in Michif, mostly referring to cultural innovations (nouns), and is closer to Quebecois French. The French school system is responsible for the borrowing of the French vocabulary into the language, but some of the vocabulary was brought by fur traders and their descendants. More study is needed to confirm this observation.

For the study of code mixing, I adopt a comparative perspective by considering other cases of code mixing with Algonquian languages. There are some striking similarities with the code mixing of French and Montagnais (East Cree) and French and Attikamek in Quebec, both of which are developing into languages with significant borrowing from French. These constitute cases of extreme borrowing rather than real mixed languages, in the same way as, for instance, Mayan languages or Chamorro borrowed extensively from Spanish. Also, cases of Cree-English and Ojibwe-English code mixing show parallels with Michif in the noun phrase: with constituent insertion, not alternation or congruent lexicalization. The data are rather homogeneous, except for the dictated French-Cree text. Still, it seems possible that the genesis of Michif was influenced by code-mixing patterns that involved Cree and French (and perhaps Ojibwe), which would probably have involved mainly Cree verbs and French nouns.

This confirms the suggestions in Chapter Five. There are three types of Cree-French mixture. One (Ile-a-la-Crosse) arose by adopting French words (nouns) into Cree, probably because of the influence of the school system and the clergy, as well as the French of fur traders and French-speaking Métis in the area. The second type is French-Cree code mixing. Here the results are somewhat contradictory since some forms of code mixing look very much like Michif, in the distribution of Cree and French elements, and other forms are rather different. Based on the limited data available, it seems possible that some form of code mixing played a role in the genesis of Michif. Code mixing of the type documented by two responses to the questionnaire in Chapter Five is too different to be a possible factor. The French part of Michif is often not grammatical in French; it appears to have a number of underlying Cree properties, showing that the process cannot have been code mixing alone. Michif still remains a third type of language mixture, different from both borrowing and code mixing. In the next two chapters I present a model for the genesis of mixed languages, in particular the aberrant case of Michif.

Ethnogenesis and Language Genesis

A Model

Michif is a peculiar language, and the Métis are a rather uncommon type of ethnic group. In this chapter I present a model for the genesis of mixed languages and the social circumstances under which they originate.

Introduction

We have seen that the Métis form a new and mixed ethnic group who speak a mixed language. I have suggested that there is some relation between these two facts. In this chapter I review this suggestion from different angles and try to formulate a model of language mixing. What kind of people speak mixed languages? Do all new and mixed ethnic groups have a mixed language? What do the new languages of these groups look like? In this way I hope to provide a model that combines social and linguistic factors. This model states under what circumstances a mixed language will emerge and which language source contributes which part to it.

"New" Languages: Pidgins, Creoles, and Mixed Languages

The Métis are a new ethnic group. We can be absolutely sure that this group did not exist before, say, the late 1600s, when the first contact of the French and Indians in the West occurred. Their identification as a separate group may have occurred even later, in the early 1800s. The Métis are a mixed group (see Chapter Three); the name of the language and the people, *Michif*, *Métif*, *Métis*, and *Mestizo*, underlines this fact. Indeed, it is one of the most conspicuous aspects of their identity. The Métis do not consider themselves Indian or white but rather a separate people, of mixed descent.

The question is, is it the newness of the Métis as an ethnic group or their mixed nature that is connected to the fact that Michif is a mixed language? To answer this question, I survey several languages that are somehow mixed or new. In this section I discuss the latter.

When a language changes, it can diverge so much from the original that at a certain moment it is considered to be another language, different from the language from which it descended. Spanish and French, for instance, both developed out of Latin. They are both daughter languages of vernacular Latin, but they are different languages now. This is the normal pattern of language change: languages are transmitted from one generation to the next and slowly change over time and along different paths in different regions, until they are divergent enough to be considered distinct languages. In this way, languages may split apart, but they are still genetically related.

However, the transmission of languages does not take place in this way in all cases. There is a significant number of new languages that can be said to have developed in a nongradual way (Thomason and Kaufman 1988: 50, 100–110, 129–199). The better known are pidgins and creoles. These two types are often lumped together, although with little or no justification. Both types of languages have quite different characteristics, and both terms cover a broad range of phenomena. Mixed languages differ from each.

Pidgins

A pidgin is no one's native language. It may arise when speakers of two or more mutually unintelligible languages are required to communicate and there is no opportunity, necessity, or desire to learn the language spoken by the others. This occurs, for instance, in trade or in work situations in which people who speak a diversity of languages are brought together. Usually the language of the economically dominant group provides the vocabulary. In situations in which there may not be a dominant group, in trade, and when only two languages are in contact, the vocabulary of the pidgin may roughly comprise both languages equally. An example is Russenorsk pidgin of the North Cape. In a few other cases, the nondominant language provides the vocabulary, for example, in some North American Indian pidgins (Drechsel 1976, 1981), perhaps because the Indians refused to learn the European languages or because the newcomers tend to learn the local language.

The grammatical system of pidgins is often rather variable and reduced and not always similar to any of the grammatical systems of the languages in contact. Pidgins are never the language of a specific ethnic group; they are always used between speakers of other languages. The vocabulary is rather limited, emphatic pronouns are used, and there is less inflection than in the source language. The following phrases are an example of pidgin English from Liberia (Holm 1989: 422) and an example from Russenorsk (from Broch and Jahr 1984b: 115), in which the Russian elements are italicized.

(1) One big pig pass all we pig come for we yard. Me take one gun and shoot for him. Me
     look he can die one time.   (West African pidgin English)

     "A pig bigger than our pigs came into our yard. I took a gun and shot at it. I saw that it
     died at once."

(2) *moja* på anner skip nåkka vin drikkom, så *moja* nokka lite *pjan*, så *moja* spaserom på lan
    på selskap anner Rusman.   (Russenorsk)

"I drank some wine on another ship, so I (am) a little drunk, so I walked-around on land
in the company of another Russian"

Creoles

It is often said that a creole language is derived from a pidgin that acquired native speakers. For this statement, however, there is little more than circumstantial evidence (except in the New Guinea area). Sometimes it is said that creoles are mixed languages,
but this is not true. In almost all cases the vocabulary of a creole language is derived
almost exclusively from one language, often that of colonial powers like English, French,
Portuguese, Dutch, Arabic, and Spanish. Although creoles can be lexically based on
any of these languages, their grammatical systems are more like one another than like
that of the language from which the vocabulary is derived. An example is Sranan Tongo,
creole English from Suriname, from a Sranan storybook (De Groot 1971: 53):

(3) wan neti wan mama sidon na sé na bedi fu en siki pikin
    one night a mother sit LOC side LOC bed of her sick child

    nanga sari na ati a luku o-fa a dé sa opo gi en
    with sad LOC heart she look how the day FUT open for her

    "One night a mother was sitting by the side of her sick child's bed. With sadness in her
    heart she was watching how the day would arrive for her."

Although the origin of pidgins and especially creoles is a matter of controversy,
there seems to be some consensus about sociolinguistic aspects of the latter: creole
languages originate in multilingual circumstances in which one language is economically dominant.

Mixed Languages

Michif, a mixed language, is unlike pidgins and creoles. Some kind of definition is
very much needed here. In the history of linguistics there has been continuous discussion of whether or not mixed languages exist (see Thomason and Kaufman 1988:
1–12). Some people have denied their existence and others have claimed that there
are no languages without at least some admixture. Part of this controversy was caused
by the fact that nonmixed languages were often used as examples of mixed languages.
For instance, English was thought to be a mixed language (see, e.g., Bailey and
Maroldt 1977) since it has both a Romance and a Germanic component. English,
however, is not a mixed language (Thomason and Kaufman 1988: 263–330). It is a
Germanic language, although with considerable lexical borrowing from French. There
is no structural influence from French of any significance.

The same is true for other languages that underwent strong lexical influence (up
to 40 percent or 50 percent of the vocabulary) and even some grammatical influence. Even in the strongest cases of borrowing discussed by Thomason and Kaufman

(1988: 100–109), the borrowing languages still belong to one language family. They did not become mixed languages. Asia Minor Greek is basically Greek, Kormakiti Arabic is basically Arabic, and so on.

To escape this pitfall, I define mixed language somewhat more precisely. To do so, I have to mention an assumption in historical linguistics: two languages belong to the same language family if both morphosyntax and lexicon have elements in common (see Haas 1969 for a historical view and Goddard 1975 for a case involving Algonquian). Thus, I define a mixed language as follows:

(4)   A mixed language is a language that shows positive genetic similarities, in significant numbers, with two different languages.

One can with equal justification claim that such a language belongs to language family A as that it belongs to language family B at the same time. This means in most of the cases that neither the lexicon nor the morphology is in itself sufficient to establish a genetic relationship between two languages. If a language shares its vocabulary with another language but it does not share its grammatical system with any other language, it is not a mixed language. For instance, a creole or a pidgin may draw its lexicon basically from one language (e.g., English), but its grammatical system is totally different from that language, as we have seen in the Sranan example. Nor is the grammatical system of a creole directly derived from any of the languages that were present in the contact situation. The grammatical system of creole languages cannot (at least in the vast majority of cases) be equated with any other existing non-creole language. Therefore, creole languages are not mixed languages: they are related to one language with respect to the lexicon, but they do not have the grammatical system in common with any other language. They are not mixed in the sense meant here, despite widespread belief to the contrary.

Some pidgins could be considered mixed languages under this definition, for example, Russenorsk. Because of its mixed lexicon it shows lexical similarities to both Russian and Norwegian. Russenorsk grammar is neither Russian nor Norwegian. There are some other examples of such pidgins, such as Trio-Ndjuka pidgin of Suriname (De Goeje 1908; Huttar 1982).

We can state that mixed languages that fall under this definition cannot as such be used for the reconstruction of a protolanguage; at most some of its parts can (see Thomason and Kaufman 1988: 206–211). Their genesis is, as they say, nongenetic, like that of pidgins and creoles.

Mixed Languages: An Overview

In this section I present some documented cases of mixed languages that follow my criterion—in more or less geographic order, starting in South America and from there going east. This list is not complete. For a more complete overview, see Norval Smith (1994; forthcoming) and Bakker and Mous (1994) and Bakker (forthcoming). I briefly discuss the way in which the languages are mixed and the sociolinguistic background, as far as these are reported in the literature (Bakker and Muysken 1994).

Media Lengua, Ecuador, South America

The first example is from South America. The language is called Media Lengua or Utilla Ingiru (little Quechua). It is spoken by Ecuadorian Amerindians, who form a geographical and cultural group between the Quechua-speaking Indians in the mountains and the Spanish-speaking Europeans in the towns in the valleys (Muysken 1980, 1981, 1988a and b). This language, a mixture of Spanish and Quechua, is spoken alongside Quechua and Spanish, both as a mother tongue and as a second language. The content words are Spanish and the grammar (phonology, morphology, syntax) is Quechua. Following is an example from Muysken (1988b: 419), in which Quechua elements in Media Lengua and their Quechua equivalents are italicized:

(5)   miza despwesitu kaza-*mu* i-*naku-ndu-ga*, ahí-*bi* buda da-*naku-n*   (Media Lengua)
      miza k'ipa wasi-*mu* ri-*naku-pi-ga*, chi-*bi* buda ku-*naku-n*   (Quechua)
      mass after house-to go-PL-SUB-TO there-LOC feast give-PL-3   (Spanish)
      yendo a la casa después de la Misa, ahí dan una boda
      "Going home after mass, they then give a feast here."

This example shows Quechua affixes attached to Spanish stems, which have been adapted to Quechua phonology.

Callahuaya or Machaj-Juyai, Bolivia, South America

A language similar to Media Lengua, called Callahuaya or Machaj-Juyai, is spoken as a ritual language by traveling Amerindian curers in Bolivia. The language is a mixture of Quechua and Pukina, the latter spoken in the area until around 1900 but now extinct. Basically the lexicon is Pukina and the grammatical system is Quechua (Stark 1972), although in some varieties the Pukina is much less extensive. An example (Quechua elements are italicized) follows:

(6)   lurisitu-*qa* yani k'ata-*puni* Pedro-*manta* k"i:-hti-*n*   (Callahuaya)
      Luwisitu-*qa* aswan hatun-*puni* Pedro-*manta* ka-sa-*n*   (Quechua)
      Luis-TOP more big-EMPH Pedro-ABL be-DUR-3
      "Luis is bigger than Pedro."

Island Carib Men's Language, Lesser Antilles, Central America

A third case may be the famous Island Carib men's language (Hoff 1994, 1995). In the 1650s the men on the Lesser Antilles were reported to speak a language different from the women. The men spoke Carib and the women spoke Arawak—at least this is what is said in some modern sources. This phenomenon was related to the historical event of the Carib conquest of Arawakan-speaking Antilles several centuries before.

  More thorough studies, however, show a different picture (Taylor and Hoff 1980; Hoff 1994, 1995). Carib men are reported to have conquered some islands of the Lesser Antilles and killed all the Arawak men, after which they took the women as their wives. The children must have learned pidginized Carib from their fathers and Arawak from their mothers. In the 1650s both women and men spoke Arawak, although with considerable lexical borrowing from Carib. However, in addressing men, the people spoke a mixture of Arawak and Carib, and when addressing women, Arawakan only. Carib was still spoken at that time, but only by men on formal occasions. The mixture is characterized by Taylor and Hoff (1980: 308) as follows: "Lexemes and some morphology from Karina [Carib], most morphology from Arawakan."

I do not agree with Taylor & Hoff that this language was a pidgin, despite the fact that the Carib items probably stemmed from continental pidginized Carib (Hoff 1994). Neither sociolinguistically nor structurally was it comparable to a pidgin. Rather it was a mixed language in which a (pidgin) Carib lexicon was combined with Arawakan morphology. The language is now extinct, although the Black Caribs in Central America still retain vestiges of the mixed register in their Garifuna language. Taylor and Hoff (1980) and Hoff (1994) cite only a limited number of phrases and words, such as the following (in which Arawak elements are italicized):

(7)   ti-ouéma-*tina*
      RES-fall-I.have
      "I have fallen."

(8)   an-eúllé-pa *nómêti*

      IT-give-NEG I.do.it

      "I do not give it."

(9)   chi-chánoumain *l-ién-rou*
      TRANS-love he-IMPERF-her
      "He loves her."

Ma'a, Tanzania, East Africa

Linguists have tried to classify Ma'a or Mbugu as either Cushitic or Bantu (see, e.g., Goodman 1971; Thomason 1983; Thomason and Kaufman 1988). Today it is being studied in detail by Mous (1994; forthcoming). The language is spoken in northeastern Tanzania. Basically, the grammatical system of Ma'a is identical to or close to Pare, a neighboring Bantu language. The lexicon consists of two parts, one set of words of Bantu origin and one of non-Bantu origin. The Bantu words are close to Pare, whereas the non-Bantu register is most closely related to southern Cushitic languages (as far as identifiable) and some from Maasai. There is hardly any doubt that the ancestors of the Ma'a were originally Cushitic speakers, who probably moved south around 300 years ago.

The mixed variety, which combines the Cushitic stems with the Bantu grammatical system, is called Inner Mbugu by Mous (1994). This is the language discussed by the other authors named in the previous paragraph. It contains a few nonproductive Cushitic morphological markers, as well as some phonemes, presumably Cushitic, such as /x/ and /ʔ/, unknown in Normal Mbugu. Inner Mbugu and Normal Mbugu share the same grammar, and the Inner Mbugu and Normal Mbugu equivalents are

complete synonyms, even in their metaphorical extensions. They have Bantu semantics. All speakers of Inner Mbugu are also fluent in Pare, and most are also speakers
of Swahili and/or of another neighboring Bantu language.

Mous argues strongly for an analysis of the genesis of this mixed language as a
register of a Bantu language with non-Bantu lexicon, not the result of borrowing Bantu
grammar into a Cushitic language. The Mbugu prefer relative isolation, and they resist
assimilation into the neighboring Bantu groups. Following is a brief text sample from
Mous (1994: 175–176), in which non-Bantu elements are italicized[1]:

(10)   íji va-*ma'a* vá-he-*hé* twáí,
       now C6–Mbugu C2.PST-C16-arrive

       kwá kubá te-vé-*dúmú*-ye va-*bó'i ká nyamálo* . . .
       with reason NEG-C2-want-APPL-PERF DEM.C2 work

       "Well, the Mbugu arrived there. Because they did not want to do this work . . ."

Basters/Griekwas, Namibia and South Africa

The fifth example is a language formerly spoken in a number of "mulatto" communities in Namibia and South Africa. Its speakers call themselves Basters, Oorlamse,
and Griekwas. They have Trekboers (Afrikaners who went north for the ivory trade
in 1800s and married local women) and Nama Hottentot and Khoekhoen ancestry.
Their history is very similar to that of the Canadian Métis (Kienetz 1983). In the mixed
language spoken by these people (along with Khoekhoen and a variety of Afrikaans),
the content words are Afrikaans, a half-creolized derivative of Dutch, and the grammatical elements are Nama (Khoekhoen or Hottentot). The mixed language is used
as an intragroup language. An example (Den Besten 1988: 26) follows (Khoekhoen
elements in Basters are italicized):

(11)   Heeltemaal-*se* natuur-*a-xu* bedorven-*he*   (Basters)
       Hoaraga-*se* =ûb-*a-xu* gaugau-*he*   (Nama/Khoekhoen)
       totally-ADV nature-CAS-PREP rotten-PASS
       Van nature helemaal bedorven   (Dutch)
       "totally rotten in nature"

This sentence was recorded in the late nineteenth century, along with a few others.

Unfortunately there are contradictory reports about whether the language is still
spoken. It is possible that some Namas speak a similar mixed language (Hans den
Besten, pers. comm.). Very little of this language exists, but it is easy to see that the
syntax and all the bound morphemes are identical to Khoekhoen and that all the lexical
morphemes are close to Germanic Afrikaans.

Romani 1: Angloromani, Great Britain, Continental Europe

An example of a mixed language from Europe is Angloromani. This is the language
spoken by Romanichal Gypsies in Britain and North America, called Poggedi jib "bro-

ken tongue" by its speakers or Angloromani by linguists (Hancock 1984b). An example (English is italicized) follows (Cornelius Price in 1897; published in Sampson 1930):

(12)   *Puri mɔnušini* and a *puri* old *rai*. They had *yek čavi*, a *rakli*, and *yeka divés* there was a *muš jali*n' on the *drom diki*n' for *būti*.

> "An old woman and an old gentleman. They had one child, a girl, and one day there was a man going on the road looking for work."

Older written sources (from the nineteenth century) show more Romani grammatical elements than are heard in the modern spoken language, and there seems to be a trend toward using more English words. Today, the grammatical elements tend to be English, and the content elements are mostly Romani. The "classical" variety of Romani, with Indic inflection, was rarely known by Angloromani speakers in the nineteenth century, with some exceptions (see Smart and Crofton 1875). Angloromani is learned in early adulthood, and today English is the first language learned.

Romani 2: Basque Romani, Basque Country, Europe

A second example from Europe is the now almost extinct language of Gypsies in the Basque country, called Errumantxela by its speakers, Motzaileen hizkuntza "sheep-shearers' language" by the local Basques, and Basque Romani by linguists (Ackerley 1929; Bakker 1991a). It was spoken in addition to Basque. Most of its speakers, after 1850 at least, probably did not know "classical" Romani. Its speakers are (and were) Gypsies who reside in the Basque Country and a group called *Kaskarotak*, who are of mixed Basque and Gypsy descent. The language has Romani stems with Basque affixes. Phonology, morphology and syntax are Basque, as well as the auxiliary, whereas the lexicon is Romani.

(13)   xau*a*, goli keau-*zak*, mol but-er-*ago* akhin-*en* d-*u-k*   (Basque Romani)
        child-DET song sing-IMP wine much-COM-COM have-FUT it-have-you
        haurr*a*, kanta *zak*, arno gehi*ago* ukan*en duk*   (Basque)
        "Child, sing, you will have more wine."

Other Para-Romani Languages in Europe and the Middle East

There are other cases of Romani mixing with the languages of the host country, in Sweden, Norway, Denmark, West Armenia, Greece, the former Yugoslavia, Turkey, Persia, Spain, Brazil, Catalonia, and Occitania (see Boretzky and Igla 1994 and Bakker and Van Der Voort 1991 and Bakker (forthcoming) for overviews). These dialects are called Para-Romani. In all these mixed Romani dialects the pattern is one and the same: the lexical material is from Romani, and the grammatical material is from the language of the host country. Those elements that have both lexical and grammatical meaning (personal pronouns, demonstratives, question elements, etc.) show some variability. These elements can be in either of the two languages or in both. Some other languages are spoken by formerly nomadic groups in many parts of Eurasia.

Senkyoshigo, Japan, East Asia

Senkyoshigo, a mixture of English and Japanese, is the in-group language of American Mormon missionaries who work in Japan (Smout 1988). In this example, the Japanese is italicized:

(14)   Hey dode, have you *benkyo*-ed your *seiten*s for our *shukai*
  today yet?   (Senkyoshigo)
  mo sukai-no tameni seiten-o benkyosita   (Japanese)
  "Hey companion, have you studied your scriptures for our meeting today yet?"

Although its speakers all speak English and Japanese, during their stay in Japan they use only Japanese (with local people) and Senkyoshigo (with their fellow missionaries). Here, again, we see that the grammatical system, including phonology, is English and the lexicon is mostly Japanese.

  This language differs from the others in that its speakers also know both source languages. It has been included here to show that any bilingual group can make up a mixed language that follows a certain procedure, but it rarely goes so far that the speakers lose command in one or both of the source languages, as they do in the other cases.

Krojo and Pecu' (Petjoek), Indonesia, Southeast Asia

At least two mixed languages are spoken in Indonesia by so-called Indo-Europeans (not to be confused with the speakers of the Indo-European languages in Eurasia), or the shortened form *Indos*, who were born to Indonesian mothers of different ethnic backgrounds and European (mostly Dutch) fathers. One of their languages, Pecu', is described by Van Rheeden (1994, 1995), and another group and their language is described by De Gruiter (1994), himself a native speaker. He grew up in Semarang, Java, in the early decades of this century. His mother was a speaker of Javanese, and his father was a Dutchman. Apparently there were many children like him. He spoke a mixture of Dutch and Javanese, with a little bit of Malay, with children of similar background. The Javanese part is only from the nonhonorific variety. According to De Gruiter (1994: 17), there are several varieties, depending on the language of the mother. The language is called Krojo in Semarang and Petjoek (/pecu'/) in Surabaja. In Surabaja it is also a mixture of Javanese and Dutch, and in Jakarta a mixture of Malay and Dutch. The etymology of *krojo* is not given; *Pecu'* is a pejorative term for an Indo. An example of the Krojo language (De Gruiter 1990: 38) in which the Dutch is italicized, follows:

(15) lho *met tas* itu kan *heef*[2] *niks*   (Krojo)
  lho nggawa tas[3] iku kan ora apa-apa   (Javanese)
  hey! bring bag you nevertheless not thing-thing
  maar dat jij je tas bij je hebt zegt toch niets   (Dutch)
  "Hey! It means nothing that you brought your bag!"

Copper Island Aleut, Northern Pacific Ocean

Copper Island was populated in the first half of the nineteenth century by Russian seal hunters and fur traders and Aleuts brought by the Russian-American Company from other areas. The company ceased to exist in 1867, and the small group of Russians, the larger group of so-called "creoles," and the largest group of Aleuts stayed on the island. The mixed language probably developed around the 1880s or 1890s; language mixture was already mentioned in 1884 (Golovko and Vakhtin 1990; Golovko 1994). Russian probably ceased to be spoken then but was again introduced in the 1940s. According to Thomason and Kaufman (1988: 234) most Russians, who were in the minority on the island, married Aleut women.

Copper Island Aleut is a mixed language, in which the Aleut verb stems have Russian tense, number, and person affixes. The personal (subject) pronouns, negators, infinitives, and conjunctions are Russian, too, as well as numerous nouns (technical terms, names for cultural innovations, and kinship terms), adverbs, and modal words. Nominal and verbal derivations are Aleut, as are nominal inflection markers, postpositions, demonstratives, and question words. Syntax is partly Russian and partly Aleut. The phonological system is a compromise between Russian and Aleut. An example, with an unusually high proportion of Russian loanwords, which are italicized[4] follows (from Golovko and Vakhtin 1990: 119):

(16) aba-qalí-*l-a-ya kada vuyána*-x tin ayug-ní-*l*.
       work-begin-PST-F-1S when war-ABS REFL.3 begin-CAUS-3S

i vot ya man akíta-x abá-*yu*.
and so I here up.to-3S.ABS work-1SG

pénsiya-m kuga ú-*yu, i vs'o ravno ya* abá*yu*
pension-RELR on.it be-1S, and all the.same I work-1S

"I began to work when the war broke out. And so since that time I work. I receive my pension, and nevertheless I work."

Peranakan Chindo, Java, Indonesia

The Peranakan Chinese are a group of descendants of Chinese traders who migrated to Java from the seventeenth century onward. Many of these Chinese traders, who used Malay as their trade language in the early days, married Javanese women. Their descendants now form a separate ethnic group, both in their own eyes and in the eyes of outsiders. They still marry within the same group rather than with Javanese. Malay (or its literary equivalent, Indonesian) and Javanese are both West Austronesian languages. The grammatical systems of the two languages show close similarities, but in their lexicon they have only 20 percent shared items.

The language of some of the Peranakan Chinese is a mixture of Malay lexicon and a Javanese grammatical system (Dreyfuss and Oka 1979, Rafferty 1982, Wolff 1983), depending on where they live. In East Java it is Javanese with Malay. The speakers all know lower Javanese as well, but only a minority of this group knows Malay or Indonesian.

Dreyfuss and Oka (1979: 250) describe the language as follows: "The majority of the content words are Indonesian, while the majority of grammatical affixes are Javanese." In their calculations, 88 percent of the grammatical affixes are from Javanese, and 90 percent of the noun and verb roots are from Indonesian. In the function words, the two languages are used evenly: 53 percent Javanese and 47 percent Indonesian. There are also a few words from Dutch, Chinese, and English—some personal pronouns, names for food, and some kinship terms. Some example sentences follow (from Dreyfuss and Oka 1979: 262–267):

(17)   *are?* ini *musti di*-kasi *oba*t tidor   (Chindo)
       child this must PASS-give medicine sleep
       bocak kuwi mesthiné di-wenehi obat tidur   (Javanese)
       anak ini mesti di-kasih obat tidur   (Indonesian)
       "This child must be given sleeping medicine."[5]

Educated Peranakans, who know both Indonesian and Javanese, may code-switch among themselves, but the way in which the two languages are mixed in Chindo is very different; in code mixing, "There were no instances in which a Javanese affix was used on an unambiguously Indonesian root, and each segment of the conversation could be easily classified as being either Javanese or Indonesian." In this variety of Chindo, Javanese affixes are, as a rule, used with Indonesian roots. Chindo differs clearly from code mixing.

Mixed Languages: Generalities and Types

A number of possible generalizations can be derived from this overview. First, all cases of mixed languages discussed here are mixtures of two languages. This does not mean that no lexical items from other languages can be borrowed. These languages behave like all other languages, so we find, for instance, English borrowings in Michif, Malay borrowings in Krojo, and borrowings from several Amerindian languages in Callahuaya. There are never more than two base languages, however. It is not known whether there are mixed languages that consist of elements from three languages. My selection may be biased in this direction as a consequence of my working definition of a mixed language, which already implies a mixture of two languages.

Second, the languages discussed in this section all must have started as, and still are, in-group languages, that is, within bilingual groups rather than as contact languages between different groups.

Third, there are striking structural parallels among the different languages in the nature of their mixture. In almost all of these cases, the mixed language combines elements from both languages in the same way: the grammar (phonology, morphology, syntax) is taken from one language and the lexicon from the other. All the mixed languages combine affixes from one language with stems from another. There are two apparent exceptions among the cases discussed here: Michif and Copper Island Aleut, in which only the verb stems have different affixes. Michif also differs from the rest in apparently having verbs from one language and nouns from the other.

Fourth, there are a number of generalities concerning the sociolinguistic background. Three main subdivisions can be made. Several of these mixed languages are spoken by groups of nomadic or seminomadic traders (the Romani cases and Callahuaya). Others are spoken by ethnically mixed groups (Copper Island Aleut, Island Carib men's language, Pecu', Krojo, and Basters/Griekwa), who are very much like the Métis. These seem to be the most conspicuous social groups with such a language. Some others are spoken by in-between groups (Senkyoshigo and Media Lengua). If we want to generalize about all of these languages, we can say that they are spoken by ethnic groups who were originally bilingual but, for some reason, wanted to distinguish themselves collectively from both groups whose languages they speak. The speakers of each of these languages form a distinct group, either a subgroup of a larger division or a completely different group. The mixed language is spoken as an in-group language. It stresses the distinctness of the group. In all of these cases it is a distinct language, for which a special name exists and which distinguishes it from other languages spoken in the area. Some of these are learned as mother tongues; others are acquired in early adulthood.

Also in all of these cases, as I remarked, the languages are split according to lexicon and grammatical system. That is, they combine the grammatical systems of one language with the lexicon of another. This is, of course, most conspicuous in mixed languages in which the grammatical system has a rich morphology: stems are combined with affixes from another language. I call this process *language intertwining*. Basically this is the combination of the grammatical system (phonology, morphology, syntax) of one language with the lexicon of another. Intertwined languages are genetically related to two languages, and therefore they do not fit into the family tree model. This term is discussed in more detail later.

Sociolinguistic and Linguistic Typology of Mixing: Language Intertwining

An intertwined language is an in-group language, and any group with sufficiently different languages can create one. It must be stressed that language intertwining has nothing to do with race mixture. We can expect similar languages to emerge between soldiers who protractedly reside in foreign territory, between pupils of foreign boarding schools, between bilingual traders, and so on. These people, however, will not lose their ability to speak the two source languages, and their form of language mixture will not receive the status of a separate language. In this, the mixed languages discussed here differ from those make-shift languages, except for Senkyoshigo.

It is clear that this process of language intertwining is more common than is often thought in linguistics. In fact, many subcultures in all kinds of societies have secret languages of a very similar type, that is, languages in which the grammatical system is the same as that of the language commonly used but part of the vocabulary is derived from other sources. Examples are all kinds of argots, slang, professional languages, and so on, in which large or small parts of the lexicon may be different from the language of the environment. These cases keep the grammatical system of the ordinary language, with replacement of the normal vocabulary by the special vocabulary. It is an effective way not to be understood by outsiders. In fact, anybody with sufficient command of a second language can create one like it with little effort. People on vacation in a foreign country who know a little of its language, for instance, may mix their native tongue with content words from the host country. However, it seldom happens that the language becomes a fixed code, a mother tongue, or even the only language spoken by individuals in a community. Therefore, the intertwined languages previously discussed are special cases.

Two Types

A number of questions naturally arise. The most obvious is, what factor(s) determine which language provides the grammatical system and which the vocabulary of the mixed language? In some cases the grammar seems to have been replaced (as in the Romani languages or Ma'a), in other cases the lexicon (Media Lengua, Griekwa, etc.). Two types can be distinguished: mixed languages spoken as "secret languages" and languages spoken as an expression of a new and mixed ethnic identity or distinction from the surrounding groups.

SUBTYPE I: NOMADS' LANGUAGES

It is perhaps easier to start with the nomadic traders who speak a mixed language as a secret language. The mixed languages mentioned here are all spoken by Gypsies, who have preserved a vocabulary related to the Indic languages from India, all of which is embedded into the grammatical systems of the languages of the different host countries. It must be stressed, however, that most of the 10 million Gypsies in the world speak the "classical," inflected Romani with an Indic lexicon and Indic grammatical system.

Not all such languages are spoken only by Gypsies. The speakers of Callahuaya, being itinerant curers, can also be considered nomads. In fact other intertwined languages are reported from non-Gypsy nomads in, for example, Afghanistan, Ireland and Scotland (Hancock 1984a), the Middle East (Kenrick 1976–1977), Turkish-speaking Asia (Ladstätter and Tietze 1994), and India.

In the case of the Gypsies, we can safely assume that at one time Romani (Gypsy) was their original language. It is not known when inflected Romani was replaced by the mixed languages, nor whether the latter were ever acquired as first languages or only learned in early adulthood (see Kenrick 1979 for Angloromani). Boretzky and Igla (1994) discuss eight mixed Romani dialects. They conclude that the mixed languages came about in a period of shift, when there were more generational differences in language (Romani vs. the local language) and competence. It is certain, however, that in these cases, the original inflected Romani has been lost at least since the middle of the nineteenth century.

It has been proposed that Media Lengua came into being through "relexification," the wholesale replacement of the vocabulary of one language by that of another (Muysken 1981; see also Bickerton 1988). It is unlikely, however, that this was the case in the Para-Romani languages, as one would expect a Romani grammatical system with borrowed vocabulary. But there are no cases of Gypsy languages that have preserved the Romani grammatical system but replaced the whole vocabulary with that of another language. It is therefore not likely that relexification played a role here, unless, of course, one accepts the "U-turn" hypothesis, first proposed by Boretzky (Boretzky 1985; Boretzky and Igla 1994). The term "U-turn" seems to have been proposed by Thilo Schadeberg. According to this theory, at first inflected Romani was lost and then the language of the host country was learned as a first language, but Romani words were still learned from the older generation or from other groups. The Gypsies kept using as many of these words as possible. This is a sort of "half-way language loss" in which people regret the loss halfway and decide to turn around—when it is already too late to save the full language.

In fact, it looks as if these Gypsy languages have preserved the original vocabulary and borrowed the grammatical system. If anything, it would rather be "regrammaticalization," the replacement of a grammatical system by a new grammatical system with preservation of the original vocabulary. Of course one must distinguish here between the historical process of shift and the linguistic process of relexification. Historically there may be a change from Romani to the host language, after which the linguistic process of relexification took place. Historically this would look like regrammaticalization, but linguistically it would still be relexification.

This wholesale grammatical replacement is highly unlikely since all languages that reportedly have grammatical borrowings have undergone considerable lexical borrowing first (Thomason and Kaufman 1988: 100–110); in other words, there are no cases of grammatical borrowing that do not also display a lot of lexical borrowing. In fact, lexical borrowing from the surrounding languages is avoided in these mixed languages of nomads. Many of the words that are usually most easily borrowed from dominant languages, such as terms for newly introduced objects, are not usually borrowed in these languages. In Angloromani the word *dikkin' mokta*, literally "looking box," is used for "television." Even clearer is the fact that many place names have Angloromani equivalents. Secrecy may play a role in some of the other cases, too, notably in Callahuaya, which is now used in ritual curing ceremonies.

I propose the following explanation for the fact that these mixed languages seemingly preserve the original lexicon and took over a different grammar: it is the most logical and discreet way to create a secret language, which can be used in such a way that even the fact that a secret language is spoken will be unnoticed by those who do not know it. It is perhaps easiest to illustrate this with an example. Imagine that you are at some location where you hear people saying this to each other:

(18) *There was a rich* mush *with* kushti-dick*ing purple* togs.
   Every divvus *his* hobben *was good.*[6]

Your first impression would be that these people speak English: it sounds like English, as there are English words and English endings. Still, it is unintelligible because almost all the content words are not English. In English this would translate as

(19)   There was a rich man with good-looking purple clothes.
   Every day his food was good.

The unknown elements are all Romani—*murš* "man," *dikhav* "I see," *dives* "day," *xaben* "food," *kushti* "good" (loan from Persian), and *togs* "clothes" (perhaps a loan from English cant)—but the words are Anglicized and derived from a Romani dialect that is no longer recoverable and seems to stand somewhat apart from the Romani dialects of the mainland. If plain Romani had been used, it would certainly have aroused the suspicion of the bystanders: why would these people suddenly speak another language? A completely different language is therefore not suitable as a secret language in this situation.

If the speakers had relexified their original language, using English words in a Romani grammatical framework, it would have been even worse: it would have sounded like a different language, intended to be unintelligible, but English words might still have been understood. It would have had no effect at all. The use of the local grammatical system with a different vocabulary is therefore the obvious choice, especially, of course, in trading contacts, where a secret language is most likely to be used (Kenrick 1979).

In short, these are secret languages, spoken with people who understand them in the presence of others who do not understand them, in order to remain unintelligible to outsiders. When people speak Angloromani, outsiders may not even notice that a secret language is being used. They may think that those Gypsies speak "bad English" or that they do not articulate well. This language is obviously not used to solve a communication gap in contacts between people who speak different languages. It is an in-group language, the utmost language of solidarity for the group members and a distancing language for nongroup members. And for these traders, all of whom speak the local languages of the non-Gypsies fluently, it is an obvious choice to embed their native vocabulary into the grammatical framework of the language of the local population. In a considerable number of Gypsy groups, the local language is spoken more fluently than the mixed language or Romani proper (Bakker and Van Der Voort 1991). This is also explained by the fact that, at least in the Angloromani speech community, the language is learned only when children enter the adult world.

I suggest here that all nomadic and bilingual groups of traders who want to use a mixed language as a secret language would use the grammatical system of the local language and the vocabulary of the nonlocal language.

SUBTYPE II: MIXED ETHNICITIES

The speakers of mixed languages of the second type are those with new ethnic identities. I also include the in-between groups such as the Indians who speak Media Lengua and the American missionaries who speak Senkyoshigo.

People of mixed origin, with parents who speak different languages, can be found in all parts of the world, but only in a limited number of cases do these people start to become a different ethnic group, like the Métis. In most cases, they will be part of the society of either the father or the mother, although sometimes slightly marginalized. In the earliest period in French Canada, for instance, the children with a French father and an Amerindian mother would live either with the mother's tribe or in the father's French society. This prevented the emergence of a separate Métis society at that time, despite the large number of mixed marriages in French Canada (as shown by Dickason 1985; see chapters Two and Three).

Elsewhere, though, these individuals of mixed origin were numerous enough to become a separate social group. They started to identify neither with their father's nor their mother's nation, and as a group, they have been marginalized by both. In many cases they have started new societies and cultures, using elements from both contributing cultures. The Basters and Griekwas, the Pecu', and the Island Carib all have such an origin. This "mixedness" is the basis of the group identity. It is striking that in the documented cases the same word is used for both the ethnic group and the language, and both denote a mixture: *Pecu'* for the Indos, *Basters* in South Africa, and of course *Métif* in Canada. This points to a narrow connection between the new, mixed identity and the new, mixed language.

Like the other mixed ethnicities, the Métis are an ethnic group that arose from the mingling of two other ethnic groups. Typically, in the first generation the fathers spoke French and the mothers spoke Cree. In the other cases, too, the mothers spoke a language different from that of the father. In the case of the Basters and Griekwas, the men spoke Afrikaans and the women Khoekhoen. In Indonesia, the men spoke Dutch and the women Javanese or Malay. On the Caribbean islands, the women spoke Arawak and the men Carib. In western Canada, the men spoke French and the women Cree. Of course, this is common to many mixed couples. Often the parents speak different languages to their children, but this is not reported to lead to the emergence of a mixed language. Apparently there are a number of social conditions to be met before the genesis of such a mixed language will occur (to be discussed later).

Let us return to the central question raised in the beginning of this chapter: which language provides the grammatical system and which one the lexicon? In the cases of the nomads' secret language, the answer for this type is very simple: the language of the mothers provides the grammatical system, and the language of the fathers provides the lexicon. This distribution is totally determined by social factors, and linguistic constraints do not play a role. The first generation of Island Carib had Arawak-speaking mothers and Carib-speaking fathers, and the mixed language therefore has a Carib lexicon and Arawakan affixes. The Basters (Khoekhoen mothers and Afrikaans fathers) speak a language with Khoekhoen affixes and an Afrikaans lexicon. The same is true for the Pecu' and Krojo speakers (Dutch lexicon and Malay and Javanese grammar).

There is an obvious explanation for the fact that the mother's language provides the grammatical system. First, it is the language best learned and known by the children. The mothers in most societies of the world take care of the children more than do the fathers, and therefore they present the primary linguistic input. If the fathers speak other languages, as in these cases, the children speak their mother's language better than their father's. Second, the men are all immigrants, whereas the women are native to the region. If the bilingual children need either of their parents' languages to converse with outsiders, it is most likely to be the language of the mothers. In fact, the better-known language, which is also the language of the region and therefore of the nearest outsiders, provides the grammatical system. This is also the case with the other mixed languages: The first generation of speakers of Media Lengua undoubtedly spoke better Quechua than Spanish. Callahuaya speakers are all fluent in Quechua; Pukina has long been extinct and may not have been widely spoken for several generations when Callahuaya emerged. The speakers of Senkyoshigo are all native speakers of American English who learned Japanese as a second language.

Social and Linguistic Conditions on Language Intertwining

Three important social conditions must be met before an intertwined language can emerge. First, there must be a significant *number* of mixed couples, and the fathers must all speak a language that is different from the one spoken by the mothers. If either the males or the females are from different ethnic or linguistic groups, an intertwined language does not seem to emerge. And only if there are sufficient children, who all speak the same two languages, can the children become a separate social or ethnic group with a mixed language.

Second, it is certainly better for the development of the new, mixed language if there are *no outside pressures* that stigmatize the newly developing mixed language. If there is a strict school system, if another group dominates the new ethnic group, or if there is pressure to integrate into another social or ethnic group, the social circumstances do not seem to be favorable for the preservation, or perhaps even the genesis, of a mixed language. The ideal situation seems to be a frontier society, where a newly arrived ethnic group, all of them males, come into contact with the local population and marry local women. Still, Pecu' may have emerged in spite of a fair amount of pressure toward the Dutch language. In many cases in Indonesia, separate schools were especially established for the Indos, where Dutch was the language of instruction. This may have stimulated the development of the mixed language instead. Krojo is still remembered by its speakers as a "language of the playgrounds" (De Gruiter 1994).

Third, the group of bilinguals must be thought of as a distinct group by outsiders, and the group members themselves must not identify with either of their parents' groups (*negative identification*). Otherwise, the members of the bilingual group remain members of an ethnolinguistic group who happen to speak a second language. In another possibility—identifying with both language groups (*positive identification*)—the bilinguals will be frequent code switchers among themselves, but no intertwined language will develop. Code switching may be the norm in these groups. When bilinguals do not think of themselves as belonging to both groups, there will be no code mixing. There is at least one case of a bilingual community where code switching is nonexistent, the Konkani-speaking Brahmins who also speak Marathi (Nadkarni 1975); the divergent factor here is that this group does not want to identify with the Marathi speakers. Only if members of a bilingual group identify with no other group than their own do they form an in-group language through the process of language intertwining. Code mixing occurs in communities where bilinguals wish to belong to both groups whose languages they speak; language intertwining occurs if they want to belong to neither.

In addition to the social conditions, there seem to be some constraints on the *types of languages* in contact. That is, at least the outcome may be unpredictable for certain types. Certainly, there are no problems in any combination of agglutinative languages and fusional languages, which constitutes the vast majority of the cases discussed here. It is hard to deduce how a polysynthetic language would behave, however. Cree is a polysynthetic language, which may account for the divergent nature of Michif (in fact, this is what I argue in Chapter Eight).

Another problem may arise when the language that should provide the grammar is an isolating language, with no bound morphemes. It is not obvious how the lexicon of another language could combine with its grammatical system in any systematic way. Perhaps an arbitrary mixture of the two lexicons would result in some cases, or perhaps the syntax would be the only component used from the "grammar" language. Malay seems close to an isolating language, and yet Pecu' basically combines Malay grammar (mainly syntax) with a Dutch lexicon.

Furthermore, there are at least two *phonological* properties that may also influence the outcome of the combination. First, the phonological distance between the two languages can be expected to be important. Most of the mixed languages have one phonological system, namely, that of the language that contributes its grammar, but some have partly mixed systems, as does Michif and possibly the language of the Basters and Griekwas and Callahuaya. We may expect problems when languages with a large number of phonemes should be integrated into a system with a small number. This would create an undesirable amount of ambiguity.

Second, when two languages have very different phoneme systems (e.g., a large number of clicks in one language vs. a purely egressive phonological system), we may expect consequences for the phonological system of the mixed language. Phonological devices that show the coherence of words—such as particular stress systems or vowel harmony, especially in agglutinative languages—may play a role, too, limiting the possibility of integrating foreign elements into the word.

Two languages seem to be exceptions, and the conditions mentioned have not been met. In Michif one would have expected Cree affixes with French stems, but it has Cree verbs and French nouns. I explain this divergence in Chapter Eight: basically Michif does, in fact, combine Cree affixes with French stems because of the polysynthetic typological characteristics of Cree. In Copper Island Aleut, another exception, one would have expected Russian stems with Aleut affixes, but in fact it has something like Aleut with Russian verb affixes and Russian loanwords. I have no explanation for this. It is possible that typological features of Aleut (for which I cannot locate an accessible grammatical study) do play a role here. Perhaps also the marriages of Russian men with Aleut women were too small in number to be significant, or the social circumstances were otherwise divergent.

Language Intertwining: The Process and the Result

An important question is, were these mixed languages created consciously or unconsciously? And were children or adults responsible? The evidence seems contradictory. De Gruiter (1994), himself a speaker of Krojo, for instance, claims that his mother already spoke Javanese heavily mixed with Dutch words, although his mother could hardly speak Dutch. Children around him commonly spoke Krojo. It is known that Angloromani is not learned as a first language today, but this does not mean that it never was. It must certainly have been adults who created Senkyoshigo. Muysken (1988b) suggests that male adolescents were the first to use Media Lengua and the evidence available seems to favor this interpretation. Just the fact that the grammatical system is not restructured or simplified and that the lexicon is fairly rich indicates that both languages were well known by their creators. These details suggest also a prime role for the first speakers beyond the level of young children. It is therefore more likely that young adults or adolescents are responsible for the creation of the mixed languages.

I have called the process of language genesis language intertwining, which creates new languages with lexical morphemes from one language and grammatical morphemes from another. In this section I give a more detailed definition of this process and a description of the social factors that led to the genesis of these languages.

The word "intertwining" is chosen for the following reasons: It suggests an intricate mixture of two (and no more than two) systems that are not necessarily of the same nature, in this case, lexicon and grammar. These two halves are combined into one organic whole, and therefore one of the components cannot be removed without damaging the other. That is, neither of the components can survive without the other. Furthermore, the term does not suggest a direction of the process, unlike "relexification," "massive borrowing," "regrammaticalization," or "massive grammatical replacement," all of which suggest the replacement of either the lexicon or the grammatical system. Not replacement, but rather combination, is the central process. Replacement is a consequence. Neither component in intertwining is more important than the other; they both have the same weight. Therefore the term "intertwining" seems most suitable for the process.

Let us call the language in intertwining that roughly provides the grammar language A, and the language that provides the lexicon language B. Several grammatical distinctions seem to play a role in the formation of these intertwined languages. First, consider the distinction between bound morphemes and free morphemes. Bound morphemes will be in language A; free morphemes tend to be in language B. Second, there is the distinction between grammatical morphemes and lexical morphemes. Bound morphemes normally will be a subset of the grammatical morphemes. Bound grammatical morphemes will occur in language A, whereas free grammatical morphemes—also called function words or system morphemes—can occur in either A or B or in both A and B. Lexical morphemes—content words—and lexical stems tend to occur in language B. It is in the free grammatical morphemes that most variation is found, both within the class of intertwined languages and within individual intertwined languages. Clitics, as bound grammatical morphemes, occur in language A.

As the mixed languages vary in the language sources for the free grammatical morphemes, both distinctions (free versus bound; grammatical versus lexical) must play a role in this process of language mixture, in degrees that have not yet been established but are worth a closer look. A detailed investigation of all the issues involved is beyond the scope of this book, but roughly the distribution appears to be as follows:

(20)

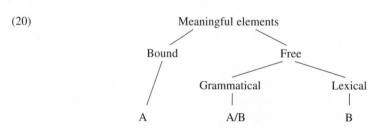

In short, once the appropriate social circumstances pertain, a few factors determine how intertwined languages are formed and which language will supply the lexicon and which the grammar. To complete the process, one may follow these steps:

1. Take the free lexical morphemes from one language and the bound grammatical morphemes from the other.
2. Try to find a solution for free grammatical morphemes. Take them from both or from either of the languages or make a mixed system.
3. If you know one language better than the other, take the grammatical system (syntax, morphology, phonology) of that language.
4. If you want the intertwined language to sound like one of the languages involved, take the grammatical system from that language.

Although this process may seem to be complex, it is not. In fact, it is very easy to follow for any bilingual person, literate or not.

A Problem in Classification

The resulting language is one that cannot be classified genetically. As mentioned, for a language to belong to a certain stock, it should have similarities with the languages of that stock both in the lexicon and in grammatical characteristics. Intertwined languages have a lexicon that belongs to language family B and a grammatical system that belongs to language family A. In other words, if one looks at the lexicon, one would classify it as a member of the family of language B; if one looks at the grammar, one would say it belongs to the family of language A.

Some languages were not recognized as intertwined by the people who studied them at the time, and there are discussions in the literature about their genetic relationship, for example, Ma'a and Mbugu (Bantu grammar and Cushitic lexicon), Basque Romani, and Michif. Goodman (1971) points out that Baumann (1894) classified Ma'a Hamitic and Cushitic, Tucker and Bryan (1957) listed it as partly Bantu, and Greenberg (1955, 1963) classified it as Cushitic. Depending on whether one looks at the lexicon or the morphology, the language is classified differently.

Another example is Basque Romani. Basque scholars who studied this language obviously recognized its grammatical system as Basque and therefore called it something like "Basque as spoken by Gypsies." When Romani scholars studied the language, however, they called it something like "Romani as spoken in the Basque Country" (see Bakker 1991a) because they recognized the vocabulary as obviously Gypsy. Each group recognized only one-half of the language and classified it accordingly.

Similarly, Michif has been classified in various odd ways, for example, as a "French Creole or almost a creole. Closest to Plains Cree" (Grimes 1988: 49). According to this classification, Michif seems to belong to two very different language families at the same time. Therefore intertwined languages must be taken as languages that defy genetic classification, like pidgins and creoles, and which have, in Thomason and Kaufman's (1988) terminology, a nongenetic origin.

After Crystallization

Once an intertwined language is formed, it can undergo the usual influences from the neighboring languages. That is, after its crystallization, other languages may also affect it. The mixed language is rarely the only language spoken by members of the group. In some cases there may be a continued need for both source languages if contacts are continued. Otherwise, if the in-group language is spoken frequently and if communication with one or both of the other language groups is no longer needed, the group will lose knowledge of one or both of the languages of the groups from which it originated. Then the in-group code of the intertwined language becomes the only code available and thus a new language. All Ma'a speakers have lost their knowledge of Cushitic, as they no longer live in a Cushitic-speaking environment, but they all speak a Bantu language in addition.There are speakers of Media Lengua who also know Quechua, others who also know Spanish, and some who know all three, but there are probably none who speak only Media Lengua. None of the speakers of Angloromani also know the British dialect of Romani, which was its source. The same is true for all or most of the speakers of the other Gypsy intertwined languages: they do not know inflected Romani.

Continued knowledge and use of either of the source languages has consequences for the nature of the intertwined language. If the source language of the grammatical system is also spoken by the community members, it will have continued lexical and grammatical influence. Most of the intertwined languages may serve as examples. Callahuaya seems to be moving toward Quechua, Angloromani is moving toward English, and Ma'a is getting more and more Bantu-like. In all these cases, the influence is both grammatical and lexical. If the source language of the lexicon is maintained, it may have continued lexical and grammatical influence on the intertwined language. This is hypothetical since there is no diachronic material on, for example, Media Lengua or the language of the Basters.

Ethnogenesis in Anthropology

Some anthropological research points to a similar direction. Moore (1994) distinguishes two ways of ethnogenesis, the cladistic and the rhizotic models. The cladistic model can be seen as the tree-branching model, which is dominant both in biology and in comparative and historical linguistics: species (languages) can become so distinct in time that they will become different species (languages). In this metaphor, one can point to the branches of a tree. The word "cladistic" is derived from the Greek word for "branch."

The rhizotic model is an alternative to the cladistic model, not to replace it, but in addition to it. The word "rhizotic" is derived from the Greek word for "root." If we use the tree metaphor once again, we look at the roots instead of the branches. One can say that different roots of a tree "merge" with one another, although it is biologically more appropriate to consider them as upside-down branches. From two entities a new one can emerge. This rhizotic model is more appropriate in some branches of science. In anthropology, the parallel with the emergence of new ethnic groups in slave societies or the mixed peoples discussed here shows itself immediately as conforming to the rhizotic model. In linguistics, the mixed languages discussed in this chapter are clearly compatible with a rhizotic classification. In fact, in comparative linguistics, the influence from other languages has long been recognized in lexical and grammatical borrowing and grammatical convergence so that the cladistic model has never been sufficient in itself. In anthropology, the merger of two or more ethnic groups into a new, hybrid group is common enough.

Summary and Conclusions

In summary, we can say that certain social conditions of bilingualism can lead to the formation of new, mixed languages. People of bilingual communities who consider themselves separate groups or who need a form of communication unintelligible to outsiders may develop such a mixed language, more or less consciously. In principle, the grammatical system of language A will be mixed with the lexical stock of language B. The languages will be mixed in the following way:

1. Bound morphemes (always of a grammatical nature) are in language A.
2. Free lexical morphemes are in language B.
3. Free grammatical morphemes can be in either language.
4. The grammatical system is that of language A.

The result is a mixed language, which I term an "intertwined" language; the process is called "language intertwining."

These languages emerge where a new ethnic group is formed through the marriages of female speakers of language A and male speakers of language B. It is clear that the social circumstances formulated here for the genesis of an intertwined language are valid for Michif, although Michif does not seem to combine the lexicon of one language with the grammatical system of another. In Chapter Eight I show that Michif is indeed a case of language intertwining, but because of the typological properties of Cree, the resulting language appears to be different from all the other cases.

The Intertwining of French and Cree

On the basis of comparable cases, discussed in Chapter Seven, I claim that under certain sociolinguistic circumstances, which are also valid for Michif, a mixed language will emerge. The model of language intertwining predicts that Michif should have the Cree grammatical system and the French lexicon, but in fact it has Cree verbs and French nouns. I argue in this chapter that the more or less polysynthetic nature of Cree morphology is responsible for the unusual distribution of Cree and French elements in Michif. Cree morphology is the key to the peculiar mixture of Cree and French, and hence to the problem of the genesis of Michif. To prove my case, I first present some background information.

I begin with historical information on linguistic studies of Algonquian morphology, especially that by Bloomfield, whose work laid the foundation for most later investigations of this language family. This is necessary to make accessible some of the specific morphological terminology I use. Then I describe Cree nominal and verbal morphology briefly, showing that it is a typical example of a polysynthetic language. I also describe French verbal and nominal morphology. In the next section I try to combine the two languages in ways known from intertwined languages, but it appears that this cannot be done. Michif is the result of a peculiar form of language intertwining caused by the typological properties of French and, especially, Cree. In this chapter, French and Cree follow their standard spellings and Michif appears in a broad phonetic transcription.

History of Algonquian Morphological Studies

The theoretical background of Algonquian linguistics is heavily influenced by the structuralist tradition, in particular by Leonard Bloomfield's studies of Algonquian. Bloomfield was trained as an Indo-European comparativist who also studied Algonquian languages from the 1920s onward. He is often taken to be an example of a linguist of the structuralist tradition, but Goddard (1987a) shows that Bloomfield's work is more multifaceted and more concerned with meaning than that of the structuralists *pur sang*. On the one hand, his work on Fox, Menomini, Ojibwe, Plains Cree, and other Algonquian languages ranks among the best descriptive and analytic work on Algonquian, culminating in his sketch "Algonquian" (Bloomfield 1946), which is still a classic in the field. He demonstrated that the comparative method used in the Indo-European tradition is also applicable to non-European languages that do not have early written sources.

On the other hand, his influence in the Algonquianist tradition seems so pervasive that the study of Algonquian languages has never really gone beyond description and comparison in the Bloomfieldian tradition, so that these languages have scarcely been analyzed in the framework of modern grammatical theories. Most of the work on Algonquian languages is done independently of linguistic theories, although it is not atheoretical, and often it is very insightful and relevant. Some Algonquianists have worked in a generative framework (Blackfoot, Ojibwe, Cree) and a few in a lexical-functional framework (Cree) (see the annual *Papers of the Algonquian Conference*, edited by William Cowan). Perhaps as a consequence of the fact that Algonquianists do not usually work in theoretical frameworks, Algonquian language data are rarely used by theoretical linguists. There are a few exceptions, such as Stephen Anderson (1992), who uses Cree and Potawatomi data in his book on morphological theory.

It is probably not only the Bloomfieldian tradition, however, that is to blame. Other Amerindian languages are also only marginally dealt with in all linguistic theories. The complexities of the languages rather than the structuralist nature of the studies is responsible for this gap. Generative grammar, for instance, is so much based on English and related Indo-European languages that this model is often not at all relevant for Amerindian languages, or their structural properties are of a completely different order. For example, Cree is typically polysynthetic, and to my knowledge no grammatical framework has ever been concerned with the nature of polysynthesis more than marginally.[1] Spencer's (1991) excellent overview of generative morphological theory deals with polysynthesis only superficially. Also, a significant portion of the descriptive and comparative work on Algonquian and other Amerindian languages does not provide morpheme-by-morpheme glosses, so it is very difficult for outsiders to grasp the structural properties of these languages.

Bloomfield's Description of Algonquian Verb Structure

Bloomfield's (1946) sketch of proto-Algonquian is still the basic source for comparative Algonquian, if taken together with Goddard's (1979) overview of later work. However, because of its compact style, the lack of morphemic glosses, and presupposed knowledge of at least one Algonquian language, it is difficult for outsiders to grasp the full richness of this study. Before discussing Bloomfield's analysis of Algonquian morphology, a brief outline of his general morphological framework is needed. Bloomfield's ideas about morphology have been most clearly outlined in chapters 13 and 14 of his book *Language* (1933) and are summarized as follows.

Morphemes, the smallest meaningful elements of a language, can be bound or free. Free morphemes can be used in isolation, or they can be combined with other free morphemes or with bound forms to form complex words. Bound forms cannot be used in isolation. Bloomfield (1933) distinguishes roots and stems as the basic units of words. Roots cannot appear as independent words. Roots are not internally analyzable, whereas stems can be complex.

Primary words are words that cannot be analyzed into smaller meaningful elements, and they can contain several bound forms (e.g., "re-ceive"). These affixlike formatives may be vague in meaning ("hamm-er"), though in Algonquian they are rather concrete. Secondary words consist of one or more roots or stems combined with one or more bound morphemes. For the formation of complex words, Bloomfield (1933) distinguishes between composition and derivation. Compounds consist of two or more free forms, for example, "blackbird." Derivation can be secondary or primary. Primary derivative words contain no free forms, only a root and another root ("per-ceive") or a root and an affixlike element ("hamm-er"), called a primary affix. Secondary derivative words have a stem form as a base, to which new formatives can be added. Inflected forms can be organized into paradigm sets. Rules of word formation form new stems, to which inflection must be added to form a real word.

How would we apply this framework to an Algonquian language such as Cree? Consider this Cree verb:

(1)   *tahkwâskwêpitêw*   (Cree)
      "He ties him fast to wood."

This verb can be broken down into the morphemes *tahko-âskw-ê-pit-ê-w*, with the following components:

(1')   *tahko-* "fixed, fast"
       -âskw- "as or with wood"
       -ê- a classificatory element referring to the preceding morpheme
       -pit- "to pull"
       -ê- an action of a third person on another third person (obviative), together with
       -w third person

The last element is the only universally accepted inflectional morpheme. The preceding vowel is sometimes taken as part of the inflection (e.g., Edwards 1954; Goddard 1990b: 450, n. 6) and sometimes as part of the verb form (e.g., Denny 1989). I follow the view that it is part of the inflection.

None of the morphemes from this string can be used in isolation; therefore a verb like this cannot be an inflected compound. Probably none of these formatives has meaning for Cree speakers when presented in isolation (unless they are trained in linguistics). These verbal stems must be taken as derivative words, and because they consist only of roots, they should more specifically be considered as primary derivatives in Bloomfield's terms. The verb consists only of bound forms. Bloomfield (1933: 241) also considers them primary derived stems. A Menomini verb like *kepa:hkwaham* "he puts a cover on it" (its Cree equivalent would be **kipâskwaham*) consists of a stem, *kepa:hkwah-*, which again consists of a root, *ke:p-* "obstruction of opening," and two primary suffixes, *-a:hkw-* "woodlike" and *-ah-* "act on animate object by tool." We could add that *-am* is the inflectional element meaning "he-it" and is traditionally called the "theme sign" of the verb (Goddard 1990b: 450, n. 6) in Algonquianist literature, which marks both transitivity or intransitivity and animacy or inanimacy of the object or subject. This Algonquian verb stem is clearly complex. It consists of four bound morphemes. Although not all verb forms are as transparent as the ones dealt with here, basically all stems are complex and follow similar patterns (Goddard 1990b). They consist of two or more bound elements. Therefore the verb stems are primary derivative words in Bloomfield's terminology. In Bloomfield's other work, he discusses stem formation in greater detail and adds a number of terms he developed especially for Algonquian languages (e.g., Bloomfield 1927, 1946).

In the overwhelming majority of cases, Algonquian verbs stems can have, and indeed do have, internal structure. They can be "obtained by abstracting inflectional elements and reduplicative syllables, and by dividing compound words" (Bloomfield 1927: 393). One problem with this procedure is that it is not always clear which elements belong to the inflectional part of the language. Which morphemes are inflectional, which ones are derivational, and which ones are primary stem formatives? I have already mentioned the controversy over the nature of the "theme" morphemes: some linguists call them inflectional; others say they are derivational morphemes and hence part of the extended, complex stems. Are the person agreement affixes the only inflectional affixes, or are affixes like causatives, reflexives, and benefactives inflectional, too? Bloomfield seems to interpret the latter categories as part of the stem, as he does different valency-changing suffixes and other derivational suffixes. The remaining strings of morphemes (i.e., after taking off reduplicated morphemes and the inflectional affixes) are classified into a number of categories. These have names like initials, medials, and finals, which together make up the stem.

This terminology follows from Bloomfield's structuralist background: the elements that form a verb stem are named after their position in the stem. Meaning plays only a subordinate role in his analysis. In his "Algonquian" (1946) sketch, he actually distinguishes a larger number of categories of elements, which together make up stems in Algonquian. The main ones are initials (also called roots), medials, and finals; there are also preverbs (which precede the verb stems), premedials, postmedials, and prefinals. Finals are subclassified as abstract finals and concrete finals, and medials and finals can be derived from a stem or a root (e.g., a nominal). Almost all of the names of these categories are names of the positions these elements take in the stem, and no reference to other grammatical or semantic categories is made.

It is not necessary here to deal with the details of this classification. Furthermore, some of these categories are fairly heterogeneous, although they also show some semantic correspondences. Bloomfield himself admits the fuzziness of his categories: "No line can be drawn between medials in this use [in nouns] and concrete noun finals. We call a suffix medial when it appears also in other uses" (Bloomfield 1946: 117). Apparently we could in theory have a verbal "stem" with the following, rather extreme, structure:

(2)   preverb – reduplication – initial (root) – premedial – medial – postmedial – prefinal –
      concrete final – abstract final

Nevertheless all of the elements within these categories have semantic features in
common. Some preverbs, for instance, are adverblike, others tense and mood markers; reduplication denotes aspect (Ahenakew and Wolfart 1983), initials denote a state,
and so on.

Additional derivational elements such as causative morphemes may follow this
stem, and inflectional elements obligatorily follow, and sometimes also precede, the
complex stem. In most cases, however, stem structure is not that complex. Still, almost all stems consist minimally of a root and a final (Goddard 1990b). There are
only three basic stem types according to Goddard: initial only, initial plus final, and
initial plus medial plus final. His Fox examples have been replaced by the Cree equivalents in the following:

(3)   nipi-w   (Cree)
      die-3
      "He dies." (only initial, with inflection)

(4)   kîsk-isw-êw   (Cree)
      severed-cut.TA-3→3'
      "He cuts him off." (initial + final, with inflection)

(5)   kîsk-ikwê-sw-êw   (Cree)
      severed-neck-cut.TA-3→3'
      "He cuts off his head." (initial + medial + final, with inflection)

Nevertheless, since all three main classes of stem-forming elements can be derived from other elements, these formatives themselves can be complex and may
consist of several elements. Goddard (1990b: 451, n. 8) further ascribes a kind of
categorial meaning to some of the formatives: "In the semantic structure of stems
like [kîsk-ikwê-sw-êw] the initial denotes a state, configuration, or the like, and the
final specifies the means by which what the initial denotes is brought about and the
inflectional valency category of the stem." By valency category he means the transitivity or intransitivity and the animacy or inanimacy of the object or subject, with
which the final agrees. Medials are characterized as "always semantically nounlike"
(Goddard 1990b: 463, n. 36).

Some of the terminology introduced here is used in the rest of this chapter. In
the next section I discuss Cree morphology specifically.

Morphology of Cree: Nouns and Verbs

Cree has three grammatical categories: verbs, nouns, and particles. Particles are not inflected (or they end in the particle ending -i), and verbs and nouns have different derivational and inflectional possibilities. I present only verbs and nouns in discussing Cree
morphology since these are the only parts to which morphological endings are attached.

Cree Nouns

As stated in Chapter Five, Cree nominal morphology does not show many complexities. There are two plural morphemes, *-ak* for animates (*simâkanis-ak* "policemen"), with *-wak* after vowels, and *-a* for inanimates (*môhkomân-a* "knives"), with *-wa* after vowels. Furthermore, there are inflectional possessive prefixes for all persons, such as in *o-môhkomân* "his knife." Some animate nouns have an additional suffix, *-im*, for example, *o-sîsîp-im-a* "his/her duck/ducks." Some morphemes can be considered more or less inflectional: the ending *-a* (or its allomorph *-wa*) is the obviative suffix—identical in form to inanimate plural noun forms—and is used to distinguish two third persons in a phrase or sentence. It does not distinguish singular or plural and in Plains Cree and Michif, at least, it is used only for animate nouns.

There are some other inflectional and derivational morphemes:

- *-ihk* is a general locative suffix, for example, *n-iskât-ihk* "in, by, on my leg." It has two allomorphs, *-ohk* (after some nouns that end in *-k* or *m*) and *-hk* (after vowels).

- *-is* the diminutive suffix (*âsokan* "bridge"; *âsokan-is* "little bridge"). It has two allomorphs, *-os* (after some nouns that end in *-k* or *-m*) and *-sis* (after nouns that end in a vowel or glide).

- *-ipan* is used for deceased persons (*ni-mosôm-ipan* "my deceased grandfather").

- *-ihkan* means "fake, imitation," for example, *awâsis* "child"; *awâsî-hkan* "doll." Unlike the others, this is of limited productivity in Plains Cree.

Cree also has prefixed adjectives, which are attached to nouns, for example, *wâpiski-wiyâs* "white-skinned person" (*wâpiski-* "white"; *wiyâs* "meat"). There are also three suffixes that derive nouns from verbs:

- *-sk* is used for "frequent V-er," for example, *mâtô-sk* "crybaby" (*mâtô-w* "s/he cries").

- *-win* creates abstract nouns (*nêhiyawê-win* "Cree language"; *nêhiyâwê-w* "s/he speaks Cree").

- *-kan* creates instruments (*cîkahwêw* "s/he chops him"; *cîkahikan* "axe").

- *o-V-w* creates agentive nouns from verbs: "person who Vs."

It could be argued that *-kan* and *-win* are nominalizations of the verb, with the derivational endings *-iwi-* "to be" and *-ikê-* "to act on someone," to which a nominalizing suffix *-n* is added. All three nominalizers are fully productive. Many, if not all, of these nominal affixes are related in form to affixes used in the verb with comparable meaning.

In short, there is very little nominal morphology. There is only one inflectional element on the noun. Cree has no overt case marking at all, nor are there conjugation classes. Even when we compare it to a language with limited morphology, like English, the latter has many more nominal derivational affixes.

Cree Verbs

Cree verb morphology has been discussed to some extent in Chapter Four, although stem formation is treated in more detail in this chapter. In this section, therefore, I repeat only that verbs can be very complex, with up to twenty morphemes. There are inflectional, derivational, and stem-formational morphemes, with fuzzy boundaries between these categories and often between the morphemes themselves. The complexity of the verb contrasts sharply with the relative simplicity of the noun. In the next section I show that Cree has structural properties that are typical of so-called polysynthetic languages: complex verbs and little nominal morphology.

Cree and Morphological Typology

The classification of languages according to their morphological properties goes back to the eighteenth century. Actually, typological classification in terms of word formation is perhaps the most common nongenetic form of language classification. Four types of languages are distinguished traditionally: isolating languages, agglutinative languages, fusional or inflectional languages, and polysynthetic languages.

Isolating languages are those that do not have bound morphemes. For every semantic concept, as well as for some grammatical concepts, there is a separate word. No language is purely isolating, but Chinese and Vietnamese are usually mentioned as closest to the prototype. Typically, words are short and not internally analyzable in isolating languages. Saramaccan or other creoles may also be given as an example (Rountree and Glock 1977: 182)[2]:

(6) nöö e i go a matu, nöö hën i go a kuun liba   (Saramaccan)
     now if you go in wood, now then you go in hill top
     "Now if you go into the woods, you go on top of a hill."

Agglutinative languages are those in which every grammatical concept is expressed by a separate morpheme. Morphemes are neatly separated from each other. Typically there are long words with many morphemes in these languages. What is expressed as many words in isolating languages is often expressed in one word in agglutinative languages. Turkish is a prime example (from Spencer 1991: 189):

(7) çalış-tır-lı-ma-malıy-mış   (Turkish)
     work-CAUS-PASS-NEG-OBLI-INFER
     "They say that he ought not to be made to work."

Isolating and agglutinative languages can be considered "ideal types" in that there is a "one meaning–one morpheme" relation. In isolating languages these meaningful morphemes are free; in agglutinative languages they are bound. The other two types differ from both.

Fusional or inflectional languages are those in which bound morphemes are used, as in agglutinative languages, but they have a composite meaning or the boundaries between the morphemes are blurred or both. Many of the European languages belong to this type.

(8) laud-o   "I praise"   (Latin)
     lauda-s   "you praise"
     lauda-t   "s/he praises"

The endings for these verbal forms have more than one meaning. The *-o* suffix means first person, indicative, active, present; the *-s* suffix means second person, indicative, active, present. Here we see that one grammatical morpheme has multiple meanings: it indicates tense, person, and mood at the same time. This is typical of inflectional languages. We also frequently find it impossible to decide on boundaries between morphemes, as in the Latin verb form *suasi* "I recommended." This form is derived from the verb *suadere* with the stem *suad-e-*, which is blended with the perfective first-person singular ending *-i*. The *-d-* of the stem has disappeared, and there is an *-s-* instead. So in this type there are bound morphemes, but they have multiple meanings and do not have clear boundaries.

Polysynthetic languages also show complex words, often with boundaries that are not easily segmentable. These languages further incorporate nounlike material into the verb, so that one word may be equivalent to a whole sentence in other languages. An example from Oneida, an Iroquoian language (Spencer 1991: 282), follows:

(9) wa-hi-nuhs-ahni:nu: John   (Oneida, Iroquoian)
     AOR-1SG.SUBJ/3M.-house-buy John
     "I bought John's house."

Plains Cree is very similar, as it has verbal forms like the following:

(10)   paw-âpisk-ahw-êw   (Cree)
     brush-metal-with tool-he/him
     "S/he brushes him (metal) with tool."

Although this typology is widely used in textbooks of linguistics, Stephen Anderson (1985, 1992) has argued that it is of very little use. First, the four language types are not discrete because languages are mostly mixtures: many languages defy strict classification in this schema. Furthermore, no grammatical properties follow from membership in any of these types. Actually, it would be more useful to formulate a number of features such as "degrees of fusion" and "ratio of bound morphemes per word" (Comrie 1989: 46). Nonetheless, for the purposes of this study, it will be useful to adopt "polysynthetic language" as a descriptive label.

Spencer (1991: 38–39) believes that polysynthetic languages have a type of compounding and therefore do not fit the traditional typology, in which "compounding" plays no role. Indeed, it is a type different from the other three. Comrie (1989:

45) distinguishes two types of polysynthetic languages: one that can have more than one stemlike element (called "incorporating") and one in which there is only one stem with blurred morpheme boundaries.

Mithun (1988: 442) argues that "polysynthetic languages do constitute a recognizable and useful morphological type," and she attempts a definition. Polysynthetic languages have many morphemes per word, but these morphemes can be combined both in agglutinative or fusional ways. They are usually concatenated in the verb, whereas the noun morphology often remains fairly simple. Thus, polysynthetic languages "share a propensity toward well-developed verbal morphology, often accompanied by comparatively little nominal morphology" (Mithun 1988: 443), which is exactly what I stated about Cree. Mithun explores the semantics of the grammatical categories expressed in the verb in polysynthetic languages. We briefly discuss these and, if applicable, give Cree examples, all of which are also valid for Michif.

The most typical verbal modifiers in the languages of the world, those for aspect, tense, and mood, are also often found in the verb in polysynthetic languages. This is true for Cree as well. The verb clearly has both mood and tense affixes. An example of a tense affix follows:

(11)   ni-kî-nohtê-wâpam-âw-ak   (Cree)
        1-PST-want-see.TA-3-PL
        "I wanted to see them." (animate)

Reduplicative prefixes mark aspect (Ahenakew and Wolfart 1983), and some other affixes also denote aspectlike things. Verbal modifiers (often adverbs in other languages) also tend to be part of the verb complex in these languages. This is true for Cree, too. There are morphemes that mean "very much," "badly," "by accident," and so on. These are often prefixed to the verb:

(12)   kî-pihci-cîk-aho-so-w   (Cree)
        PST-by.accident-chop-TA.by.tool-REFL-3
        "He chopped himself by accident."

Several categories that are marked on the noun in other languages are expressed in the verb in polysynthetic languages. Mithun mentions number, gender, and case markers. In the verb in example (11) we see the plural-marking morpheme -ak for a plural object. The verb form -wâpam- indicates that the object is animate. The equivalent of this verb for an inanimate object would be the following:

(13)   ni-kî-nohtê-wâpaht-ên   (Cree)
        1-PST-want-see.it-4
        "I wanted to see it/them." (inanimate)

We have already seen in these examples that the verb forms agree with both subject and object. Mithun also mentions datives and benefactives, instrumentals, comitatives, and locatives as being expressed verbally in polysynthetic languages. All of these are indeed expressed as part of the verb in Cree:

(14)   nit-atoskê-stamaw-êw   (Cree)
       1-work-BEN-3SUBJ/3.OBJ.
       "I work for him." (benefactive)

(15)   wît-api-m-êw   (Cree)
       COMIT-sit-TRANS?-3SUBJ/3OBJ
       "He sits with him." (comitative)

(16)   it-ohtê-w   (Cree)
       there-go-3
       "He goes there." (locative)

An example of an instrumental is the morpheme -*ahw*- "him by tool" in (12), where it is realized as -*aho*-.

These are the typical features of a polysynthetic language according to Mithun. It is clear that Cree is an example of this type. All the typical polysynthetic features mentioned by Mithun are valid for Cree. Its verbs show the complexity of other languages of this type and express roughly similar semantic concepts. Mithun (1988: 451) calls these verbs "derivationally complex stems," which implies that new verb stems can be formed from derivational formatives in a productive way. These verbs tend to be highly lexicalized, with idiosyncratic meaning. The productivity of the lexicon in polysynthetic languages also means that new words can easily be created for new concepts, and this is commonly done. In most Algonquian languages, borrowing has been somewhat unusual, at least until recently (Pentland 1982: 105), although it is becoming more and more common (Rhodes 1985: xxv). This productivity of word formation is also true for Cree. Furthermore the nominal morphology is predicted to be relatively simple in such a language. Indeed, there are only a few derivational suffixes, such as a diminutive; there are possessive affixes; and there is only one syntactic affix in the noun, which marks the obviative, as we have seen. Therefore, in all respects Cree appears to belong to the polysynthetic type of language (Denny 1989).

Given that Cree belongs to this language type, we must ask whether the morphemes are added in an agglutinative or in a fusional way. There appear to be a number of processes that blur the morpheme boundaries. For instance, the ending -*êw* in (14) means third-person subject, third-person object, with one morpheme for two concepts. Furthermore, in example (15) the stem morpheme -*ohtê*- "to go" is -*ohtâ*- in first or second person. In example (12) the morpheme combination -*ahoso*- "self with tool" is actually -*ahw*- "with a tool," with -*iso*-, the reflexive suffix. Sometimes epenthetic vowels or consonants are used, such as the -*t*- between the vowel final prefix *ni*- and the vowel final stem *atoskê* "to work" in example (14). Nevertheless, in many cases the boundaries are clear, so we should say that Cree is a polysynthetic language with partly agglutinative, partly fusional morphology.

Summary: Cree Morphology

In summary, the Cree verb appears to consist of inflectional prefixes and suffixes and derivational affixes; the stems seem to consist of derivational elements. Typologically, Cree is a typical polysynthetic language, one that generally shows relatively simple noun derivation and inflection and the marking of large amounts of information in the verb. The verb includes information on grammatical functions of its arguments, the gender and number of its arguments, adverbial modifying elements, and prepositionlike elements.

Morphology of French

French morphology differs very much from that of Cree. Although in standard French all kinds of inflectional affixes are written, many of these are not pronounced in any dialect and one can wonder whether they ever were (Denis Dumas, pers. comm.). Therefore, the French here is written not in standard spelling but in a phonological transcription. Furthermore, in any discussion of French morphology we must account for the category of clitics.

Affixes versus Clitics

It is typical for French, as well as many other Romance languages, to have a number of clitics. Clitics make up a category of morphemes between the free and the bound. They have no stress and cannot occur by themselves. They must be attached to other words, including inflected words, but they are not inflectional. An example from English is 's, in "he's a carpenter." In French there are clitics that attach to verbs and that are commonly accepted as prime examples of this morphosyntactic category, but one can argue—somewhat more controversially—that some parts of the noun phrase are also cliticlike in behavior. An example of a series of verbal clitics in French follows:

(17) Je le lui donne [žllwidɔn]   (French)
      I it him give
      "I give them to him."

Although written as separate words, the elements *je* and *le* can only cooccur with the verb stems; they are not pronouns. Pronouns can also be added to the sentence, as in (18), where they have emphatic meaning:

(18) Moi je le lui donne à Pierre le livre   (French)
      Me I it him give to Pierre the book
      "*Me*, I give the book to *Pierre*."

Sentences like these are very common in colloquial French. These clitics are close to becoming inflectional elements.

In the noun phrase, too, one could argue that the possessive elements *mon, ton/ta, son/sa*, and *leur(s)* and the articles *le, la*, and so on are clitics. In emphatic forms, full pronouns are used, such as *moi* in (20):

(19) mon livre   (French)
        "my book"

(20) le/mon livre à moi   (French)
        the/my book to me
        "*My* book"

The same may be true to a certain extent for the articles, which share a number of features with clitics (see a subsequent section for Michif).

French Verbs

Verb conjugation is fairly simple in French. Many of the verbal paradigms are rarely used in colloquial speech, and what is left can be reduced to a few forms:

(21) A typical verbal paradigm[3]:

Present tense		*Past tense*	
žə-marš	"I walk."	žə-marš-e	"I walked."
ty-marš	"You walk."	ty-marš-e	"You walked."
il/ɛl-marš	"He walks."	il/ɛl-marš-e	"S/he walked."
ɔ̃-marš[4]	"We walk."	ɔ̃-marš-e	"We walked."
vu-marš-e	"You (PL) walk."	vu-marš-e	"You walked."
il/ɛl-marš	"They walk."	il/ɛl-marš-e	"They walked."

Past participle	*Infinitive*
marš-e	marš-e

In these most common and productive verbal paradigms of colloquial French, there are only two forms, the "bare" form and the one ending in *-e*. The latter marks past participles, infinitives, second-person plural forms, and all past-tense forms. The elements that are traditionally considered to be personal pronouns are cliticized to the verbs, as suggested by the hyphens in the paradigms. There are hardly any productive derivational verb suffixes in French.

This overview of French morphology is, of course, a gross simplification, although not far from the truth. There are a few common verbs (such as "to be" and "to have") that show more complexity and some paradigms for synthetic tenses and moods (future, subjunctive, etc.), but these are not often used in colloquial speech.

French Nouns

French nouns do not have any case markers or other inflectional elements that mark grammatical functions, number, gender, or anything else, although they have procliticlike elements that mark number, gender, and possession. Whereas there is no French nominal inflection, its derivational system is complex. Reference grammars (e.g., Corbeau 1951) list hundreds of derivational morphemes. For some semantic functions, scores of morphemes are listed. For instance, more than twenty morphemes form abstract nouns from verbs, six different morphemes form nouns that denote female persons, ten morphemes are used to denote ethnic origin (e.g., *Holland-ais*), and so on. Among these, there are also many irregular and unproductive forms.

French has articles that mark the gender and number of the noun. An article (including the partitives for noncount nouns), a numeral, or a possessive element has to be present with all French nouns. This is an indication of a somewhat closer connection between nouns and modifiers of the noun phrase than, for example, in English. The articles and possessives are cliticlike elements that attach to the noun. Clitics can develop into possessive prefixes, similar to those in Cree.

Another indication of the fairly close link between French articles, as well as adjectives, and the noun is the existence of a phonological process across word boundaries: the liaison. If the noun starts with a vowel, a connecting consonant, derived from an underlying phoneme, is normally placed between the preposed article or adjective and the noun:

(22) /animal/   "animal"
      /l-animal/   "the animal"
      /œ̃-n-animal/   "an animal"
      /œ̃ pǝti-t-animal/   "a small, little animal"
      /le-z-animo/   "the animals"
      /le gro-z-animo/   "the fat animals"

This is true for French (although it depends on region and class of speakers whether liaison is consistently applied) but not for Michif, where these liaison consonants have become part of the noun (see Chapter Four).

Michif Articles, Possessives, and Adjectives: Prefixes, Clitics or Independent Words?

We have some reason to assume that French articles, possessive prefixes, and prenominal adjectives are more similar to prefixes in Michif than to clitics (as they are in French). They are certainly not independent words. There are a number of arguments in favor of this view. I have already mentioned the obligatory presence of one of these elements before a French noun. There are other arguments that can be raised for Michif only, not for French.

First, numerals in Michif (but not in French) are also placed outside the article-plus-noun combination, as in (23). Second, in Cree there are adjectival prefixes that attach to the noun stem. These are not often used in Michif, but if they are, they precede the French article or possessive marker, as in (24):

(23) trwa: li: zariñæl
      three the moose
      "three moose"

(24) *kIsčI*-mi:-grăpe:r
      great-my.P-grandfather
      "my ancestors"

On the other hand, the article in (23) does not denote definiteness here. On the other hand, it is not really a dummy element since singular indefinite noun phrases have a singular indefinite article, as in (25) and (26):

(25) *pe:jak* æ̃ nɔm
    one a man
    "one man"

(26) *uškajI*-jæ̃-ša:r
    new-a-car
    "a new car"

Most French adjectives are placed after the noun. Some French adjectives, however, are placed between the article and the noun in Michif, as well as in French (*le petit enfant*). If we accept the French articles as clitics, we would be forced to concede that the intervening adjectives are clitics, too. There is some reason to do so, at least in Michif. Whereas gender distinctions are completely absent for postposed adjectives in Michif, in preposed French adjectives the distinct masculine and feminine forms are usually maintained. This may point to a more intimate link between prenominal adjectives and the noun than is the case with postnominal adjectives. All this may be the result of Cree influence since possessives and adjectives are prefixed in Cree and Cree has no articles. Cree makes no overt distinction between definite and indefinite noun phrases, a fact that may have contributed to the loss of the definite-indefinite distinction in the plural (as shown in example 23).

It is not clear what the status of the French article in Michif is. It is a cliticlike element that preserves some of the gender and number features of the French article, but it seems to have lost some of the semantics of (in)definiteness of French.

Summary: French Morphology

French nouns are not overtly inflected, but they have a complex and an irregular derivational system. The French verb has no inflectional or derivational endings of any importance. The only inflectional element it has, (-*e*), has several interpretations. Some of the French grammatical elements, however, tend to cliticize or perhaps even become prefixes in Michif. Apart from these, one could say that the nominal system is complex in derivation and simple in inflection. The verb is simple in inflection and not very complex in derivation.

The Intertwining of French and Cree

I have shown that Cree verb morphology is very complex and noun morphology fairly simple. Colloquial French has no inflectional noun morphology, but it apparently has a few proclitics and an irregular, complex nominal derivation. French verbs do have pronouns cliticized onto them but no inflection to speak of.

We have seen in Chapter Seven that the languages involved in language intertwining are of several types but that the process still yields roughly the same result.

If sociolinguistic circumstances such as those undergone by the Métis stimulate the genesis of a new, mixed language, the grammatical system of the mother's language and the lexicon of the father's language will intertwine. In this section I show that we run into numerous problems if we try to intertwine French and Cree in the same way in which the other languages, discussed in Chapter Seven, are intertwined. When we try to combine French lexicon and Cree grammar, we immediately face a complex issue: what is grammar and what is lexicon in Cree?

It is not easy to distinguish inflection from derivation in Cree verbs, and derivation is not easily distinguished from stem formation. It is therefore obvious that difficulties arise if we try to separate stems from affixes.

Cree Verbs

If we want to strip Cree verbs of their affixes, we are confronted with numerous and serious problems. Consider a Cree verb form such as the following:

(27)   nôhtê-wâp-am-ito-w-ak   (Cree)
       want-look-AN-REC-3-PL
       "They want to see each other."

Where is the boundary between stem and affixes? It is clear, if we start from the right, that the morphemes *-ak* ("plural subject/object") and *-w* ("third-person subject") are bound, inflectional morphemes, thus belonging to the class of grammatical elements, not lexical elements. The morpheme *-ito-* "each other" is also clear: it is a productive derivational morpheme, as well as a grammatical morpheme, that marks reciprocity.

From then on, however, things are unclear: is *-am* a lexical element or a grammatical morpheme? Is it part of the stem or a derivational suffix? The traditional analysis is that it is an abstract final, or a "theme sign," and part of the stem since there are different stem forms for animate and inanimate objects: *wâpam-* for animate objects and *wâpaht-* for inanimate objects. One can also say that these are a kind of agreement morpheme: they agree in gender with the object or subject noun. If one follows Stephen Anderson's (1982: 587) definition of inflection ("inflectional morphology is what is relevant for the syntax"), it would even be an inflectional suffix. In some cases, part of these stems shows similarities in shape with inflectional morphemes. One could also argue that the two different stem forms are part of a two-member paradigm. Both *-am* and *-(a)ht* also occur in other verb stems for animate and inanimate verbs, respectively. The inflectional morphemes that follow these stems also differ according to the animacy or inanimacy of the object or subject.

(28a)   wâpam-êw   (Cree)
       see.AN-3→3' (AN)
       "He sees him."

(28b)   wâpaht-am   (Cree)
       see.INAN-3→4 (INAN)
       "He sees it."

In this case (as in most cases of Cree verbs) it is clear that these stems are etymologically related, but other verbs have completely different stems for animate or inanimate subjects or objects. Note in example (29) that the word for "fish" in Cree is animate and the word for "meat" is inanimate.

(29a)   ni-wî-*môw*-âw kinosêw   (Cree)
        1-VOL-eat.AN-3 fish (AN)
        "I am going to eat fish."

(29b)   ni-wî-*mîci*-n wiyâs   (Cree)
        1-VOL-eat.INAN-3→4 meat (INAN)
        "I am going to eat meat."

Therefore it is best to consider the verbs *wâp-am-* and *wâp-aht-* as paired stems (as in the Algonquianist tradition), one for animate objects and one for inanimate objects. These stems are very much connected with the arguments of the verb, as they agree in gender with the object or the subject.

The next element in the verb form (27) is *wâp-*. It looks superficially like a lexical element with the meaning "to see," but this could actually be considered a formative or root (as *wâp-* or *-âp-*) with a less concrete meaning, something like "visibility" or "clearness." We find the same element in verbs and nouns such as the following:

(30a)   wâp-iw   (Cree)
        "He sees"; i.e., "He is not blind."

(30b)   wâp-an
        "it is dawn, east"

(30c)   wâp-ahki
        "tomorrow," i.e., "when it gets light"

(30d)   wâp-os
        "(white-tailed) hare"

(30e)   wâp-ôhô
        "white owl"

(30f)   wâp-iskâw
        "It is white."

(30g)   kit-âp-aht-am
        "S/he observes it."

(30h)   kîmôt-âp-iw
        "S/he looks secretly."

It could therefore be argued that formatives like *wâp-*, *-am*, and *-aht* are grammatical rather than lexical elements. Their meanings are more abstract than usual for lexical elements. If one asks a Cree speaker for the meaning of either of these formatives, for instance, he or she will not be able to answer. There is also a structural argument for the statement that they are grammatical elements: these morphemes can never be used in isolation because they do not have independent meaning. At least two of these formatives have to be combined to create lexical stems with concrete meanings. Native speakers do know the meanings of these combinations but not the individual formatives.

Another consideration involves movement verbs. All these verb stems consist of at least two bound morphemes, often with little or no lexical meaning if taken alone but generally freely combinable. If one takes one morpheme from the first column and one from the second (31), the result is usually an existing and almost always an intelligible combination.

(31)	pim-	"along"	-paht-	"run"
	papâm-	"about"	-ohtê-	"go"
	most-	"on foot"	-âsi-	"sail"
	sipwê-	"away"	-îwi-	"take with"
	it-	"someplace"	-ihâ-	"fly"
	is-	"in such a way"	-payi-	"start"
	wak-	"curved"	-pici-	"move oneself"
	wayawî-	"outside"	-iska-	"on water"
	paci-	"wrong"	-isi-	"be"
	kîmôti-	"in secret"	-âtisi-	"live"

The verb stems must consist of two or more formatives (initials and finals), which make up the stem only in combination. The meanings in the examples are much concreticized for the sake of clarity. A translation like "to sail" may sound verblike, but it could also be translated as "by wind."

The final element to be discussed in the Cree verb of example (27) is the morpheme *nôhtê-* "want," which precedes the stem *wâpam-*. This is one of a great number of so-called preverbs that can be placed before the stem of the verb. They can often be equated with auxiliaries in European languages. Again, they have grammatical rather than lexical meaning, and again they cannot be separated from the verb stem; only other preverbs can be placed between the stem and the preverbs. These preverbs can be preceded by other prefixes: tense and mood prefixes and person prefixes (for first and second person). In the verb complex, the clearest boundary is probably between the so-called stem, starting with an initial or reduplicative element, and the preverbs (Goddard 1990b).

The structures discussed are typical of Cree or Algonquian verbs. The verb in (27) had only initials and finals. Medials are also common. Three typical Cree verbs, with initial and final elements and some with medials, are given here as illustrations (examples from Wolfart 1971):

(32) mihkw-âpisk-isw-êw   (Cree)
     INIT-MED-FIN-INFL
     red-stone-by.heat-3→3'
     "He makes the stone red hot."

(33) kâs-ihkwê-n-êw   (Cree)
     INIT-MED-FIN-INFL

wash-face-by.hand-3→3'
"He washes his face with his hands."

(34)   pim-âp-am-êw   (Cree)
        INIT-MED-FIN-INFL
        along-see-AN-3→3'
        "He sees him pass."

Thus, every Cree verbal "stem" consists of a number of smaller units, which are bound morphemes. There are many hundreds of these elements and they should be considered open-class categories. Native speakers can combine most of these morphemes freely to create new verbal stems with subtle shades of meaning.

In conclusion, we can state that it is impossible to separate the affixes from the stem in a nonarbitrary manner. Furthermore, the stem also consists of smaller formatives. Taken in isolation, the smallest formatives beyond the phoneme have a rather abstract meaning, but when several of them are combined a meaningful stem can be the result. There are bound morphemes in a codependent relation. Also, the stem agrees in gender with the object or subject. Cree verbs are therefore closely knit units that consist solely of affixes.

Cree Nouns

In Cree nouns, it is generally easy to separate the affixes from the stems. The only inflectional affixes for nouns are the locative *-ihk* (allomorph *-ohk*), the inanimate plural–animate obviative *-(w)a*, the animate plural *-ak*, and the possessive prefixes and suffixes, as illustrated in (35) and (36).

(35a)   maskisin   (Cree)
         "a shoe, the shoe"

(35b)   maskisin-ihk
         shoe-LOC
         "on, in the shoe" (locative)

(35c)   maskisin-a
         shoe-PL
         "shoes" (plural inanimate)

(35d)   ni-maskisin
         1-shoe (possessed noun)
         "my shoe"

(36a)   nâpêw   (Cree)
         "a man, the man" (proximate)

(36b)   nâpêw-ak
         "men, the men" (plural)

(36c)   nâpêw-a
         man-OBV
         "the (other) man, the (other) men" (obviative)

There are also a few derivational forms, such as the diminutive suffix *-(s)is* (*nâpêsis* "boy"; *maskisinis* "little shoe").

The unmarked, proximate form of Cree nouns is usually identical to the noun root. Only in the case of dependent stems (nouns with obligatory possessive prefixes) is it difficult to say where the noun ends and the affix starts. In these cases, stem and affix form an organic whole:

(37)   nistikwân "my head"
       *(i)stikwân "a head, someone's head"
       mistikwân "a head, someone's head" (*mi-* is a prefix that marks nonpossession)

Nouns can also have prefixes that are equivalent to adjectives in English. These prefixes cannot be used in isolation, for instance, *oski-mînisa* "fresh berries" (Wolfart 1973a: 76); *oski-* (prefix) "young, new"; *mînisa* "berries." Here, too, the boundaries between stem and prefix are clear.

Thus, apart from the dependent stems, it poses no problems if one wants to separate the root from its affixes.

French Stems and Cree Affixes

The language intertwining model predicts that Cree affixes are combined with French nominal and verbal stems. On the one hand, this seems possible in principle for nouns. Cree nouns are not necessarily complex, but some can be. We have seen that French nouns have no inflectional affixes, although there are some prenominal elements that look like clitics. It would therefore be no problem to add affixes from other languages to French nominal stems. For Cree nouns (in contrast to verbs), it is virtually always possible to mark a firm boundary between the nominal stem and the affixes and between the adjectivelike prefixes and the noun. Only in a small subgroup of nouns are the boundaries between stem and affix fuzzy. These nouns have diminutive *-os* instead of *-is* and locatives *-ohk* instead of *-ihk* because of an underlying final *-w* in the stem. There are also different forms for vowel-final and consonant-final nouns, but these are perfectly predictable. The adjectivelike prefixes are also easily separable from the stem. Their meaning is concrete enough. Therefore, it must in principle be possible to combine French nominal stems with Cree affixes. Neither French nor Cree nouns nor the combination of the two is problematic.

On the other hand, it is obvious that we face problems if we try to combine Cree verbal affixes with French verbal stems according to the predictions of the language intertwining model. It would be impossible to decide where the Cree verbal affixes start and where the stem ends (as I have argued previously). For example, are the elements *-am-* and *-(a)ht-* agreement morphemes or part of the stem? The boundaries between the morphemes are often unclear.

It may be best to consider the whole Cree verb as consisting of bound morphemes, perhaps on a gliding scale of paradigmaticality, grammaticalization, and lexicality (see some of the problems discussed in Goddard 1987b and 1990a). Then a logical step follows if we want to combine grammar A (Cree) with lexicon B (French). The whole Cree verb would belong to the grammatical part of the language and not to the lexical part. Bound morphemes, as grammatical morphemes, are derived from the language of the grammatical system. Therefore, I conclude that it is impossible to combine the Cree verb stems or affixes with the affixes or stems of other languages, with the possible exception of other Algonquian language. It should be possible, however, to add Cree nominal affixes to French nouns.

The integrity of the Cree verb cannot be violated. It cannot be broken down into a grammatical part and a lexical part. There seem to be two possibilities for intertwining the Cree grammatical system with non-Algonquian stems: combining the Cree verb with French nouns stems (as in Michif) or using a Cree auxiliary combined with borrowed verb forms. Both strategies leave the Cree verbs intact.

Thus, if we were to combine Cree grammar with French lexicon, one of the two possible results would basically be Cree verbs and French nouns. Still, one would expect the French nouns to have Cree affixes, and that is exactly what Michif looks like. Cree is the language that provides the grammar (including the whole verbal complex), and French is the language that provides the lexicon. It is a form of language intertwining, as in the other cases in Chapter Seven, but because of the peculiar structure of the Cree verb, the grammatical part includes the whole verbal complex. In the remainder of this chapter I illustrate my point with a number of structural peculiarities of Michif that corroborate this analysis and a few apparent counterexamples.

Michif Structure and the Language Intertwining Hypothesis

The hypothesis just suggested can be formulated as follows. The structure of Michif is the result of the combination of Cree grammar with French lexicon—a process I term language intertwining. The grammatical and bound elements are Cree, and the lexical and free elements are French. The verb is totally Cree because the verb consists only of grammatical and bound elements, which can have lexical meaning in a polysynthetic language.

This hypothesis about the lexical and grammatical structure of Michif predicts a number of factors (discussed in the following sections). First, we would expect Cree grammatical elements that are not bound morphemes also to appear in Michif. One can think of possible particles like adverbs, question words, personal pronouns, and so on, in addition to French elements (see Chapter Seven). Second, as Cree nominal affixes can easily be separated from the noun itself, we would expect to see the Cree nominal affixes attached to French nouns. Third, when Cree nominal stems can be verbalized by means of affixes, one would expect French forms to be integrated into the Cree verb; but when roots or initials are used in Cree to form the verbs, this should be impossible. Fourth, there are a few French verb forms with Cree affixes, perhaps contrary to our expectations. Further, one would expect French nouns to be incorporated into Cree verbs if incorporation is indeed a productive syntactic process. Finally I discuss a number of apparent counterexamples in the Michif data.

Free Grammatical Morphemes in Cree

The presence of Cree demonstratives in otherwise French noun phrases in Michif has startled some researchers, particularly since it seems to be the only major exception to the generalization that the verb phrase is Cree and the noun phrase is French (Thomason and Kaufman 1988: 228–233). Some examples follow:

(38) *anIma* lι li:v
      that.INAN the book
      "that book"

(39) *ana* lɔm
      this.AN man
      "this man"

These demonstratives agree in number and animacy (of the corresponding Cree noun) with the nouns they modify. Cree *masinahikan* "book" is inanimate; *nâpêw* "man" is animate. Because demonstratives—especially the Cree ones, which show gender and number agreement—have more grammatical meaning than lexical meaning, it is not at all surprising that this category is drawn from the language that provides the grammatical part of the language.

It will come as no surprise that other free grammatical elements can be of Cree origin as well, especially in the more Cree-oriented dialects like that of Camperville. In all dialects, question words, postpositions, and personal pronouns are derived from Cree. Some categories of free grammatical morphemes can be derived from both French and Cree, such as prepositions, negators, and conjunctions. Numerals are the only elements that are always derived from French, although one would also expect them to be derived from Cree. There may be social reasons for this exception: perhaps the more numeracy-oriented nature of the French people is responsible. In the same way, in some Amerindian languages English numbers are commonly used (e.g., Bella Coola in British Columbia, as well as by many Cree speakers).

French Nouns with Cree Affixes

In the following discussion of the attachment of Cree nominal affixes to French nouns, I deal with each affix individually.

OBVIATION AND PLURAL

Obviation and plural cannot be clearly distinguished in Plains Cree. Obviative forms are neutral for number. Only animate nouns can be marked for obviation, and they are marked with the suffix *-(w)a*. The animate proximate (i.e., nonobviative) plural is marked with the noun suffix *-(w)ak*. The inanimate plural is marked with the suffix *(w)a* on the noun, the same suffix that also marks the animate obviative.

Both *-(w)a* and *-(w)ak* are found as plural markers on Cree nouns in Michif. Neither the animate plural morpheme *-(w)ak* nor the inanimate plural *-(w)a* was ever combined with French nouns in my material (except for two or three cases, like *oilers-a*). Only the French plural marker *li:* (< French *les*) is used to pluralize French nouns. The French indefinite plural marker *di:* (< French *des*) is only used in fixed French expressions, so that it can be said that *li:* is the only productive plural marker, used for both animate and inanimate nouns and in both definite and indefinite noun phrases. Cree does not distinguish between definite and indefinite nouns overtly.

The Cree obviative suffix -*(w)a*, however, is added to both French nouns and to Cree nouns in all dialects known until now, although its use seems to be more restricted in Michif than in Plains Cree (see Chapter 4). First, in Michif it is not used after a third-person possessive construction, whereas it is obligatory in Cree:

(40) o-têm-a   (*o-têm)   (Cree)
       his-dog-OBV

(41) sū šǽ   (*sū šǽ-wa)   (Michif)
       "his dog"

Second, the use of the obviative seems to be more restricted in Michif than in Plains Cree, even when it distinguishes subject and object in the sentence. Whereas in Plains Cree it seems to be used for all animate nouns, Michif has a kind of "animacy hierarchy" for obviation. Overt marking is obligatory with personal names; it is often (but not always) used with humans, sometimes with animals, and never with inanimates. Furthermore, postnominal French adjectives never receive obviation markers.

(42) Pi:tər lı bɔ̃ džy-*wa ki:-pImIčIsahw-e:w*   (obligatory)
       Peter the good God-OBV PST-follow-3→3'
       "Peter was a disciple of Jesus."

(43) Pi:t iva dɔ̃ti: lı marɔ̃-*wa*   (optional)
       Pete he-goes tame the wild.horse-OBV
       "Pete is going to tame the wild horse."

The obviative subject agreement morpheme -*yi*- (/jI/), which is used for third-person subjects possessed by another third person, is still marked overtly in the verb, even though (in Michif at least) it is not marked overtly in the noun phrase. In (44) this suffix is not used in Cree or in Michif since the possessor is not a third person. In (45), where the subject is a third person possessed by another third person, obviation is overtly marked on the noun and on the verb in Cree, but only on the verb and not on the noun in Michif.

(44a) ni-stês   *nipâ-w*   (Cree)
        my-brother sleep-3

(44b) mū frɛ:r   *nIpa:-w*   (Michif)
        "My brother is sleeping."

(45a) cân o-stês-a nipâ-yi-w   (Cree)
        John his-brother-OBV sleep-OBV-3

(45b) bæčts[5] sū frɛ:r *nIpa:-jI-w*   (Michif)

(45c) *bæčts sū frɛ:r-a nIpa:-jI-w*   (Michif)
        John his brother-(OBV) sleep-OBV-3
        "John's brother is sleeping."

This -*yi-*/ -*ji-* suffix is also used occasionally with nouns, indicating that the noun is possessed by an obviative possessor. A Cree example (from Wolfart 1973b: 18) and a Michif example follow:

(46)   ôhi nâpêw-a kâ-nipahâ-yi-t o-wîkimâkan-iyi-wa itohta-h-êw   (Cree)
        that.OBV man-OBV COMP-kill-OBV.SUBJ-3 his-wife-IYI-OBV take-3→3
        "He took there that man who had killed his (own) wife."

(47)   *ka:h-ki:htwa:m e:-wu:če:m-a:t* su frɛ:r-*IjIw*
        REDUP-again COMP-kiss-3→3 his brother-OBV.POSS
        "She repeatedly kissed his brother."[6]

In any case, Cree nominal obviation suffixes are used with French nouns in Michif.

<small>SUFFIX -*IPAN* "DECEASED"</small>

The derivational suffix -*ipan* was probably originally a verbal suffix-marking preterite. It is rare in contemporary Cree verbs (Wolfart 1973b: 49). In Cree it can be productively added to nouns that denote humans who are no longer alive:

(48)   ni-mosom-ipan   (Cree)
        my-grandfather-deceased
        "my deceased grandfather"

This affix, also used productively in Michif, is added to French nouns:

(49)   mũ vjø-*Ipan*
        "my deceased husband"

It is even used occasionally with English nouns when one is speaking English: "his first wife-*ipan*." A few speakers used the suffix with verbs, a phenomenon also existent, but rare, in modern Plains Cree. I have only a few examples:

(50)   Ralph L. *ki:-nagamu-h-pan*
        Ralph L. PST-sing-?-PRET
        "Ralph L.[7] was a singer, used to sing."

(51)   *kaja:š tanIgana:tagwe: aja:w-ak-Ipan* ǣ minuš.
        long.time.ago wish.DUB? have.AN-1→3-PRET IAMS cat
        "Long ago I wished I had a cat."

<small>PREFIXED ADJECTIVES</small>

Cree has no separate categories of adjectives. The equivalents of adjectives are either modifying elements prefixed to the noun or verbs functioning as a kind of relative clause. These Cree relative clauses, as verbal forms, exist in Michif, too, as expected. As predicted, there are also examples of Cree "adjectives" prefixed to French nouns, although these are not very common. Some examples follow:

(52)   *napakI-*lı-pwɛsũ
       flat-the-fish
       "flatfish" (Cree *napaka-w* "he is flat")

(53)   lı šɛf *ki:-ataw-e:w uškajI-*jæ̃-ša:r
       DAMS chief PST-buy-3→3 new-IAMS-car
       "The chief bought a new car."

(54)   *kIsčI-*mi:-grãpe:r dã lı kanada *uscI-w-ak*
       great-1.POSS.PL-grandfather in DAMS Canada be.from-3-PL
       "My ancestors came from Canada."

POSSESSIVE MARKING: DEPENDENT AND INDEPENDENT STEMS

Cree possessives can be of two kinds, both marked with affixes. There are dependent stems with obligatory possession marking and independent stems with optional possession marking. Dependent stems are mostly inalienable possessions such as body parts and kin. The affixes are prefixes with singular possessors or prefix-suffix combinations in which the suffixes mark plurality or obviation:

(55)   *nI-*   "my . . ."   *nI-X-Ina:n*   "our (EXCL) . . ."
       kI-   "your . . ."   *kI-X-Ina:n*   "our (INCL) . . ."
       o-   "his . . ."   *kI-X-Iwa:w*   "your (PL) . . ."
       o-X-IyIw   "his Y's . . ."   *o-X-Iwa:wa*   "their . . ."

There are a few grammatical differences between dependent stems and independent stems (see Chapter Four, example 123): first, dependent stems have an obligatory possessive prefix; second, dependent stems have a separate prefix *mi-*, which marks nonpossession, whereas independent stems have no such prefix; third, dependent stems never have an epenthetic consonant between the prefix and a vowel-initial noun.

On the basis of the intertwining hypothesis, one would expect Cree possessive affixes to occur with French nouns. This is only partly borne out by the facts. I recorded no French forms with only Cree affixes, but I have several hybrid forms in my data in which French nouns have French possessive "prefixes" and Cree possessive suffixes (as in Cree, where forms with plural possessors combine possessive prefixes and suffixes), as in *sa-tāt-Iwa:w* "their aunt" (Cree *o-tôsis-iwâw-a*). The plural suffix of the possessed noun refers to the plurality of the possessor. Another example follows:

(56)   John *tahkuht-am* li: fiy *anIhI* si: zarɛj-*Iwa:w*
       John bite-3→4 AP girl dem-OBV 3.POSS.PL ear-3.PL
       "John bites the girls' ears."

Most Michif speakers, however, use the forms *lø tāt* "their aunt" or *lø zarɛj* "his/her ear(s)." I have no explanation for the fact that Cree suffixes appear but not prefixes. Perhaps this occurs because French already has "prefixes."

It is striking that a French possessive element is obligatory with French nouns whose Cree equivalents would be dependent stems. A question such as "How do you say 'head' in Michif?" is answered either with "It depends whose head" or with *ma tête, ta tête,* or *sa tête* but never *la tête* or *tête,* which would be the answer given by speakers of French. Apparently the alienable-inalienable distinction is still important in Michif, despite the disappearance of the prefixed Cree dependent stems. The French possessive element may function as a prefix in Michif rather than a cliticized element, as it does in French. The continued use of the plurality suffixes in possessives also points to Cree semantics in the possessive system.

LOCATIVE MARKING: *-IHK* AND *DA*

Cree has a locative marker, *-ihk,* with an allomorph, *-ohk.* One would expect this suffix to be added to French nouns, but this is not the case. Instead, the preposition *dã* (often pronounced as [da:] or [da]) is used, from French *dans* "in." There are two remarkable aspects of Michif locatives, however, that show Cree influence.

The preposition *da* is used as a general locative preposition in Michif, meaning "in," "on," and "at," whereas *dans* in French can mean only "in." The preposition *da/dã* apparently copies the wider functions of the Cree locative. In the light of the following, it does not seem possible to say simply that there has been a process of generalization of meaning. The *da* preposition in Michif is sometimes combined with other Cree or French adpositions in Michif—which is not possible in French. If it is combined, the meaning would be different. An example follows:

(57)   ãnarjɛr dã lɪ ša:r
       in-back in the car
       "behind the car"

In French this would mean "in the back of the car" and not "behind the car," as in Michif. The latter would be *derrière la voiture.* This *da* is used with both French and Cree adpositions.

(58)   dã lɪ frɪdž *uhčl*
       LOC the fridge from
       "out of the fridge"

(59)   *utahk* dã lɪ ša:r
       behind LOC the car
       "behind the car"

Although it may seem strange at first sight, this is obviously a direct copy of the Cree construction, in which several locative adpositions govern nouns in the locative case:

(58')   tahkascikan-ihk ohci   (Cree)
        fridge-LOC from
        "out of the fridge"

(59')   otahk otâpânask-ohk   (Cree)
         behind car-LOC
         "behind the car"

I conclude that *da* in Michif has exactly the same function as *-ihk* in Cree: a general locative marker instead of a preposition that denotes only "inside," as in French, and a kind of "case marker" for some adpositions. Apparently French *dans* took over the functions of the Cree suffix *-ihk*. As shown in Chapter Five, it seems as if the preposition *da* is very frequent, just because it took over many other functions that the French preposition does not have. Why this occurred is not clear yet. It may have to do with the fact that there are two allomorphs for the Cree locative, but this does not seem to be a sufficient reason.

DIMINUTIVE *-IS* AND *PETIT*

The last nominal affix used in Cree is the derivational suffix *-is* (allomorphs *-sis* and *-os*), which is the diminutive suffix. Contrary to our expectations, there are no instances of *-is* used with French nouns in any dialect of Michif. The only thing one can notice is the relatively frequent use of the French adjective *pči* (< F. *petit* "little"), which may have taken over the function of the Cree diminutive.

SUMMARY

If we summarize the use of Cree nominal endings with French stems, we see that three Cree affixes are used extensively with French stems in Michif, although all in fewer contexts than in Cree (obviative, *-ipan*, and prefixed adjectives). Three Cree affixes have French equivalents that have taken over the functions of the Cree affixes (dependent possessive affixes, diminutives, and locatives). One could say that these are French in shape and relative position to the noun but Cree in function. Only one Cree affix is not used in Michif with French elements—the plural marker—but here again the French element may have taken over Cree functions because the French distinction between definite and indefinite plurals is lost in Michif.

Finally, we can say that the noun phrase consists of French stems, with French syntax, but semantically it is almost entirely Cree. Some Cree suffixes are used overtly, and in those cases in which Cree affixes are not used, French elements appear to function very much like Cree affixes.

French Nouns as Part of Cree Verbs

For the use of French nouns with Cree verb affixes in verbalization constructions, I have predicted the possibility of replacing these Cree nouns by French nouns but not Cree roots or initials. Here, boundaries between nominal stems and verbal affixes are clear. It is perhaps best to illustrate this case with two verbal suffixes, which both mean "to be"—one that is attached to initials or roots (*-IsI-*) and one that is attached to stems (*-IwI-*).

-IwI- AND *-IsI-*

In Cree, the suffix *-iwi-* can be added to nouns to mean something like "to be an X." An example from Cree follows:

(60) ê-awâsis-iwi-yân   (Cree)
      COMP-child-be-1
      "when I was a child"

This suffix is also used in Michif, but apparently only with French nouns and adjectives, not with Cree stems:

(61) lı tã *ka:*-lı-rwɛ-*hIwI-t*
      the time REL-the-king-BE-3.AN
      "the time when he was king"

(62) la-brɛm-*Iw-an*
      the-fog-BE-4
      "It is foggy."

(63) lı-sæl-*Iw-an*
      the-dirty-BE-4
      "It is dirty."

This suffix is productive in all varieties of Michif. All examples in our data have French nouns and adjectives; none of them have Cree nouns. This is what we would expect if the lexicon is French and the grammatical system is Cree. It seems that only French nouns can combine with this verbalizing suffix.

There is also a similar suffix, *-IsI-*, meaning roughly "to be." This, however, is added to roots or initials and is not found in the Michif data with French nouns. It is fairly common with Cree roots (initials) in Michif. An example (existing in both Cree and Michif) follows:

(64) maskaw-IsI-w   (Michif, Cree)
      strong-be-3
      "He is strong."

The difference between these two suffixes in combination with French stems is that in the one case the element is used with stems and in the other with roots. Only *-IwI-*, which combines with nominal stems, is used in Michif with French stems because of its easy separability: it is combined with stems rather than roots. Other Cree affixes show similar patterns.

NOUN + *-IHKÊ-*

The suffix *-ihkê* can be added to nouns (but not roots) in Cree to form a verb "to make X," as in (65):

(65)   maskisin-ihkê-w   (Cree)
       shoe-make-3
       "S/he makes shoes."

This is possible with French nouns and adjectives in Michif also:

(66)   *mi:na ka*-lı-budæ̃-*Ihke:-w*
       again FUT-the-sausage-make-3
       "She will be sulky again." (lit. "She will make sausage again.")

(67)   *mjœht-am* alãtu:r sa mæ̃zũ *e:*-lı-*žali:-hke:-t*
       like.TI-3→4 around her house COMP-DAMS-nice-make-3
       "She likes to make her garden beautiful."

OTHER AFFIXES ATTACHED TO STEMS

Other affixes are attached to nominal stems rather than roots. The pair *-inâkosiw* "he
looks like X" and *-nâkwan* "it looks like X" (and its related form *-imâkwan* "it smells
like X" and some others) are added to stems, as well as *-ihkâsow* "he pretends X."
Some examples follow:

(68)   miyo-nâkw-an   (Cree)
       good-look.II-4
       "It looks good."

(69)   dılɛt-*Ina:kw-an*   (Michif)
       milk-look.like.II-4
       "It looks milky."

(70)   maci-mâkw-an   (Cree)
       bad-smell.II-4
       "It smells bad."

(71)   lagrɛs-*Ima:kw-an*   (Michif)
       grease-smell.II-4
       "It smells greasy."

(72)   atoskê-hkâso-w   (Cree)
       work-pretend.AI-3
       "S/he pretends to be working."

(73)   lı-bɔs-*Ihka:šu-w*   (Michif)
       DAMS-boss-pretend.AI-3
       "He acts as if he is the boss."

Only Cree affixes that can attach to stems, not Cree affixes that attach only to roots,
can be added to French stems. No Cree stem formatives or affixes that attach to roots
are used with French lexical material in the data.

French Verbs with Cree Verbal Affixes

A few French verbs can be used (or perhaps are always used) with Cree verbal morphology, which might seem to pose problems for our hypothesis. Some examples
follow:

(74)   *gi:*-lı-ga:ž-i:-*n* syr lı brǭ
       1.PST-DAMS-bet-INF-1 on the brown
       "I betted on the brown one."

This also occurs with some English verbs:

(75)   *kahkIja:w* lı-sɛlıbre:t-i:-*w-ak* lı kæt dı žujɛt
       all DAMS-celebrate-INF-3-PL the four of July
       "All celebrate the Fourth of July."

(76)   *dawe:ht-a:na:n* ɛn batri: *ka:*-lı-ča:rdž-i:-*t*
       1.need-11 DAFS battery REL-DAMS-charge-INF-3
       "We need a battery charger."

In all cases, the French (or English) verbs apparently have the infinitive form—ending in /i:/ (< F. *-er*)[8]— and they are preceded by the French definite article, whether
they are nouns, adjectives, or verbs.

One cannot argue, for two main reasons, that the combination of French verbs
and Cree morphology is a more recent development of the language. First, it must
predate the diaspora of the Métis, as the phenomenon exists in all Métis communities for all Michif speakers. It also occurs in communities where French ceased to be
spoken to any significant degree a long time ago (as in Turtle Mountain). Second, all
Michif speakers make the combinations in exactly the same way, in all communities. It is so peculiar that it does not resemble a process that could have developed
twice in exactly the same fashion. It is not used by French-Cree bilinguals and not in
communities like Ile-a-la-Crosse.

As an explanation I suggest that these French verbs did not have a Cree equivalent when the French or English concept was introduced into the Métis community.
Because of the widespread knowledge of French, a new Cree term was not coined,
as in most Cree-speaking communities; instead the French term was borrowed. In
some cases the Cree word with an equivalent meaning is also used, but that word is
limited to the more Native-oriented activities. I do not have many examples in my
data. The meanings of the French verbs used in this construction are "to bless" (in
church), "to arrange" (furniture), "to embroider," "to plaster," "to witness" (in court),
"to stutter," "to bet" (with money), "to vote," "to domesticate," "to mix" (plaster),
"to paint" (house, furniture), and "to haggle." The English verbs thus used are "to
charge," "to celebrate," "to haul," "to settle" (a disagreement), "to deal," "to save"
(money), "to can," "to box" (as a sport), "to gamble," "to park" (a car), "to collect"
(money), and also on one occasion "to trust." This list is exhaustive as far as my data
are concerned. These verbs seem to denote activities mainly associated with nonna-
tives. Therefore they may be lexical borrowings, which fill lexical gaps, rather than

the result of language intertwining. It still seems a productive way of spontaneously borrowing English items for which a speaker does not know the Cree equivalent.

It is remarkable that in each case in which French elements are used with Cree verbal affixes, the French element is preceded by the French definite article. Although this phenomenon is not yet fully understood, its function might be to mark the fact that what follows *le* or *la* must be interpreted as a foreign, non-Cree item. The end point of the foreign element, even the English verbs, is marked by the French (perhaps the infinitive) marker *-i:*[9] as a "flag," which shows the boundary between the foreign element and the native endings. These flags warn the listener not to subject to Cree verb stem derivation the elements that are found between two flags. This interpretation is parallel to Drapeau's (1980) explanation of the obligatory use of the French definite article with French nominal borrowings into Montagnais, even when this would be incorrect in French (e.g., *le ski*): it is used to flag foreign elements in the language. The article and infinitive morphemes would function as markers of the boundaries of the foreign elements. If not marked as such in the Cree verb, the foreign element would be subject to a Cree morphological analysis into initial, finals, and so on to make up its meaning, which is undesirable. This hypothesis is preliminary and requires closer investigation.

Looking at all the instances of these verbs in the data (some thirty tokens in all), it is striking that some derivational and inflectional affixes are used with them but not with others. The preverbs, the causative suffix, and the obviative and possessive agreement suffix *-yi-* are used, as well as the inflectional personal agreement markers (which are obligatory), but strikingly enough, not the direction markers (see Chapter Four for a brief explanation). These direction markers are sometimes considered derivational and sometimes inflectional by Algonquianists.

Of course, this whole issue raises the question, if it is in principle possible to combine French verbs with Cree verbal affixes in this way, why was it not done throughout the language? I do not have a solid explanation for this, but some aspects may play a role. First, it seems rather burdensome to add two extra dummy morphemes to each verb form. This would go against the economy of the language.

Second, it is apparently impossible to add the Cree direction markers to these stems. Their absence could lead to undesirable ambiguities since they are one of the main markers of grammatical functions in both Cree and Michif.

Third, there are phonological problems. If the whole intertwined language were to use these French verbs in a Cree grammatical framework, the French words would need to be adjusted to Cree phonology, as in the other cases. Cree has one of the smallest phoneme inventories of the world and could never integrate French words, as French has a large phoneme inventory.

Fourth, the meanings of the verbs indicate that they are lexical borrowings. Either they denote nontraditional activities that do not exist in the Cree or Métis world or the traditional Métis activities are different from those of the outsiders.

Finally, it is possible that the patterns of code mixing, which must have preceded the crystallization of the Michif language, hindered the use of Cree affixes with French verbs. In Chapter Six, I suggest that code-mixing patterns may favor French nouns and Cree verbs. It is possible that the mixed forms are only used for the French verbs that denote more or less "foreign" activities. There seems to be a parallel with Navaho-

English code mixing (mentioned in Chapter Six), in which a few English verbs have Navaho affixes; normally, however, the English verb is used with helping verbs that mean "to make" or "to do."

In short, there are several arguments to explain the existence of these French verbs. It is, on the one hand, a corroboration of the hypothesis that in Michif it is not borrowing but something else—what I call language intertwining—since borrowing apparently occurs in a different way. On the other hand, it shows that a combination of Cree affixes with French verbs is possible in exceptional cases, although it remains an unsolved question why not all French verbs are treated in the same way.

Noun Incorporation

Nouns can be incorporated into verbs in Plains Cree, but not much is known about the constraints and possibilities of noun incorporation in this language because it has been studied only by few researchers (Wolfart 1971; for a theoretical approach see Mellow 1989). It is my impression that incorporation is much less productive now than it was in the 1920s, when Bloomfield (1930, 1934) collected his texts in Plains Cree. It is certain that the incorporated nouns have a form that is almost always different from the noun in isolation. The forms are rarely identical (*iskwêw* "woman"; incorporated form -*iskwêw*-), as in the following example:

(77)   nôcih-iskwêw-ê-w   (Cree)
        chase-woman-CLASS-3
        "He chases women."

The incorporated noun is sometimes similar: *atim* "dog," incorporated form -*astim*-; *maskisin* "shoe," incorporated form -*askisin*-:

(78)   kêt-askisin-ê-n-ê-w   (Cree)
        take.off-shoe-CLASS-by.hand-DIR-3
        "He take off his shoes."

Sometimes the forms show no formal relationship (*ni-sit* "my foot," -*isk*- "foot"; *n-êstakay* "my hair," incorporated form -*ânisk*-) as in this:

(79)   kaskitêw-âniskw-ê-w   (Cree)
        black-hair-CLASS-3
        "He has black hair."

Furthermore, some nouns cannot be incorporated, for example, *nâpêw* "man." For this reason, noun incorporation is possible only for nouns that have an incorporated equivalent, and it is therefore not a purely syntactic process. It is not stems that are incorporated but rather affixes with a nounlike meaning. These affixes are not necessarily etymologically related to the corresponding nouns. In fact, roots are incorporated, not stems. The prediction that the incorporation of French nouns will not be possible in Michif is borne out by the facts. Incorporated nouns are found in Michif, but these are the Cree-derived nounlike "infixes" (medials), as in the examples. This is what one would expect since these elements are grammatical affixes rather than lexical elements.

The only example I have come across so far, which only vaguely resembles incorporation, is the following:

(80) æ kana:r *ka:*-lt-vɛr-*lštIkwan-e:-t*
      a duck REL-the-green-head-CLASS-3
      "a duck that has a green head, mallard"

In this example the incorporated noun is Cree, but it is modified by a French adjective.

Mellow (1989) argues that incorporation in Cree is a syntactic process. Many of his arguments are sound, but there are important counterarguments: syntactic analysis seems to be of very limited productivity in contemporary Cree, and the incorporated form of the noun is rarely identical to the free form of the noun, which also makes the full productivity of noun incorporation doubtful.

In short, these two factors—affixes are incorporated, not stems, and incorporation is of limited productivity—explain why French nouns cannot be incorporated into Cree forms.

Some Apparent Counterexamples

Two structural features of Michif deserve mention, as they might be taken as counterexamples to the intertwining hypothesis (French lexicon and Cree grammar) proposed here.

LACK OF FRENCH VERBS WITH CREE NOMINALIZING SUFFIXES

First, we would expect that the Cree nominalizing affixes *-sk*, *-kan*, and *-win* would be attached to French verbal stems rather than to Cree stems. These suffixes are used productively with Cree verbs in Michif, but it is not possible to attach them to French verbs, perhaps because of the great amount of irregularity in nominalization in French. Another explanation may be that these suffixes are in fact combinations of the nominalizing suffix *-n* and two verb suffixes, *-iwi-* "to be" and *-ikê-* "to do something to things," and therefore too much blurred. Neither seems sufficient as an explanation. It is also possible that the availability of Cree verbs—the central element of the sentence—with productive nominalization possibilities made preservation of French patterns superfluous. It is striking, though, that French derivational suffixes are productively added to French nouns in Michif (see Chapter Four).

FRENCH ARTICLES WITH CREE NOUNS

The second problem is the fact that Cree nouns (whether real nouns or nominalized verbs), if used in Michif, are regularly but not always preceded by French articles or possessive markers, especially the less common nouns (see Chapter Four, examples 105 and 106).

(81)   lı *we:pIn-Ike:-wIn*
      DAMS throw-INTRANS-NOM
      "garbage"

(82) ɛn *pu:ju:-šk*
      IAFS quit-ITER
      "a quitter"

This contradicts the prediction of my model that Cree nominal affixes would be added to French stems. One preliminary explanation may be that the result of the language intertwining process was unconsciously analyzed by speakers of Michif as having Cree verbs and French nouns, so that Cree nouns, when they were used, were interpreted as belonging to the French noun phrase, thus obtaining a French article. Another possibility is that these Cree nouns are thought to be borrowings into French. They often have the article that would be required if the noun had been French, with the exception of the verbalized Cree nouns formed with the *-win* and *-kan* suffixes, which appear to be always masculine in Michif.

Conclusions: Cree Morphology and Michif

In this chapter we have seen that Cree nominal morphology is almost nonexistent and that Cree verbal morphology is extensive. The latter differs significantly from, say, Indo-European languages. Apart from personal agreement morphemes for subject and object, which are considered part of the inflectional morphology, there are a number of derivational affixes that mark grammatical function changes and gender changes. The greatest difference, however, is that Cree verbs, when stripped of these combinations of derivational and inflectional affixes, can still be subdivided into smaller morphological formatives. Cree stems always consist of a number of bound morphemes, which is almost unknown in Indo-European languages except for small classes such as the English words "per-ceive," "de-ceive," "con-ceive," "con-fer," and "de-fer" (but not, e.g., *"per-fer"; see Spencer 1991: 86), but these examples are still rather different. Although these morphological formatives of the stem in Cree often have strongly idiomatic or lexicalized meaning, it is possible to make new combinations with them productively. Speakers are able to ascribe a meaning to new formations when they hear them. Nevertheless, it is very hard to ascribe meanings to the formatives themselves. They only have a clear meaning when they are combined into larger units.

In conclusion, I claim that Michif arose through a process I call language intertwining. The social circumstances were such that a new, mixed language was needed. Most often the result of the process will be a language with the grammatical system of language A (the language of the first-generation mothers) and the lexicon of language B (the language of the first-generation fathers). Michif seems to be different from the other cases of language intertwining because we must think of its whole verb complex as consisting only of affixes; thus the verb in total must be Cree. It appears to be impossible in general to combine Cree affixes with French verb stems, as in the other cases of intertwining (Chapter Seven), and so Michif seems to be on the surface a mixture of Cree verbs and French nouns. On closer scrutiny, however, there appears to be a number of Cree affixes used with French stems, as one would expect.

We have seen that the predictions of the language intertwining hypothesis are mostly corroborated by the data, which show the existence of French lexical stems (both nouns and verbs) with Cree grammatical affixes. When the Cree affix is not used, there is a French element that functions unlike its French source but exactly like the Cree element it replaces, with only few exceptions. We also find Cree grammatical elements when these are free morphemes.

In the next chapter I attempt to pinpoint as precisely as possible the place and the time when Michif arose, based on the historical and geographical information given earlier and the comparative material on Cree and French dialects.

The Source Languages of Michif

French, Cree, and Ojibwe

Introduction

In the foregoing chapters we have seen that Michif, which combines Cree and French elements, is a language in its own right. It is a so-called intertwined language spoken by the Métis people. The Métis are a consequence of the Canadian fur trade, during which European men married Amerindian women. Their children were bilingual, and they more or less combined the grammatical system of the mother's language with the lexicon of the father's. From this combination the Michif language emerged, a language with Cree verbs and French nouns.

I cite historical and linguistic evidence for the fact that Michif must have crystallized before the 1840s, when some of the Michif-speaking communities were established and when people who are today remembered as Michif speakers were born (see Chapter Six). There are, however, some indications that Michif arose around or before 1810.

In this chapter I study the source languages of Michif. Although linguists have classified Michif as a mixture of Plains Cree and Canadian French, this generalization is incorrect at two points. First, both the French and the Cree components differ from their supposed source languages. These differences must be explained. Second, most linguists have ignored remarks by Michif speakers that their language not only contains French and Cree elements but in fact is a mixture of Cree, French, and Saulteaux. The presence of the Saulteaux (Ojibwe) elements in all dialects of the Michif language may provide a key to its origin and to its first speakers.

The French Component of Michif

The French component of Michif differs considerably from standard European French, even to the extent that some of it is not recognizable to Parisians. It is, not surprisingly, much closer to Canadian French and even closer to prairie Canadian French. In fact, the French dialect with which Michif is most closely related is the form of French spoken in the prairie provinces by Métis, members of the same nation as the Michif speakers. Métis French is the source language for Michif. In fact, this French is also called Michif by its speakers. Métis French, as well as Louisiana Cajun French, is probably the most divergent dialect of standard French in North America. Nevertheless, it remains a dialect of French, not a creole or creoloid. One could set up the following continuum for the French dialects.

(1) Parisian French → Quebecois French → Acadian (?) → western Canadian French →
     Métis French → French component of Michif

Canadian French

European French is an official language in Canada. Federal services are conducted in both French and English, and something approaching European French is taught in the schools. A variety close to European French is most often used in the media. Because of more intensive contacts between the two continents, official Quebecois moves closer to European French with every generation. French is the sole official language only in the province of Quebec. The province of New Brunswick is officially bilingual. There are two main dialects of Canadian French, Quebecois (of Quebec) and Acadian (Nova Scotia and New Brunswick), from which dialects in other areas are usually derived. Michif shares traits with both. Both dialects date from the early period of settlement and show archaic trends, as well as, of course, innovations. I mention some of the more striking points in which Canadian French differs from European French (based on Hewson 1989).

LEXICON

Canadian French differs from standard European French, first, in having a number of words for items unknown in the Old World. Most of these are names for flora and fauna and other natural phenomena, such as *bleuet* "blueberry" and *poudrerie* "snowstorm." Among them are Amerindian loanwords, mostly from Micmac, Montagnais, and Algonquin (Ojibwe) and a few from Abenaki, Mohawk, and Huron (Faribault 1993). Some examples are *carcajou* "wolverine" and *micouane* "big spoon" (from Ojibwe *e:mekkwa:n* "big spoon").

A second lexical difference is the influence of maritime vocabulary on everyday speech (Dulong 1970; Hewson 1983) because, in the early days, most transportation involved a body of water. Some of the early settlers may have come from seafaring families. The verb *embarquer*, for example, originally meant only "to embark," but in Canada it is also used for stepping into a car. Third, many words have a different meaning in Quebec French than in European French. The verb *embarquer*, just mentioned, is an example. Finally, Canadian French has English loanwords, which are often different from English borrowings in European French, for example, "raftsman" and "fun."

MORPHOLOGY AND SYNTAX

In morphology and syntax there are also differences, and here I mention only a few. Some verbs are regularized. For instance, in France the verb *mourir* has the standard forms *je meurs* "I die" and *je suis mort* "I am dead," whereas in Canada one hears *je mours* and *j'ai mouru*. Some adjectives have feminine forms in Canada, which they do not have in standard French, such as *pourri-te* "rotten."

The order of the clitics with respect to the verb is sometimes different, for example, *Ne parlez-moi-z-en pas* "Do not talk to me about it" for standard European French *Ne m'en parlez pas*. The *-z-* is an example of false "liaison." In these cases, the consonant is not derived from an underlying consonant. An example of a syntactic difference is the question construction. Whereas European French has *Quand est-ce que tu pars?* for "when do you leave," Canadian French has *Quand pars-tu?* One can also hear *Tu viens-tu?* in Canadian French.

PHONOLOGY

Most obvious to outsiders, however, are the phonological differences. In some cases, words are pronounced in an archaic way, for example, in Canada the final consonants of *bout* "end" and *icitte* "here" (standard *ici*). The standard phoneme sequence /wa/ is often pronounced [wɛ] in Canada, for example, /franswɛ/ for *François*.

As for the vowels, the most conspicuous Canadian differences are in the length and the tendency to have diphthongs for long vowels, for example, /sejz/ for *seize* "sixteen." Some nasal vowels have shifted in place of articulation so that, for instance, the nasals /œ̃/ and /ɛ̃/ merge. Standard /ɛ/ is often pronounced in Canada as [a] in closed syllables, especially before /r/, for example, [vart] *verte* "green" (feminine).

In Canadian French, the consonants /t/ and /d/ are spirantized before high front vowels, for example, [tˢy etˢydᶻi] for *tu étudies* "you study." Final consonant clusters are often simplified, as in the final "r" in [kat] *quatre* "four." Finally, the /h/ is still pronounced in Canada, as in [la haš] *la hache* "the axe."

There are, of course, many more differences, but there is insufficient space to discuss all of them. Many of these Canadian dialectal traits, which were originally formulated for Quebecois, can also be found in some way or other in the French used by the Métis and the French part of Michif. The reader may have noted some in the text and the examples in other chapters. The point of interest here, however, is the phonological difference between Métis French, the source language for Michif, and its supposed source language, eastern Canadian French.

Métis French versus Quebecois French

In this discussion of the French component of Michif versus Quebecois French, I take Métis French as the point of comparison. This language is the source language for Michif and, as far as the noun phrase is concerned, virtually identical to Michif. It makes no sense to compare Métis French to Parisian French since the former is evidently more closely related to Quebecois French. There are some differences, however, between Métis French and other French dialects in Canada. As these differences may have arisen under the influence of the Native languages spoken by the early generations of Métis, they may shed some light on the "substrate" languages of Métis French, and therefore on the ethnic groups who would become the Métis nation.

LEXICON

Métis French differs lexically from other Canadian French dialects. Although the bulk of the lexicon is also known in conservative western Canadian, Quebecois, or Acadian French dialects, some lexical items seem to be typically Métis: *boulet* ([bulε] for "ankle" (it means "fetlock" in standard French), *ponque* [pɔ̃k] for "rectum" (possibly related to the Ojibwe word for "farting" *boogidi*), and so on. Many Michif words of French origin have meanings that differ from other dialects, for example, French *taureau* "bull," Michif *tu:ru* "pemmican"; French *biche* "female deer," Michif *bɪš* "elk"; French *cérise* "cherry," Michif *sriz* "[certain] berry"; French *griv* "thrush," Michif *grɪv* "robin" (see Papen 1984b). Furthermore, all Métis French dialects use a number of Cree or Ojibwe words that differ in number and kind from place to place. For instance, the words for "bee" and "ant" are Ojibwe; the words for "chokecherries," "grandmother" and "grandfather," and some other kinship terms are Cree.

MORPHOLOGY AND SYNTAX

Some linguistic differences between Métis French and Quebecois French have been discussed in Chapter Three, and I repeat three grammatical differences here:

- In Métis French, possessives are formed as possessor – possessive pronoun – possessed, not as in the French possessed – preposition – possessor (*Pierre son cheval* vs. *le cheval à Pierre*).

- There is no gender difference in the personal pronouns when referring to persons in Métis French, for example, *Ma femme, il est malade* "My wife, he is ill" or *Les femmes, ça coupait le bois* "The women, it used to cut wood" (Douaud 1985). Feminine forms are also used to refer to males: *Mon vieux, elle est dans la maison* ("My husband, she is in the house").

- Numerals are placed before articles and nouns instead of between them, as in French (this is the Michif construction; it is not known whether it also exists in Métis French).

The possessive construction is a straight calque from the Algonquian (Cree and Ojibwe) construction (see Chapter Three). The lack of gender in pronouns is also undoubtedly an influence from the Cree and Ojibwe languages since Algonquian languages make no distinction between masculine and feminine (or male and female) in pronouns. Cree Indians, even some with a university degree, confuse English masculine and feminine pronouns when they speak. The Algonquian influence on the position of the numeral cannot easily be claimed. Cree has no articles. The particular Michif order may be due to the fact that numerals, like other quantifiers, can be easily separated from the noun phrase to which they belong, in Michif as in Cree or Ojibwe. Perhaps the possibility of this movement stimulates the article and noun to become a closer syntactic unity in Michif. In any case, these grammatical deviations from Canadian French seem to be the consequence of Cree or Ojibwe influence.

PHONOLOGY

Three phonological differences are discussed in Chapter Three:

- There is the raising of /e/ to /i/ and the raising of /o/ to /u/ (and also often /œ/ to /y/).
- In Michif, all sibilants within one word are harmonized: either they are all palatalized or none are.
- Whereas Quebecois French has spirantized /t/ (realized as [tˢ]) and /d/ (realized as [dᶻ]), Métis French has the affricates /č/ and /dž/.

These are not the only phonological differences:

- There is the labialization of velars before back vowels in Métis French. Words like *goudron* and *cochon* are often pronounced [gwadrũ] and [kwašũ] in Métis French.
- There is alternation between palatalized velar stops and palatalized alveolar stops. These seem to be in free variation, for example, /sæ̃čɛm/ or /sæ̃kjɛm/ "fifth" (F. *cinquième*); /lamɩričæ̃/ "American" (F. *l'Américain*). Some forms may be hypercorrect, such as /la mwa:ki/ (also /moči/) "half" (F. *la moitié*) and /aparkjæ̃/ (F. *appartient*).
- Some speakers of Métis French use /I/ for the schwa, for example, *mu nɩvœ* "my cousin." This, again, may be an influence from Cree, as Cree does not have schwas but does have short /I/.

Although the differences between Métis French and Canadian French are less important than the similarities, some of them are so conspicuous (notably mid-vowel raising) that Métis French is readily distinguishable from all other French dialects. What are the origins of the deviations in Métis French phonology? Here Amerindian influence is rather difficult to establish.

Merger of *e/i*

The most conspicuous difference between Canadian French and Métis French is the rule of mid-vowel raising (/e/ > /i/; /o/ > /u/). For the raising of /o/ to /u/, it is easy to point to an Amerindian source. In Cree and Ojibwe—and in all Amerindian languages of the fur-trading area except Assiniboine—[o] and [u] are variants (allophones) of the same phoneme.

The raising of /e/, however, is somewhat obscure. A few languages are spoken in the fur-trading area in which /e/ and /i/ are merged. Strikingly, the dialect of Plains Cree that merged with Métis French does *not* show this phenomenon: /e/ and /i/ are separate phonemes in the Cree component of Michif but not in the French part. This suggests strongly that mid-vowel raising had already taken place in Métis French *before* the two languages intertwined. The merger of /e/ with /i/ has been attested to only in some Woods Cree dialects in northwestern Manitoba and northeastern Saskatchewan (see Starks 1987 and Brightman 1989) and in the northern dialect of Plains Cree, spoken in the woodlands of Alberta and northwestern and central Saskatchewan (see Pentland 1978a). I am not aware of any Ojibwe dialects in which these phonemes have merged.

Because all Cree dialects that exhibit this merger are spoken in the woodlands north of the prairies, this is where one should look if this change in Métis French is caused by Amerindian languages. However, this area is probably too far to the west to have been an influence on Red River French, although it is true that Woods Cree was formerly also spoken further east, near Hudson Bay. Some of the early sources of Woods Cree (notably Isham's 1743 material from York Factory and MacKenzie's 1790 word lists from the English River (Rich 1949; Lamb 1970) seem to show this merger of /e/ and /i/; thus a Cree dialect formerly spoken more to the east toward Hudson Bay may in principle be the source of the /e/ and /i/ merger.

I think there are two possible causes for this merger. One possibility is that Métis French had merged the two vowels in analogy with the merger of /o/ and /u/ (undoubtedly caused by an Amerindian language), as a consequence of which all mid-vowels were raised. The other possibility is that widespread bilingualism and extensive use by French fur traders of some Cree dialects of the woodlands in which /e/ and /i/ were merged had triggered the raising. The latter seems historically possible. Whatever is the cause, the change must have taken place before Métis French mixed with Plains Cree.

Alternation of *wa/o*

The productive optional labialization of velars before back vowels (/ekosɛ/ vs. /ekwasɛ/ "Scotchman") in Métis French is also of uncertain origin. It is also found after /m/, for example, *mutũ* next to *mwatũ* "sheep." As this is not an unusual phonological process after velars in the languages of the world, it may be a spontaneous change. There is a possibility, however, that there is an Algonquian source, even though in Cree and Ojibwe it is not limited to postvelar contexts. Several words in Algonquian have cognates that either have /wa/ or /o/, for instance, the following proto-Algonquian forms (Aubin 1975, nbr. 2146):

(2)   **waΘa:kw-* versus * *oΘa:kw* "evening (yesterday)"

These alternants with /o/ and /wa/ are found in many Algonquian languages. In a number of cases, some of the daughter languages of proto-Algonquian have a form with /wa/ and others with /o/. In the word for "muskrat," for example, Cree has /wa/ and Ojibwe /o/: Cree *wacask*, Ojibwe *waššašk* and *ossask* (Aubin 1975, nr. 2143). In Ojibwe, the variation between /o/ and /wa/ seems to be most prevalent. Rhodes (1985) sometimes gives both forms in his dictionary of the eastern dialects. He also has entries such as *wakaan* "farm animal," plural *ookaanag* (with suffix *-ag*). J. Randolph Valentine (1994: 141) shows that more northern and western dialects of Ojibwe (Saskatchewan, northern Manitoba, northwestern Ontario) have more words with *wa-*, whereas the other dialects have *o-*.

Furthermore, in a few cases, the Cree part of Michif has a -*kwa*- cluster, whereas Cree has a -*ko*- cluster, for example Michif *šišikwat* and Cree *sisikoc* "unexpectedly." There are also variants within Cree dialects, for example, Swampy Cree *opâsin* and Plains Cree *wapâsin* "small narrows" (Faries 1938: 388). It is therefore possible that people who spoke French and several of these Algonquian languages, or several Ojibwe dialects, introduced an equivalent of the variant forms they had noticed in Cree and Ojibwe into their French. Ojibwe would then be its most likely source. The French *voyageurs* must have known Ojibwe since they traveled mainly through Ojibwe territory. It would be a borrowing of allophonic variation.

Other Features

Some of the other phonological differences between Métis French and Canadian French are more easily explained: they are influences from Cree and Ojibwe. Something like sibilant harmony also exists in Cree, in which /s/ and /š/ are not distinctive and do not co-occur as allophones within one word. The absence of the schwa in Métis French and its replacement by /I/ can also be a Cree influence since Cree has no schwa and the /I/ is closest to this central vowel. For the alternation between /k/ and /č/ before high vowels, I have no explanation. The process seems natural enough not to demand an external cause.

In summary, it is clear that Métis French has been influenced by Native languages, the most likely being Cree and Ojibwe. Some syntactic differences are calques in these two languages. For phonology, the situation is somewhat more obscure. The /o/ and /wa/ alternation suggests knowledge of both Cree and Ojibwe—if it indeed reflects the dialectal differences that may have triggered it. For some other features, it can be Ojibwe, as well as Cree, influence. Cree influence will come as no surprise, but the lexical adoption of undoubtedly Ojibwe words suggests that not only Cree but also Ojibwe influenced Métis French on nonlexical levels, too.

The Cree Component of Michif

The Amerindian component of Michif, as stated repeatedly, is closest to the Plains Cree dialect, and therefore I compare here the Cree component of Michif with Plains Cree. For the latter, I use as comparison the western dialect of the upstream people (see following sections). It would have been more appropriate to compare Michif with the eastern variant of the downstream people, but nothing has been published about this variant. It seems to be very close to the upstream variant, in any case. When I speak about the Plains Cree dialect here, I am referring to the southern Plains Cree dialect of the upstream people. I first discuss briefly the position of Plains Cree among the Cree dialects and then the subdialects of Plains Cree.

Cree Dialects

The linguistic label "Plains Cree" is used for those western Cree dialects in which the proto-Algonquian consonant *1 became /j/, written as "y" in standard Cree. For instance, the reconstructed proto-Algonquian word for "person" is **elenyiwa*, but in Plains Cree it is *iyiniw*.

Cree is divided into a number of dialects, which are distinguished according to the reflex of this sound *l. Most of them are named after the geographical features of the area where most of its speakers can be found. Thus, the dialect that has /j/ (spelled "y") is called Plains Cree, the dialect with "n" is called Swampy Cree, the dialect with /ð/ ("th") is called Woods or Rock Cree, the dialect with "l" is called Moose Cree (around Moose Factory), and finally the "r" dialect of Quebec is called Tête-de-Boule Cree or Attikamek. The eastern Cree dialect (east coast of James Bay), which also has /j/, is called Quebec Cree (Cris Quebecois or James Bay Cree). Table 9.1 illustrates the different dialects with the words for "me," "person," and "no."

This diversity for the reflex of proto-Algonquian */l/ is not typical of Cree alone; one can find the same reflexes in many other Algonquian languages as well (see, e.g., Pentland 1978a). Ojibwe, for instance, also has or had dialects with /l/ and /r/ in addition to widespread /n/, and Montagnais has /j/, /l/, and /n/ dialects (and /r/ dialects in the past).

It is clear from table 9.1 that the "y" reflex of proto-Algonquian *l is typical of Plains Cree, as is the Cree part of Michif (see map 2 for Cree dialects). Quebec Cree also has "y," but it is in other respects rather different from the Cree component of Michif. For instance, whereas Michif and Plains Cree have /k/, Quebec Cree often has /č/. Whereas Michif and Plains Cree have /e:/, Quebec Cree has /a:/. In addition, the geographical location makes it unlikely that Quebec Cree was the source of Michif Cree. Therefore, there is no doubt that Michif is closer to Plains Cree.

In other respects, too, it is closer to Plains Cree than to any other Cree dialect. However, there are some differences between the Cree part of Michif and Plains Cree, to be discussed later in this chapter. One thing I must mention here is that the Cree component in Michif lost more of its complexity than Plains Cree, and Plains Cree lost more of its complexity than the Cree dialects from which it most likely derives.

Plains Cree is most closely related to western Swampy Cree (eastern Manitoba), Moose Cree (west coast of James Bay, Ontario), and Woods Cree. Moose Cree is spoken only in a small area. The other dialects, including Plains Cree, are spoken over wide areas (see map 3), but they seem relatively homogeneous—which suggests a recent geographical expansion. They differ only marginally in phonology, lexicon, and grammar. Plains Cree verbal morphology, however, is considerably less complex than Moose Cree (Ellis 1983). Plains Cree is certainly the least complex of

TABLE 9.1 Cree Dialects According to Their Reflex of Proto-Algonquian *l

	*l > ?	Example words		
		Person	Me	No
Plains	y	iyiniw	niya	namôya
Swampy	n	ininiw	nina	môna
Woods	ð	iðiniw	niða	namôða
Moose	l	ililiw	nila	namôla
Attikamek	r	irinu	nira	namôra
Quebecois	y	iyiyi	niya	nemawî

all Cree dialects, as Wolfart (1973b: 43, n. 55) remarked: "There is a striking contrast between the relatively simple verb paradigms attested in Plains Cree texts and
the immense proliferation of forms which Ellis (1971) reports for the Swampy and
Moose dialects of eastern James Bay."

The Cree verb in Michif is even more simplified than the Plains Cree verb. Michif
has no dubitative forms and no changed conjuncts, and neither of the two preterite
forms that are attested to for Plains Cree. In the verb, Michif has more analytic forms
than Plains Cree (see Chapter Five). It must be mentioned that contemporary Plains
Cree is in the process of losing just these same categories, too, undoubtedly as a consequence of the universal knowledge of English among the Cree. Wolfart (1973b:
44) remarked that already his Plains Cree texts from the 1960s had significantly fewer
dubitative forms than Bloomfield's texts from the 1920s. Also, people familiar with
non-Plains dialects of Cree and Montagnais find the Cree part of Michif simplified,
even, said one, as "the way children speak." This double process of simplification
(Cree → Plains Cree → Michif Cree) is doubtlessly connected with the fact that Plains
Cree was a lingua franca and often used by people for whom it was not a first language (see the following section). Matters are complicated somewhat by the existence of several subdialects of Plains Cree, which are now described.

Dialects of Plains Cree

The origin of the Cree Indians of the prairies, the Plains Cree, is a little controversial. Some claim that they came to the prairies from the east as recently as 200 years
ago (e.g., Mandelbaum [1940] 1979); others claim that the Crees have lived in the
prairie provinces since prehistoric times (e.g., James Smith 1976, 1981; Russell 1991).
Part of this controversy is caused by a confusion of the Plains Cree *language* and the
Plains Cree *people*. The language is spoken on the plains but also in the woodlands—
at least a Cree dialect with the reflex "y" for *l. There is not only a geographical and
cultural difference between the Plains Cree speakers of the plains and those of the
woodlands but also a few minor dialect differences. One can distinguish between
the dialects of the eastern and western bands in the prairies and between the Plains
Cree dialects of the woodlands (northern Plains Cree) and those of the prairies (southern Plains Cree).

EASTERN PLAINS CREE AND WESTERN PLAINS CREE

The Plains Cree people traditionally subdivide themselves into two main groups, the
upstream people and the downstream people (with reference to the Saskatchewan
River). Both of these are again subdivided into a number of bands (Mandelbaum
[1940] 1979). The upstream people live in the western region, along the North
Saskatchewan River and to the south of the Battle River. They include the House
People, the Parklands People, and the River People. The Downstream People live in
the southeastern region, that is, in the Qu'Appelle River Valley and north. They include the Calling River People, the Rabbitskins, and the Touchwood Hills People.

The cultural and linguistic differences between these two main groups were
considered by Mandelbaum to be "not of major order": "The dialectal differences among

Plains Cree bands are minor, being chiefly matters of vowel length and degree of nasalization" (Mandelbaum [1940] 1979: 11–12). Unfortunately this cannot be confirmed by linguistic studies since all linguistic work on Plains Cree is based on the dialects of the upstream (western) groups. All of their subdivisions were studied: the River People by Bloomfield (1934), the House People by Ahenakew (1987b), and the Beaver Hills People by Edwards (1954) and Wolfart (1973b). No work at all, however, has been published on the Plains Cree language of the Downstream People.

This is a blank field in Cree studies, as well as a regrettable gap for the study of the origins of Michif since the Plains Cree component of Michif differs systematically in a number of points from the published accounts of Plains Cree (to be discussed); it could be that the Cree part of Michif is identical to the dialect of the Downstream subdivision of the Plains Cree. Geographically, these eastern bands are, of course, closer to the speakers of Michif since Michif is spoken in the region adjacent to the eastern boundaries of the Plains Cree area. If "nasalization" is indeed one of the features in which the two divisions differ, it may well be the case that it is present only in these eastern dialects of Plains Cree. In any case, nasal vowels have not been reported for the upstream dialects, although the Cree component of Michif has some nasal vowels. It seems that southeastern Saskatchewan Plains Cree indeed has some nasal vowels, so that it may be similar in that respect to the Cree part of Michif. Furthermore, this dialect borders the Ojibwe language, which has nasal vowels, so that areal influence is very possible.

NORTHERN PLAINS CREE AND SOUTHERN PLAINS CREE

There is also a difference between the Plains Cree language spoken in the woodlands and that on the prairies. Wolfart (1973b: 11) distinguishes a "northern" variant and a "southern" variant of Plains Cree, which are mutually intelligible. He does not indicate the differences, but it is known from Pentland (1978a), for example, that the main difference between the two is the fact that /e:/ becomes /i:/ in northern Plains Cree. That language has only three long vowels (/i:/, /a:/, and /u:/), whereas southern Plains Cree has four (/i:/, /e:/, /a:/, and /u:/). This is true not only for Alberta but also for Saskatchewan, where the Crees in the Northwest speak northern Plains Cree (see map 2). The fusion of /e/ with /i/ is a feature shared with the Woods Cree dialects of Saskatchewan and Manitoba (Pentland 1978a; Starks 1987; Brightman 1989). We could roughly say that the dialects of the woodlands do not have the contrast, whereas the dialect of the plains does. The Cree component of Michif preserves the /e/ and /i/ contrast and is thus identical to the prairies dialect of Plains Cree. A further difference is that some northern Plains Cree dialects also have *-twâw* in the third-person plural conjunct, whereas other dialects have *-cik*. Michif belongs to the latter group.

From my own observations, I want to add that the distribution of conjunct and independent order verb forms differs significantly between the woodlands dialect and the dialect of the plains. In the woodlands, conjunct forms are commonly used in main clauses, whereas this does not occur on the plains. In the woodlands dialect, there seems to be an aspectual difference between the two verbal orders.

Clearly Michif belongs to southern Plains Cree rather than northern Plains Cree. The Cree part of Michif is therefore related to the language of the plains Crees rather than the woodland Crees. In other respects, however, it will appear to share some traits with the Cree dialects spoken in the woodlands to the east rather than with the western ones.

Michif versus Plains Cree

Plains Cree and Michif Cree differ from each other in phonological, morphological, and lexical aspects. Syntactic differences are more difficult to assess. They are certainly present, but the overall adoption of French noun phrases changed the language so radically that it cannot be ascertained which differences would be attributable to their intrusion. Furthermore, Cree syntax is not yet well understood, so it is much more difficult to study. I do not, therefore, discuss syntactic differences between Michif and Plains Cree.

I first mention some phonological differences and then morphological and lexical differences between the two languages, and I compare those with other languages spoken in the area to see whether Michif shows similarities with other Native languages when it differs from Plains Cree.[1]

PHONOLOGY

Michif phonology is discussed in Chapter Four. The phonology of the Cree component of Michif is close, but not identical, to Plains Cree. Not all the phonological differences are discussed here, nor are the morphophonological processes of vowel coalescence.

Merger of the Sibilants /s/ and /š/

The most salient difference is the nature of the sibilants. Proto-Algonquian had two sibilants, /s/ and /š/. This contrast is preserved in several of the Algonquian languages, such as Ojibwe, including the Saulteaux dialect—except for the dialect in the Qu'Appelle Valley, which has only /š/ (Pentland 1978a: 119). In Plains Cree, however, these have merged into /s/. In Michif Cree, too, the contrast is lost, but they have merged into /š/. Michif Cree shares this sibilant with the eastern dialects of Cree, from the west coast of James Bay eastward (Rhodes and Todd 1981), and with the southwestern Saskatchewan dialect of Ojibwe (see map 2).

Cree /c/ and Michif /č/

The reflex of proto-Algonquian *\/č/ is /č/ in Michif and /c/ in Plains Cree. Both /s/ and /c/ are alveolar consonants in Plains Cree but palatal in Michif. Michif shares this variation with Moose Cree and Ojibwe but, as far as is known, not with other Cree dialects.

Nasal Vowels

Plains Cree has no phonemic nasal vowels, whereas Michif Cree shows nasal vowels in a number of Cree words. Some vowels are nasalized under the influence of an adjacent /n/, for example, nIwa:pahtã̃ "I see it" (also nIwa:pahtæn), whereas the Cree equivalent is niwâpahtên [niwa:pahte:n]. Some of the Cree words that are systematically nasalized in Michif are *ūhī* (animate obviative and inanimate plural demonstrative) and some other demonstratives, the question element *čī*, and some lexical elements like *mǣkwač* "in the meantime, while." Nasal vowels in Michif Cree are /ū:/, /æ:/, and /ī:/—all long vowels. I have no data with nasal /ã:/, so I suspect it does not exist in the Cree part of Michif.

This nasalization may have been influenced by Ojibwe or French, which both have nasal vowels. In standard French (and probably Canadian French) high vowels cannot be nasalized, and in Ojibwe all vowels can be nasal. As /i/ can be nasalized in Michif and Ojibwe but not in French, Ojibwe influence is more plausible. Another argument for Ojibwe influence is that at least some of the Michif words with nasal vowels are nasal in the Saulteaux dialect, too, such as Michif *mǣkwač* and Saulteaux *mẽ:kwa:*.

The Disappearance of Preaspirated Stops

The phonological differences between Plains Cree and Michif Cree, previously discussed, are valid for all varieties of Michif. The phenomenon discussed here, however, is not valid for all speakers; but speakers who exhibit this phonological feature can be found in all Michif-speaking communities, so this must have been a variation before the Métis dispersal.

Plains Cree has a set of preaspirated consonants: /ht/, /hp/, /hc/, /hk/, and /hw/, for example, *pêhtam* "he hears it," *ahpêtikwê* "maybe," *mihcêt* "many," *wâpahki* "tomorrow," and *pakamahwêw* "he beats him." These are common in Michif, too, but some Michif speakers do not use the aspirated /ht/ or /hč/ consonants; they consis tently replace the preaspiration with /s/ before /t/ and /č/ but not before the other phonemes. They say *pe:stam* and *misče:t* but *ahpe:tIkwe*, *wa:pahkI*, and *pakamahwe:w*.

This preconsonantal /s/ may have emerged from an interdental voiceless fricative /θ/. The Algonquianist Truman Michelson recorded some Turtle Mountain Plains Cree in 1911–1912, when this language was apparently still spoken there in addition to Michif. Both of his informants consistently used forms like *niwâpaΘtän* (Michelson 1939: 76, and the "Fort Totten" material in Michelson 1912, which is actually Turtle Mountain Cree).[2]

Is this change of /ht/ and /hč/ into /st/ and /sč/ an independent development in Michif Cree, or does it have parallels in other Cree dialects or Algonquian languages? It has not been attested to in Plains Cree. Woods Cree and some dialects of northern Plains Cree have lost the preaspiration, having a lengthening of the preceding vowel instead. Ojibwe, including the Saulteaux dialect, has geminate stops, whereas Cree has preaspirated stops. The only dialects with a parallel development are Tête-de-Boule Cree (Cooper 1945: 39; Béland 1978) and some Manitoba Swampy Cree dialects (Pentland 1978a: 112, 126), which also have /st/ clusters when Plains Cree has /ht/.

The Voiced-Voiceless Opposition: No Voicing between Vowels

In Plains Cree "voicedness" is not distinctive in the phonological system. Stops tend to be voiced between vowels—/k/ is more often voiced than /p/ between vowels, /p/ more often than /t/—but they are always voiceless in the initial position. In Michif, the situation is quite different. Stops are rarely if ever voiced between vowels. Cree *mâka* "but," for instance, is phonetically [ma:ga] in Plains Cree but [ma:ka] in Michif Cree. In Ojibwe, voicing of stops between vowels is even more frequent than in Cree.

The Voiced-Voiceless Opposition: Word-initial Voicing

Initial stops in Michif are voiced according to a vowel elision rule: the first- and second-person prefixes *ni-* and *ki-* can lose their vowels between two stops, subsequently leading to a conflation of the two adjoining consonants. The /n/ triggers voicing of the stops. Plains Cree, Saulteaux, and Michif can be said to represent three stages in the development of the *ni-* prefix.

(3) *Plains Cree*   *Saulteaux*   *Michif*

    ni-k-   ng-   g-
    ni-t-   nd-   d-
    ni-p-   mb-   b-
    ni-s-   nz- (?)   ž-
    ni-c-   ndž- (?)   dž-

Michif resembles Saulteaux, which has prenasalized stops, more than it does Plains Cree. Most speakers of Michif are not aware that, for example, the first syllable in *gi:-wa:pam-a:w* "I saw him" has an underlying form *ni-ki:-*, which is the Plains Cree form. Furthermore, the second-person prefix *ki-* disappears before verbs (roots or other prefixes) that start with *k-*. Thus Plains Cree *ki-ki:wa:n* "you go home" is rendered *ki:wa:n* in Michif. As a result, the Cree part of Michif is unusual among the Algonquian languages, having a contrastive phonological distinction between voiced and voiceless stops, for example, in *gašta:n* "I am able" vs. *kašta:n* "you are able" (Plains Cree *ni-kaskihta:n* vs. *ki-kaskihta:n*).

This voicing also occurs elsewhere in Michif words. When a short /i/ disappears, it may cause the adjacent consonants to be voiced. For instance, Cree *pimipahtâw* "he runs" is *pimbahta:w* in Michif. This process is, of course, valid only for the Cree part of the language, although neither the Saulteaux prenasalized consonants nor the Michif voiced consonants are unique in this process of initial voicing. We find these same developments in some other dialects of central Algonquian languages (Rhodes and Todd 1981).

I suspect that there is a connection between the loss of optional voicedness in the intervocal position and the presence of the feature <voicedness> in initial stops in particular contexts. It is possible that the contrast between voiced and voiceless stops became phonologically distinctive in the initial position in Michif, when the vowel elision rule was introduced. This led to phonetically and phonologically voiceless stops in intervocal positions.

In table 9.2 I compare these phonological features with a number of dialects of Cree and Ojibwe, chosen because they can be expected to have been involved in the genesis of Michif and/or sufficient documentation was available. Because I had to rely on sometimes brief sources, there may be errors in this table.

It is clear that Michif Cree phonology is not identical to that of any of the other languages considered in this section. Nevertheless, it seems closer to the eastern varieties of Cree (Moose Cree, Tête-de-Boule Cree, and eastern Swampy Cree) in having palatal sibilants and /sC/ instead of preaspirated consonants, in at least a sub-

TABLE 9.2 Some Phonological Peculiarities of Michif Compared to Cree and Ojibwe Dialects

	(A) *s/š*	(B) *č*	(C) *nasals*	(D) *hC/sC*	(E) *k-g*	(F) *ni-nd-d*
Michif	š	č	+	hC⌐C	k-g	d
Northern Plains Cree	s	c	–	hC/⌐C	k/g	ni/nd
Southern Plains Cree	s	c	–(?)	hC	k/g	ni
Moose Cree	s/š	č	–	hC	k/g	ni
West Swampy Cree				hC/⌐C		
East Swampy Cree	s/š			sC/hC		
Tête-de-Boule Cree	s/š	c/č	+	⌐C/sC	k/g	ni
Woods Cree	s	c	–	⌐C	k/g	ni
Severn Ojicree	s/š	č	–(?)	hC/CC	k/g	ni
Saulteaux Ojibwe	s/š-š	č	+	CC	k/g	nd
Minnesota Ojibwe	s/š	č	+	C (?)	k/g	nd
Eastern Ojibwe	s/š	č	+	CC/hCC	k/g	ni
Assiniboine	s/š	c	+	sC	k/g	—

Blank spaces indicate that the sources do not provide the appropriate information.

(A) When a column is headed by two phonemes separated by a slash, there is an opposition between two sibilants in the language mentioned in the row. Saulteaux is variable.

(C) The symbol "+" means that there are nasal vowels; "–" means that they are not reported.

(D) The letters "hC" indicate preaspirated consonants; "sC" indicates /sC/ instead of /hC/ before dental stops; "CC" means that the dialect has geminates instead; "⌐C" means compensatory lengthening of the vowel preceding the disappeared preaspiration.

(E) The use of "k/g" indicates that at least some stops are normally voiced between vowels; "k-g" means that there is a contrast in some places.

(F) The letters "ni" indicate that the personal prefix is not reduced, "nd" that the vowel has disappeared and a prenasalized stop is used in first-person forms, and "d" that the two consonants have conflated into a voiced stop. This is, of course, not the case only with words that start with "t."

set of the cases. It is also closer to Ojibwe dialects at a number of points. This suggests phonological connections both with Ojibwe and with eastern Cree dialects.

MORPHOLOGY

The inflectional morphology of the Michif verb differs in several aspects from Plains Cree in ways not reported in Rhodes's (1977) description of Michif Cree verbal morphology. The following forms of the verbs in the independent order differ systematically from Plains Cree:

- The first-person inclusive form ("we," including "you") for verbs and pronouns has the affixes *ki-* and *-na:n* in Michif but *ki-* and *-naw* in Cree. For example, the Michif pronoun is *kIjana:n* "you and me"; the Cree pronoun is *kiyanaw*. In Michif "we (INCL) are eating it" is *kI-mi:čI-na:n*; in Cree it is *ki-mîci-naw*.

- The affix that indicates plurality of the object in first- or second-person plural forms is *-ik* in Michif but *-ak* in Plains Cree. For instance, *ni-wa:pam-a:na:n-ik* "we see them" in Michif is *ni-wâpam-ânân-ak* in Cree.

- The ending for the third-person inverse form (obviative subject, proximate object) is *-iku* in Michif but *-ik* in Plains Cree, for example, Michif *wa:pam-iku* "s/he is seen, someone sees him/her" and Cree *wâpam-ik*.

- The future conjunct marker is *či-* in Michif but *(ki)ta-* in Cree, for example, Michif *pɔkɔ čI-šIpwe:hte:ja:n* "I have to go" and Cree *piko ta-sipwêhtêyân*.

This is, of course, not a significant portion of the verb morphology of Cree; there are scores of verb affixes, which yield hundreds of inflected forms for each verb (see Chapter Four). Nevertheless, it is striking that we find these same deviant forms in apparently all Michif-speaking communities. In table 9.3, I represent these morphological traits for a number of dialects of Cree and Ojibwe.

Two things strike us when we look at these data. First, in all of these forms, when Michif differs from Plains Cree, the morphology appears to be identical to that of Saulteaux. It is also striking that Michif and Saulteaux share some of these morphological features with Cree dialects spoken to the east. The similarities with the geographically nearest Cree dialects (Swampy Cree, Woods Cree, and Plains Cree) are less significant than those with, for instance, Moose Cree. For example, the conjunct marker *či-* and the inverse marker *-iku* are both used in the eastern dialects of Cree (Moose Cree and Tête-de-Boule) that are spoken in Ontario and Quebec but not in the dialects adjacent to the Michif area (Woods Cree, western Swampy Cree, and

TABLE 9.3 Some Morphological Peculiarities of Michif Compared to Cree and Ojibwe Dialects

Types of variation	ki-naw/ki-na:n	-ak/-ik	-ik/-iku	(ki)ta-/či-
Michif	**-na:n**	**-ik**	**-iku**	**či-**
Northern Plains Cree	-naw	-ak	-ik	(ki)ta-
Southern Plains Cree	-naw	-ak	-ik	(ki)ta-
Moose Cree	-naw	-ak/-ik	-iku	(ki)či-
West Swampy Cree			-ik	(ki)ta-
East Swampy Cree				
Tête-de-Boule Cree	-nanu	-ak	iku	kata, kicci
Woods Cree	-naw	-ak	-ik	(ki)ta-
Severn Ojicree	-na:n	-ak	-ik	či-
Saulteaux Ojibwe	-na:n	-ik	-iku	či-
Minnesota Ojibwe	-naw	-ak	-igun	dži-
Eastern Ojibwe	-na:n	-ik	-ik	či

Plains Cree). Michif is also closer to Ojibwe dialects in these divergent forms. Apparently Michif shares some morphological traits with eastern Cree dialects and Ojibwe. For morphology and phonology, the results are similar.

LEXICON

The Michif verb lexicon is very close to that of Plains Cree, but some Michif verbs consistently differ from those in Plains Cree. In addition, Michif nouns that are not French or English are often Ojibwe rather than Cree. Some of the non–Plains Cree forms found consistently in Michif are shown in table 9.4.

In some cases the only difference is a reflex of proto-Algonquian *l or a derived form used with the same meaning. In other cases the stem is different. Again, when Michif words differ from Plains Cree, they appear to be virtually identical to the Saulteaux forms. I suspect the last form will have a Saulteaux equivalent, too, but I have been unable to verify this.

FURTHER DIFFERENCES

There are also some differences of degree between Michif and Plains Cree. Some constructions are more actively used in Michif, such as impersonal forms (unspecified actor) and passive forms (in -*Ika:šo*- and -*Ika:wI*). Reduplication, still very productive in Plains Cree (Ahenakew and Wolfart 1983), does not often occur in Michif Cree (but see Chapter One for examples). Changed conjunct forms, rare in contemporary Plains Cree, are probably nonexistent in Michif. I have no unambiguous examples in my data. Also, delayed imperatives are often replaced with the simpler direct equivalents. Several synthetic constructions (benefactives) are being replaced by analytic forms at a more rapid rate in Michif than in Plains Cree (see Chapter Five). However, in some cases Michif seems more conservative than Plains Cree. Michif speakers in Camperville use -*Ipan* preterites, which are rare in contemporary Plains Cree.

In conclusion, the phonological and morphological differences between Plains Cree and the Cree part of Michif are few in number. When they differ, Michif ap-

TABLE 9.4 Some Non–Plains Cree Words in Michif

	Plains Cree	Michif	Saulteaux
"To dance"	nîmihito-	ni:mi-	ni:mi-
"To write"	masinahikê-	ušipe:hike:-[3]	ošipi:ke:(n)-
"Girl"	iskwêsis	kwezæs[4]	(ik)kwe:zẽs
"To be called"	isiyihkâso-	išinihka:šo-	išinikka:so
"Eat with someone"	wîcimîcisom-	witušpam-	wi:toppam-
"Bee"	âmô	jãmū	ãmõ
"Ant"	êyikôs	ɛnikūs	enikūs
"My namesake"	nikwêmês	gwæmæ	[Ojibwe niiyawen'enh] (?)

pears to share features most often with the Saulteaux dialect of Ojibwe and/or with some of the Cree dialects spoken to the east, which seems to confirm the fact that the speakers of the Cree dialect of the Plains indeed came from the woodlands south of Hudson Bay. The Crees in the woodlands north of the prairies may have lived there much longer. The differences between the Cree part of Michif and Plains Cree may reflect differences between downstream and upstream Plains Cree, or they may be different developments of the same dialect, one spoken by the Métis and the other by Indians.

This argument suggests an influence from Saulteaux and Ojibwe and possibly a more easterly origin of the dialect. This finding is in line with historical facts. Ojibwe was one of the languages used in the fur trade in the east, and many Ojibwe women married French fur traders. There were also many Ojibwe speakers who spoke Plains Cree as a second language, and Plains Cree was the lingua franca of the northern plains. I deal with the background of the Ojibwe elements in the following section.

The Ojibwe Component of Michif

It is striking that Michif speakers often characterize their language not as a mixture of Cree and French but as a mixture of Cree, Saulteaux (Ojibwe), and French. This is what many speakers tell me, and it can also be found in print from time to time, for instance, in a history book by the Cree-speaking Métis author Anne Anderson from Alberta. She writes the following about the Fishing Lake Métis colony in Alberta in the 1930s: "Most of the children spoke good Cree. The language was mostly Cree and some Saulteaux. Once the schools were running on a fairly organized schedule, the English language was spoken more regularly. *The elders spoke a mixture of French, Cree and Saulteaux*" (1985: 389; my emphasis). Apparently in this community, and presumably in other communities in Alberta, Michif was given up in favor of Cree early in this century and is no longer spoken there.

Patrick Gourneau (1980: 9–11), a Turtle Mountain Chippewa, describes the Michif language of his reservation in his tribal history book as "a jargon involving a unique mixture of French, Cree, Plains-Ojibway, and English. French and Cree Indian's words dominate the jargon." Dusenberry (1985: 122), an anthropologist who worked with the Montana Métis in the 1950s, described their language as "a composite of Indian tongues, usually Cree and Chippewa, and French. Often a few English words were added."

In earlier chapters of this book, it has become clear that there is indeed a consistent Ojibwe element in Michif (Bakker 1991b) and that many Michif speakers are aware of it. There is linguistic evidence for an Ojibwe substrate in Michif, and in this section, I present historical confirmation. First, I give some additional information on Plains Cree as a second language of the western Plains Ojibwes since this is a key element in the explanation of the Ojibwe elements. Then I show that some Ojibwe cultural elements still play a role in Michif culture. In the next section I make plausible the argument that many of the early Frenchmen and Métis married Ojibwe women rather than Cree women. I also briefly touch on the use of Ojibwe and French in the Great Lakes fur trade and perhaps even the existence of a mixed language in that area. All these facts stress the historical importance of the Ojibwe people for the Métis and the Michif language.

Cree as a Second Language for the Plains Ojibwe

In contrast to some other Cree dialects, the Plains dialect has been recorded since only relatively recent times. Woods Cree sources go back to the seventeenth century, but Plains Cree vocabularies were first published as late as 1809 (Alexander Henry) and 1820 (Daniel Harmon), after which many others followed. Before these, only two Plains Cree words were recorded, one from the Fort Qu'Appelle Valley and the other from an unknown location (Pentland 1978a).[5]

David Pentland (1978a) noted that the earliest Cree words (as far as they can be identified as such) were recorded in an area well outside the Cree area as it is known today. The Michigan place name *Oulaministik*, or Manistique River, must be Cree and was recorded as early as 1717. This is *l*-dialect Cree, not Plains Cree. Sault Sainte Marie, on the north shore of Lake Superior, has a Cree name, Baouichtigouian (*pâwistikwêyâw* "the rapids"), and east of there, around Thunder Bay, there is Kaministikwia (*kâ-ministikwêyâw* "Island River"), recorded around 1750. All three place names refer to localities that are in Ojibwe country, and the nearest Crees today are several hundreds or even thousands of kilometers away. Historical atlases, however, and historical sources (Mandelbaum [1940] 1979; Harris 1987; Tanner 1987) show that Cree speakers were living in the Thunder Bay and Sault Sainte Marie area and around Lake of the Woods on the Minnesota, Ontario, and Manitoba border in the eighteenth century.

There are some indications that not all those Indians who spoke Cree were in fact ethnically Cree. The Cree name for the river in Michigan was recorded from a guide who was "probably an Ojibwe" (Pentland 1978a: 104). In other cases, too, Cree words may have been recorded from Ojibwe speakers.

In Chapter Two I discuss the extensive use of lingua francas by Indians. For the Ojibwes living on the prairies, who were originally from the Minnesota woodlands, Cree was the lingua franca (David Pentland, pers. comm.). They spoke it as a second language since Plains Cree speakers had been living adjacent to their territory in the north. James Howard (1965: 7) also states that "many [Plains Ojibwe] do speak Cree as second or third language. . . . One prominent family in the Turtle Mountains was given the English name 'Cree' because of this ability to speak the Cree language." This Cree-Ojibwe bilingualism led to some confusion in the past: were its speakers Cree or Ojibwe? Howard discusses some of these dilemmas:

> Although the Plains-Ojibwa recognize their linguistic and historical relationship to the Woodland Ojibwa, and may sometimes refer to their *language* as *Ótšɪpwè* (Ojibwa) they never, when speaking their own language, refer to their *tribe* by that name. Sometimes, when speaking English, they may refer to their dialect of Ojibwa as "Cree", or to themselves as either "Chippewa" or "Cree" which has led incautious whites to draw incorrect conclusions regarding their identity. (James Howard 1965: 7)

If we take into consideration Rhodes's (1982) discussion of lingua francas used in the Great Lakes area (see Chapter Two), we can easily extend his findings to the area west of the Great Lakes. Rhodes showed that the Native people of the Great Lakes usually knew a second language, which was often that of the groups living immediately north of their habitat, and it was generally the language used for communication with outsiders (Pentland, pers. comm.). Some Plains Ojibwes and the woodland Ojibwes south of Lake of the Woods, such as those of Red Lake, Minnesota, of (probably Plains) Cree, lived south of Cree speakers in the eighteenth century. In Manitoba, supposedly the cradle of Michif, speakers of Plains Cree have now almost disappeared: there are perhaps fewer than ten, mostly Métis. The Ojibwes of Minnesota apparently continued to transmit Cree to the younger generations after the Crees had moved away.

There is ample documentation for the intermarriage of Ojibwes and Crees (Steinbring 1981: 245) and of joint bands of Crees and Ojibwes (e.g., Hickerson 1956). Already in 1790 Edward Umfreville remarked: "These two nations have always been in strict alliance with each other, and many of the Ochipawas [Ojibwes] live in promiscuous manner among the Ne-heth-aw-as [Crees], and upon very friendly terms with them" (Umfreville 1790: 179). It is therefore not surprising that the Plains Ojibwes spoke Cree in addition to Ojibwe.

Ojibwe Traces in Contemporary Michif Culture

As stated in Chapter Three, Métis mythology is a mixture of French, Cree, and Ojibwe mythology. The Ojibwe element is prominent (Rhodes 1987). The culture hero of the Manitoba Plains Ojibwe is called Nanabužu. In all Michif dialects, its equivalent is Nɛnabuš. This latter form is used only by Indians east of Lake Superior (John D. Nichols, pers. comm.). It occurs, for instance, in the eastern Ojibwe and Ottawa stories recorded by Bloomfield (1958) as *ne:nepoš*. All myths in Jones (1917), which were recorded on the northeast shore of Lake Superior and in Minnesota, west of Lake Superior, have Nänabushu. Rhodes (1985: 290) lists both Nenbozho and Nenbosh, the first as a form used in Walpole Island and Curve Lake, Ontario; the latter, as a general southern Ojibwe form from the eastern Great Lakes. This terminology may point to an influence on Michif from Ojibwe dialects in the east.

There are also indications of widespread Cree-Ojibwe bilingualism among the Métis in the past. A fair number of speakers I interviewed remembered that their parents and grandparents spoke Ojibwe (Saulteaux), as well as Michif. Furthermore, some descendants of the Red River Métis in Manitoba speak Ojibwe as their first language. In addition, I recorded a mixed Cree-Ojibwe song in five different Métis communities—Saint Lazare, Fort Qu'Appelle Valley, Camperville, Sainte Madeleine, and Turtle Mountain—in five slightly different versions. One of the versions of the song is as follows (Ojibwe elements are italicized):

(4) *geget niminwendam*   "Really I like it."   (Cree-Ojibwe)
    e:-utihkumija:n   "that I am lousy"
    tahtwa:w *gigi:že:ba*   "every morning"
    nina:nisucina:(?)   "I crack them."

The first line is always Ojibwe, the second line Cree, the third line a mixture of Ojibwe and Cree, and the fourth line possibly Ojibwe. Two of the singers, when asked, said they do not understand the song, probably because they do not know Ojibwe. A song like this could have originated only in a period when both languages were widely known in the communities. The fact that it is so widespread now means that it is old; thus, it must predate the Métis dispersion. This is another indication that Ojibwe was spoken widely among the Métis in the nineteenth century (see also Chapter Six).

Languages Spoken by Indian Women in the Early Métis Community

In this section I discuss the Indian groups from which the early French Canadians and early Métis chose their marriage partners. It is possible to check this information without access to the archival sources because Sprague and Frye (1983) published a significant amount of valuable genealogical information on the Red River Métis and their ancestors. In the table Genealogies of Red River Households, they list approximately 4000 marriages and other genealogical, religious, and ethnic data gathered from archival sources. A few of these marriages involve Indian women, but unfortunately the sources do not give ethnic information about them. Most Indian women are listed only with first names, and even when family names are given, there is no mention of tribal affiliation, although some family names provide a clue. I list all of these in table 9.5. In these cases, a man has married an Indian woman who has a surname identical to an Indian tribal name. I choose 1812 as a rather arbitrary end date of my data since we can be sure that at that time the adult Métis had already identified themselves as a separate nation. The women had to have been born before that date.

There are two indications that these names are indeed tribal affiliations. First, none of them appears among the men, which could have been possible if they were real family names. In one case the first name is not given, only "Cree," which may mean just "Cree woman."

Second, in the period before 1812, seventeen Indian women with a possible tribal affiliation can be identified. Most of their husbands are Roman Catholic French Canadians, so their children would be first generation Métis. One of these women is possibly Shoshoni ("Serpent"; see Mandelbaum [1940] 1979: 9); one Atsina ("Gros Ventre"); two Assiniboine; two Cree; and eleven Saulteaux, the Canadian name for Plains Ojibwe. Of course, this cannot be taken be a reliable random selection, but it may be seen as circumstantial evidence that a significant portion, if not the vast majority, of the Amerindian ancestors of the Red River Métis were Ojibwe rather than Cree, despite the fact that the Amerindian component of Michif is Cree rather than Ojibwe.

Ojibwe must have been an important language for the early Métis, as it was the first language of many of their mothers and wives. Many of the Ojibwes, however, spoke Cree as a second language, as I have shown. Peers (1987) further documented the contacts of the Ojibwe Indians with the Red River settlement, confirming my conclusions in Chapter Six, which are based on early sources of Métis language use. Ojibwe was one of the Métis languages in the early days, and many Ojibwes spoke Cree as a second language.

TABLE 9.5 Women with Possible Tribal Affiliations in the Red River Settlement Born before 1812 and Their Husbands

Indian woman	Born	Husband (religion, birthplace)
Saulteaux, Bethsy	1767	Short, James (Prot., Orkneys)
Cree, ? [no first name]	1772	Flammand, Joseph
Saulteaux, Charlotte	1783	Morisseau, Antoine
Saulteaux, Josephte	1783	Bercier, Alexis (RC, Can.)
Saulteaux, Madeleine	1785	Ledoux, Baptiste (RC, Can.)
Cree, Josephte	1786	Lavallee, Ignace
Assiniboine, Louise	1787	Beuton, Angus (Eur.)
Saulteaux, Marie	1787	Lambert, Antoine (RC, Can.)
Saulteaux, Marguerite	1790	Gariepy, Baptiste (RC, Can.)
Serpent, Marguerite	1793	Patenaude, Michel (RC, Can.)
Saulteaux, Charlotte	1794	Lepine, Baptiste (RC, Can.)
Assiniboine, Angelique	1800	Sutherland, Pierre (? his children are RC)
Saulteaux, Marie	1800	McNab, Thomas (Prot., Métis)
Grosventre, Josephte	1800	Fleury, Louison (RC, Can.)
Saulteaux, Catherine	1801	Ducharme, Pierre (RC, Can.)
Saulteaux, Josephte	1810	Racette, Charles (RC, Métis)
Saulteaux, Geneviève	1810	Desjarlais, Jean Baptiste

Data from D. N. Sprague and R. P. Frye, *The genealogy of the first Métis nation. The development and dispersal of the Red River settlement 1820–1900* (Winnipeg: Pemmican Publications, 1983).

Language Use and Mixture in the Great Lakes Fur-trading Area

In this chapter we have seen the influence of the Ojibwes on the Michif language and mythology and the frequency of Ojibwe marriage partners for the French Canadians and Métis around 1800. There are some indications that the influence of the Ojibwe people and language may go back even further and that preceding developments in the Great Lakes area had some influence on the Red River Métis.

A mixture of French with Ojibwe may already have been spoken in the Great Lakes area, where Ojibwe was the lingua franca. Henry Schoolcraft, who spent the winter of 1834 in Michilimackinack, or Mackinack, then a major center on the fur trade route from western Canada to Montreal, wrote about the inhabitants of the village:

> Society here is scarcely a subject of remark. It is based on the french element of the fur trade—that is, a commonality who are the descendants of French or Canadian [i.e., French Canadian] boatmen and clerks or interpreters who have invariably married Indian women. The English, who succeeded to power after the fall of Quebec, chiefly withdrew, but have also left another element in the mixture of Anglo-Saxons, Irishmen or Celts, and Gauls, founded also upon intermarriages with the natives. Under the American rule, the society received an accession of a few females of various European and American lineage. . . . In such a mass of diverse

elements the French language, the Algonquin [i.e., Ojibwe], in several dialects, and the English, are employed. And *among the uneducated, no small mixture of all are brought into vogue* in the existing vocabulary. (Schoolcraft 1851: 458–459; my emphasis)

This quotation shows that there was also a mixture of Ojibwe, French, and English in the Great Lakes area, suggesting a connection with the local Métis population. There are some additional indications that there was, indeed, such a mixed language: Brayet.

Brayet: Ojibwe and French?

A language that is now, as far as I know, extinct and about which information would be most welcome is Brayet. It is supposed to be a mixture of Ojibwe and French, formerly spoken around the Great Lakes. My only source is Margaret Stobie, who says that Bungee[6] "has its French counterpart in Braillais, which grew up between Saulteau [sic] and Quebecois along the southern trade route from Sault Ste. Marie through the Lake of the Woods passage and on west" (Stobie 1970). The Brayet language is mentioned again by Stobie (1971) as a mixture of French and Ojibwe. Unfortunately, she does not give any sources, neither for the name (which I have never seen elsewhere) nor for the general information. It is not known how Ojibwe and French were mixed, nor do we know where and when. If the model outlined in chapters Seven and Eight is correct, it should be similar to Michif. We have no language data for Brayet, only the twentieth-century references by Stobie.

The etymology of the name is the only clear thing. It is derived from the French (perhaps Canadian) word *braguette*, meaning "breechclout." In northwestern Saskatchewan Métis French, it has also taken on the derived meanings "Indian" and "diaper" (Community of Ile-a-la-Crosse 1990). This French word must have been part of the vocabulary of the English-speaking North West Company fur traders at least in that area since the English River Book gives "a Bryette" as the translation for the Cree word *assesian* "breechclout" (Duckworth 1990: 6). North West Company men also received "braillets" as part of their equipment and clothing (Innis 1970: 240, n. 244).

A mixture of French and Ojibwe is also mentioned by Peterson (1981: 178–179) when she refers to the Métis of the Great Lakes around 1800. Would this be the same language as Brayet? Because of a lack of sources, it is impossible to answer this question. Except for oral information from a Minnesota Métis in 1990 that his now deceased grandfather spoke a mixture of French and Indian, which in his own view was "very different" from Michif (as judged from examples in the dictionary of Laverdure and Allard 1983), no further data on this language are known.

There seems to be a historical connection between the Great Lakes Métis and the Red River Métis. Most of the family names of the former that are cited in Peterson's (1978) study recur among early Red River settlers—LaFramboise, Fisher, Bertrand, Blondeau, Amiotte, and so on (see Sprague and Frye 1983). It is known that some of the mixed French-Ojibwe families from the Great Lakes moved to the Red River forks in the early 1800s (Peterson 1978: 61; 1985), so there probably is continuity between the two Métis societies. It is therefore possible that these Métis brought a mixed language with them from the Great Lakes to the Red River settlement. If so, it would have been an Ojibwe dialect (perhaps Ottawa), mixed with French.[7]

The *voyageurs*, who cannot always be clearly distinguished from Métis or people of mixed ancestry, were already reported as speakers of mixed French and Indian in the Red River settlement in the 1820s (Ross [1856] 1962). They may mark another language link between the Great Lakes and the Red River area.

All we can conclude is that probably a mixed language that consisted of Ojibwe and French elements developed around the Great Lakes and that may be associated with the mixed marriages of French traders with Ojibwe women. It may have been brought by some to the Red River settlement.

Ojibwe and Michif

In the preceding sections, I have cited ample historical indications that Ojibwe speakers were important to the Métis around 1800. In short, there was an Ojibwe influence on the Métis and the Michif language from three possible sources. First, the *voyageurs* probably spoke Ojibwe, as well as French, since their canoe routes went through Ojibwe territory and it is known that they spoke Indian languages well. Second, the Métis from the Great Lakes who settled in the Red River settlement probably spoke Ojibwe or perhaps even a mixture of Ojibwe and French. Third, the Indian women whom the French men married in the Red River settlement were mostly Ojibwe. These women undoubtedly also spoke Cree, and different Ojibwe dialects may have been involved, certainly Saulteaux, the language of the Plains Ojibwe women. Some eastern dialects of Ojibwe, possibly Ottawa or southwestern Ojibwe, were also spoken.

Linguistic evidence for the Ojibwe influence on Michif has been cited in several places in this book. Ojibwe has had a lexical, morphological, and phonological influence on the Cree part of Michif, and possibly also a phonological and lexical influence on the French part. One can safely say that there is an Ojibwe substrate in the Cree part of Michif, elements that one would expect when many Ojibwe speakers speak Cree as their second language.

The question that now comes to mind is, why is Michif not a mixture of Ojibwe and French? Why is it a mixture of Cree and French?

Michif: Ojibwe, French, and Cree Come Together

I have shown that there was a considerable number of Ojibwe speakers in the first Red River Métis families. In fact, there were so many that one has to ask why Michif is not a mixture of Ojibwe and French. The reason is the following: Plains Cree was the lingua franca of the Plains, where the Métis bison hunters spent much of their time between the 1820s and 1840s (see chapters Three and Six).

Plains Cree as a Lingua Franca

In Chapter Two, I cite Rhodes's (1982) study of lingua francas of the Great Lakes. He does not deal with the Plains, but there is much evidence for the use of Plains Cree as a lingua franca, and as one of the source languages of Michif, it is important to know which Native groups so used it. That Plains Cree was a lingua franca on all the northern Plains and some of the adjacent woodlands is clear from many sources. The Plains Cree joined bands of different groups and intermarried with Assiniboines, Blackfoot, Ojibwe, Saulteaux, Monsoni, Algonquin, Dakota, Athapaskan, Shoshoni, "Sonnants," Sarcee, and Crow (Sharrock 1974: 115), some of whom were allied to the Crees, whereas others were enemies. The Plains Cree language was and is used not only by the Crees but also by the Assiniboines, Saulteaux, Chipewyan and Dene, Blackfoot, and even some Kutenai and Shuswap.

Assiniboines

There is abundant evidence of Cree-speaking Assiniboines over almost three centuries, although the Assiniboines are a Siouan-speaking group. In almost any fur-trading source one finds references to joint parties of Assiniboines and Crees (see, e.g., Hickerson 1956; Sharrock 1974). The Assiniboines lived south and southwest of the Plains Cree, but during the modern period they have shared significant expanses of tribal territory. Many Canadian Assiniboines today know Plains Cree. Douglas Parks (pers. comm., 1990) reports: "In Saskatchewan most Assiniboine speakers, at least on the Mosquito-Grizzly Bear's Head and White Bear reserves, are bilingual in Cree. In fact, on those reserves Cree is everyone's daily language."

The same is true for the Alberta Stoneys. Their language underwent significant influence from Plains Cree. Taylor (1981b: 12) states: "Long contact with the Crees, and the passage of many generations of Cree bilingualism, have also brought some Cree lexical items and loan translations to the Stoney lexicon."

This Assiniboine knowledge of Cree must be several centuries old. A Cree-speaking Assiniboine was interpreter for the French explorer La Vérendrye on the Plains in 1738–1739 (Taylor 1981a: 179). This Cree-Assiniboine bilingualism dates from at least the end of the seventeenth century. As early as 1695, a Jesuit missionary already wrote: "The *Kriqs* and *Assiniboëls* are allied together. . . . Many *Assiniboëls* speak *Kriq* and many *Kriqs Assiniboël*" (Thwaites 1896–1901: 66, 107–109; cited in Sharrock 1974: 105).

This period of mutual bilingualism is related to the fact that the Crees and Assiniboines were allied probably since at least the 1660s (Sharrock 1974: 104). There were many intermarriages, which even led to the emergence of a mixed-blood band called the Cree-Assiniboines by the traders, *nêhipwatak* by the Crees (the word *nêhiyaw* means "Cree" and *pwat* means "Sioux"), and "young dogs" by the Saulteaux and Crees. This group "spoke both languages, but neither correctly" (*Fort Pelly Journal* 1837 and HBC records; cited in Sharrock 1974: 111). It is very possible that this tribe spoke a mixed language, as do the Métis, although I am at a loss concerning how Cree and Assiniboine would have been mixed since both the social circumstances and the typological properties of the languages are unusual. In any case, the point is that there is a long tradition of Cree-speaking Assiniboines.

Ojibwe

The knowledge of Cree by the Plains Ojibwe has already been discussed and will not be repeated here. A recent language survey in Saskatchewan (Fredeen 1991) shows that considerable numbers of Ojibwes still know Cree as a second language.

Chipewyan and Dene

In Chipewyan communities bordering on the Plains Cree area, such as Patuanak in Saskatchewan and Fort Chipewyan in Alberta, Cree is spoken as a second language by many (Scollon and Scollon 1979; Krauss and Golla 1981: 80). Plains Cree is used as a church language in Patuanak and other Chipewyan communities. That the use of Cree by the Chipewyans is already a few centuries old is clear from older sources. Alexander MacKenzie reported that Chipewyans who came to trade with him in the late eighteenth century used Cree: "[The Chipewyans] have a smattering of the Knistenaux [Cree] tongue, in which they carry on their dealings with us" (Lamb 1970: n. 149, 240; cited in Silverstein 1973; see also Taylor 1981a: 179).

The early records also mention numerous individual Chipewyans who spoke Cree, such as the chief who accompanied MacKenzie (Silverstein 1973: 14); the woman, Thanadelthur, who was to persuade her people in 1714 to trade with the English, although she may have learned this language when she was a slave of Cree Indians (Van Kirk 1980: 66–67); or a family encountered near Great Slave Lake who spoke Cree and French and Chipewyan in 1821 (Brown 1980: 126). The oldest myth text printed in Cree was actually recorded in 1880–1881 by Emile Petitot from a Chipewyan. Wolfart (1990b) shows that it contained a few grammatical flaws, probably because the person who had given the text to Petitot was not a native speaker.

Other Athapaskan-speaking Nations

Alexander Henry mentions knowledge of Cree among the Sarcees at the end of the eighteenth century. The Sarcees now live in central Alberta: "Most of them have a smattering of the Cree language, which they display in clamorous and discordant strains, without rule or reason." (Coues 1897: 2, 737; cited in Silverstein 1973: 14). "Even the Blackfoot and the Sarcees can also speak Cree a bit, because they often camped with that nation in time of peace" (Lacombe 1874a: xi).[8] Among the Beavers, too, who live in northern Alberta, there were at least some who could speak Cree: "Many Chipewyans whose language is so difficult to learn, understand Cree, like their allies, the Beavers of Peace River" (Lacombe 1874a: xi).[9]

Blackfoot Confederacy

Silverstein (1973: 13–14) mentions that Cree was spoken by the Piegans of the Blackfoot Confederacy at Rocky Mountain House in Alberta in 1810, for which Alexander Henry was his source. In the Cree oral history of war between the Blackfoot and Crees, some Blackfoot are reported to speak Cree: "Then the Blackfoot called out, in Cree . . ." (Bloomfield 1934: 38–39).[10] Knowledge of Cree by the Blackfoot is also reported by Lacombe (1874a: xi).

Other Nations

The Palliser expedition met a Shuswap chief who knew at least some Cree in 1859 (Spry 1963: 253; see also earlier in this chapter). The Shuswap live in southeastern

British Columbia, on the west side of the Rocky Mountains, and speak a Salishan language. A few centuries ago they were still living on the prairies. Cree has also been reported among the Kutenai, who speak a language isolate, with no known relatives. The Kutenai apparently have never lived in areas adjacent to the Crees, but still the Palliser expedition in 1859 met at least one Kutenai who spoke Cree (Spry 1963: 137). The year before, none of the Kutenai whom the expedition met spoke Cree, so it was not widespread.

Among the Dakotas or Sioux, Cree was used as a lingua franca, according to James Howard (1965: 7; see also Spry 1963). I am unaware of other sources, but this is nonetheless very likely.

I have no data on the Gros Ventre, who now live in Montana but who used to live in the Canadian prairies. I suspect that there were Cree bilinguals there, too.

MÉTIS AND WHITES

Cree was also used as a lingua franca between Métis and English-speaking "half-breeds" and possibly white people in the Red River settlement in the 1860s: "Thus a man whose usual language is English, and one who speaks French alone, are enabled to render themselves mutually intelligible by means of Cree, their Indian mother tongue, though each is totally ignorant of the civilized language ordinarily used by the other" (Hargrave 1871: 75, 181; also cited in Stobie 1967–1968: 75).

According to an 1890 newspaper article on the Manitoba senate, Cree (or perhaps Ojibwe) seems to have been used even there: "In those days there were three official languages—English, French and Indian—in use. It is related that Dr. O'Donell, exasperated at the use of more Indian (in the Senate) than he considered necessary, said, 'I don't see anything in our acts permitting the use of Indian'. Still, it was not discontinued" (cited in Stobie 1970).

Finally, Lacombe confirms the widespread use of Cree among all the prairie nations:

> The Cree language is the one most widely spoken in the Northwest. With this language, if needed, one can communicate with any tribe of this area. As the language has approximately the same grammatical rules as Saulteaux and part of the words come from the same roots and have the same pronunciation, the Cree language is largely intelligible for a Saulteaux. Only the accent is more determined in Saulteaux than in Cree. The Assiniboines, whose language is the same as the one spoken by the Sioux, and who are the friends and the allies of the Crees through marriages, almost all understand Cree a bit, and some speak it very well. (1874a: xi)[11]

It is clear that in all the tribes adjacent to Plains Cree territory, there are people who speak the Plains Cree language, perhaps more so in the past than today. Among the Ojibwe to the east, the Assiniboines to the southwest, the Blackfoot to the west, and the Chipewyans to the north, knowledge of Plains Cree must have been reasonably widespread, despite the fact that some of these nations were enemies of the Cree. Even among some of the nations in places not adjacent to the Plains Cree area, there were speakers of Cree, such as the Shuswap, Sarcee, and Kutenai. Only in the case of the Assiniboines do the Cree seem to have known their partners' language, too. In summary, Plains Cree was undoubtedly the lingua franca of the northern plains and the adjacent woodlands.

What relevance does this have for the origin of Michif? Of course, the most obvious repercussion is the fact that the Amerindian ancestors of the Métis need not have been Plains Cree Indians; they could have originated from any of the groups who spoke Plains Cree as a second language. For some of these groups, it would have been the language used with outsiders. As we have seen, the Métis trace the Amerindian side of their ancestry to the Saulteaux, Cree, and Assiniboine nations (Crawford 1983a: viii), all speakers of Plains Cree. It is among these tribes that one must find the ancestors of the speakers of Michif. There is one obvious place where the Métis met with the Assiniboines, Crees, and Ojibwes: at the bison hunt and the winter camps in the parklands.

The Métis and the Plains

I have already mentioned the paradoxical fact that Michif is a language usually associated with the fur trade, which took place in the woodlands, whereas Michif contains mostly elements of the Cree dialect of the Plains, where the role of the fur trade was insignificant. The solution for this paradox must be sought in the historical circumstances in the early Red River Settlement. Michif is the language the Métis used in the bison hunt and in the winter camps. These hunts took place on the prairies, and the wintering camps were built in the parklands immediately adjacent.

The Métis bison hunters of Saint François Xavier and Baie Saint Paul used their land in the Red River settlement just as a base. The mainstay of their lives was their travels west and south into the prairies in search of bison. In the west, they were joined by groups of Indians (see Chapter Three), but they were the largest ethnic group there. Several groups of Indians hunted bison around 1800 on the northeastern Plains (North Dakota, Montana, southwestern Manitoba, and southern Saskatchewan) when the Métis started their hunts: Assiniboines, Crees, and Ojibwes, as well as their enemies, the Sioux. In the first three groups, Plains Cree was generally spoken, as already shown. Some of the Métis spent the winters with these Indians. The importance of the non-Cree Indians in the bison hunt may be illustrated by the fact that the whole organizational system of the "provisional government" of the hunt, with chiefs and scouts, was copied directly from Assiniboine bison hunters (Barkwell 1991). The Métis would later use this as a base for their provisional government of Manitoba.

Most of the Métis spoke Ojibwe, Cree, and French, whereas the Indians all spoke Cree, as well as Assiniboine or Ojibwe. It is only natural that Cree would be the contact language between the Métis and these Indians: it was the language that all the people involved had in common. Because of the growing importance of the bison hunt after 1821, and hence their increasing contact with Cree-speaking Indians, Ojibwe became less and less important to the Métis. They became accustomed to speaking more Cree when they traveled to the hunting grounds and winter camps, slowly abandoning Saulteaux.

Although Amerindian-French code mixing must have been common among most *voyageurs* and people of mixed ancestry from the moment of the very first mixed marriages and resulting bilingual children, it was only in these hunting camps that the mixture solidified into a fixed code. Here the language must have taken the form of Cree verbs and French nouns. This pattern may have been prevalent in code mixing, too. The genesis, or at least the codification, of the Michif language is intimately connected with the emergence of a Métis identity. The crystallization had been preceded by different kinds of code mixing, notably Ojibwe-French.

The Métis bison hunters were involved in two additional activities connected with the bison hunt. One was the pemmican trade, in which they traded dried bison meat with settlers and the Hudson's Bay Company. The other was the freighting of goods with their Red River carts along the trails west and south, in the tracks of their hunting trips. Perhaps these trading activities also stimulated the use of Michif, although it was certainly not used in trade contacts with non-Métis.

Michif was used only as an in-group language by the Métis. It was not used with outsiders, so that its existence remained unknown to the outside world until a few decades ago. The languages used with outsiders were French, Ojibwe, and Cree. It was probably only after the massive dispersal of the Métis from the 1860s onward that their knowledge of French, Cree, and/or Ojibwe was completely lost, so that Michif became the only language spoken by several thousands of people much later. Before those languages fell into disuse, however, Michif must have been the language they felt most comfortable with.

This scenario explains a number of factors, some of which have remained enigmatic until now. It sheds light on why the Cree dialect is the Plains Cree of the prairies rather than a Cree dialect (Swampy, Woods, or Rock Cree) of the woodlands. It accounts for the Ojibwe substrate in the Cree part of Michif. It explains why Plains Cree is somewhat more simplified than other Cree dialects and why the Cree part of Michif is slightly more simplified than Plains Cree: after all, it was learned by many as a second language. It explains why Michif today is spoken in locations associated with the Métis wintering camps. It indicates why the sources of the early 1800s about the Red River settlement mention mostly Ojibwe as a language spoken by the Métis and not Cree. It also explains why Cree was more and more mentioned as a language of the Métis after the 1840s. It suggests why only the descendants of the Métis bison hunters speak Michif and not the descendants of the Métis farmers and fishermen. It explains why the Ojibwe influence seems to come from both the Great Lakes dialects and the Plains dialect.

Conclusions

The early Métis must have spoken at least Ojibwe, French, and Cree. There must have been some impetus that made them shift from Ojibwe to Cree. This impetus is the bison hunt, which took place to the west of their summer settlement at Red River, where Métis joined Assiniboine, Cree, and Plains Ojibwe bands, who all spoke Cree as a first or second language. Cree was the only language known to all of them, as only the Ojibwes spoke Ojibwe. The Ojibwe element in Michif would be older. It is possible that it came from the Great Lakes area, where Ojibwe was the lingua franca and where some of the ancestors of the Red River Métis originated. There are some indications that a mixed language was spoken there, which also may have been used by *voyageurs* and Métis who came to the Red River settlement from that area. The Cree element started to dominate after the beginning of the organized bison hunts in the 1820s.

The Genesis of Michif

This book deals with the origin of the mixed language Michif. Not much is known about the genesis of mixed languages, although some recent research uncovered many new facts. This is the first book that studies the birth of a new, mixed language. If the attempts to save the language do not succeed, it will effectively die out within one or two decades, as its speakers have exchanged their language for the all-encroaching English. It will not have survived two centuries.

Michif appears to be unique within the group of mixed languages, seemingly having a dichotomy of verbs from one language and nouns from another. All other mixed languages have a lexicon from one language and a grammar (phonology, morphology, syntax) from another. The intriguing question about Michif is why it is mixed in this way.

The birth of Michif (and other mixed languages) can be approached only from an interdisciplinary perspective. I hope I have shown that a combination of typological linguistic, historical linguistic, sociolinguistic, anthropological, ethnohistorical, and historical data can yield interesting results, each confirming the conclusions drawn from other fields.

Michif is a language that is associated with the fur trade. Nevertheless, it did not emerge in the trade contacts between the fur traders and the Natives. It is certain that it was not the trade language used between these two groups not only because there are absolutely no indications for this use in the historical documentation. If it was the language used in trade contacts, it should have been mentioned in the contemporary documents. Furthermore, we know from other cases of trade relations in the world that these contacts lead to simplified forms of the language of one group or to a simplified compromise between the languages of both groups. Michif is not a simplified form of either French or Cree. Although both the French and the Cree components are slightly altered from the source languages, these alterations simplify both components only a tiny bit, not what one would expect in cases of trade languages. In fact, Michif seems to combine the most complex parts of both languages. The Cree verb is infinitely more complex than the French verb, and the French noun, with its arbitrary genders and definite-indefinite distinction, is more complex than the Cree noun. In trade contacts, the source languages tend to lose a large part of their bound morphemes and semantic distinctions such as gender and number. This did not occur in Michif. So, both for historical and linguistic reasons, Michif cannot have been a language used in trade contacts.

Was it a language spoken by the first generation of Métis children, who were "Métis" in the sense of being a distinct group of mixed Amerindian and European ancestry? It is known that relations between Europeans and Amerindians had produced several generations of children before there was a distinct group with a specifically Métis identity. In the beginning these children were often raised as Indians in the tribes of their mothers, sometimes as Europeans, or both at the same time. It was only around 1800 that a separate group of Métis, calling themselves *Bois Brulés* or *Halfbreeds*, appeared in what was then called the Northwest. It would more likely be in those years that Michif would emerge since it was only then that the Métis formed a distinct ethnic group.

In the historical sources, however, there are no references to a language like Michif spoken by the Métis. There are numerous allusions to language mixing by the Métis by commentators from the 1820s on, and perhaps even from before that date. It can be argued that people would not mix languages in the presence of outsiders unless it was their usual way of speaking. If this is correct, these observers may be referring to Michif. This seems to be corroborated by the oral history of the Métis. Two persons, one born around 1842 and the other in 1825, were remembered by their great-grandchildren, who are now in their 70s and 80s, to be speakers of Michif, among other languages. None of the people I interviewed had any idea when the language had started, which means that it must have started a long time ago. Michif is spoken today in communities that already existed in the 1840s, which also points to the emergence of the language early in that century. Its speakers are descended from Métis bison hunters who gathered in Saint François Xavier (Red River settlement) and Pembina (on the Red River in Minnesota) for the annual bison hunts between the 1820s and 1870s. The dialects of Michif spoken by their descendants are so similar that they must stem from a common source.

Michif is a mixture of French and Cree. The first Métis, however, must have had quite a few Ojibwe women among their mothers and wives, probably even a majority. In those scarce cases in which it is possible to learn the nationality of the women who were marriage partners of the French, a considerable majority appear to be Ojibwe. References to Saulteaux (Plains Ojibwe) ancestry in oral history also point to this fact. Other mothers were mostly Assiniboines and Crees. All these tribes have in common the fact that Cree was spoken as a second language in their communities. This can explain the loss of many of the lesser used inflectional paradigms of the Cree part of the language, as well as a number of linguistic features in which Michif differs from Cree.

The numerical majority of the Ojibwes among the people who provided the input for the Amerindian component of Michif is responsible for the small but clear influence from Ojibwe—notably the Saultaux dialect—on Michif. Ojibwe nouns and verb stems, a few verb endings, and phonological influence from Ojibwe support the theory that speakers of Ojibwe were somehow involved in the genesis of Michif. There are two possible explanations for these Ojibwe elements.

The first explanation is that the ethnic Ojibwes spoke Cree as a second language, which was probably spoken by western Ojibwes for many generations as a lingua franca in the area adjacent to Cree territory. But why, then, would they teach their children Cree? This is likely only if the mothers of the first generation were ethnically diverse and if they all spoke Cree as a second language. This is possible, as it is known that Cree was widely used by all tribes in the areas adjacent to Cree territory. Their children would have needed Cree for communication with other Indian-European children, which may have reinforced its presence.

The other explanation is that people from the east (French *voyageurs* and fur traders, who must have spoken Ojibwe; Ojibwe Indians; or mixed Ojibwe-French families from the Great Lakes) brought the Ojibwe language with them to the Red River settlement in the early 1800s. It would only be there that Cree became important. Already in the early 1800s the Métis around Red River were reported to hunt bison. Massive Métis bison hunts started in the territory of the Cree, Assiniboine, and Ojibwe Indians and in the territory of their enemies, the Sioux. Groups of these Indians (except for the Sioux) joined the Métis hunts. The Métis also had wintering camps near the Indians of the prairies. All four groups (Cree, Assiniboine, Ojibwe, and Métis) spoke Cree as their first or second language, stimulating the use of Cree in the hunts and winter camps. The result would logically have been a Cree-French mixture with an Ojibwe substrate, and Ojibwe would fall into disuse.

It may be asked whether Michif was not originally French-Cree code mixing and Cree with French borrowings. Michif appears to differ structurally from both languages, however. In the Cree dialects that borrowed from French, notably that of Ile-a-la-Crosse, borrowing appears to be limited to nouns and their governing prepositions and possessives, which only amounts to about 14 percent and 10 percent, respectively, of the tokens in these categories. The French words are borrowed with the definite articles, as is common for French borrowings in many languages. In Michif and code mixing, however, indefinite articles are also used.

There are also linguistic differences between French-Cree code mixing and Michif, which point to an independent origin. In code mixing, there appears to be a rather arbitrary mixture of French and Cree, as in other reported cases of code mixing. There is no verb-noun dichotomy, as in Michif. In the Montagnais (eastern Cree) community of Betsiamites, code mixing is so extensive that the Montagnais-French mixture is becoming a mother tongue for the children. Although it is different from Michif, for example, in the use of French verbs (with a Montagnais helping verb "to do") and in the much lower frequency of French nouns, it suggests the possibility that code mixing played an indirect role in the genesis of Michif. However, I argue that not code mixing, but a process called language intertwining, was decisive in Michif's birth.

The Métis speak a mixed language because they have a mixed identity. They do not feel that they belong to either of the groups whose languages they speak. They are a new ethnic group, born out of the meeting of two very different peoples: French Canadian fur traders and Amerindian women. They identify themselves as Métis, and although they recognize their European and Amerindian ancestry, they do not feel a part of either. Their traditional culture combines elements from both, but it also shows numerous innovations unique to the Métis as well.

In similar circumstances elsewhere in the world, comparable events have occurred:

a new ethnic group arose whose members speak a new language. Such new languages are typically mixed, through a process that I call language intertwining. The first generation of children born of these mixed-language marriages is typically bilingual, speaking the languages of both the mother and the father. Since the fathers come from a different area and the mothers speak an indigenous language, these children have more opportunity to speak the language of the mothers than that of the fathers. In addition, these children were probably raised by the mothers (and/or other women who speak the same language), providing more language input in the maternal language than in the paternal one. So there are several reasons why these first-generation children speak the language of their mothers better than the language of their fathers. In the case of the first-generation Métis, they must have spoken better Cree than French.

In general, when there are many mixed couples with bilingual children, they can start to speak a mixed language. When the mothers of the first generation speak a language different from the fathers, the new mixed languages of their descendants, if they are a considerable group, appear to combine the grammatical system of the mothers' language and the lexicon of the father's. They intertwine the vocabulary of the father's language into the grammatical framework of the mother's language. In fact, in Michif the same thing occurred, but because of the typological features of Cree, the process led to the atypical result of a language with French nouns and Cree verbs. It can be argued that Michif has a Cree grammatical system, which includes verbs, and a French lexicon, which is mostly nominal. In Cree verbs it is impossible to separate the affixes from the stem. In fact, the whole verb consists only of affixes and should therefore be considered part of the grammatical system of the language. The result of this process is a language with Cree verbs, demonstratives, personal pronouns, and question words and French articles, nouns, and prepositions. French nouns can have Cree affixes.

It must have become clear that there is still more to learn about Michif. First, a thorough study of Métis mythology is needed while the elders who have grown up in the narrative tradition of the old days are still here to share their stories. In addition, data on the eastern dialect of Plains Cree are lacking, and it is not known in which ways it differs from the Cree that has been recorded in print. It probably shares a number of features with the Cree part of Michif. The influence of the Assiniboine language on Plains Cree would be worth exploring, including the question of whether some of the mixed Cree-Assiniboine bands in southeastern Saskatchewan still speak a mixed language, as they were reported to do in the past.

Michif is a unique language in many respects. It is unclassifiable genetically and therefore comparable with the duck-billed platypus or the panda in biology. Does it belong to the Algonquian or to the Indo-European (Romance) language family? Even as a mixed language it is unique. With its verb-noun dichotomy it looks completely different from the other mixed languages of the world. The process by which it arose must have been the same, I have argued, only the result is different because of the typological features of Cree. Unfortunately, many of the Métis still live in conditions of poverty, are victims of discrimination, and maintain fewer and fewer of the traditions of their ancestors. I hope that this book can at least assuage some sorrow for the people whom I respect and love. It is a matter of deep regret that human languages that are threatened with extinction—especially those as unique as Michif—do not receive as much attention as animals in the same situation.

NOTES

Chapter 1

1. The abbreviations in the glosses are defined in the beginning of the book.

2. Examples of mixed-lexicon pidgins are Trio-Ndjuka pidgin of Suriname (De Goeje 1908) and Russenorsk (Fox 1983; Broch and Jahr 1984a and b).

3. It remains to be explained, however, why the Turkish verbs are borrowed with all the Turkish inflections (see Igla 1991) instead of just the root, to which Romani inflection would be added. This falls outside the scope of this study.

4. I am very grateful to Professor Van Holk of the Slavic Languages Department of the University of Groningen for his valuable assistance with the data on this language. The Copper Island Aleut glosses were provided by Evgenij Golovko of Saint Petersburg, to whom I also express my thanks.

Chapter 2

1. Even some of these groupings are contested by specialists, so the actual number of families may be higher.

2. ". . . les Vagabonds, qui avoient pris du goût pour la liberté d'une vie errante & pour l'indépendance, restèrent parmi les Sauvages, dont on ne les distinguoit plus, que par leurs vices. On eut recours en divers tems aux Amnisties, pour rappeller ces Transfuges, & d'abord elles furent assez inutiles."

3. "M. de Denonville revient ensuite aux Coureurs de Bois dont il dit que le nombre est tel, qu'il dépeuple le Pays des meilleurs hommes, les rend indociles, indisciplinables, débauchés, & que leurs Enfans sont élévés conme des Sauvages."

4. "Le nombre des Canadiens en impose aux indigènes, leur influence s'étend de jour en jour, et ils s'assurent de leur estime par la générosité de leurs présents."

Chapter 3

1. Murray Hamilton first alerted me to the subject of this section.
2. The French name is Cendrillon. An Acadian version of the fairy tale is "Cendrillouse," from which the Michif name may be derived (Haden 1948).
3. Wolfart (1990a) shows that the "Sesame Open" story in Bloomfield (1930: 340) must have come to the Sweetgrass Cree through a French intermediary, as the Cree formula *nikotwâsik iskwahtêm, pâskihtêpayih* "Six door, open!" can only be a misunderstanding of "sésame" as "sixième." I want to add that the source was probably Métis, as both words would be pronounced [si:zæm] in Michif, where the sibilants are harmonized and the mid-vowel /e/ is raised to /i/.
4. This is the same word as *âpihtawikosisân*, given in a previous section.
5. "Isolé de la société blanche, le Métis l'est également de la société indigène."
6. For bibliographies on Métis languages, see Nichols (1985) and Bakker (1989a).

Chapter 4

1. Rhodes's phonetic transcription has been adjusted to the system used here.
2. According to Christoph Wolfart and David H. Pentland, eastern Plains Cree has nasal vowels (pers. comm.).
3. The word bæčɪs is derived from French "Jean-Baptiste" and is sometimes taken as the Michif equivalent of "John."
4. "I think he will not go" would probably be:žɪ pãs *e:ka šI-Ituhte:-t*.
5. This form is masculine, although it clearly refers to a female person.
6. In northwestern Saskatchewan, where Cree is used with French nominal borrowings, English nouns virtually always have the gender of the equivalent French nouns; see Hogman (1981).
7. We do not have second-person plural forms in our data, although both Rhodes (1977) and Orser (1984) do. These seem to be rather marginal.
8. Lynn Drapeau (pers. comm.) suggested an Algonquian source for *da/dã*, but I find that unlikely. The word *anta* "there" is rare in Plains Cree, and it would not explain the commonly nasal character of *dã*. Nevertheless, some form of conflation of the French and Cree form cannot be excluded.

Chapter 5

1. I estimate the number of speakers of Plains Cree in Manitoba at fewer than ten.
2. "La population [de la réserve de Turtle Mountain], essentiellement formée de métis canadiens recrutés parmi les descendants d'hivernants de Pembina, de Saint-François-Xavier, de la Montagne de Bois . . . doit aux avantages de toute sorte qui lui sont assurés d'éviter la déchéance matérielle des groupes de prairie. Elle ne subit pas les effets démoralisants de l'hostilité ou du mépris des Blancs, ni les répercussions d'une concurrence qu'elle ne peut soutenir."
3. "When the first traders came to northern Saskatchewan they brought a language with which they tried to educate the people of the area. Some of our forefathers went to school where they learned to read and write in French. These people integrated some of these words into our language that we now speak today" (Community of Ile-a-la-Crosse 1990).
4. This information was first conveyed to me by Murray Hamilton.
5. Some Michif speakers say *parla*. The etymology of this word is unclear, though undoubtedly French. It is also used by the Métis in Yellowknife.

6. French *ça prend* "it takes," "one has to"; Cree *čI-šIpwe:hte:ja:n* or *ta-sipwêhtêyân* "that I will go."

7. Cree *piko* "one has to."

Chapter 6

1. The undated typescript by Schindler may be older but not by much.

2. ". . . le langage familier et pittoresque, qui distinguait déjà les Bois-Brulés."

3. Although this is not really a contemporary source, Spry followed the contemporary sources closely, in particular the report made by the expedition member Dr. Hector.

4. "Les métis ne vivent pas en pleine forêt comme les Indiens. Ils s'établissent en bordure des villes des blancs, ou forment de véritables colonies, un petit monde à part, comme, par exemple, à Camperville sur le lac Winnipegosis, où se parle un langage extraordinaire composé de cris et de français."

5. "Notre grande occupation sera envers les sauvages, mais pour les prêcher il faudroit les poursuivre de campements en campements, ce qu'il n'est guère possible de faire avant de savoir leurs langues. Je me suis occupé jusqu'à présent en partie à apprendre le Saulteux."

6. ". . . il se trouve bien des obstacles à leur prompte instruction [des Brulés which means Métis]; et voici les principaux: Leurs différentes langues que nous n'entendons pas. . . ."

7. French missionaries had established a language study center at Lac des Deux Montagnes.

8. "D'ailleurs c'est là [St. François Xavier] où j'aurai le plus de facilité d'étudier la langue sauvage que je désirois apprendre, mais en laquelle je crains bien de ne pouvoir réussir, faute de moyens suffisans. Je comprends néanmoins combien il est nécessaire de la savoir; car ce n'est pour ainsi dire qu'avec les femmes métives et plusieurs enfans qui comprennent très peu le françois qu'on peut avancer l'oeuvre de Dieu. Pour la plus grande partie des Canadiens et des anciens métifs, ce sont malheureusement de bien pauvres chrétiens."

9. "Mgr. Provencher ramena du Canada, en 1831, M. Belcourt, homme d'intelligence et d'énergie, désireux de se consacrer à la conversion des sauvages. Naturellement on commença par les plus proches. Les Sauteux furent l'objet des premières tentatives d'évangélisation."

10. The original vocabulary is in the University of Rochester Library. I am grateful to Karl Kabelac for making this available.

11. Bungee is a dialect of English influenced by Gaelic, Cree, and Ojibwe, formerly spoken in the northern part of the Red River Settlement by descendants of Orkneymen and Scottish traders and their Indian wives (Scott & Mulligan 1951; Stobie 1967–1968; Blain 1987, 1989, 1994).

12. "Les Cris ont trois R différents, le plus fréquent a quelque rapport avec le R gras des Provençaux."

13. I am grateful to Dwayne Desjarlais of Ile-a-la-Crosse, Cree coordinator of the Rossignol school, for making this available to me.

14. Some examples of each of the categories under 14: (a) *buenas dias* "good day", *adios* "goodbye" (Topping 1980: 11, 17); (b) *gi Eneru gi bente i unu gi mit siette sientos sisenta i sinko* "January 21, 1765" (ibid. 276); (c) *otra semana* "next week", *asta despues ta'lo* "until later" (ibid. 115, 17); (d) *unu, dos, tres, kuatro*, etc. (ibid. iii–iv); (e) *noskuantos dias* "a few days" *todu* "all" (ibid. 294, 12) (f) *pues* "then" *asta ki* "until" (ibid. 17, 348); (g) *pot fabot* "please" (ibid. 16); *siempre* "always", *mas* "most" (i) *este* "this" *no* "isn't it" (ibid. 70, 342).

15. This is obviously a borrowing from English, used in many Cree dialects.

Chapter 7

1. The numbers in the glosses preceded by "C" refer to the Bantu noun classes and their concord markers.

2. The word *heef* is based on the Dutch verb *hebben* "to have"; compare *hij heeft* "he has."

3. The word *tas* is a Dutch borrowing in Javanese.

4. I am grateful to A. G. F. van Holk for his help in this matter. The interlinear interpretation was kindly provided by Evgenij Golovko, to whom I also express my thanks.

5. I am grateful to Hadewych van Rheeden and Jan van der Veerdonk for the Javanese and Indonesian translations.

6. This example comes from a religious tract in Angloromani.

Chapter 8

1. However, a book on polysynthetic languages, written in a generative framework, has recently been published (Baker 1995).

2. From the story "fa fii höndi pakia" ("How to Hunt Peccary"). The spelling is taken from the book.

3. Some dialects (among them standard French) pronounce the past tense ending /e/ as /ɛ/.

4. The standard form in -ɔ̃ like *nous marchons*, is not often used in colloquial speech.

5. This (bæčɪs) is a common Métis name derived from the French Jean-Baptiste.

6. Cree does not distinguish between males and females in pronouns; the gender in the English pronouns is chosen to make clear that the subject kisses someone else's brother. That distinction is clear in Cree and Michif but not in an English sentence such as "He kissed his brother," where "his" can refer to "he" or to someone else.

7. Ralph L. was a local singer in Camperville who died.

8. It can just as well be a past participle form. I have no examples of French verbs that have distinct forms for the infinitive and the participle.

9. There is no Cree morpheme *i:*.

Chapter 9

1. My sources for the languages discussed here are the following: *General*: Pentland 1978a; MacKenzie and Clarke 1981; Rhodes and Todd 1981. *Michif*: fieldwork 1988, 1990. *Southern Plains Cree*: Bloomfield 1934; Wolfart 1973b; Ahenakew 1987a and b. *Eastern Ojibwe and Odawa*: Bloomfield 1958; Rhodes 1976, 1985. *Moose Cree*: Ellis 1983. *Woods Cree*: Howse 1844; Pentland 1978b; Starks 1987; Brightman 1989. *Tête-de-Boule Cree*: Cooper 1945; Béland 1978; fieldwork 1993. *Saulteaux*: Voorhis 1977. *Eastern Swampy Cree*: Pentland 1978a. *Western Swampy Cree*: Pentland 1978a; Rhodes and Todd 1981; Beardy 1988. *Severn Ojibwe and Ojicree*: Todd 1971; Wolfart 1973a; J. R. Valentine (pers. comm.). *Minnesota Ojibwe*: Kegg 1983. *Assiniboine*: Levin 1964.

2. In his fieldwork on Turtle Mountain Cree in 1911–1912, on only one occasion was Michelson not able to obtain an Algonquian noun—most of them are Cree, and a few are Ojibwe—because his informants "use French word." Other features also point to the fact that Michif was more commonly spoken by his informants. This is clear from his field notes (Michelson 1911–1912), which were kindly made available to me by the National Anthropological Archives in Washington. The Cree he recorded is virtually identical to the Cree component of Michif.

3. David Pentland commented that he had recorded this same form from Swampy Cree speakers in eastern central Manitoba. My Swampy Cree informants (northern central Manitoba) use the Plains Cree form.

4. Note that neither /z/ nor /s/ is part of the phonological system of the Cree part of Michif.

5. I thank David H. Pentland, who first suggested (in print or in conversation) many of the ideas presented here. Nevertheless, he may not agree with the points I am making.

6. Bungee (Blain 1987, 1989, 1994) is the language associated with the retired Hudson's Bay Company Scots and Orkneymen who had married Indian women and who had settled in Red River. It is basically a dialect of English, with Orkney and Scottish influence, and a little Cree and Ojibwe admixture.

7. In a relevant remark, Thomas (1985: 248) comments on a paper on Michif: "Michif, as he [Crawford 1985a] describes it, appears to be basically Cree-Ojibwa in structure but with a sizable French vocabulary, particularly in nouns. I have heard of areas where the opposite process has taken place, that is, where the language is French in structure but Ojibwa in content. The language spoken by a large part of the population on the Garden River Ojibwa reserve near Sault Ste. Marie, Ontario, is such an example." When I tried to verify this observation on this reserve in 1987, I was unable to find any trace of a mixed language. A man in his 90s knew some French, in addition to his first language, Ojibwe, but he denied the existence of such a mixture, and so did an anthropologist who had made a study of this reserve. I have serious doubts about the existence of the mixed language Thomas describes.

8. "Même les Pieds-Noirs et les Sarcis peuvent parler un peu aussi le cris, ayant souvent campé avec cette nation, dans les temps de paix."

9. "Grand nombre de Montagnais dont la langue est si difficile comprennent le cris, ainsi que leurs confrères, les *Castors* de la rivière de La Paix."

10. The original Cree text (in standardized spelling):

kîtahtawê kâ-matwê-pîkiskwê-t awa âyahciyiniw ê-nêhiyawê-t . . .
suddenly COMP-audibly-speak-3 this enemy COMP-speak.Cree-3

11. "La langue crise est la plus parlée dans le Nord-Ouest. Avec cet idiome, dans le besoin, on peut se mettre en rapport avec n'importe quelle tribu de ce pays. Ayant les mêmes règles grammaticales à peu près que la langue Sauteuse, une partie des mots venant des mêmes racines et ayant souvent la même prononciation, la langue crise peut se faire comprendre en grande partie par un Sauteux. Seulement l'accent est bien plus déterminé en sauteux qu'en cris. Les Assiniboines, dont la langue est la même que celle des Sioux, et qui sont les amis et alliés des Cris par les mariages, comprennent presque tous un peu le Cris, et quelques-uns le parlent très-bien."

References

Ackerley, Frederick George. 1929. Basque Romani. *Journal of the Gypsy Lore Society*, 3rd series, 8(2): 50–94.

Ahenakew, Freda. 1987a. *Cree language structures: A Cree approach*. Winnipeg: Pemmican Publications.

Ahenakew, Freda, ed. 1987b. *Wâskahikaniwiyiniw-âcimowina. Stories of the House People*. Winnipeg: University of Manitoba Press.

Ahenakew, Freda, and H. C. Wolfart. 1983. Productive reduplication in Plains Cree. In *Papers of the Fifteenth Algonquian Conference*, ed. William Cowan, 369–377. Ottawa: Carleton University.

Albers, Patricia C. 1993. Symbiosis, merger, and war: Contrasting forms of intertribal relationships among the historic Plains Indians. In *The political economy of North American Indians*, ed. John H. Moore, 94–132. Norman: University of Oklahoma Press.

Anderson, Anne. 1985. *The first Metis. A new nation*. Edmonton: Uvisco Press.

Anderson, Stephen R. 1982. Where's morphology? *Linguistic Inquiry* 13: 571–612.

Anderson, Stephen R. 1985. Typological distinctions in word formation. In *Language typology and grammatical description*, ed. Timothy Shopen, vol. 3, 3–56. Cambridge: Cambridge University Press.

Anderson, Stephen R. 1992. *A-morphous morphology*. Cambridge: Cambridge University Press.

Andrews, G. A. 1985. Cree commentary and vocabulary. In *Metis outpost. Memoirs of the first schoolmaster at the Metis settlement of Kelly Lake, B.C., 1923–1925*, 301–308. Victoria, B.C.: Pencrest Publications.

Appel, René, and Pieter Muysken. 1987. *Language contact and bilingualism*. London: Edward Arnold.

Aubin, George. 1975. *A proto-Algonquian dictionary. Mercury Series—Canadian Ethnology Service Paper* 29. Ottawa: National Museum of Man.

Backus, Ad. 1992. *Patterns of language mixing. A study in Turkish-Dutch bilingualism*. Wiesbaden: Harrassowitz.

Backus, Ad. 1996. Two in one. Bilingual speech of Turkish immigrants in the Netherlands. Tilburg: Tilburg University Press.

Bailey, Charles-James N., and K. Maroldt. 1977. The French lineage of English. In *Langues en contact—pidgins—créoles—Languages in contact*, 21–53. Tübingen: G. Narr.

Baker, Mark. 1995. The polysynthesis parameter. Oxford: Oxford University Press.

Bakker, Peter. 1988–1989. Canadian fur trade and the absence of creoles. *Carrier Pidgin* 16(3): 1–2.

Bakker, Peter. 1989a. Bibliography of Métis languages. *Amsterdam Creole Studies* 10: 41–47.

Bakker, Peter. 1989b."The language of the coast tribes is half Basque." A Basque-Amerindian pidgin in use between Europeans and Native Americans in North America, ca. 1540–ca. 1640. *Anthropological Linguistics* 31(3/4):117–147.

Bakker, Peter. 1989c. Relexification: The case of Michif (French-Cree). *Vielfalt der Kontakte. Beiträge zum 5. Essener Kolloquium über Grammatikalisierung: Natürlichkeit und Systemökonomie. Band II*, ed. Norbert Boretzky, Werner Enninger, and Thomas Stolz, 119–137. Bochum: Studienverlag Dr. N. Brockmeyer.

Bakker, Peter. 1990a. A Basque etymology for the word "Iroquois." *Man in the Northeast* 40: 89–93.

Bakker, Peter. 1990b. The genesis of Michif: A first hypothesis. In *Papers of the Twenty-first Algonquian Conference*, ed. William Cowan, 12–35. Ottawa: Carleton University.

Bakker, Peter. 1991a. Basque Romani—A preliminary grammatical sketch of a mixed language. In *In the margin of Romani: Gypsy languages in contact*, ed. Peter Bakker and Marcel Cortiade, 56–90. Amsterdam: Publications of the Institute for General Linguistics, University of Amsterdam, 58.

Bakker, Peter. 1991b. The Ojibwa element in Michif. In *Papers of the Twenty-second Algonquian Conference*, ed. William Cowan, 11–20. Ottawa: Carleton University.

Bakker, Peter. 1991c. Review of Sarah Grey Thomason and Terrence Kaufman, "Language Contact, Creolization and Genetic Linguistics." *Canadian Journal of Linguistics* 36(2): 171–176.

Bakker, Peter. 1994a. Is John Long's Chippeway (1791) an Ojibwe pidgin? In *Papers of the Twenty-fifth Algonquian Conference*, 14–31. Ottawa: Carleton University.

Bakker, Peter. 1994b. La traite des fourrures et les noms des tribus. Quelques ethnonymes amérindiens vraisemblement d'origine basque dans le Nord-Est. *Recherches Amérindiennes au Québec* 24(3): 17–24.

Bakker, Peter. 1996. Hudson Bay traders' Cree: A Cree pidgin? In *nikotwâsik iskwâhtêm, pâskihtêpayih! Studies in honour of H. C. Wolfart*, ed. John D. Nichols and Arden C. Ogg, 1–34. Winnipeg: Algonquian and Iroquoian Linguistics, Memoir 13.

Bakker, Peter. forthcoming. Language intertwining: Genesis and structure of mixed languages.

Bakker, Peter, and Anthony P. Grant. 1995. Interethnic communication in Canada, Alaska and adjacent areas. In *Atlas of languages of intercultural communication in the Pacific, Asia, and the Americas*, ed. Stephen A. Wurm, Peter Mühlhäusler, and Darrell T. Tryon 1107–1169. Berlin: Mouton de Gruyter.

Bakker, Peter, and Maarten Mous, eds. 1994. *Mixed languages. Fifteen case studies in language intertwining*. Amsterdam: Institute for Functional Research in Language and Language Use.

Bakker, Peter, and Pieter Muysken. 1994. Mixed languages. In *Pidgins and creoles. An introduction*, ed. Jacques Arends, Pieter Muysken, and Norval Smith, 41–52. Amsterdam: John Benjamins.

Bakker, Peter, and Robert A. Papen. In press. Michif: A mixed language based on French and Cree. In *Contact languages: A wider perspective*, ed. Sarah G. Thomason. Amsterdam: J. Benjamins.

Bakker, Peter, and Hein van der Voort. 1991. Para-Romani languages: An overview and some speculations on their genesis. In *In the margin of Romani: Gypsy languages in contact*, ed. Peter Bakker and Marcel Cortiade, 16–44. Publications of the Institute for General Linguistics, University of Amsterdam.

Baraga, Bishop. 1878–1880. *A dictionary of the Otchipwe language*. Montréal: Beauchemin et Valois. Reprinted 1992, St. Paul: Minnesota Historical Society Press.

Barkwell, Lawrence J. 1991. Early law and social control among the Métis. In *The struggle for recognition: Canadian justice and the Métis nation*, ed. Samuel W. Corrigan and Lawrence J. Barkwell, 7–37. Winnipeg: Pemmican Publications.

Barkwell, Lawrence J., David N. Gray, Ron H. Richard, David N. Chartrand, and Lyle Longclaws. 1989. Languages spoken by the Métis, appendix 4. *Manitoba Métis Federation Inc.—Submission to the Aboriginal Justice Inquiry. Research and analysis of the impact of the justice system on the Métis*. Winnipeg: Manitoba Métis Federation.

Baumann, Oskar. 1894. *Durch Massailand zur Nilquelle*. Berlin.

Bear, Glecia et al. 1992. *Kôhkominawak otâcimowiniwâwa. Our grandmothers' lives as told in their own words*, ed. and trans. Freda Ahenakew and H. C. Wolfart. Saskatoon: Fifth House Publishers.

Beardy, L. 1988. *Pisiskiwak kâ-pîkiskwêcik. Talking animals*, ed. H. C. Wolfart. Winnipeg: Algonquian and Iroquoian Linguistics.

Beaudet, Jean-François. 1992, Automne. "Aussi insensés que les pauvres Indians." Les coureurs de bois et l'univers spirituel Amérindien. *Religiologiques*, 41–61.

Béland, Jean-Pierre. 1978. Atikamekw morphology and lexicon. Ph.D. thesis, University of California, Berkeley.

Bickerton, Derek. 1988. Relexification. *Journal of Pidgin and Creole Languages* 3(2): 277–282.

Bishop, Charles A. 1975. The origin of the speakers of the Severn dialect. In *Papers of the Sixth Algonquian Conference*, ed. William Cowan, 196–208. *Mercury Series—Canadian Ethnology Service Paper* 23. Ottawa: National Museum of Man.

Blain, Eleanor. 1987. Speech of the lower Red River settlement. In *Papers of the Eighteenth Algonquian Conference*, ed. William Cowan, 7–16. Ottawa: Carleton University.

Blain, Eleanor. 1989. The Bungee dialect of the Red River settlement. M.A. thesis, University of Manitoba.

Blain, Eleanor. 1994. *The Red River dialect*. Winnipeg: Wuerz Publishing.

Bloomfield, Leonard. 1927. The word-stems of Central Algonquian. *Festschrift Meinhof*, 393–402. Hamburg: L. Friedrichsen.

Bloomfield, Leonard. 1930. *Sacred stories of the Sweet Grass Cree*. Ottawa: King's Printer. Reprinted 1976, New York: AMS Press; Saskatoon: 1994 Fifth House.

Bloomfield, Leonard. 1933. *Language*. New York: Holt, Rinehart & Winston.

Bloomfield, Leonard. 1934. *Plains Cree texts*. New York: American Ethnological Society. Reprinted 1974, New York: AMS Press.

Bloomfield, Leonard. 1946. Algonquian. In *Linguistic structures of native America*, ed. Harry Hoijer, 85–129. *Viking Fund Publications in Anthropology* no. 6. New York: Viking Fund.

Bloomfield, Leonard. 1958. *Eastern Ojibwa: Grammatical sketch, texts and word list*. Ann Arbor: University of Michigan Press.

Boas, Franz. 1911. Introduction. In *Handbook of American Indian languages*. Bureau of American Ethnology, bulletin 40, part 1; 1–83. Washington D.C.: U.S. Government Printing Office.

Boeschoten, Hendrik. 1991. Asymmetrical code-switching in immigrant communities. In Papers for the Workshop on Constraints, Conditions and Models, London, 27–29 September 1990, 85–100.

Boisvert, David, and Keith Turnbull. 1985. Who are the Métis? *Studies in Political Economy* 18: 107–128.

Boretzky, Norbert. 1985. Sind Zigeunersprachen Kreols? In *Akten des 1. Essener Kolloquiums über Kreolsprachen und Sprachkontakte*, ed. Norbert Boretzky, Werner Enninger, and Thomas Stolz, 43–70. Bochum: Studienverlag Dr. N. Brockmeyer.

Boretzky, Norbert, and Birgit Igla. 1994. Romani mixed dialects. In *Mixed languages. Fifteen case studies in language intertwining*, ed. Peter Bakker and Maarten Mous, 35–68. Amsterdam: IFOTT.

Boteler, Bette. 1971. The relationship between the conceptual outlooks and the linguistic description of disease and its treatment among the Chippewa and/or Cree Indians of the Turtle Mountain Reservation. Unpublished thesis, University of North Dakota, Grand Forks.

Brightman, Robert A. 1989. *Âcaðôhkîwina and âcimôwina. Traditional narratives of the Rock Cree Indians. Mercury Series—Canadian Ethnology Service Paper 113.* Hull: Canadian Museum of Civilization.

Broch, Ingvild, and Ernst Håkon Jahr. 1984a. Russenorsk: A new look at the Russo-Norwegian pidgin in northern Norway. In *Scandinavian language contacts*, ed. P. Sture Ureland and Iain Clarkson, 21–65. Cambridge: Cambridge University Press.

Broch, Ingvild, and Ernst Håkon Jahr. 1984b. *Russenorsk: Et Pidginspråk i Norge.* Oslo: Novus.

Brody, Jill. 1987. Particles borrowed from Spanish as discourse markers in Mayan languages. *Anthropological Linguistics* 29: 507–532.

Brown, Jennifer. 1980. *Strangers in blood. Fur trade company families in Indian country.* Vancouver: University of British Columbia Press.

Burley, David V., and Gayel A. Horsfall. 1989. Vernacular houses and farmsteads of the Canadian Métis. *Journal of Cultural Geography* 10(1): 19–33.

Campbell, Maria. 1973. *Halfbreed.* Toronto: McClelland & Stewart.

Canfield, Kip. 1980. A note on Navaho-English code-mixing. *Anthropological Linguistics* 22: 218–220.

Chapdelaine, Claude, and Greg Kennedy. 1990. The identity of the prehistoric occupants of the Temiscouata area. In *Papers of the Twentieth Algonquian Conference*, ed. William Cowan, 72–83. Ottawa: Carleton University.

Charlevoix, P. F. X. de. 1744. *Histoire et description générale de la Nouvelle France.* Paris: Rollin Fils.

Community of Ile-a-la-Crosse. 1990. Community Michef retention project. Unpublished paper.

Comrie, Bernard. 1989. *Language universals and linguistic typology*, 2nd ed. Chicago: University of Chicago Press.

Cooper, John M. 1945. Tête-de-Boule Cree. *International Journal of American Linguistics* 11: 36–44.

Corbeau, L. J. 1951. *Grammaire du français contemporain.* Zutphen: Thieme.

Corrigan, Samuel W., and Lawrence J. Barkwell. 1991. *The struggle for recognition: Canadian justice and the Métis nation.* Winnipeg: Pemmican Publications.

Coues, Eliott. 1897. *New light on the early history of the greater Northwest*, 2 vols. New York: Francis P. Harper.

Cowie, Isaac. 1913. *The Company of Adventurers on the great buffalo plains. A narrative of seven years in the service of the Hudson's Bay Company during 1867–1874.* Toronto: William Briggs.

Crawford, John. 1973a. Linguistic and sociolinguistic relationships in the Michif language. *Proceedings of the Linguistic Circle of Manitoba and North Dakota* 13: 18–22.

Crawford, John. 1973b. Some sociolinguistic observations about Michif. *Proceedings of the Linguistic Circle of Manitoba and North Dakota* 8: 18–21.

Crawford, John. 1976. Michif. A new language. *North Dakota English* 4(1): 3–10.

Crawford, John C. 1983a. Introduction. In *The Michif dictionary. Turtle Mountain Chippewa Cree*, ed. Patline Laverdure and Ida Rose Allard, vii-x. Winnipeg: Pemmican Publications.

Crawford, John C. 1983b. Speaking Michif in four Métis communities. *Canadian Journal of Native Studies* 3: 47–55.

Crawford, John C. 1985a. Dialects of Michif: A beginning. *Proceedings of the Linguistic Circle of Manitoba and North Dakota* 25: 14–15.

Crawford, John C. 1985b. What is Michif? Language in the Metis tradition. In *The new peoples. Being and becoming Métis in North America*, ed. Jacqueline Peterson and Jennifer S. H. Brown, 231–241.Winnipeg: University of Manitoba Press.

Dahlstrom, Amy. 1987. Discontinuous constituents in Fox. In *Native American languages and grammatical typology*, ed. Paul D. Kroeber and Robert E. Moore, 53–73. Bloomington: Indiana University Linguistics Club.

Dahlstrom, Amy L. 1991. *Plains Cree morphosyntax*. New York, London: Garland.

Dahlstrom, Amy. 1995. *Topic, focus and other word order problems in Algonquian*. The Belcourt Lecture, 25 February 1994. Winnipeg: Voices of Rupert's Land.

De Goeje, C. H. 1908. De "handelstaal" der Joeka's met de Trio's en Ojana's. In *Verslag der Toemoekhoemak-expeditie*, 204–219. Leiden: E. J. Brill.

De Groot, A., ed. 1971. *Jorka-Tori*. Paramaribo: Varekamp & Co.

De Gruiter, V. E. 1994. *Het Javindo—de Verboden Taal*, 2nd rev. ed. Den Haag: Moesson.

Delâge, Denys. 1985. *Le pays renversé. Amérindiens et Européens en Amérique du Nord-Est, 1600–1664*. Montréal: Boréal Express.

Delâge, Denys. 1991. Des Amérindiens dans l'imaginaire des Québécois. *Liberté* 33(4): 15–28.

Delâge, Denys. 1992a. Les influences Amérindiennes sur la culture matérielle des colons de la Nouvelle-France. In *L'Archéologie et la rencontre des deux mondes. Présence européenne sur des sites amérindiens*, ed. Michel Fortin, 173–203. Québec: Musée de la Civilisation.

Delâge, Denys. 1992b. L'influence des Amérindiens sur les Canadiens et les Français de la Nouvelle-France. *Lekton* 2(2): 103–191.

Delâge, Denys. 1992c. La religion dans l'alliance Franco-Amérindienne. *Anthropologie et Sociétés* 15(1): 55–87.

Den Besten, Hans. 1988. Die Niederländischen Pidgins der alten Kapkolonie. In *Beiträge zum 3. Essener Kolloquium über Sprachwandel und seine bestimmenden Faktoren, vom 30.9–2.10 1987 [sic: 1986] an der Universität Essen*, ed. Norbert Boretzky, Werner Enninger, and Thomas Stolz, 9–40. Bochum: Studienverlag Dr. N. Brockmeyer.

Denny, J. Peter. 1989. The nature of polysynthesis in Algonquian and Eskimo. In *Theoretical perspectives on native American languages*, ed. Donna B. Gerdts and Karin Michelson, 230–258. New York: State University of New York Press.

Dickason, Olive P. 1980. A historical reconstruction for the northwestern Plains. *Prairie Forum* 5(1): 19–37.

Dickason, Olive P. 1985. From "One Nation" in the Northeast to "New Nation" in the Northwest: A look at the emergence of the Métis. In *The new peoples. Being and becoming Métis in North America*, ed. Jacqueline Peterson and Jennifer S. H. Brown, 19–36. Winnipeg: University of Manitoba Press.

Douaud, Patrick C. 1980. Métis: A case of triadic linguistic economy. *Anthropological Linguistics* 22: 392–414.

Douaud, Patrick C. 1982. All mixed: Canadian Metis sociolinguistic patterns. In *Sociolinguistics Working Paper* 101. Austin: Southwest Educational Development Laboratory.

Douaud, Patrick C. 1985. *Ethnolinguistic profile of the Canadian Métis. Mercury Series— Canadian Ethnology Service Paper 99.* Ottawa: National Museum of Man.

Douaud, Patrick C. 1989. Mitchif: Un aspect de la francophonie Albertaine. *Journal of Indigenous Studies* 1(2): 69–79.

Dowse, Thomas. 1877, August 30. Manitoba and the Canadian Northwest. *Chicago Commercial Advertiser.*

Drapeau, Lynn. 1980. Les emprunts au français en montagnais. In *Inuktitut et langues Amérindiennes au Québec. Cahiers de linguistique* 10, 29–49. Québec: Presses de l'Université de Québec.

Drapeau, Lynn. 1991, August. Michif replicated: The emergence of a mixed language in northern Québec. Paper presented at the Tenth International Conference on Historical Linguistics, Amsterdam.

Drapeau, Lynn. 1995. Codeswitching in caretaker speech and bilingual competence in a Native village of Northern Québec. *International Journal of the Sociology of Language* 113: 157–164.

Drapeau, Lynn, and Peter Bakker. 1994, July. Typological constraints on code-mixing: The case of three Algonquian languages in contact with French. Paper presented in the Session on Code-Switching, World Congress of Sociology, Bielefeld, Germany.

Drechsel, Emanuel J. 1976. "Ha, now me stomany that!" A summary of pidginization and creolization of North American Indian languages. *Linguistics* 173: 63–82. Reprinted 1976 in *IJSL* 7: 63–81.

Drechsel, Emanuel J. 1981. A preliminary sociolinguistic comparison of four indigenous pidgin languages of North America (with notes towards a sociolinguistic typology in American Indian linguistics). *Anthropological Linguistics* 23(3): 93–112.

Dreyfuss, Gail Raimi, and Djoehana Oka. 1979. Chinese Indonesian: A new kind of language hybrid? In *Papers in pidgin and creole linguistics* 2, 247–274. *Pacific Linguistics Series, no 57.* Canberra: Research School for Pacific Studies.

Duckworth, Henry. 1990. *The English River book. A North West Company journal and account book.* Montreal: McGill Queen's University Press.

Dulong, Gaston. 1970. L'influence du vocabulaire maritime sur le franco-canadien. In *Phonétique et linguistique romane: Mélanges offertes a M. Georges Straka*, 331–338. Strasbourg: Société de Linguistique romane.

Dusenberry, Verne. 1985. Waiting for a day that never comes: the dispossessed Métis of Montana. In *The new peoples. Being and becoming Métis in North America*, ed. Jacqueline Peterson and Jennifer S. H. Brown, 119–136. Winnipeg: University of Manitoba Press.

Eccles, W. J. 1983. *The Canadian frontier, 1534—1760*, rev. ed. Albuquerque: University of New Mexico Press.

Edwards, Mary. 1954. *Cree, an intensive language course.* Meadow Lake: Northern Canada Evangelical Mission.

Ellis, C. Douglas. 1971. Cree verb paradigms. *International Journal of American Linguistics* 37: 76–95.

Ellis, C. Douglas. 1983. *Spoken Cree. West coast of James Bay.* Edmonton: Pica Pica Press.

Ellis, C. Douglas. 1990. *"Now then, still another story—" Literature of the western James Bay Cree: Content and structure.* Winnipeg: Voices of Rupert's Land.

Erasmus, P. [ca. 1850.] 1976. *Buffalo days and nights.* Calgary: Glenbow Institute.

Evans, Donna. 1982. On coexistence and convergence of two phonological systems in Michif. *Work Papers, Summer Institute of Linguistics/University of North Dakota Session* 26: 158–173.

Fabian, Johannes. 1982. Scratching the surface: Observations on the poetics of lexical borrowing in Shaba Swahili. *Anthropological Linguistics* 24: 14–50.

Faribault, Marthe. 1993. L'emprunt aux langues amérindiennes. In *Français du Canada—Français de France III*, ed. Hans-Josef Niederehe and Lothar Wolf, 199–215. Tübingen: Max Niemeyer Verlag.

Faries, Richard, ed. 1938. *A dictionary of the Cree language as spoken by the Indians in the provinces of Quebec, Ontario, Manitoba, Saskatchewan and Alberta*. Toronto: Church of England in Canada. (Rev. ed. of dictionary by E. A. Watkins, 1865.)

Fishman, J. A. 1977. Language and ethnicity. In *Language, ethnicity and intergroup relations*, ed. Howard Giles, 15–57. London: Academic Press.

Fox, James A. 1983. Simplified input and negotiation in Russenorsk. In *Pidginization and creolization as language acquisition*, ed. R. Andersen, 94–108. Rowley: Newbury House.

Fredeen, Shirley M. 1991. *Sociolinguistic survey of indigenous languages in Saskatchewan: On the critical list*. Saskatoon: Saskatchewan Indigenous Languages Committee.

Gilman, Rhoda R., Carolyn Gilman, and Deborah M. Stultz. 1979. *The Red River trails. Oxcart routes between St. Paul and the Selkirk settlement 1820–1870*. St. Paul: Minnesota Historical Society.

Giraud, Marcel. 1945. *Le Métis canadien. Son rôle dans l'histoire des provinces de l'Ouest*. Paris: Institut d'Ethnologie.

Goddard, Ives. 1975. Algonquian, Wiyot and Yurok: Proving a distant genetic relationship. In *Linguistics and anthropology: In Honor of C. F. Voegelin*, ed. M. Dale Kinkade, Kenneth L. Hale, and Oswald Werner, 242–262. Lisse: Peter de Ridder Press.

Goddard, Ives. 1978. Eastern Algonquian languages. In *Handbook of North American Indians, Vol. 15, Northeast*, ed. Bruce G. Trigger, 70–77. Washington D.C.: Smithsonian Institution.

Goddard, Ives. 1979. Comparative Algonquian. In *The languages of native America: Historical and comparative assessment*, ed. Lyle Campbell and Marianne Mithun, 70–132. Austin: University of Texas Press.

Goddard, Ives. 1981. Synonymy. In *Subarctic: Handbook of North American Indians* 6, ed. June Helm, 370–371. Washington, D.C.: Smithsonian Institution.

Goddard, Ives. 1987a. Leonard Bloomfield's descriptive and comparative studies of Algonquian. In *Leonard Bloomfield. Essays on his life and work*, ed. Robert A. Hall, Jr., and Konrad Koerner. Amsterdam: John Benjamins. Reprinted 1987 in *Historiographica Linguistica* 14(½): 179–217.

Goddard, Ives. 1987b. Post-transformational stem-derivation in Fox. *Papers and Studies in Contrastive Linguistics* 22: 59–72.

Goddard, Ives. 1990a. Paradigmatic relations. *Special session on general topics in Amerindian linguistics. Berkeley Linguistics Society* 16: 39–50.

Goddard, Ives. 1990b. Primary and secondary stem derivation in Algonquian. *International Journal of American Linguistics* 56(4): 449–483.

Goddard, Ives. 1994. The west-to-east cline in Algonquian dialectology. In *Papers of the Twenty-fifth Algonquian Conference*, 187–211. Ottawa: Carleton University.

Golovko, Evgenij. 1994. Mednyj Aleut or Copper Island Aleut: an Aleut-Russian mixed language. In *Mixed languages. Fifteen case studies in language intertwining*, ed. Peter Bakker and Maarten Mous, 113–121. Amsterdam: IFOTT. Institute for Functional Research on Language and Language Use.

Golovko, Evgeni V., and Nikolai B. Vakhtin. 1990. Aleut in contact: The CIA enigma. *Acta Linguistica Hafniensia* 22: 97–125.

Goodman, Morris. 1971. The strange case of Mbugu. In *Pidginization and creolization of languages*, ed. Dell Hymes, 243–254. Cambridge: Cambridge University Press.

Gourneau, Patrick (Aun nish e naubay). 1980. *History of the Turtle Mountain Band of Chippewa Indians*. Turtle Mountain: Patrick Gourneau.

Greenberg, Adolph M., and James Morrison. 1982. Group identities in the boreal forest: The origin of the northern Ojibwa. *Ethnohistory* 29(2): 75–102.

Greenberg, Joseph. 1955. *Studies in African linguistic classification*. New Haven: Yale University Press.

Greenberg, Joseph. 1963. *The languages of Africa*. Bloomington. Indiana University Press.

Greenberg, Joseph. 1987. *Language in the Americas*. Stanford: Stanford University Press.

Grimes, Barbara F. 1988. *Ethnologue. Languages of the world*, 11th ed. Dallas: Summer Institute of Linguistics.

Haas, Mary R. 1969. Grammar or lexicon? The American Indian side of the question from DuPonceau to Powell. *International Journal of American Linguistics* 35: 239–255.

Haase, Martin. 1992. *Sprachkontakt und Sprachwandel im Baskenland. Die Einflüsse des Gaskognischen und Französischen auf das Baskische*. Hamburg: Helmut Buske.

Haden, Ernest F. 1948. La petite Cendrillouse. *Les Archives de Folklore* 3: 21–34

Hancock, Ian. 1984a. Shelta and Polari. In *Language in the British isles*, ed. Peter Trudgill, 384–403. Cambridge: Cambridge University Press.

Hancock, Ian. 1984b. The social and linguistic development of Angloromani. In *Romani rokkeripen to-divvus. The English Romani dialect and its contemporary social, educational and linguistic standing*, ed. Thomas Acton and Donald Kenrick, 89–134. London: Romanestan Publications.

Hanzeli, V. E. 1969. *Missionary linguistics in New France: A study of seventeenth century and eighteenth century descriptions of American Indian languages*. The Hague: Mouton.

Hargrave, Joseph James. 1871. *Red River*. Montreal: John Lovell.

Harmon, Daniel Williams. 1820. *A journal of voyages and travels in the interior of North America*. . . . Andover: Flagg & Gould.

Harris, R. Cole. 1987. *Historical atlas of Canada. Vol. I. From the beginning to 1800*. Toronto: University of Toronto Press.

Harrison, Julia D. 1985. *Métis. People between two worlds*. Vancouver/Toronto: Glenbow-Alberta Institute and Douglas and McIntyre.

Haugen, Einar. 1950. The analysis of linguistic borrowing. *Language* 26: 210–232.

Havard, V. 1879. The French half-breeds of the Northwest. In *Annual report of the Board of Regents of the Smithsonian Institution . . . for the year 1879*, 309–327. Washington, D.C.: U.S. Government Printing Office.

Heller, Monica. 1991. The politics of code-switching: Processes and consequences of ethnic mobilisation. In *Papers for the Workshop on Impact and Consequences: Broader considerations*. Strasbourg: European Science Foundation.

Helm, June ed. 1981. *Subarctic. Handbook of North American Indians* 6. Washington, D.C.: Smithsonian Institution.

Henry, Alexander. 1809. *Travels and Adventures in Canada and the Indian Territories between the Years 1760 and 1776*. New York.

Hewson, John. 1983. The speech of nations. *Canadian Journal of Linguistics* 28: 33–46.

Hewson, John. 1989. *The French language in Canada*. St. John's: Memorial University of Newfoundland.

Hickerson, Harald. 1956. The genesis of a trading post band: The Pembina Chippewa. *Ethnohistory* 3(4): 289–345.

Hoff, Berend. 1994. Island Carib, an Arawakan language which incorporated a lexical register of Cariban origin, used to address men. In *Mixed languages. Fifteen case studies in language intertwining*, ed. Peter Bakker and Maarten Mous, 161–168. Amsterdam: IFott Institute for Functional Research of Language and Language Use.

Hoff, Berend. 1995. Language contact, war, and Amerindian historical tradition. The special case of the Island Carib. In *Wolves from the sea. Readings in the anthropology of the native Caribbean*, ed. Neil L. Whitehead, 113–138. Leiden: KITLV Press.

Hogman, Wes. 1981. Agreement for animacy and gender in the Buffalo Narrows dialect of French/Cree. *MASA: Journal of the University of Manitoba Anthropology Students' Association* 7: 81–94.

Holm, John. 1989. *Pidgins and creoles. Vol. II. Reference survey.* Cambridge: Cambridge University Press.

Howard, James H. 1965. The Plains-Ojibwa or Bungi: Hunters and warriors of the northern prairies. With special reference to the Turtle Mountain Band. *South Dakota Museum Anthropology Papers* 1. Reprinted 1977, *Reprints in Anthropology* 7. Lincoln, Neb.: J. and L. Reprint Co.

Howard, Joseph Kinsey. 1952. *Strange empire. A narrative of the Northwest.* New York: William Morrow.

Howse, Joseph. 1844. *A grammar of the Cree language; with which is combined an analysis of the Chippewa dialect.* London: J. G. F. and J. Rivington.

Huttar, George. 1982. A Creole Amerindian pidgin of Suriname. *Society for Caribbean Linguistics, Occasional Paper* 15.

Huxley, Selma, ed. 1987. *Los Vascos en el marco Atlantico norte. Siglos XVI y XVII.* Donostia: Eusko Kultur Egintza Etor S.A.

Huyshe, Captain G. L. 1871. *The Red River expedition.* London/New York: Macmillan; Toronto: Adam, Stevenson.

Igla, Birgit. 1989. Das Romani von Ajia Varvara. Deskriptive und historisch-vergleichende Darstellung eines Zigeunerdialekts. Ph.D. thesis, Ruhr Universität Bochum.

Igla, Birgit. 1991. On the treatment of foreign verbs in Romani. In *In the margin of Romani: Gypsy languages in contact,* ed. Peter Bakker and Marcel Cortiade, 50–55. Amsterdam: Publications of the Institute for General Linguistics, University of Amsterdam.

Innis, Harold A. 1970. *The fur trade in Canada.* Toronto: University of Toronto Press.

Jackson, Michael. 1974. Aperçu de tendances phonétiques du parler français en Saskatchewan. *Canadian Journal of Linguistics* 19(2): 121–133.

Johnson, Alice M., ed. 1967. *Saskatchewan journals and correspondence: Edmonton House, 1795–1800; Chesterfield House, 1800–1802.* London: Hudson's Bay Record Society.

Jones, William. 1917. *Ojibwa texts* 7. Leiden: American Ethnological Society Publications.

Kane, Paul. [1859] 1968. *Wanderings of an artist among the Indians of North America. From Canada to Vancouver's Island and Oregon through the Hudson's Bay Company's territory and back again.* London: Longman, Brown. Reprinted 1968, Edmonton: Hurtig Publishers.

Kegg, Maude. 1983. *Nookomis gaa-inaajimotawid. What my grandmother told me,* ed. John D. Nichols. St. Paul: Minnesota Archaeological Society.

Kenrick, Donald. 1976–1977. Romanies in the Middle East. *Roma* 1(4): 5–8; 2(1): 30–36; 2(2): 3–39.

Kenrick, Donald. 1979. Romani English. *Romani sociolinguistics,* ed. Ian F. Hancock. *International Journal of the Sociology of Language* 19: 111–120. Reprinted 1984 in *Romani rokkeripen to-divvus. The English Romani dialect and its contemporary social, educational and linguistic standing,* ed. Thomas Acton and Donald Kenrick, 79–88. London: Romanestan Publications.

Kienetz, Alvin. 1983. The rise and decline of hybrid (Metis) societies on the frontier of western Canada and southern Africa. *Canadian Journal of Native Studies* 3(1): 3–21.

Krauss, Michael, and Victor K. Golla. 1981. Northern Athapaskan languages. In *Subarctic. Handbook of North American Indians* 6, ed. June Helm, 67–85. Washington, D.C.: Smithsonian Institution.

Krosenbrink-Gelissen, L. E. 1989. The Metis National Council: Continuity and change among the Canadian Metis. *ERNAS. European Review of Native American Studies* 3(1): 33–42.

Lacombe, Albert. 1874a. *Dictionnaire de la langue des Cris.* Montréal: Beauchemin & Valois.

Ladstätter, Otto and Andreas Tietze. 1994. *Die Abdal (Äynu) in Xinjiang.* Wien: Verlag der Österrreichischen Akademie der Wissenschaften.

Lamb, W. Kaye, ed. 1970. *The journals and letters of Sir Alexander MacKenzie [1789–1819].* Cambridge: Cambridge University Press.

Lang, Geo. 1990, April. Le discours du coureur de bois mesuré à l'aune des langues mixtes. Paper read at the conference on Avant 1860: Discours et langages au Canada, Toronto.

Lang, Geo. 1991. Voyageur discourse and the absence of fur trade pidgin. *Canadian Literature* 131: 51–63.

Lang, Georges. 1994. Trajets parallèles et destins divers du voyageur Canadien-français et du bandeirante brésilien. In *Les discours du Nouveau Monde au XIXe siècle au Canada français et en Amérique latine,* ed. Marie Couillard and Patrick Imbert. New York: Legas.

Lavallee, Guy A. S. 1988. The Metis people of Saint Laurent, Manitoba. An introductory ethnography. M.A. thesis, University of British Columbia, Vancouver.

Lavallee, Guy A. S. 1990, May. The Michif French language. A symbol of Metis group identity at St. Laurent, Manitoba. Paper presented at the Annual Meeting of the Canadian Anthropology Society, Calgary.

Laverdure, Patline, and Ida Rose Allard. 1983. *The Michif dictionary. Turtle Mountain Chippewa Cree.* Winnipeg: Pemmican Publications.

Leavitt, Robert M. 1985. Confronting language ambivalence and language death: The roles of the university in Native communities. *Canadian Journal of Native Studies* 5: 262–267.

Lederman, Anne. 1988. Old Indian and Métis fiddling in Manitoba: Origins, structure and question of syncretism. *Canadian Journal of Native Studies* 8(2): 205–230.

Lee, David. 1989. The Métis militant rebels of 1885. *Canadian Ethnic Studies* 21(3): 1–19.

Lefebvre, Claire, and John Lumsden. 1989. Les langues créoles et la théorie linguistique. *Canadian Journal of Linguistics* 34: 249–272.

Lesage, Germain. 1946. *Capitale d'une solitude.* Ottawa: Éditions des Études Oblates.

Levin, Norman Balfour. 1964. *The Assiniboine language.* Bloomington: Indiana University Press.

Longpré, Robert. 1977. *Ile-a-la-Crosse 1776–1976. Sakitawak bi-centennial.* Ile-a-la-Crosse: Ile-a-la-Crosse Local Community Authority.

Lussier, Antoine S. 1980. Un métis écrit un lettre. In *The other Natives. The/les Métis,* Vol. III, ed. Antoine S. Lussier & Bruce Sealey, 167–170. Winnipeg: Manitoba Métis Federation Press and Editions Bois Brulés.

McDougall, John. 1903. *In the days of the Red River rebellion: Life and adventures in the Far West of Canada (1868–1872).* Toronto: W. Briggs.

MacKenzie, Marguerite, and Sandra Clarke. 1981. Dialect relations in Cree/Montagnais/ Naskapi: Verb paradigms. *Recherches Linguistiques à Montréal* 16: 135–192.

MacLean, Hope. 1982. *Indians, Inuit and Métis of Canada.* Toronto: Gage.

MacLeod, Margaret, and W. L. Morton. 1963. *Cuthbert Grant of Grantown.* Toronto: McClelland & Stewart.

Mailhot, José. 1985. Implementation of mother-tongue literacy among the Montagnais: Myth or reality? In *Promotion of Native writing systems in Canada,* ed. Barbara Burnaby. Toronto: OISE Press.

Mandelbaum, David G. [1940] 1979. *The Plains Cree. An ethnographic, historical, and comparative study. Canadian Plains Studies* 9. Regina: Canadian Plains Research Center, University of Regina.

Mellow, Dean. 1989. A syntactic approach to noun incorporation in Cree. In *Actes du vingtième Congrès des Algonquinistes*, ed. William Cowan, 250–261. Ottawa: Carleton University.

Menovshchikov, G. A. 1969. O nekotoryx social'nyx aspektax èvoljucii jazyka. In *Voprosy social'noj linguistiki*, 110–134. Leningrad: Nauka.

Messing, Gordon M. 1987. *A glossary of Greek Romany, as spoken in Agia Varvara (Athens)*. Columbus, Ohio: Slavica.

Meyer, David. 1987. Time-depth of western Woods Cree occupation of northern Ontario, Manitoba and Saskatchewan. In *Papers of the Eighteenth Algonquian Conference*, ed. William Cowan, 187–200. Ottawa: Carleton University.

Michel, Fernand. 1866. *Dix-huit ans chez les sauvages. Voyages et missions de Mgr. Henry Faraud, évêque d'Anemour, vicaire apostolique de MacKensie, dans l'extrême nord de l'Amêrique Brittanique. D'après les documents de Mgr, l'évêque d'Anemour par Fernand-Michel*. . . . Paris/Bruxelles: Régis Ruffet.

Michelson, Truman. 1911–1912. Turtle Mountain Chippewa (Cree), fieldnotes, file 2703, Algonquian, Misc. Washington, D.C.: National Anthropological Archives, Smithsonian Institution.

Michelson, Truman. 1912. Preliminary report on the linguistic classification of Algonquian tribes. *Bureau of American Ethnology Annual Report* 28: 221–290b.

Michelson, Truman. 1939. Linguistic classification of Cree and Montagnais-Naskapi dialects. *Bureau of American Ethnology Bulletin* 123: 67–95.

Michif Languages Committee. 1985, June 26–28. Report of the Michif Languages Conference, Winnipeg, Manitoba.

Mishaegen, Anne de. 1946. *Dans la forêt canadienne*. Bruxelles: La Renaissance du Livre. Dutch trans. 1947, *In de Canadeesche wouden*, Naarden: Rutgers.

Mithun, Marianne. 1988. System-defining structural properties in polysynthetic languages. *ZPSK. Zeitschrift für Phonetik, Sprachwissenschaft und Kommukikationsforschung* 41(4): 442–451.

Moine, Louise. 1979. *Remembering will have to do*. Saskatoon: Saskatchewan Indian Cultural College.

Moore, John H. 1994. Putting anthropology back together again: The ethnogenetic critique of cladistic theory. *American Anthropologist* 96(4): 925–948.

Moravcsik, Edith A. 1975. Verb borrowing. *Wiener Linguistische Gazette* 8: 3–31.

Morgan, Lewis Henry. 1993. *The Indian Journals, 1859–1862*. New York: Dover Publications. Originally published 1959, Ann Arbor: University of Michigan Press.

Morison, Samuel Eliot. 1971. *The European discovery of America. The northern voyages A.D. 500–1600*. New York: Oxford University Press.

Mous, Maarten. 1994. Ma'a or Mbugu. In *Mixed languages. Fifteen case studies in language intertwining*, ed. Peter Bakker and Maarten Mous, 175–200. Amsterdam: IFOTT.

Mous, Maarten. In press. Ma'a or Mbugu. *SUGIA. Sprache und Geschichte in Afrika*.

Muysken, Pieter. 1980. Sources for the study of Amerindian contact vernaculars in Ecuador. *Amsterdam Creole Studies* 3: 66–82.

Muysken, Pieter. 1981. Half-way between Quechua and Spanish: The case for relexification. In *Historicity and variation in Creole studies*, ed. A. R. Highfield and A. Valdman, 52–78. Ann Arbor, Mich.: Karoma.

Muysken, Pieter. 1988a. Lexical restructuring in Creole genesis. In *Beiträge zum 4. Essener Kolloquium über Sprachkontakt, Sprachwandel, Sprachwechsel, Sprachtod*, ed. Norbert Boretzky, Werner Enninger, and Thomas Stolz, 193–209. Bochum: Studienverlag Dr. N. Brockmeyer.

Muysken, Pieter. 1988b. Media Lengua and linguistic theory. *Canadian Journal of Linguistics* 33(4): 409–422.

Muysken, Pieter. 1991. Needed: A comparative approach. In *Papers for the Symposium on Code-switching in Bilingual Studies: Theory, significance and perspectives*, 253–272. Strasbourg: European Science Foundation.

Muysken, Pieter. 1997. The Language Fortress. Ms., University of Amsterdam.

Myers-Scotton, Carol. 1992. Constructing the frame in intrasentential code-switching. *Multilingua* 11(1): 101–127.

Myers-Scotton, Carol. 1993. *Duelling languages. Grammatical structure in codeswitching.* Oxford: Clarendon Press.

Nadkarni, M. V. 1975. Bilingualism and syntactic change in Konkani. *Language* 51: 762–683.

Newman, Peter C. 1985. *Company of adventurers. Vol. I. The story of the Hudson's Bay Company.* Harmondsworth: Penguin Books.

Nichols, John D. 1985, June 26–28. Bibliography of language in Metis communities. In Michif Languages Committee, Report of the Michif Languages Conference, Winnipeg, Manitoba.

Nichols, John D. 1992, October. "Broken Oghibbeway": An Algonquian trade language. Paper read at the Twenty-fourth Algonquian Conference, Ottawa.

Nichols, John D. 1995. The Ojibwe verb in "Broken Oghibbeway." *Amsterdam Creole Studies* 12: 1–18.

Nortier, Jacomine. 1989. *Dutch and Moroccan Arabic in contact: Code switching among Moroccans in the Netherlands.* Dordrecht: Foris.

Nute, Grace L. 1931. *The voyageur.* New York and London: D. Appleton. Reprinted 1987. St. Paul: Minnesota Historical Society.

Nute, Grace L. 1942. *Documents relating to Northwest missions, 1815–1827.* Minneapolis: Minnesota Historical Society.

Orser, Lori. L. 1984. Mitchif: A problem in classification. M.A. thesis, University of Kansas, Lawrence.

Oudin, Anne-Sophie, and Lynn Drapeau. 1993. Langue et identité ethnique dans une communauté montagnaise bilingue. *Revue Québecoise de Linguistique* 22(2): 75–92.

Owen, Roger C. 1965. The patrilocal band: A linguistically and culturally hybrid unit. *American Anthropologist* 67: 675–690.

Pannekoek, Frits. 1991. *A snug little flock. The social origins of the Riel resistance 1869–70.* Winnipeg: Watson & Dwyer.

Papen, R. A. 1984a. Un parler français méconnu de l'Ouest Canadien: Le Métis. "Quand même qu on parle français, ça veut pas dire qu'on est des Canayens!" In *La langue, la culture et la société des francophones de l'Ouest*, ed. Pierre-Yves Mocquais, André Lalonde, and Bernard Wilhelm, 121–136. Regina: Institut de Recherche du Centre d'Etudes Bilingues.

Papen, R. A. 1984b. Quelques remarques sur un parler français méconnu de l'Ouest Canadien: Le Métis. *Revue Québecoise de Linguistique* 14(1): 113–139.

Papen, R. A. 1986a, April. Le Michif: Un cas de symbiose linguistique. Paper read at the Ve Colloquium of Creole Studies, La Réunion.

Papen, R. A. 1986b. On the possibility of linguistic symbiosis: The case of Michif. Paper read at Linguistics at UCSD: The First Twenty Years Colloquium, University of California, San Diego.

Papen, R. A. 1987a. Can two distinct grammars coexist in a single language? The case of Métif. In *Papers from the Tenth Annual Meeting of the Atlantic Provinces Linguistics Association*, ed. A. M. Kinloch. Fredericton: University of New Brunswick Press.

Papen, R. A. 1987b. Linguistic variation in the French component of Métif grammar. In *Papers of the Eighteenth Algonquian Conference*, ed. William Cowan, 247–259. Ottawa: Carleton University.

Papen, R. A. 1987c. Le Métif: Le nec plus ultra des grammmaires en contact. *Revue Québecoise de Linguistique Théorique et Appliquée* 6(2): 57–70.

Papen, R. A. 1988. Sur quelques processus phonologiques, morphologiques et lexicaux du Métif. In *Papers from the Eleventh Annual Meeting of the Atlantic Provinces Linguistics Association*, ed. R. M. Babitch et al., 107–115. Shippagan: University of Moncton.

Payment, Diane. 1991. *Otipemisiwak. The free people*. Ottawa: Canadian Government Publishing Centre.

Peers, Laura L. 1987. Rich man, poor man, beggarman, chief: Saulteaux in the Red River settlement. In *Papers of the Eighteenth Algonquian Conference*, ed. William Cowan, 261–270. Ottawa: Carleton University.

Pelletier, Emile. 1975. *Exploitation of Métis lands*. Winnipeg: Manitoba Metis Federation Press.

Pentland, David H. 1978a. A historical overview of Cree dialects. In *Papers of the Ninth Algonquian Conference*, ed. William Cowan, 104–126. Ottawa: Carleton University.

Pentland, David H. 1978b. Proto-Algonquian *sk in Woods Cree. In *Linguistic studies of Native Canada*, ed. Eung-Do Cook and Jonathan D. Kaye, 189–202. Lisse/Vancouver: Peter de Ridder Press/University of British Columbia Press.

Pentland, David H. 1982. French loanwords in Cree. *Kansas Working Papers in Linguistics* 7: 105–117.

Peterson, Jacqueline. 1978. Prelude to Red River: A social portrait of the Great Lakes Métis. *Ethnohistory* 25: 41–67.

Peterson, Jacqueline. 1981. The people in between: Indian-white marriage and the genesis of a Métis society and culture in the Great Lakes region, 1680–1830. Ph.D. thesis, University of Illinois, Chicago.

Peterson, Jacqueline. 1985. Many roads to Red River: Métis genesis in the Great Lakes region, 1680–1815. In *The new peoples. Being and becoming Métis in North America*, ed. Jacqueline Peterson and Jennifer S. H. Brown, 37–71. Winnipeg: University of Manitoba Press.

Poplack, Shana. 1980. "Sometimes I'll start a sentence in Spanish Y TERMINO EN ESPANOL": Toward a typology of code-switching. *Linguistics* 18: 581–618.

Powell, J. V. 1891. Indian linguistic families north of Mexico. In *Seventh Annual Report*. Bureau of American Ethnology, 1–142. Washington, D.C.: U.S. Government Printing Office.

Préfontaine, R. 1980. Le parler Métis. In *The other Natives. The/les Métis*, Vol. III, ed. Antoine S. Lussier and D. Bruce Sealey, vol. III, 162–166. Winnipeg: Manitoba Métis Federation Press and Editions Bois Brulés.

Priest, Gordon E. 1985. Aboriginal languages in Canada. *Language and Society* 15: 13–19.

Proulx, Paul. 1991. Review of John D. Nichols, ed., *Statement made by the Indians. Canadian Journal of Linguistics* 36(2): 113–213.

Rafferty, Ellen. 1982. Discourse structure of the Chinese Indonesian of Malang. In *NUSA. Linguistic Studies in Indonesian and Languages in Indonesia* 12. Jakarta: Universitas Atma Jaya.

Rhodes, Richard. 1976. A preliminary report on the dialects of eastern Ojibwa-Odawa. In *Papers of the Seventh Algonquian Conference*, ed. William Cowan, 129–156. Ottawa: Carleton University.

Rhodes, Richard. 1977. French Cree—A case of borrowing. In *Actes du Huitième Congrès des Algonquinistes*, ed. William Cowan, 6–25. Ottawa: Carleton University.

Rhodes, Richard. 1982. Algonquian trade languages. In *Papers of the Thirteenth Algonquian Conference*. ed. William Cowan, 1–10. Ottawa: Carleton University.

Rhodes, Richard. 1985. *Eastern Ojibwa-Chippewa-Odawa Dictionary*. Berlin: Mouton.

Rhodes, Richard. 1986. Métchif: A second look. In *Actes du Dixseptième Congrès des Algonquinistes*, ed. William Cowan, 287–296. Ottawa: Carleton University.

Rhodes, Richard. 1987. Les conte Métif-Métif myths. In *Papers of the Nineteenth Algonquian Conference*, ed. William Cowan, 297–301. Ottawa: Carleton University.

Rhodes, Richard. 1992. Language shift in Algonquian. *International Journal of the Sociology of Language* 93: 87–92.

Rhodes, Richard, and Evelyn M. Todd. 1981. Subarctic Algonquian languages. In *Subarctic. Handbook of North American Indians* 6, ed. June Helm, 52–66. Washington, D.C. Smithsonian Institution.

Rice, Keren. 1989. *A grammar of Slave*. Berlin: Mouton de Gruyter.

Rich, E. E., ed. 1949. *James Isham's observations on Hudsons Bay, 1743, and notes and observations on a book entitled "A voyage to Hudsons Bay in the Dobbs galley," 1749.* Hudson's Bay Company series 12. Toronto: Champlain Society.

Roe, F. G. 1935. The Red River hunt. In *Transactions of the Royal Society of Canada*, section II, 171–218.

Ross, Alexander. [1856] 1962. *The Red River settlement. Its rise, progress, and present state, with some account of the native races and its general history to the present day.* Minneapolis: Ross & Haines.

Rountree, Catherine, and Naomi Glock. 1977. *Saramaccan for beginners.* Paramaribo: Summer Institute of Linguistics.

Russell, Dale R. 1991. *Eighteenth century western Cree and their neighbours.* Ottawa: Canadian Museum of Civilization.

St.-Onge, Nicole. 1985. The dissolution of a Métis community: Pointe à la Grouette, 1860–1885. *Studies in Political Economy* 18: 149–172.

St.-Onge, Nicole. 1990. Race, class and marginality in an interlake settlement: 1850–1950. In *The political economy of Manitoba*. Regina: Canadian Plains Research Center, University of Regina.

St.-Onge, Nicole. 1992. Variations in Red River: The traders and freemen Métis of Saint Laurent, Manitoba. *Canadian Ethnic Studies* 14(2): 1–21.

Sampson, John. 1930. Two stories of Cornelius Price. *Journal of the Gypsy Lore Society,* 3rd series 9(2): 49–57.

Sankoff, David, and Shana Poplack. 1987. Adposition and article in Finnish-English code-switching. Unpublished paper, Université de Montréal, Québec.

Sauvé, Louise, ed. 1989. *Peuples autochtones de l'Amérique du Nord. De la réduction à la coexistence.* Sainte-Foy: Télé-Université, Université de Québec.

Schindler, Jenny. n.d. *Introduction. The Turtle Mountain Mitchif.* Belcourt.

Schoolcraft, Henry. 1851. *Historical and statistical information respecting the history, condition and prospects of the Indian tribes of the United States.* Philadelphia: Lippincott, Grambo.

Scollon, Ronald, and Suzanne B. Scollon. 1979. *Linguistic convergence: An ethnography of speaking at Fort Chipewyan, Alberta.* New York: Academic Press.

Scott, S. Osborne, and D.A. Mulligan. 1951, December. The Red River dialect. *The Beaver* 42–45.

Sealey, D. Bruce, and Antoine S. Lussier. 1975. *The Métis. Canada's forgotten people.* Winnipeg: Pemmican Publications.

Sharrock, Susan R. 1974. Crees, Cree-Assiniboines, and Assiniboines: Interethnic social organization on the far northern plains. *Ethnohistory* 21(2): 95–122.

Sherzer, Joel. 1976. *An areal-typological study of American Indian languages north of Mexico.* Amsterdam: North-Holland.

Silverstein, M. 1973 ms. Dynamics of recent linguistic contact. Overlong version to appear in *Handbook of North American Indians* Vol. 16, ed. by Ives Goddard.

Slobodin, Richard. 1966. *Metis of the Mackenzie district*. Ottawa: Canadian Research Centre for Anthropology, Saint-Paul University.

Smart, B. C. and H. D. Crofton. 1875. *The dialect of the English Gypsies*. London: Asher.

Smith, James G. E. 1976. On the territorial distribution of the western Woods Cree. In *Papers of the Eighteenth Algonquian Conference*, ed. William Cowan, 414–435. Ottawa: Carleton University.

Smith, James G. E. 1981. Western Woods Cree. In *Subarctic. Handbook of North American Indians* 6, ed. June Helm, 256–270. Washington, D.C.: Smithsonian Institution.

Smith, Norval. 1994. An annotated list of creoles, pidgins and mixed languages. In *Pidgins and Creoles. An Introduction*, ed. Jacques Arends, Pieter Muysken, and Norval Smith, 331–374. Amsterdam: John Benjamins.

Smith, Norval. forthcoming. *The book of younger languages. A bibliographical guide to pidgins, creoles and mixed languages*.

Smout, Kary D. 1988. A missionary English from Japan. *American Speech* 63(2): 137–149.

Spencer, Andrew. 1991. *Morphological theory. An introduction to word structure in generative grammar*. Oxford: Basil Blackwell.

Sprague, D. N. and R. P. Frye. 1983. *The genealogy of the first Métis nation. The development and dispersal of the Red River settlement 1820–1900*. Winnipeg: Pemmican Publications.

Spry, Irene M. 1963. *The Palliser expedition. An account of John Palliser's British North American exploring expedition 1857–1860*. Toronto: Macmillan.

Spry, Irene M. 1985. The Métis and mixed-bloods of Rupert's Land before 1870. In *The new peoples. Being and becoming Métis in North America*, ed. Jacqueline Peterson and Jennifer S. H. Brown, 95–118. Winnipeg: University of Manitoba Press.

Stark, Louisa R. 1972. Machaj-Juyai: Secret language of the Callahuayas. *Papers in Andean Linguistics* 1(2): 199–227.

Starks, Donna. 1987. An introduction to Woods Cree: The case of South Indian Lake. In *Papers of the Eighteenth Algonquian Conference*, ed. William Cowan, 335–344. Ottawa: Carleton University.

Statement, 1817. Statement respecting the Earl of Selkirk's settlement upon the Red River in North America. . . . London: John Murray.

Statistics Canada. 1984. *Canada's Native people*. Ottawa: Ministry of Supply and Services.

Steinbring, Jack. 1981. Saulteaux of Lake Winnipeg. In *Subarctic. Handbook of North American Indians* 6, ed. June Helm, 244–255. Washington, D.C.: Smithsonian Institution.

Stewart, W. A. 1962. Creole languages in the Caribbean. In *Study of the role of second languages in Asia, Africa and Latin America*, ed. F. A. Rice, 34–53. Washington, D.C.: Center for Applied Linguistics.

Stobie, Margaret. 1967–1968. Background of the dialect called Bungi. *Historical and Scientific Society of Manitoba* III(24): 65–75.

Stobie, Margaret. 1970, July 13. Bungi—Sound of history. *Winnipeg Free Press*.

Stobie, Margaret. 1971. The dialect called Bungi. *Canadian Antiques Collector* 6(8): 20.

Taché, A. A. 1869. *Esquisse sur le Nord-Ouest de l'Amérique*. Montréal: Charles Payette.

Tanner, Helen H. 1987. *Atlas of Great Lakes Indian history*. Norman: University of Oklahoma Press.

Taylor, Allan R. 1981a. Indian lingua francas. In *Language in the USA*, ed. Charles F. Ferguson and Shirley Brice Heath, 175–195. Cambridge: Cambridge University Press.

Taylor, Allan R. 1981b. Variation in Canadian Assiniboine. *Siouan and Caddoan Linguistics* 4: 9–16.

Taylor, Douglas R., and Berend J. Hoff. 1980. The linguistic repertory of the Island-Carib in the seventeenth century: The men's language—A Carib Pidgin? *International Journal of American Linguistics* 46(4): 301–312.

Thomas, Robert K. 1985. Afterword. In *The new peoples. Being and becoming Métis in North America*, ed. Jacqueline Peterson and Jennifer S. H. Brown, 243–251. Winnipeg: University of Manitoba Press.

Thomason, Sarah G. 1983. Genetic relationship and the case of Ma'a (Mbugu). *Studies in African Linguistics* 14(2): 195–231.

Thomason, Sarah Grey, and Terrence Kaufman. 1988. *Language contact, creolization and genetic linguistics*. Berkeley: University of California Press.

Thwaites, Ruben G. 1896–1901. *Jesuit relations and allied documents*. Cleveland: Burrows Brothers.

Todd, Evelyn M. 1971. A grammar of the Ojibwa language: The Severn dialect. Ph.D. thesis, University of North Carolina, Chapel Hill.

Topping, Donald M. 1980. *Spoken Chamorro. With grammatical notes and glossary,* 2nd ed. Honolulu: University Press of Hawaii.

Tough, Frank. 1989. Race, personality and history: A review of Marcel Giraud's "The Metis in the Canadian West." *Native Studies Review* 5(2): 55–93.

Trigger, Bruce. 1976. *The children of Aataentsic: A history of the Huron people to 1660,* 2 vols. Montreal: McGill Queen's University Press.

Trudel, Marcel. 1960. *L'esclavage au Canada français*. Québec: Presses Universitaires Laval.

Tucker, A. N., and M. Bryan. 1957. *Linguistic survey of the northern Bantu borderland,* vol. IV. Oxford: Oxford University Press.

Tucker, Sarah. 1851. *The rainbow in the north*. London: James Nisbet.

Turgeon, Laurier. 1982. Pêcheurs basques et Indiens des côtes du Saint Laurent au XVIe siècle: Perspectives de recherche. *Etudes Canadiens/Canadian Studies* 13: 9–14.

Turgeon, Laurier. 1990. Basque-Amerindian trade in the Saint Lawrence during the sixteenth century: New documents, new perspectives. *Man in the Northeast* 40: 81–87.

Turtle Mountain Indian Reservation. 1985. *Turtle Mountain Indian Reservation. Belcourt, North Dakota. St. Ann's Centennial. 100 Years of Faith, 1885–1985*. Belcourt. Turtle Mountain Indian Reservation.

Umfreville, Edward. 1790. *The present state of Hudson's Bay. . . .* London: Charles Stalker; Reprinted 1954, ed. W. Stewart Wallace. Toronto: Ryerson Press.

Valentine, J. Randolph. 1994. Ojibwe dialect relations. Ph.D thesis, University of Texas, Austin.

Valentine, Lisa Philips. 1995. *Making it their own: Severn Ojibwe communicative practices*. Toronto: University of Toronto Press.

Valentine, Lisa Philips. 1994. Code switching and language leveling: Use of multiple codes in a Severn Ojibwe community. International Journal of American Linguistics 60: 313–341.

Van Hout, Roeland, and Pieter Muysken. 1995. Insertion, alternation, congruent lexicalization. Corpus-based approaches to bilingual speech. In *Summer school on code-switching and language contact*, 302–306. Leeuwarden: Fryske Akademy.

Van Kirk, Sylvia. 1980. *"Many tender ties." Women in fur-trade society, 1670–1870*. Winnipeg: Watson & Dwyer.

Van Kirk, Sylvia. 1985. "What if mama is an Indian?": The cultural ambivalence of the Alexander Ross family. In *The new peoples. Being and becoming Métis in North America*, ed. Jacqueline Peterson and Jennifer S. H. Brown, 207–217. Winnipeg: University of Manitoba Press.

Van Kirk, Sylvia. 1991, September. By code and canoe: George Nelson's manuscript journals, 1821–1822. Paper presented at the Sixth North American Fur Trade Conference, Mackinac Island.

Van Rheeden, Hadewych. 1994. Petjo: The mixed language of the Indos in Batavia. In *Mixed languages. Fifteen case studies in language intertwining*, ed. Peter Bakker and Maarten Mous, 223–237. Amsterdam: IFOTT.

Van Rheeden, Hadewych. 1995. Het Petjo van Batavia. Ontstaan en structuur van de taal van de Indo's. Amsterdam: Publikaties van het Instituut voor Algemene Taalwetenschap.

Voorhis, Paul. 1977. *Saulteaux phrase book, based on the dialects of Manitoba*. Brandon, Manitoba: Brandon University, Department of Native Studies.

Vrooman, Nicholas. 1984. *Turtle Mountain Music*. New York: Folkways.

Wade, Mason. 1968. *The French Canadians, 1760–1967. Vol. I: 1760–1911*. Toronto: Macmillan.

Weaver, Deborah. 1982. Obviation in Michif. *Work Papers, Summer Institute of Linguistics/ University of North Dakota Session* 26: 174–262.

Weaver, Deborah. 1983. The effects of language change and death on obviation in Michif. In *Actes du Quatorzième Congrès des Algonquinistes*, ed. William Cowan, 261–268. Ottawa: Carleton University.

Weinreich, Uriel. 1953. *Languages in contact*. The Hague: Mouton.

Weston, Lori Orser. 1983. Alternative structures in a mixed language: Benefactives and dubitatives in Michif. In *1982 Mid-America Linguistics Conference papers*, ed. Frances Ingemann, 427–432. Lawrence: University of Kansas.

Wolfart, H. C. 1971. Plains Cree internal syntax and the problem of noun-incorporation. In *Proceedings of the Thirty-eighth International Congress of Americanists*, vol. 3, 511–518.

Wolfart, H. C. 1973a. Boundary maintenance in Algonquian: A linguistic study of Island Lake, Manitoba. *American Anthropologist* 75: 1305–1323.

Wolfart, H. C. 1973b. *Plains Cree: A grammatical study*. Philadelphia: American Philosophical Society.

Wolfart, H. C. 1978. How many obviatives: Sense and reference in a Cree verb paradigm. In *Linguistic studies of Native Canada*, ed. Eung-Do Cook and Jonathan D. Kaye, 255–272. Lisse/Vancouver: Peter de Ridder Press/University of British Columbia Press.

Wolfart, H. C. 1989. Prosodische Grenzsignale im Plains Cree. *Folia Linguistica* 23(3/4): 327–334.

Wolfart, H. C. 1990a. One thousand and one nights: The Orient and the far Northwest. In *Actes du 20ème congrès des Algonquinistes*, ed. William Cowan, 370–395. Ottawa: Carleton University.

Wolfart, H. C. 1990b. The supplement to Petitot's Dieu-Lunaire text. *International Journal of American Linguistics* 56: 580–586.

Wolfart, H. C. and Freda Ahenakew. 1987. Notes on the orthography and the glossary. In *Wâskahikaniwiyiniw-âcimowina. Stories of the House People*, ed. Freda Ahenakew, 113–126. Winnipeg: University of Manitoba Press.

Wolfart, H. C. and Janet F. Carroll. 1981. *Meet Cree: A guide to the Cree language*. Edmonton: University of Alberta Press.

Wolff, John U. 1983. The Indonesian spoken by the Peranakan Chinese of East Java: A case of language mixture. In *Essays in honor of Charles F. Hockett*, ed. F. Agard et al., 590–601. Leiden: E. J. Brill.

Wood, L. A. 1915. *The Red River colony. A chronicle of the beginnings of Manitoba*. Toronto: Glasgow, Brook.

Wood, Major. 1850. Pembina settlement. Letter from the secretary of war, transmitting report of Major Wood, relative to his expedition to Pembina settlement, and the condition of affairs of the north-western frontier of the Territory of Minnesota, March 19, 1850. 31st. Cong, 1st sess, House of Representatives, ex. doc. nr. 51.

Woodley, Ken. 1978. Economics and education in a Métis community. In *The other natives. The/les Métis* vol. II, ed. Antoine S. Lussier and D. Bruce Sealey, 129–154. Winnipeg: Manitoba Métis Federation Press and Editions Bois Brulés.

Zeilig, Ken, and Victoria Zeilig. 1987. *Ste. Madeleine: Community without a town. Métis elders interview.* Winnipeg: Pemmican Publications.

Index of Languages, Personal Names, and Geographical Names

Senkyoshigo, 200, 203, 206, 208, 209
Severn Ojibwe, 181, 187, 258, 284n1
Sharrock, S., 38, 56, 57, 174, 271
Sherzer, J., 29
Shuswap, 165, 271–273
Silverstein, M., 15, 272
Simpson, 168, 176
Sioux, 30, 39, 41, 43, 44, 56, 57, 65, 75,
    129, 174, 271, 273, 274, 279
Slobodin, R., 60
Smart, B., 199
Smith, Norval, 195
Smith, James, 44, 256
Smout, K., 200
Southern Plains Cree, 146, 254, 257, 258
Southwestern Ojibwe, 42, 43, 270
Spanish, 23, 42, 64, 69, 179, 183, 185, 189,
    191, 193, 194, 196, 208, 212
Spencer, A., 220, 221, 246
Sprague, D., 164, 171, 173, 175, 267–269
Spry, I., 58, 164, 166, 272, 273
Sranan, 194, 195
Stark, L., 196
Starks, D., 253, 257, 258, 284n1
Statement, 54, 55, 64, 71, 168, 176, 194,
    229
Statistics, 75, 122
Steinbring, J., 266
Stewart, W., 23
Stobie, M., 59, 166, 167, 174, 269, 273
Stoney, 271
Suriname, 14, 194, 195
Swampy Cree, 45, 122, 130, 134, 136,
    254–256, 258–260, 262, 275, 284n1,
    285n3
Sweden, 199

Taché, A., 177
Tanner, A., 43, 265
Taylor, Allan, 15, 271–272
Taylor, Douglas, 196–197
Thomas, R., 60, 270, 285n7
Thomason, S., 4, 13, 20, 43, 193–195, 197,
    201, 205, 211, 234
Thwaites, R., 34, 271
Tietze, A., 199
Todd, E., 39, 86, 258, 260, 284n1
Topping, D., 185
Touchwood Hills, 57, 172, 173, 256
Tough, F., 58

Trigger, B., 15, 42, 101, 103, 183, 187
Trio-Ndjuka pidgin, 14, 195
Trudel, M., 52, 64
Tucker, A., 211
Tucker, S., 54, 168, 176, 211
Turgeon, L., 31
Turkish, 19, 20, 22, 113, 199, 179, 204,
    220
Turnbull, 60
Turtle Mountain(s), 27, 57, 59, 61, 76, 79,
    113, 118, 122, 122–125, 129, 130,
    134–137, 139, 141, 144, 146, 147,
    155, 159, 161, 163, 170–173, 242,
    259, 264–266

Umfreville, E., 266

Vakhtin, N., 20, 201
Valentine, J. Randolph, 253, 258, 284n1
Valentine, Lisa Philips, 181, 186
Van Der Voort, H., 199, 206
Van Holk, A., 20, 201, 281n4, 284n4
Van Hout, R., 180
Van Rheeden, H., 200
Van Kirk, S., 49, 50, 166, 272
Vérendrye, 167, 176, 271
Voorhis, P., 258, 284n1
Vrooman, N., 125

Wade, M., 31–33
Walhalla, 123, 172, 173
Weaver, D., 89, 153
Weston, L., 3, 111, 153, 282n7
Willowbunch, 122, 132, 172, 173
Winnipeg, 54, 55, 58, 62, 76, 163, 174
Wolfart, H. Chr., 5, 7, 69, 82, 84, 89, 99,
    146, 177, 218, 222, 230, 232, 236,
    244, 256–258, 263, 272, 282n2,
    282n3, 284n1
Wolff, J., 201
Wood, L., 6, 109, 167–169, 175
Wood Mountain, 59, 122, 172, 173
Woodland Ojibwa, 265
Woodley, K., 126
Woods Cree, 45, 253, 255, 257–259, 262,
    265

York Factory, 37, 47, 253

Zeilig, K. & V., 127

Subject Index

DATE DUE

DEC 1 5 2009	
DEC 0 8 2010	